Shopping for a Better World

Shopping for a Better World:

The Quick and Easy Guide to All Your Socially Responsible Shopping

THE COUNCIL ON ECONOMIC PRIORITIES

Benjamin Hollister

Rosalyn Will

Alice Tepper Marlin

AND

Stephen Dyott, Sylvia Kovacs, and Laurie Richardson

SIERRA CLUB BOOKS

SAN FRANCISCO

The Sierra Club, founded in 1892 by John Muir, has devoted itself to the study and protection of the earth's scenic and ecological resources—mountains, wetlands, woodlands, wild shores and rivers, deserts and plains. The publishing program of the Sierra Club offers books to the public as a nonprofit educational service in the hope that they may enlarge the public's understanding of the Club's basic concerns. The point of view expressed in each book, however, does not necessarily represent that of the Club. The Sierra Club has some sixty chapters coast to coast, in Canada, Hawaii, and Alaska. For information about how you may participate in its programs to preserve wilderness and the quality of life, please address inquiries to Sierra Club, 730 Polk Street, San Francisco, CA 94109.

Royalties earned by CEP will be used for further corporate social responsibility research

LIBRARY OF CONGRESS CATALOGING IN PUBLICATION DATA
Shopping for a better world : the quick and easy guide to all your socially responsible shopping / the Council on Economic Priorities.
p. cm.
Includes index.
ISBN 0-87156-471-8
1. Marketing (Home economics)—United States—Handbooks, manuals, etc. 2. Shopping—United States—Handbooks, manuals, etc. 3. Social responsibility of business—United States—Handbooks, manuals, etc. 4. Commercial products—United States—Evaluation—Handbooks, manuals, etc. 5. Grocery trade—United States—Evaluation—Handbooks, manuals, etc. I. Council on Economic Priorities.
TX356.S59 1994
363.7'0525—dc20 94-8231
CIP

Production by Amy Evans
Cover design by Bonnie Smetts
Book design and composition by Park Press

Printed in the United States of America on acid-free paper containing a minimum of 50% recovered waste paper, of which at least 10% of the fiber content is post-consumer waste

10 9 8 7 6 5 4 3 2 1

Contents

Acknowledgments

The Council on Economic Priorities would like to thank everyone who made this book possible. We especially wish to acknowledge the generous financial support of the Teresa and H. John Heinz III Charitable Fund, the Flow Fund, and the Marie C. and Joseph C. Wilson Foundation. A special vote of gratitude to Sheila Ratner, our Administrative Director. Thanks also to Sean Moulton and Ken Scott, who worked on CEP's environmental research. We are grateful for the hard work of our research interns: Elizabeth Ascoli (Haverford); Heidi Beehler (SUNY Binghamton); Marisa Donalds (Princeton); Robin Goldstein (Brandeis); Lifan Hung (University of Washington, Seattle); Loretta Kazanecki (National Audubon Expedition Institute, Lesley College); and Elisabeth Lerner (New York University). A heartfelt thank you to the criteria committee of our Board of Directors: Beth Smith, Albert Hurwit, M. D., Anne S. Davidson, Tyna Coles, Carole Robbins, John T. Connor, Jr., Joseph W. Garton, Kate Rand Lloyd, Henry Morgan, Arthur H. Rosenfeld, and George Wallerstein. Our appreciation also goes to our knowledgeable advisors: Howard Adams, Richard Adams, Melanie Adcock, Mark Albion, Lindsay Audin, Randy Barber, David Brower, James Cannon, Louis Clark, Archie Colander, Barry Commoner, Maurice Culver, Jennifer Davis, Jerome Dodson, Albert Donnay, Jack Doyle, Edythe Flemings Hall, Dana Friedman, Terry Gips, Lenore Goldman, Denis Hayes, Randall Hayes, Alex Hershaft, John A. Hoyt, Marv Hrubes, Joseph Kinney, Debbi Liebergot, Joel Makower, Michael Mariotte, Michael McCloskey, Susan Meeker-Lowry, Keith Mestrich, Gwen Morgan, Richard Perry, George Riddick, Steven Ross, Ruth Ruttenberg, Ray Scannell, Robert Schwartz, Joan Shapiro, Timothy Smith, Henry Spira, Jonathan Tasini, Ann Taylor, Joe Uehlein, and Eric Utne. We also wish to thank Erik Migdail, Editor, Sierra Club Books, and Joe Spieler, CEP's book agent, for their wisdom and guidance throughout the preparation of this book.

CEP Board of Directors and Staff

Preface

An architect friend of mine, one who has thought at length about the ways in which products and services are designed, likes to point out that most advertising is aimed at consumers with lifestyles rather than people with lives. The truth goes beyond advertising. Almost all of us at some point in our lives buy into the essential falsehood of the modern marketplace: that we are consumers. This book is a guide to buying our way out.

Consumerism represents a one-dimensional view of our relationship with products. No matter how extensively times may change, consumerism remains steadfast in its core belief that we human beings have the capacity to care about only one thing at a time. The "thing" may change: in the '80s, it was status; in the '90s, we crave security. But whether it appeals to materialism or fear, consumerism is always about one thing—a lifestyle measured in terms of products. Consumers are people defined by their parts, by specific desires and particular needs. Consumers have the same relationship to real people as cardboard cut-out figures do, except the cardboard figures have more depth.

The trouble with consumerism is that it suggests a world in which people are merely extensions of products, when the reverse is true. People are not extensions of products. The things we buy are extensions of ourselves—of our values, beliefs, dreams, and needs, real and perceived. Our lives are much more complicated than consumerism allows. Yes, we want clean kitchens. But we also want safe drinking water, equal opportunity for everyone's daughters and sons, safe and fair working conditions, and an environment in which nature's gift of creation can continue.

Can we have all these things and clean sinks, too? The consumer in us instinctively answers, "No." We fear the painful trade-offs that we have been duped into believing must be required. Lurking in our well-indoctrinated minds is the image of the cave that we suspect we are being asked to return to, a world without modern conveniences.

This fear stems from consumerism's doctrine that what is being offered at any one time is the best that can be offered. Despite all its promises, consumerism is more about limits than about possibilities. It says we cannot have a car that is safe, stylish, *and* energy efficient. It says we cannot have cleaning products that work well *and* are environmentally benign. It says we cannot impose social objectives on manufacturers *and* expect them to produce affordable products.

The truth is, we can. Innovative people and companies have begun to demonstrate, in the marketplace, how well-designed products and systems can fulfill their primary functions without sacrificing other things that also genuinely matter to us.

We can encourage this trend by rewarding those companies and products that see us for the multi-dimensional beings we are, with lives that are rich, complex, and valuable. Adam Smith's invisible hand will do more to spank corporations into responding than a thousand exhortations from political leaders ever could.

Teresa Heinz
Chair, Heinz Philanthropies
Vice Chair, Board of Trustees, Environmental Defense Fund
March, 1994

Shopping for a Better World

What Is Shopping for a Better World?

American consumers over the last few years have had to learn all over again how to ride out tough times and manage with shrinking paychecks. It hasn't been easy. Yet even with less money to spend in real terms, your purchases and those of your neighbors can lead to real changes in corporate policy. Your choice of what car, washing machine, computer, or even breakfast cereal to buy may make more difference than you think, especially if you let companies know that social and environmental records affect your choices. Companies wield tremendous power, but individuals can influence corporate practices and can actually help change the world. It's the simple, positive activism of casting your economic vote conscientiously.

How much do you really know about each company you support with your hard-earned dollars? Does it pour toxic materials into our rivers and atmosphere? Does it aggressively promote cigarettes even though an estimated 2.5 million people die every year as a consequence of smoking? Or does it invest in pollution prevention, donate significant portions of its profits to charity, revitalize local communities, and value the expertise of women and minorities at the highest levels of management? *Shopping for a Better World* provides you with the information you need to select products made by companies whose policies and practices you support. Not only can you find out what company makes your favorite products but you can also see that parent company's social record at a glance—all in one convenient reference guide.

Of course, whether you are purchasing a refrigerator or sneakers, no one but you can decide which products to buy for yourself and your family. Quality, safety, or price may be of paramount importance. If a certain brand is on sale, or is the only brand of sport shoes your teenager will wear, chances are that's what you'll bring home. But keep in mind that product differentiations created by advertising can be artificial, trivial, or just plain misleading. *Shopping for a Better World* was created to enable you to cut through advertising hype to reality.

Shopping for a Better World empowers you by making it easier to write or call companies on our Honor Roll and X-rated list. Their addresses are included with profiles beginning on page 76.

Companies want your business. The Council on Economic Priorities (CEP) has learned that the sensible ones will listen if enough people inform them that company social and environmental performance matters. Managers know that for every customer who bothers to write, 200 to 500 more feel the same way and will vote silently with their pocketbooks. Apparently a lot of you are doing so. *Fortune* magazine, in a January 1991 cover story by Faye Rice, reported, "Today's tougher U.S. consumers...are insisting on high-quality goods that...come from a manufacturer they think is socially responsible." And an *Adweek* review of CEP's supermarket guide stated, "[The] wildly successful checklist for the checkout, which weighs in on whether the companies behind the products are doing the right thing, has companies increasingly paying attention."

Shopping to Effect Positive Change

The Council on Economic Priorities first released *Shopping for a Better World: The Quick and Easy Guide to Socially Responsible Supermarket Shopping (SBW)* in December 1988. Many of you let us know the guide was just what you were looking for. What happened next?

- Since then, nearly a million books in our *SBW* series have been sold. (Please see page 395 to order other guides in our series.)
- In an early CEP poll of buyers of the guide, an impressive 78 percent of the 968 respondents said they had "switched brands" because of *Shopping for a Better World* ratings; 98 percent told us that all issues CEP rates were important to them; 64 percent referred to the *Shopping for a Better World* ratings whenever they shopped; and 97 percent considered the environment their top or near-top priority.
- More than 60 percent of Americans indicated they would switch brands or stores to purchase from companies that support particular social causes, according to a 1993 Cone/Roper Benchmark Survey on Cause-Related Marketing. Respondents were most impressed with companies that direct aid to causes for a year or more, thus demonstrating long-term commitment. Forty-eight percent would support companies that "donate money to a cause

through a foundation or nonprofit agency"; 29 percent applauded firms that "allow employees time off to volunteer for a cause or issue." "To succeed in the 1990s," says Edward Keller, executive vice president for marketing at Roper, "products have to meet not only the price and quality demands of consumers, but their personal values as well."

- Readers not only are joining our nationwide membership, but many are also helping to create a new spirit of corporate cooperation by writing to companies. They criticize bottom ratings and praise top ones. When a company like Perdue sports a row of question marks (?), these consumers want to know why.
- More companies, including Pfizer, Reebok, and The Gap, are working with CEP to eliminate "?" ratings. Companies that never answered CEP's complete questionnaire before are now providing more information, including privately held companies like L'Oreal, Mars, and Health Valley Natural Foods. Private firms generally do not disclose social information to private organizations. In the process, some discover good programs they were not aware of, and poor policies that need review. A number have even thanked CEP for prodding them to self-examination! Corporate willingness to disclose complete or partial information has steadily increased from 34 percent of companies surveyed our first year to 69 percent our fourth year. Disclosure in 1993 and 1994, when we queried many new companies in industries unfamiliar with CEP, reached roughly 60 percent each year.
- Citing positive corporate responses to CEP's Campaign for Cleaner Corporations (C3) recommendations, an independent panel of judges in December 1993 removed Cargill, General Motors, Georgia-Pacific, and USX from CEP's list of egregious corporate polluters. Seven of the eight companies originally named in 1992 met with CEP and C3 judges over the next year to find out how they might improve their environmental performance. Only Rockwell refused. Four companies that showed little or no improvement remained on the 1993 list, and six new corporate polluters were named. (Please see page 391 for more information.) A new list is announced every December.

- New Consumer, a British research organization modeled after and allied with CEP, has now published several books, including *Changing Corporate Values* (Kogan Page Ltd., 1991), *Shopping for a Better World* (Kogan Page Ltd., 1991), *The Global Consumer* (Victor Gollancz, 1991), and *Good Business* (School for Advanced Urban Studies, 1993). CEP is working with New Consumer on *The Transnational Corporation in a Host Country: Policy and Practice in the Developing World*, a study of sustainable development and human-rights initiatives by transnational corporations in developing countries.
- In Japan, leading journalist and author Mitsuko Shimomura surveys the corporate social responsibility of major Japanese companies. Results are published annually in book form. The 1993 survey is entitled *Social Contribution: A Report on 111 Japanese Corporations.* Led by Ms. Shimomura, who consulted with CEP on *Shopping for a Better World* research methods, the publishing giant Asahi Shimbun has established a grant-giving foundation. One of its operating projects is to conduct the annual company-by-company assessment of Japanese corporate social responsibility. Each year, Asahi covers more companies. Groups in Germany, Australia, Canada, and Holland are working on similar research.
- Alice Tepper Marlin, founder and executive director of CEP, won the 1990 "Right Livelihood Award" for "the courage and vision to show the directions in which the Western economy must develop if it is to contribute to—instead of harm—global security and the well-being of humanity." The award is presented annually in the Swedish Parliament on the day preceding the Nobel Prize presentations. In 1990, Ms. Marlin was named *Adweek's* "Woman of the Year," largely because of the impact of *Shopping for a Better World.*

CEP Helps You Shop for a Better World

The Council on Economic Priorities (CEP), an independent, non-profit public-interest research organization, is supported by a nation-wide membership as well as by individual and foundation grants. It stays on the edge of emerging social issues that affect you and your community.

Over the years, CEP has painstakingly gathered and documented facts in its major studies and research reports on subjects you want to know about—subjects as diverse as child care, air pollution, occupational safety, and the politics of defense contracting.

In 1969, when the Council on Economic Priorities was founded, few corporations acknowledged their responsibility for environmental stewardship, charitable giving, or fair employment. Today, that climate has changed. CEP, our members, and millions of consumers like you have helped change it.

CEP's goal is to inform and educate the American public and provide incentives for corporations to be good citizens, responsive to the environment and to the social concerns of all their stakeholders: employees, neighbors, investors, and consumers.

Our major recent publications include *Students Shopping for a Better World* (Ballantine Books, 1993), a guide to help young people ages 12 to 20 shop more responsibly for clothing, cosmetics, fast food, sneakers, and the like; *Shopping for a Better World: The Quick and Easy Guide to Supermarket Shopping* (Ballantine Books, 1992); *The Better World Investment Guide* (Prentice-Hall, 1991), which traces the history of the ethical investing movement, profiles major ethical funds, and rates 100 publicly held companies (out of print, but available in libraries); and *Building a Peace Economy* (Westview, 1991), which details the economic consequences of the end of the Cold War.

CEP has researched and released in-depth environmental analyses of more than 150 major U.S. corporations, including many in the oil, aerospace, food, beverage, paper products, apparel, timber, chemical, and electric-utility industries. The reports not only give detailed data on toxic releases, OSHA violations, waste and energy policies, and litigation, but also compare each company's environmental performance with that of its major competitors. (To order Corporate Environmental Data Clearinghouse [CEDC] Reports, see page 396.)

SCREEN, CEP's institutional investment research service, rates the social records of 800 companies, including the Standard & Poor's

500, and adds more each year. Institutional investors such as The Calvert Group, Covenant Investment Management, Dreyfus Corporation, Merrill Lynch, and Rockefeller & Co. depend on CEP for regular, updated information that helps them in their investment decisions. So do brokers and high-net-worth individuals. In addition to ratings, one-page profiles and quarterly news updates are provided for SCREEN subscribers. In-depth reports on specific issues, companies, and benchmark practices are available by special arrangement. Manufacturers such as Levi Strauss & Co. use SCREEN ratings as a factor in selecting vendors and our benchmark research service in developing policy and monitoring internal social and environmental performance.

CEP celebrated its 25th anniversary in 1994 at our America's Corporate Conscience Awards ceremony. The annual awards gala honors corporations for outstanding citizenship. James Preston, Chairman and CEO of Avon Products, Inc., and George Harvey, CEO of Pitney Bowes, have served as chairpersons over the years. Well-known celebrities Mike Wallace, Bill Moyers, Jane Pauley, Coretta Scott King, Ed Begley, Jr., Gloria Steinem, George Plimpton, and Joanne Woodward have been among the emcees and presenters of these coveted awards. (See page 388 for more information.)

Join us! All CEP members receive a free copy of *Shopping for a Better World* and CEP's monthly *Research Report*. To join, simply send in the order form at the back of this book.

About Using This Guide

The ratings in this new *Shopping for a Better World* are divided into two main sections. The first section lists alphabetically all the companies that appear in the guide (see page 62). The second section is arranged by product category (e.g., Baby Food or Bread) (see page 110). Within each product category, brand names are arranged alphabetically. The company that makes each product is identified by an abbreviation, found next to the product name.

As you shop, look for the company or the brand name of the product you'd like to know more about. Each entry is followed by ten columns. The first contains the abbreviation for the parent company that makes the product. (See Company Names and Abbreviations index on page 324.) The information in the next nine columns applies to that specific company. All the products made by that company or its subsidiaries will have the same rating. *Shopping for a Better World* rates companies according to their performance in the following issue areas: Environment, Charitable Giving, Community Outreach, Women's Advancement, Advancement of Minorities, Family Benefits, Workplace Issues, and Disclosure of Information. Military Contracts and Animal Testing, previously under separate columns, are now flagged in the Extras column.

Eight issues are rated using letter grades A, B, C, D, and F—providing you with a concise "report card" on the social responsibility performance of each company. A "?" means that despite much searching, we could not find sufficient information to assign a rating. Please see About the Ratings, below, for detailed explanations of each rating.

The final column, labeled Extras, contains important information about a company that is not revealed by the ratings alone. The About Extras section on page 16 explains each phrase.

About the Ratings

This section explains the ratings used throughout *Shopping for a Better World*:

- "A" indicates outstanding performance.
- "B" means above-average performance.
- "C" means moderate performance or a mixed record.
- "D" means below-average performance.
- "F" indicates poor performance or little evidence of a good record.

Wherever possible, CEP has sought to distribute the companies equally among these ratings. Unless indicated otherwise, a rating of "?" means insufficient information.

Environment

Companies are evaluated in 13 areas of corporate environmental performance:

1. Toxic Releases: in absolute terms and as a percentage of sales.
2. Environmental Policy: scope and accountability, measurable goals, senior level or board responsibility, U.S. laws followed abroad.
3. Packaging: packaging quantity, use of recycled materials.
4. Office Recycling: materials included, implemented companywide.
5. Use of Raw Materials/Waste Reduction: source-reduction programs, reuse/recycling materials in manufacturing process, switch to nonhazardous materials, disposal techniques.
6. Toxics Reduction: participation in EPA's 33/50 program, elimination of heavy metals from inks and dyes, waste tracked by the Resource Conservation and Recovery Act, use of chlorofluorocarbons and ozone-depleting chemicals.
7. Community Health: impact of operations on community health, compliance with right-to-know regulations.
8. Energy Conservation: lighting and equipment efficiency, provisions for carpooling and alternative transport, use of alternative energy sources.
9. Natural Resources: impact of operations on natural resources, extraction procedures, use of ozone-depleting chemicals.
10. Accidents.
11. Superfund Sites: number relative to industry competitors.
12. Compliance Issues: compliance with various environmental statutes.
13. Environmental Technologies.

Companies are rated based on a weighted average of performance in each of these categories. The size of the company and type of industry are also considered.

Note: Environmental ratings for companies with worldwide operations are based primarily on their U.S. operations, supplemented by assessment of their global environmental impact, where data is available to CEP.

Charitable Giving

Total worldwide cash donations (including direct corporate giving, foundation giving, and matching gifts) for the most recent year is figured as a percentage of the average of three previous years' pretax worldwide earnings. For companies taking a loss for two or more of the last three years, no calculation was made and their rating is a "?".

In-kind (noncash) giving may constitute a large part of a company's charitable giving. Due to inconsistencies in the measurement of the monetary values of these donations, however, CEP is not able to factor it into large-company total giving, except for those on the threshold between two ratings or whose in-kind giving alone is so substantial that it ensures them a top grade.

A: 1.6 percent or more of net pretax earnings given to charity.
B: 1.1 to 1.6 percent of net pretax earnings given to charity.
C: 0.8 to 1.1 percent of net pretax earnings given to charity.
D: 0.5 to 0.8 percent of net pretax earnings given to charity.
F: Less than 0.5 percent of net pretax earnings given to charity.

Community Outreach

Companies are evaluated in three areas of community impact: outreach programs, volunteer efforts, and effect of operations on local residents.

A: Focused outreach programs, strong record of promoting volunteerism, and generally positive impact of operations on nearby communities.
B: Generous, though less developed, programs with positive impact; or strong programs and moderate adverse community impact.

C: Modest community programs or mixed record.

D: Little or no evidence of programs designed to benefit community, or modest programs with significant negative impact highlighted by major lawsuits or citizen campaigns against company.

F: Significant negative impact on local communities with little or no evidence of programs designed to benefit community.

Note: Ratings in this category apply to U.S. operations only.

Women's Advancement

CEP looks at representation of women on a company's board of directors and among its corporate officers and subsidiary and division presidents. Where information is available, these ratings are adjusted up or down according to Equal Employment Opportunity Commission reports on percentages of women among officials and managers, programs established to facilitate women's advancement, purchasing from women-owned firms, representation of women among the top 25 salaried officers at the company, and lawsuits.

A: 10 percent or more female representation on the board of directors or among top officers.

B: 7 to 10 percent female representation on the board of directors or among top officers.

C: 4 to 7 percent female representation on the board of directors or among top officers.

D: Some female representation on the board or among top officers, though less than 4 percent.

F: No women on the board or among top officers.

Women's Advancement is only one indication of a company's responsiveness to its female employees. See the Family Benefits and Workplace Issues categories for other information on how companies are responding to the changing workforce.

Advancement of Minorities

CEP looks at representation of minorities on a company's board of directors and among its corporate officers and subsidiary and division presidents. Where information is available, these ratings are adjusted up or down according to Equal Employment Opportunity Commission reports on percentage of minorities among officials and managers, programs established to facilitate minority advancement, purchasing from minority-owned firms, banking with minority-owned banks, representation of minorities among the top 25 salaried officers at the company, and lawsuits.

A: 9 percent or more minority representation on the board of directors or among top officers.

B: 4 to 9 percent minority representation on the board of directors or among top officers.

C: 2½ to 4 percent minority representation on the board of directors or among top officers.

D: Some minority representation on the board or among top officers, though less than 2½ percent.

F: No minorities on the board or among top officers.

N: Neutral. Some small companies have too few employees to reflect the national demographics and/or are in geographic locations that do not reflect national demographics.

Advancement of Minorities is only one indication of a company's responsiveness to minority employees. See the Family Benefits and Workplace Issues categories for other information on how companies are responding to the changing workforce.

Note: Ratings in this category apply to U.S. operations only.

Family Benefits

CEP rates companies on a numerical scale that measures the extent and balance of family benefits offered in five major areas:

1. Leave: maternity, paternity, family, and personal.
2. Day Care: on- and near-site day care centers.
3. Flexibility: part-time return to work following parental leave, flextime, compressed work week, job-sharing, and flexplace.
4. Dependent Care: child, elder, and disabled-dependent care services.
5. Education: on-site seminars, caregiver fairs, and education materials.

The company receives a rating based on its composite score in relation to other companies under consideration.

If a benefit is in an experimental stage or in the process of being implemented, CEP counts it as a "yes." A benefit still in the research stage is counted as a "no." The size of the company and type of industry are also considered. A benefit granted through "departmental discretion" or on a "case-by-case basis" is counted as a "no" for large companies. CEP feels that only a companywide written policy can eliminate the possibility of discrimination. For small companies, however, handling employee needs on a case-by-case basis is common and can be managed fairly. CEP credits case-by-case benefits for small companies only.

Note: Ratings in this category apply to U.S. operations only.

Workplace Issues

Companies are evaluated in five work-related areas:

1. Medical/Retirement Coverage: medical coverage, retirement plan, savings plan, life insurance.
2. Labor Relations: employee relations (strikes, etc.), National Labor Relations Board charges, grievance procedures for nonunionized employees, worker-management teams on strategic-planning issues, salary differentials.
3. Workplace Safety: worker injury rates, Occupational Safety and Health Administration violations, ergonomic and other worker-safety programs, policy regarding use of video display terminals.
4. Worker Involvement/Development: profit sharing, employee stock ownership, employee suggestion program, in-house skills/literacy/career training, tuition reimbursement for work-related courses, fitness/wellness programs, employee assistance program, worker/management teams on operational issues.
5. Displaced Worker Assistance: no-layoff policy, relocation assistance, severance pay, outplacement services, job-training assistance, provision for notice.

Companies are rated based on a weighted average of performance in each of these categories. The size of the company and type of industry are also considered.

Note: Ratings in this category apply to U.S. operations only.

Disclosure of Information

A: Company provides complete and current materials on its social programs and policies either by fully completing CEP's questionnaire or by providing comparable information in printed matter or phone interviews.

B: Company provides extensive yet incomplete information on its social programs and policies either by partially completing CEP's questionnaire or by providing comparable information in printed matter or phone interviews.

C: Company provides some specific information on social programs and policies though many key questions left unanswered.

D: Company answers few questions or comments on programs and policies only in general terms. Thus, response is not detailed enough to give any real indication of the company's performance.

F: Company provides only the most basic information: an annual report, proxy statement and 10-K, or less.

For ratings by company see page 62; for ratings by product see page 110.

About the Research

In preparing this guide, the Council on Economic Priorities used information gathered in several ways:

1. questionnaires filled out by the companies themselves.
2. printed material from, or phone interviews with, company officials.
3. specialized institutions or publications such as the AFL-CIO and trade unions, American Association of Fund-Raising Counsel Trust for Philanthropy (NY), Asahi Shimbun Foundation (Japan), Atlantic States Legal Foundation (NY), *Black*

Enterprise (NY), Catalyst (NY women's research organization), *Catalyst* (VT social-investment publication), Center for Auto Safety (DC), Center for Science in the Public Interest (DC), Center for the Study of Commercialism (DC), Citizens Clearinghouse for Hazardous Waste (VA), Citizens for a Better Environment (CA), Coalition of Labor Union Women (NY), Cone Communications (MA), Conservation and Renewable Energy Inquiry/Referral Service (MD), Consumers United for Food Safety (WA), *Corporate Crime Reporter* (DC), The Data Center (CA), Earth Island Institute (CA), Environmental Action Coalition (NY), Environmental Action Foundation (DC), Environmental Defense Fund (NY), Environmental Law Institute (DC), Families and Work Institute (NY), Food and Water, Inc. (MD), The Foundation Center (NY), Friends of the Earth (DC), Government Accountability Project (DC), Greenpeace (DC), The Humane Society of the United States (DC), Independent Sector (DC), Interfaith Center on Corporate Responsibility (NY), Johns Hopkins Center for Alternatives to Animal Testing (MD), Labor Research Association (NY), Motor Voters (CA), National Anti-Vivisection Society (IL), National Association for the Advancement of Colored People (NJ), *Boycott Quarterly* (WA), National Leadership Coalition on AIDS (DC), National Safe Workplace Institute (IL), National Toxics Campaign (MA), National Women's Economic Alliance Foundation (DC), The Natural Resources Defense Council (NY), New Consumer (Unit-ed Kingdom), Nuclear Free America (MD), Nuclear Information and Resource Service (DC), People for the Ethical Treatment of Animals (MD), Renew America (DC), Rainforest Action Network (CA), Rocky Mountain Institute (CO), Sierra Club Legal Defense Fund (CA), Social Ventures Network (CA), United Nations Environment Program (NY), William McDonough Architects, Inc. (NY), Work/ Family Directions (MA), Working Committee on Community Right to Know (DC), Worldwatch Institute (DC).

4. business and public libraries, especially for such resources as

Taft Corporate Giving Directory, *National Data Book*, *Monthly Labor Review*, Bureau of National Affairs publications, Nexis and Lexis.

5. federal government agencies such as the Bureau of Labor Statistics, the Environmental Protection Agency, Occupational Safety and Health Administration, U.S. Department of Agriculture, U.S. Small Business Administration, National Labor Relations Board, and state and regional regulatory agencies.
6. advisors who are experts in our various categories (complete list in Acknowledgments, on page ix).

After months of research, we sent each company our ratings with a request for corrections and updates. All comments from companies and advisors were considered when making final ratings.

The Council looks for comprehensive, comparable data, a task that is far more difficult in some areas than in others. For example, definitive data is publicly available on charitable contributions, making this issue easy to compare. Categories such as Environment and Workplace Issues are extremely complex, so that even with substantial information, data were not always comparable company to company. Foreign companies also do not always present comparable data. Our ability to obtain and verify data is much stronger for the domestic operations of U.S. companies.

Where firms cooperated with CEP's efforts by answering all or most of our survey, a more complete picture emerges. CEP thanks the cooperating companies for providing us with comprehensive information while some of their peers did not.

Disclaimer

The ratings in this guide are based on information current as of January 1994 and in some instances earlier. The data were gathered from the following:

1. the companies themselves
2. government agencies, libraries, specialized centers, and citizens groups
3. advisors who are experts in our chosen categories

CEP claims no predictive value for its ratings; a company may change its behavior tomorrow.

CEP claims no knowledge of programs or problems not in the public domain or voluntarily submitted by the companies themselves or other sources.

CEP is a nonpartisan organization that does not endorse any product or company.

CEP ratings apply to the company as a whole and not to individual subsidiaries and divisions. Additionally, we do not purport to rate individual products alone. For such evaluations, we refer you to such sources as Consumers Union and The Center for Science in the Public Interest. Our ratings are based entirely on factual information, so it is up to each consumer to decide which companies he or she wants to support.

About Extras

The Ratings Charts that begin on page 62 include a section called "Extras." Extras comprise additional information about the social impact of a company that is not reflected in a rating. Some Extras are positive, some are negative, and some are neutral.

100 Percent Profit to Charity. Newman's Own, the natural-foods company founded by actor Paul Newman, donates 100 percent of its profits (more than $56 million since 1982) to charities. Perhaps best known of the 400 recipients is the Hole-in-the-Wall-Gang Camp for children with life-threatening diseases. Children who ordinarily spend much of their lives in the hospital are given the chance—free of charge—to form friendships and develop skills and confidence in an outdoor setting.

Animal Testing. Many individuals and organizations have become concerned with corporations that use animals in their research. Efforts to end the use of animals in testing on consumer products have been successful at many large cosmetics companies such as Revlon and Avon. Other companies continue to test on animals though they do not make medical products. Pain is often inflicted on animals to develop nonessential consumer products such as new shades of lipstick and new kinds of hairspray.

Roughly 20 million animals are used in lab research each year. The majority are rats and mice; some are dogs, cats, and rabbits. Testing by consumer-products companies accounts for a tiny fraction of all research animals; the majority are used by drug companies and in government, academic, and medical research—often resulting in life-saving medical advances. Many tests aim to protect worker health as they use materials over extended time periods and in enclosed areas.

Animals will continue to be used until we find good alternatives. So we need to make sure that they are used only for good reasons and in cases where no effective alternative to their use has been found. The aim of the test must be to protect the health of workers, find cures, and save lives. Meanwhile, we must make sure that such uses are as humane as possible.

Some companies, such as Tom's of Maine and The Body Shop, were established with the principle of no animal testing. Others, such as Colgate-Palmolive and Procter & Gamble, have substantially reduced the number of animals used and/or actively joined the search for alternative test methods.

Animal-rights activists disagree over what testing is acceptable. The cures for polio and diabetes, for example, were found through research that used animals to test for life-saving medicine and to gather knowledge about biological processes. Without more animal-testing research, we might never find a cure for AIDS or cancer. Developing new treatments for diseases has been so beneficial for sick human beings that most people feel animal testing was worth it. Others feel that we have no right to kill an animal, no matter how great the benefits. Whatever you believe, there's no doubt that careful procedures and sharing information can safely reduce the number of animals used.

Food and Drug Administration testing guidelines for new consumer products have long been murky and a source of frustration to both companies and animal-welfare advocates. In June 1993, the NIH Revitalization Act was passed, directing the National Institutes of Health (NIH) to create a plan to conduct or support research into methods of experimentation that do not require the use of animals, that reduce the number of animals used, and that produce less pain and distress in animals. It further mandates research to establish the validity and reliability of these methods. Though the law should increase government involvement in the development and validation of alternatives, no funds were appropriated for implementation.

CEP gives companies credit for investing in research on alternatives and for decreasing the number of animals tested. We recommend you seek out and read information on all sides of this issue.

The animal-protection movement has raised public awareness about the use of animals for safety testing, especially for cosmetics and household products. L'Oreal has now joined Revlon and Avon in ending animal testing for their products. Procter & Gamble has made impressive strides to reduce the numbers of animals necessary for testing. Many other companies, too, have committed substantial sums to investigating alternatives to animal testing. With the founding of the Johns Hopkins Center for Alternatives to Animal Testing 10 years ago, and development or expansion of other research centers dedicated to developing alternatives, some tests that relied on animals have been replaced with nonanimal tests.

For every animal used in testing, millions of animals suffer from birth to slaughter through factory farming—the raising, transport, and slaughter of animals on factory farms. Read the Factory Farming Extra (page 21) to learn more about this issue.

Because animal testing is such a controversial issue, the Extras section not only explains which companies are testing, but also identifies those that have demonstrated a commitment to research and/or use alternatives. An Extra for animal testing is not given if a company does no testing. Companies that do conduct tests on animals receive one of six messages:

1. **Animal Testing: Nonmedical Products.** These are companies that manufacture no medical products yet test their products on animals. They may make such products as

cosmetics or industrial chemicals. (Humans do come into contact with these chemicals, especially workers at industrial plants, so here there is a *medical purpose*.) In the last five years, the companies in this group have not reported any effort to reduce the number of animals they use and/or have not spent significant resources (under $250,000 annually) researching alternative testing methods.

2. **Animal Testing: Medical Products.** These drug/pharmaceutical manufacturers conduct tests on animals. Like those in the above category, these companies have neither significantly reduced the numbers of animals they use (by 40 percent or more) nor substantially contributed to the advancement of alternative research methods (under $250,000 annually) over the last five years.
3. **Animal Testing: Medical and Nonmedical Products.** These companies perform tests for both medical and nonmedical products. Like those in the above category, these companies have neither significantly reduced the numbers of animals they use (by 40 percent or more) nor substantially contributed to the advancement of alternative research methods (under $250,000 each year) over the last five years.
4. **Animal Testing: Nonmedical Products, Significant Alternative Efforts.** Although these companies test on animals for products that do not serve a medical purpose, they have reduced the numbers of animals tested by at least 40 percent over the last five years and/or made financial commitments of $250,000 annually or more to explore alternative test options.
5. **Animal Testing: Medical Products, Significant Alternative Efforts.** These companies conduct research on animals to further medical knowledge but, unlike those in category two, have reduced the number of animals used by at least 40 percent over the last five years and/or donated $250,000 annually to researching alternative testing methods.
6. **Animal Testing: Medical and Nonmedical Products, Significant Alternative Efforts.** These companies perform tests for both medical and nonmedical products. They have

reduced the numbers of animals tested by at least 40 percent over the last five years and/or made financial commitments of $250,000 annually or more to explore alternative test options.

For companies with any of these Extras, there may be some adjustment made for company size. To learn more about animal welfare issues, contact The Humane Society of the United States, 2100 L Street, NW, Washington, DC 20037. It offers information about fur issues, dissection in schools, animal testing, factory farming, and many environmental issues as well.

CEP's Campaign for Cleaner Corporations (C3). C3, begun in 1992, identifies some of the nation's worst corporate environmental performers in their respective environmentally risky industries. An independent panel of judges chooses the companies based on CEP's research, and the Council recommends measures to improve their environmental-management ratings. Activists contact the companies and urge them to follow CEP's recommendations. Each year, companies that act on our recommendations and show substantial improvement are removed from the list, and new polluters are named to it. For more information, please see page 391.

CEP Award. Through our annual America's Corporate Conscience Awards, CEP honors companies for outstanding records in environmentalism, charity, equal opportunity, community action, and responsiveness to employees. A panel of judges selects the winners. For information on the Corporate Conscience Awards, please see page 388.

CEDC Report. CEP's Corporate Environmental Data Clearinghouse (CEDC) has produced an in-depth, comprehensive environmental report on this company. Please see page 395 to order.

CERES Principles. Responding to the disastrous Exxon *Valdez* oil spill in 1989, the Coalition for Environmentally Responsible Economies (CERES) wrote the CERES Principles, which set forth a 10-

point commitment to a healthy environment. CERES urges all corporations to sign the principles, which include the following: (1) protection of the biosphere; (2) sustainable use of natural resources; (3) reduction and disposal of wastes; (4) wise use of energy; (5) risk reduction; (6) marketing of safe products and services; (7) damage compensation; (8) disclosure; (9) employing environmental directors and managers; and (10) allowing an annual environmental audit.

In 1993, Sun Oil Company and H.B. Fuller became the first two Fortune 500 companies to sign. General Motors joined in February 1994. At that time, there were 71 other signatories. In signing, a company makes a pledge to uphold the principles by using only environmentally friendly policies and methods, and to submit an annual progress report to CERES and to the public. Although CERES has no enforcement power, it identifies companies that aren't following the principles and urges them to do better.

Tobacco. Though CEP includes in this guide food products made by two major U.S. cigarette manufacturers, RJR Nabisco and Philip Morris, we do not list cigarettes. Because the manufacture and promotion of cigarettes is responsible for 1,000 deaths a day in the U.S. alone, CEP does not consider any brand of cigarettes a socially acceptable choice. These addictive products are aggressively marketed by producers, especially to women, minorities, and youth. Health officials and consumer activists have objected for years to billboard advertising in poorer urban neighborhoods where, they claim, people are dying in disproportionate numbers from diseases related to smoking.

As antismoking groups work to ban all print and outdoor cigarette ads, the tobacco industry is using direct marketing, such as mail offers, magazines, posters, and sponsorship of televised sporting events. It is also handing out free "samples" on busy street corners—as it did long ago in the U.S.—in countries where regulations are few and health warnings often are not required and not provided.

Factory Farming. The small family farm has largely given way to huge, modern complexes engaged in intensive animal production. In the broiler industry, chickens routinely have less than one square foot of living space per bird. Birds are genetically selected for their rapid weight gain. As a result, they often have difficulty supporting their own weight and develop painfully crippled legs. Maintaining dense populations of animals in a confined indoor space increases the likelihood of disease. The U.S. Department of Agriculture estimates that roughly one-third of all raw poultry in this country carries Salmonella or Campylobacter bacteria. The agency maintains that proper cooking and handling by consumers will prevent illness. However, the poultry industry (and meat industry) have resisted providing labels with this information to consumers. Safe handling labels on raw meat and poultry products finally appeared in May, 1994.

Veal calves are often kept in narrow stalls too small for the animals to turn around in. To give the meat a light color, the calves are fed a liquid, iron-deficient diet that can cause anemia and lower resistance to disease. Most beef cattle are fed high-calorie grain diets with little roughage, sometimes leading to liver disease. When this condition is prevalent, traces of antibiotics administered to the cattle may be found in meat sent to market.

Fair Share. The National Association for the Advancement of Colored People (NAACP) is the oldest civil-rights organization in the United States. In December 1981, the NAACP created the Fair Share Program. The program seeks to establish a relationship between the African-American community and corporate America to ensure that a fair share of dollars spent by African-American consumers are reinvested back into their communities in the form of jobs and business opportunities. The Fair Share Program promotes the following:

- Minority vendor programs for purchases of goods and services from African-American contractors, professionals, and financial and insurance institutions.
- Aggressive affirmative-action programs and opportunities for the advancement of African-Americans into senior management positions.

- Representation of African-Americans on corporate boards.
- Philanthropic contributions to worthy African-American organizations and causes.

Foreign-Based Company. Foreign companies present a challenge to corporate-responsibility researchers because the U.S. and foreign countries have dramatically different standards in several areas. In an effort to obtain more accurate and usable information for our readers, CEP in 1991 revised its research methods for evaluating transnational corporations headquartered abroad. Our questionnaire now asks the company to provide *worldwide* data for charitable giving, women's advancement, and animal testing. It requests domestic (*U.S. only*) information for minority advancement, community outreach, family benefits, and workplace issues. In the environment category, a two-part questionnaire asks for separate information about domestic operations and those outside the U.S.

Heart-Valve Suits. Shiley Incorporated, a subsidiary of Pfizer Inc., manufactured a prosthetic heart from 1979 to 1986, when the device was withdrawn due to a small percentage of reported strut fractures. Over 80,000 of these heart valves are in use around the world, as a means to extend the lives of patients whose own hearts had become diseased. By 1990, when the company reported that at least 394 Bjork-Shiley Convexo-Concave valves had broken and 252 patients had died, a class-action suit was filed by Public Citizen's Health Research Group on behalf of 55,000 U.S. heart-valve recipients. Soon after, the Food & Drug Administration (FDA) directed Shiley Incorporated and Pfizer to establish a notification and registry system (which they did through the MedicAlert Foundation) to let patients and doctors know of the danger.

In 1992, *Lancet* published findings by Dutch researchers that the fracture rate for 60-degree Shiley valves might be as much as five times higher than previously supposed. The report said that some patients should consider replacement of the risky valves. As a result, Pfizer was asked by the FDA to send a special alert with this new information to doctors and valve patients.

There is, however, alarming new information. According to a January 1994 letter to FDA Commissioner David Kessler from Dr. Sidney Wolfe, Director of Public Citizen's Health Research Group, a new Dutch study of explanted heart valves randomly chosen from 24 patients at risk showed that seven of them had the kind of strut fractures that preceded total valve failure. This indicates a fracture rate even higher than that previously stated, which was based only on reported fractures. (Many cases may have gone unreported because valve fracture symptoms resemble other episodes of heart malfunction.) Wolfe's letter asked that the FDA require Shiley and Pfizer to immediately renotify all valve patients and their doctors to help them make reoperation decisions.

Increasing TRI. The Toxic Release Inventory (TRI) is an EPA-designated facility-by-facility report on releases of 308 toxins and 20 chemical categories. CEP's methodology for assigning environmental ratings takes into account the TRI as adjusted for sales. It also incorporates the change in TRI as adjusted for sales from 1988 to 1990. Environmentalists and the media have spotlighted top emitters of TRI by state and nationwide. The vast majority of companies have significantly reduced their releases of these hazardous chemicals. The Extra specifies that a company's unadjusted TRI numbers have *increased.*

Infant Formula. There are two separate issues in the infant formula debate:

1. **Free Supplies to Developing Countries.** The morality of corporate donations of supplies of infant formula to hospitals in developing countries has been questioned for years. These free or subsidized samples are used as a marketing tool. The health implications can be severe. If breast feeding is interrupted in the early stages of postnatal care, the production of breast milk ceases. Upon leaving the hospital the mother, now dependent on the costly formula, may mix it with contaminated water or dilute it to make it last longer. These practices often result in "Bottle Baby Disease," which can lead to death. In 1981, the World Health Organization

(WHO) and UNICEF (United Nations International Children's Emergency Fund) established an International Code to regulate the marketing of breast-milk substitutes. This code is intended to be applied universally, including in the U.S.

During 1992 and 1993, according to the Interfaith Center on Corporate Responsibility, the governments of 122 nations officially told companies to end these supplies. As participants in UNICEF's Baby Friendly Initiative, AHP, Nestle, Bristol-Myers Squibb, and Abbott Labs have committed to ending free supplies in developing countries that request such action. According to ICCR Director Tim Smith, there has been positive movement, but investigators have found violations (by all companies) in a few countries.

2. **Direct Advertising to Mothers in the U.S.** The WHO Code is intended to be applied universally. However, Bristol-Myers Squibb, Gerber, and Nestle—in violation of this nonbinding code—are spending millions of dollars on TV and magazine ads that promote new formulas directly to mothers in the United States. These practices have been condemned by groups as diverse as the American Academy of Pediatrics and the National Council of Churches. A broad-based campaign to end direct advertising has begun. (Abbott Labs and American Home Products Corporation have not advertised infant formula in the U.S., but they maintain that the WHO code does not apply to industrialized countries.)

Military Contracts. This Extra refers to companies that have conventional weapons-related and/or fuel contracts totaling $500,000 or more reported in 1993 for fiscal year 1992. Contracts for food, clothing, and other basic supplies are not counted.

Nuclear Weapons. This Extra refers to companies that have nuclear-weapons-related contracts of any amount reported in 1993 for fiscal year 1992. These may include contracts for nuclear weapons or their components, and/or systems aiding launch, guidance, delivery, or deployment of nuclear weapons.

On-Site Day Care. A small but growing number of U.S. corporations offer child care at the workplace. Campbell Soup Company subsidizes 50 percent of the tuition for more than 100 children of its employees in its headquarters in Camden, New Jersey. It has also helped upgrade day-care facilities throughout the Camden area. Other companies offering on-site/near-site day care in at least one location include Apple Computer, Ben & Jerry's, Chrysler, Dayton Hudson, Hershey, Johnson & Johnson, Nike, and S.C. Johnson & Son, Inc.

Pesticide-Sterilization Suits. In 1989, the first of several groups of consolidated suits brought by nearly 1,000 Costa Rican farmworkers charged that Standard Fruit Co. (a subsidiary of Dole Food Company, Inc.) had for years used pesticides in Central America that were banned in the U.S. The company used dibromochloropropane (DBCP) on banana plantations in Costa Rica until 1979, when cases of alleged worker sterility influenced the Costa Rican government to outlaw further use of the pesticide. The company then sent leftover DBCP to Honduras, a country where health protection for workers was far less stringent. There, many more workers allegedly became sterile.

In March 1990, a Texas Supreme Court ruled that the personal-damage suit against Standard Fruit (Dole), and the developers of DBCP (Dow Chemical and Shell Oil Company) could be tried in the U.S. Before the case could come to trial, however, the defendants settled out of court for an undisclosed sum. The *Corporate Crime Reporter* put the amount at $20 million, citing a "confidential source."

Dole is critical of CEP's continued inclusion of this Extra. "It is unfair from our (the Company's) point of view. It leaves the mistaken impression that Dole is the same now as it was years ago. Today," said Dole's spokesperson, "we provide workers with an enormous amount of training on handling pesticides. Every application is supervised; we use special application equipment. Safety and environmental concerns are taken into account."

According to Dole, in 1992 Dow and Shell conducted medical testing that indicated reproductive impairment among Dole's Costa Rican workers. Within three months, Dole put together medical teams to get in touch with current and former workers in that country. Doctors tested them "to determine different levels of impairment" and, where indicated, offered compensation.

But Charles Siegel, a Dallas-based lawyer handling more than 12,000 new sterilization allegations from several countries, claims that "Dole and its representatives in Costa Rica require releases from workers before they are examined by company doctors. By signing these releases, the men are no longer represented in the suit. The company can compensate them," says Siegel, "far, far less than they would expect to receive in litigation in the U.S." In late 1993, Charles Siegel sought and won a permanent injunction against the original three defendants, plus Occidental Chemical Company, and Chiquita Brands, Inc., enjoining them and their representatives from having contact of any kind with workers exposed to DBCP. However, the defendants have removed all cases to Federal Court (as of April 1994).

Profiles. A more in-depth account of this company appears in the Honor Roll or X-rated section, beginning on page 76.

Same-Sex Partner Benefits. Lotus Development, a software manufacturer, pioneered the offering of health benefits to same-sex domestic partners in 1991. Now, more companies or divisions of companies have decided to offer these benefits, including Apple Computer, Ben & Jerry's, Levi Strauss & Co., MCA (Matsushita), and HBO and Warner Brothers (Time Warner).

Small Companies. You may wonder why CEP has included small businesses—with fewer than 100 employees—along with corporate giants with tens of thousands of employees. Not only do small companies make up 99 percent of all U.S. companies, but they often also lead the way in innovative management, provision of organically grown products, prevention of cruelty to animals, and responsiveness to employees and consumers. Of the more than three million companies with fewer than 20 employees, an estimated 200,000 have sprung up just in the last few years. Some 80 percent of new ventures go out of business every year.

In 1993, none of the small companies studied by CEP had military contracts. Not only do they avoid animal testing, but they usually are also strong advocates for animal welfare. Most small companies we analyzed recycle raw materials, use recyclable packaging, and take steps to ensure no toxic chemicals are used in the manufacturing process.

Some small businesses, particularly those with a majority of female employees, often have considerable flexibility in work arrangements: employees may work at home, work part-time or on alternative schedules, or bring children to work with them. Companies report that these arrangements cost little and have resulted in greater productivity, higher morale, and lower turnover. In the areas of Family Benefits, Minority Advancement, and Workplace Issues, however, small companies rarely do as well as large ones.

Few very small companies rated "C" or higher in Minority Advancement. If an enterprise employing fewer than 15 employees is based in a region with few minorities, it rarely has the capacity to seek them elsewhere to fill positions on its board or in top management. So CEP has given very small companies with no minorities in top management or on the board a "neutral" rating in this category.

Workplace Principles. In 1988, the Citizens Commission on AIDS (now defunct) developed the Workplace Principles, a 10-point "bill of rights" on AIDS issues in the workplace. The Washington-based National Leadership Coalition on AIDS was formed by business leaders to promote corporate action on AIDS. It asked companies and organizations nationwide to adopt the Workplace Principles and abide by them. Signatories pledge not to discriminate against workers with AIDS, to educate all employees about how AIDS is spread (and how it isn't), to keep medical records confidential, and to not require HIV screening as part of hiring practices. More than 400 companies and organizations have endorsed the Workplace Principles.

About Students Shopping for a Better World

Drawing on the firsthand experiences of people ages 12 to 20 through interviews and focus groups, CEP released *Students Shopping for a Better World* (Ballantine Books) in 1993. It highlights the issues that socially conscious young people consider most important: the environment, equal employment opportunity, animal testing for consumer products, and corporate willingness to disclose information.

Readers meet teens who are actively working to achieve positive change. They learn that this age group collectively spends more than $80 billion a year—and see how purchasing more selectively, according to one's values, has begun to make a difference.

Students Shopping for a Better World assigns report-card grades "A" through "F" in five areas for 166 companies that make or sell clothes, snacks, compact discs, tapes, personal-care products, fast food, and sporting goods. Down-to-earth discussions show how to choose a socially responsible career, handle money responsibly, and protect oneself from the excessive influence of high-powered corporate advertising.

Here are some corporate and other developments since CEP released the student guide:

- Among the "Top Teen Brands," The Gap and Reebok in 1993 greatly improved their disclosure. Reebok completed CEP's questionnaire, thereby zooming from "F" to "A" in disclosure. The Gap left out one important piece of information, and therefore rated a "B."
- Levi Strauss & Co., following its pioneering human-rights guidelines, decided not to do business in China or Burma, unless there are changes in repressive government policies in those countries. It audited 700 contractors and subcontractors for compliance, obtaining concrete improvements at a quarter of them and dropping 5 percent that were recalcitrant.
- L'Oreal ceased all animal testing in 1993.

- Youth for Environmental Sanity (YES!), based in Santa Cruz, California, has brought an environmental-education message to more than 150,000 kids at school assemblies nationwide. At each stop, members tell audiences about *Students Shopping for a Better World* and distribute copies. YES! has now reordered more guides for future tours.
- A new book, *Green at Work: Finding a Business Career that Works for the Environment* (Island Press, 1992), includes a resource list of company contacts in environmental positions who can provide information on a corporation's environmental-management practices and programs.
- REM, the popular music group, gave out 3,200 *Students Shopping for a Better World* guides with its Christmas 1993 fan-club package.
- In Fall 1992, a group called FUTURES was founded by Tara Kneller at Syracuse University to promote corporate social responsibility. FUTURES encourages other schools to set up their own active chapters and to study local businesses. Ms. Kneller, a policy-studies major, was selected as one of 85 Truman Scholars in 1993. Faculty advisor William D. Coplin, Ms. Kneller, and a group of other Syracuse University students created a *Teacher's Guide to Students Shopping for a Better World.* It is being used in high-school and college classes from Massachusetts to Texas to Washington State, and in Aruba, Dutch West Indies. (To order, see page 395.)
- The Social Venture Network (415-771-4308) established Students for Responsible Business. This membership organization sponsors an internship program open to MBA students in many schools across the country. Offering a newsletter and speakers to explain the program, the group also compiles a résumé book for second-year students, which is distributed to members of Social Venture Network and Businesses for Social Responsibility (202-842-5400), a consortium of companies committed to working for corporate accountability.
- Lyn Wong, who teaches home economics at Simi Valley High School in Ventura County, California, reports that students in her

classes are very concerned about environmental issues (*Los Angeles Times*, October 21, 1993). She decided to use *Students Shopping for a Better World* and similar publications to help inform intense discussions about such things as rainforest destruction and the environmental impact of timber cutting in the Northwest. Ms. Wong and some other "home ec" teachers in Ventura County also initiated a statewide competition on home energy conservation and other environmental issues.

- The Foundation for a Creative America awarded prizes in Fall 1993 to several young inventors at a Washington, D.C., ceremony. Among the winners were Van Thanh Doan of Oklahoma, who came up with a lab test to screen out highly toxic drugs before reaching the animal trial stage, and Kurt Beswick of Florida, who invented an offshore drilling platform designed to be environmentally safe.

Companies Reach Out to Youth—and Sometimes Exploit Them

Education. Over the last few years, corporations increasingly have targeted young people as a potentially bottomless pot of gold. Whittle Communications' Channel One is now beamed to kids in more than 12,000 schools across the country. The roughly 10-minute "news" show is accompanied by two minutes of advertising. Guess whose study found out that the children watching Channel One had acquired "little" or "no better" knowledge of events in the news than other kids? Whittle's very own study! Now entrepreneur Chris Whittle is raising money to build his own chain of "technologically integrated" schools (*Fortune*, 11/16/92). It's called the Edison Project, and Whittle hopes to start up by September 1996.

Environmental Education. Corporations, especially those with environmental weaknesses, have noted with interest the national groundswell of environmental education in schools. It has given them yet another avenue by which to reach young minds: company-sponsored environmental curricula. Though not used by all teachers who receive the free "educational" packages, the curricula are welcomed by many schools. According to *Environmental Action* (September/October 1991), Browning-Ferris Industries' "Mobius Curriculum: Understanding the Waste Cycle" and Keep America Beautiful's "Waste in Place" program were in use in more than 45 states in Fall 1991. Browning-Ferris is a waste-management firm and Keep America Beautiful was founded by the beverage industry. Both of these, as well as Dow Chemical and Procter & Gamble, promote plastics recycling without citing real problems connected with continued high production of plastics. For example, their public-relations material does not mention that plastics production uses huge amounts of toxic chemicals, and that the U.S. has been recycling only about 4 percent of plastics.

You can challenge companies to show true commitment to the environment. Randy Light, assistant coordinator of San Francisco's recycling-education program, suggests that corporations donate money to state funds to design independent educational curricula. This would help differentiate between environmental protectors and profiteers.

Advertising. Young consumers may not realize how much ads can have to do with their emerging buying habits. American consumers are hit with "up to 3,000 marketing messages a day," according to *Newsweek*. Did you know that advertising has grown to be a $130 billion-a-year industry? That's billions spent on convincing folks to buy things they often don't need, further encouraging a disposable society. The more stuff we buy, the more ends up in landfills (now over 1,500 pounds per person, per year).

Michael Jacobson and Ronald Collins, co-founders of the nonprofit Center for the Study of Commercialism in Washington, D.C., have come up with an interesting thought: "media literacy" classes to help kids in elementary and high schools better understand and cope with the commercialized society in which they live. CEP thinks this is a great idea, sort of like classes in self-defense.

Shopping for Generous Charitable Giving

Corporations have pitched in more readily in the last three decades to alleviate problems in housing, education, and child care, forging important ties with community groups. While the deepening recession in the early nineties meant some corporations had to curtail expenditures, "companies [said] they can't back away from their investment in the community," says Edmund Burke, Executive Director of the Center for Corporate Community Relations at Boston College. Many corporations listened to consumers, environmentalists, and their own employees. A 1993 Cone/Roper survey showed that 60 percent of Americans were willing to switch brands or stores to buy from companies supporting social causes they believe in. A study conducted by the New York–based Research and Forecast organization found that 50 percent of workers felt more loyal to their company when the CEO was involved in community relations.

Though many companies did cut back on cash gifts, most found other ways of helping. Learning how to give "smarter" led to more in-kind gifts like food products to Second Harvest hunger-alleviation programs, computers to high schools, and printing services for local nonprofits. Executives now spend more time in planning sessions with community groups. Companies strengthen volunteer programs by offering paid hours off for employees performing volunteer work, small cash awards to organizations where employees volunteer, and/or annual recognition of outstanding volunteers. Some firms institute job-training programs for disadvantaged youths, or set up partnerships with local governments to revitalize communities.

Colgate-Palmolive, for example, followed up on its commitment to inner-city youth by collaborating with the New York City School Construction Authority to rebuild and renovate the Wadleigh School, a junior high school in Harlem. Colgate-Palmolive provided startup funds plus planning and budgeting expertise for the school, which has components specializing in science and technology, alternative arts, and writing and publishing. Digital Equipment, Polaroid, and New England Telephone participated in a Middle

School Math Project conducted by the nonprofit Education Development Center in Massachusetts. Company volunteers conducted math classes, substituting for 32 teachers from seven school systems, while those teachers attended training seminars to update their knowledge and enhance teaching techniques.

Sara Lee Corporation and Dole Food Company are among the large contributors to Second Harvest; Giant Food has a long-standing partnership with the Maryland Food Bank.

Corporate giving as a percentage of pretax net income rose steadily for 16 years until it reached a peak of almost 2 percent in 1985. Then in 1991 and 1992, reflecting the economic downturn, corporate generosity dropped to $6 billion—just over 1.6 percent. These national figures include in-kind donations and are figured as a percentage of domestic, rather than worldwide, pretax earnings. They thus tend to be higher than CEP figures. There is no standard measure of the value of in-kind donations, so it is difficult for CEP to incorporate this type of giving into our rating criteria. Neither cause-related marketing proceeds nor in-kind donations are included in our charity ratings for large companies, which are calculated as a percentage of worldwide pretax earnings. If, however, a company's primary form of philanthropy is through product donations, as is the case with many supermarkets, then CEP does consider in-kind donations when making a rating. For small companies, we consistently included in-kind giving in our calculations.

For foreign-based companies, charitable giving is seldom as common as it is in the United States. And multinational companies based in the United States that give generously here may give little in other countries where they operate.

You can help shape the future of charitable giving:

- Support nonprofit organizations you know spend most of their money on important programs, and minimal amounts on promotion or advertising. To ascertain spending on fundraising and administration, call the National Charities Information Bureau (212-929-6300).

- Ask your employer to match your gifts generously, giving at least $2 for every $1 you donate.

- Ask your employer to donate money to the organizations where you volunteer, or to allow a few paid hours a month for such activities.
- Help raise money for your favorite causes.
- Select products made by companies rated "A" or "B."

Shopping for Equal Opportunity

The U.S. Department of Labor estimates that three-fourths of all new entrants into the workforce in the 1990s will be minorities or women. A comparison of earnings patterns doesn't inspire hope, but some companies are making efforts to change this situation.

For 1993, Bureau of Labor Statistics (BLS) average-wage figures for full-time workers show the following:

- Black Americans earned $370 per week.
- Hispanic Americans earned $335 per week.
- White Americans earned $478 per week.
- Women working full-time earn only 71 cents for every $1 a man earns, according to the U.S. Bureau of the Census.
- Many boards of directors of major companies still do not have even one female participant; a greater number lack members of minority groups.

As CEP researched the composition of corporate boards and upper management over the last 25 years, it has seen an almost universal pattern: slow but steady movement from a token woman to two or maybe three women at the top in many large corporations. While few minorities are yet on company boards, their numbers are also slowly increasing in senior management. One hopeful sign is that even with the recent round of downsizing and layoffs, about 37 percent of the companies we studied in 1993 have healthy ratings for minority advancement—roughly the same as in 1992. More companies are instituting diversity-awareness programs to help employees understand each other better, thereby helping to remove some of the old barriers to advancement.

Some companies, such as Avon, General Mills, and IBM, have upward-mobility committees and/or mentoring programs in place to eliminate barriers to the advancement of qualified women and minorities. They advertise in women's and minorities' publications and/or regularly review their personnel managers' records in hiring women and minorities.

In 1993, according to Catalyst, the New York–based women's research organization, 500 women held 721 directorships at Fortune 1000 companies. The latter number represents only 6 percent of all directorships. Minorities had even less representation.

It is possible for corporations to support equal employment opportunity even if minorities make up only a small portion of the surrounding population or if the company is in an industry where the pool of qualified women applicants is limited. Some companies, even small ones, have appointed minorities from other geographic areas to their boards.

Companies may choose to keep funds in banks owned by minorities or women, or in greenlining banks like Shorebank in Chicago (a winner of CEP's Silver Anniversary Award in April 1994), which has turned its entire neighborhood around by making local home-mortgage and small-business loans available to minorities.

By seeking out suppliers among businesses owned by minorities or women, companies provide invaluable experience and revenues. PepsiCo, for example, has a $228 million minority purchasing program. The growth of minority purchasing and banking programs has been encouraging. In 1972, purchasing programs reported $86 million in business. The National Minority Suppliers Development Council (NY) states that by 1992 (the latest year for which figures are available), purchasing programs it monitors reached $20.5 billion. Among the Fortune 500 companies, 170 participate as national members.

Greater opportunity is being extended to people with disabilities, thanks to a new federal law passed in 1990. The Americans with

Disabilities Act (ADA) ensures equal employment rights and access to public businesses for the 43 million citizens of the U.S. who are disabled.

General Mills' Red Lobster subsidiary in 1990 opened up jobs in its restaurants to more than 1,000 developmentally disabled people across the country. The parent company operates a Disability Awareness Council to help educate employees and remove attitudinal barriers concerning people with disabilities. PepsiCo's Pizza Hut subsidiary runs a Jobs Plus program at its restaurants and delivery facilities for more than 1,500 people with developmental disabilities.

You can help carry on the dream of Martin Luther King, Jr.:

- Encourage your place of work to break the "glass ceiling" when promoting and to seek out banks and suppliers owned or operated by women, minorities, or people with disabilities.
- Let your elected representatives know you support enforcement of Equal Employment Opportunity laws.
- Practice equal opportunity and teach your children to do the same.
- Join organizations that speak out for equal employment opportunities.
- Select products made by companies rated "A" or "B" in Women's Advancement and Minority Advancement.

Shopping for Our Right to Know

Consumers, investors, employees, and nonprofit groups working in the public interest all need access to facts and figures in order to form knowledgeable opinions about corporations. A company's willingness to share information on its basic operations and its social endeavors is essential to this effort, and is an indication of good corporate citizenship.

Until recently, most corporations resisted providing comparable data on social initiatives. Attempts to require companies to do so by law have been largely unsuccessful.

Though a majority of firms still do not publish information on social performance, many companies with a definite commitment to social responsibility have made it a priority. More and more companies are adding a small section to their annual reports discussing their "commitment" or "public responsibility."

While some publish glowing reports on recycled paper, full of feel-good pictures and words that provide little substantive information on the company's social programs, others routinely inform the public of the social impact of their operations, in measurable terms and using a format comparable year to year and among companies. Bristol-Myers Squibb Company, Ben and Jerry's, Sears, J.C. Penney, General Motors, Home Depot, and Kimberly-Clark are among those providing substantive information either in separate social-responsibility reports or in sections of their annual reports. Of the 191 companies rated in this book, 90 cooperated fully by providing extensive information, 27 provided more limited information, and 75 gave us little or no information. Please see page 13 (About the Research) for how CEP gathered information.

Let companies know that you want information about their social performance:

- Ask companies that did not cooperate (they received a "D" or an "F" for Disclosure) to provide information for our next edition.
- Urge members of Congress and the Securities and Exchange Commission to require annual disclosure of comparable data on corporate social performance.
- Encourage companies to publish meaningful social-responsibility reports, often called social audits or stakeholder reports.
- Select products made by companies rated "A" or "B" in Disclosure.

Shopping for a Thriving Community

Walk through any community in America—is it vital? Thriving? Or are there shuttered businesses and homes for sale on every block? Most cities and towns have had reversals tied to the recent recession. When companies restructure and lay off thousands of employees, the severity of the dislocation caused depends to a large extent on how the corporation handles it. It may offer extensive retraining, generous severance pay, or a chance to transfer within the company. Or it may merely hand out pink slips. In some cases, companies simply pull up stakes with little notice and leave a community for another one where labor or taxes are cheaper. That has led to American ghost towns.

Even before the economy weakened, however, the lack of affordable housing for low- and middle-income families and of quality public education had taken a sad toll on communities across the nation. Increasingly, the corporate community has heard and begun to respond with innovative community-outreach programs.

Companies can invest in low-cost housing in a variety of ways: the construction of new housing; the refurbishment of existing housing; or the revitalization of entire neighborhoods. S.C. Johnson & Son, Inc., for example, supports the Racine Habitat for Humanity and is an active member in the Racine County Economic Development Corporation (Wisconsin). Procter & Gamble organized an equity fund of $4.5 million from Cincinnati companies to provide housing for low-income people in the community. Brooklyn Union Gas Company's Cinderella Project (Area Development Fund) worked with local banks, development corporations, and foundations to develop some 5,000 residential housing units and 30 commercial units since 1989.

Corporations can also contact experienced intermediaries for help in evaluating local housing needs and managing housing programs. The Local Initiatives Support Corporation (LISC) in New York City, the Enterprise Foundation (EF) in Columbia, Maryland, and the National Equity Fund (NEF) in Chicago, Illinois, are three such intermediaries. They act as financial go-betweens, distributing corporate funds to local community organizations.

Their work is having an impact. For example, LISC has collaborated with 875 community-development groups to create more than 44,000 housing units. In its first six years, NEF raised $620 million from 100 corporations and created more than 15,000 affordable homes in 62 cities nationwide.

By staking these organizations with grants and investing in the consortia they put together, companies provide housing and can also aid their own workforce. Affordable housing near company workplaces aids both in recruitment and in retention of employees. Employee productivity is also positively affected because workers don't have to worry about excessive traveling time and expenses.

Thoughtful companies have realized that without a decently educated pool of workers to choose from, the proximity of residences to the workplace will not matter. So they are responding with imaginative programs: Adopt-A-School, literacy projects, vocational training, employment programs, and volunteer and tutoring projects. With these programs, companies hope to breathe new life into the school systems they depend on.

Adopt-A-School can be a fine example of a program that brings the corporate world and the community together. A business may help students prepare for the job market by supplying public schools with updated equipment, enhancing incentives for good academic performance, and placing employees in schools as instructors or counselors.

Schools should be wary, however, of companies that use them primarily as marketing extensions—where the emphasis is on familiarizing young minds with brand names rather than on improving the quality of education, or when the corporate financial and staff commitment is minimal and lacks substance.

A company's greatest resource—and link to the community—is its employees. Volunteerism is a positive way to help the community and a visible way to enhance the company's name. Through executive assistance to community organizations, paid release time for employees, grants to organizations for which employees volunteer, job banks, and involvement of retired employees, communities may receive much help to address local problems.

To make your community a better place, you can do any or all of the following:

- Volunteer at a community center, public-interest group, or school.
- Encourage your employer to establish a strong volunteer program, to invest in affordable housing, and to support local schools.
- Join a local organization that promotes housing and economic development or public-education efforts.
- Consider a career in community work or teaching.
- Support companies rated "A" or "B" in Community Outreach.

Shopping for Family Benefits

A high degree of productivity, superior morale, and low absenteeism among workers are like money in the bank to corporations. Yet it has taken most companies years to comprehend that changes in family structure and the economy are creating a workforce burdened with worry—and that something must be done to help.

Nevertheless, relatively few corporations provide a truly family-friendly environment. In 1991, only 37 percent of women in companies of 100 or more were covered even by unpaid maternity leave. Only 8 percent of full-time employees were eligible for any kind of child-care assistance. Companies that want to help families must be willing to examine long-entrenched ideas. Once new policies are introduced, companies must check to ensure they are followed by managers in every part of the company. US West, for example, found that employees in some locations were not enjoying the same excellent family benefits as employees in other areas. It worked hard to rectify the situation and was once again listed among *Working Mother*'s "100 Best Companies" in 1993.

The urgent need for corporate family benefits has moved beyond concerns about child care to encompass the broader area of dependent care. Americans have achieved greater longevity than ever before. For many people with aging parents, however, this can create anxiety as they struggle to fit doctor visits and personal care into days already crowded with work. One-quarter of all families with children under age 18 are headed by a single parent (U.S. Census Bureau, 1991). In two-parent families, both mother and father in the workforce is now the norm, not the exception. Thus, dealing with work and family demands is especially difficult for the "sandwich generation"—those employees with growing families and responsibility for elder care.

Corporate health indicators such as the degree of active employee involvement, turnover, and absenteeism, may begin to show that companies committed to easing work/family strains have simply found it to be good business. A 1992 Families and Work Institute (FWI) study of companies that included Johnson & Johnson and AT&T indicated a positive relationship between use of strong family support systems and higher morale and productivity. Among Johnson & Johnson workers who availed themselves of family leave and flexible scheduling, absenteeism was about half that of the total company workforce. It cost AT&T as much as 32 percent of an employee's annual salary to provide several months' unpaid parental leave—but the company could lay out 150 percent of salary if it replaced the worker. Another study, which University of Chicago researchers conducted at Fel-Pro, Inc. (auto-parts manufacturer, Skokie, IL) backed up FWI findings. Employees using the company's generous family-friendly policies are high performers, "more active in team problem solving and almost twice as likely to submit suggestions for improvements" (*Business Week*, June 18, 1993). Fel-Pro won an Honorable Mention for Employee Responsiveness at CEP's Corporate Conscience Awards ceremony in 1990.

Elder Care. The U.S. General Accounting Office (GAO) reports that there were 26 million Americans aged 60 or over in 1965. This number jumped to 42 million in 1990. By the year 2030, an estimated 83 million (nearly 28 percent of the population) will be 60 or over. The percentage of working people who are primary caregivers for an elderly relative has grown from 10 percent in 1980 to more than 20 percent in 1992, according to the Families and Work Institute. And employees providing elder care may well reach more than 40 percent of the workforce by the turn of the century.

Resource and referral (R&R) services are the most effective way for a company to aid employees with responsibility for elder care, according to Andrew Scharlach, a professor of aging at the University of California at Berkeley (*Wall Street Journal*, June 21, 1993). He estimates that the annual cost to employers for absenteeism and turnover among workers who must care for disabled or elderly dependents is roughly $2,500 per employee. Still, says Mr. Scharlach, though caregivers could save considerable time and money by using R&R services, less than 20 percent of workers do so.

Most of the companies on *Working Mother*'s "100 Best Companies for Working Mothers" list do provide resource and referral for elder care. Some, such as Home Box Office, also offer seminars and support groups for caregivers. Other corporations meet elders' needs in different ways: Lancaster Laboratories (Lancaster, PA), a consultant in the environmental, food, and pharmaceutical fields, has an on-site center where employees' elderly relatives may come during the day. The Stride Rite Corporation (Cambridge, MA), though not on the 1993 *Working Mother* list, established the nation's first company-run intergenerational child-and-elder day-care center.

In June 1991—two years before family-leave legislation was passed—Nordstrom (Seattle, WA) extended its companywide leave policy to provide up to 12 weeks off (unpaid) in any 24-month period for employees caring for elderly parents. NationsBank (Charlotte, NC), fifth-largest bank in the U.S., has exceptional work/family programs, including a $10 million Dependent Care Fund, to be used for startup and continuing support of both elder- and child-care programs for its employees.

Many progressive companies hire work/family coordinators. NationsBank has created a staff dedicated to the development and management of family programs.

Child Care. In the early nineties, as working parents twice saw President George Bush veto family-leave legislation, a group of 11 corporations decided to do something. They organized and helped obtain funding for the American Business Collaboration for Quality Dependent Care (ABC Collaborative), which over 1992 and 1993 allocated more than $26 million for elder- and child-care programs in

25 states. Those founding companies were Allstate Insurance (80 percent owned by Sears, Roebuck & Co.), Amoco, AT&T, Eastman Kodak, Exxon, IBM, Johnson & Johnson, Motorola, Travelers Insurance, Work/Family Directions, Inc., and Xerox. Some 133 other corporations have now joined ABC to help support its projects in their communities.

Family Leave: Welcome and Long Overdue. Signaling support for U.S. families, President Bill Clinton in February 1993 signed into law the Family and Medical Leave Act (FMLA). This legislation requires employers of 50 or more persons to provide up to 12 weeks' unpaid leave for childbirth, adoption, or serious illness of the employee or a close family member. Employees are guaranteed the same job or an equivalent one, and health-care benefits are maintained by the employer during the leave. The U.S. still lags behind other industrialized countries in this area. Japan and several European countries provide more extensive leave, often paid, for childbirth and illness.

The Milwaukee-based National Association of Working Women (also called "9 to 5") continues its efforts to strengthen the legislation, and seeks a national policy of extended, paid coverage. You may reach 9 to 5 at 800-522-0925.

Shopping for a Better Workplace

Not every employee aspires to become chief executive officer; not every employee seeks a job in management. Nor is everyone qualified. But all people who work expect to be treated fairly and with respect. At socially responsible companies, all receive a competitive salary, comprehensive health insurance, pension plans that can move from job to job, the right to organize without intimidation, in-house education programs or tuition reimbursement, and job security or adequate notice with opportunities for retraining or outplacement. Workers who participate in profit sharing or employee stock ownership plans (ESOPs) tend to feel a personal stake in their company's success. Critics argue, however, that ESOPs are sometimes offered as substitutes for good employee benefit plans and compensation.

Safety at work is still a huge problem in the U.S. But a comprehensive Occupational Safety and Health Administration (OSHA) reform measure reintroduced in 1994 would address many problem areas. It would set up worker/management safety and health programs at every business with 11 or more full-time employees and extend OSHA coverage to public employees who have been excluded up to now. From 1970 to 1990 the number of workplace fatalities dropped. But workplace injuries tripled. "Every day in America, 17 people die on the job and more than 16,000 workers are injured," says Joseph Dear, Assistant Secretary of Labor for Occupational Safety and Health. In 1992, workplace injuries cost employers $115 billion.

Advances in computer technology and engineering have transformed the way our offices and factories function. But the benefits of technology can be offset by new threats to the environment and to workers' health. Computer screens emit low-level radiation. Certain types of assembly-line work or data-processing jobs may lead to carpal tunnel syndrome (repetitive motion injuries). Exposure to asbestos or other dangerous substances may cause fatal illnesses that are not detected until years later.

Carpal-tunnel injuries account for an increasing number of workplace illnesses in today's automated society. The Bureau of Labor Statistics says that cumulative-trauma disorders accounted for 62 percent of the 457,000 occupational illnesses in 1992, compared with 48 percent of the 240,900 workplace illnesses in 1988. Cases of repetitive-motion disorders are spreading from blue-collar jobs to jobs that involve white-collar work with blue-collar rhythms and discipline. Data-entry workers are particularly susceptible. Supermarket checkers and cashiers have also experienced these disorders. OSHA plans to issue guidelines that may eventually become mandatory for cutting the incidence of cumulative-trauma disorders. Meanwhile, better workplace and equipment design and regular scheduling of breaks could reduce the risks of these disorders.

Some companies also make a point of announcing policies of nondiscrimination based on sexual orientation. Progressive workplaces support the right of all individuals to work regardless of race, religion, gender, ethnicity, sexual orientation, or other "identifiers." One of the most pressing issues of the 1990s has been the AIDS epidemic and the impact it has had on the workplace. Socially responsible workplaces ensure confidentiality to those who want it, and encourage affected workers to stay on the job as long as possible.

To reflect evolving workplace issues and advisor recommendations, CEP strengthened its rating criteria in 1992. To earn a top rating, companies now must offer comprehensive medical and pension benefits, have in place some mechanism for handling employee grievances, and be free of significant OSHA violations and National Labor Relations Board cases.

For a discussion of equity for disabled workers, please read Shopping for Equal Opportunity. For a discussion of family benefits in the workplace, including dependent care and flexibility, please read Shopping for Family Benefits.

Here's how you can show your support for a better workplace:

- Make sure your own workplace adheres to local and federal rules and regulations.
- See that your office workplace provides regular breaks, ergonomic seating, and company-subsidized eye examinations for operators of video display terminals.
- Support or join groups that promote workplace safety.
- If your workplace already offers good programs, take advantage of them so you can improve your skills, do a better job, and advance.
- Avoid patronizing companies with documented records of poor safety, and write to the chief executive officer informing him or her of your action.
- Look for the union "bug" or other union identifiers on items you buy. If your company has unions, become a member.
- Make yourself heard where you work. If your company has a newsletter that solicits employee input, take the time to write in with suggestions to improve the workplace.
- Select brands made by companies rated "A" or "B."

Shopping for a Greener World

Since Earth Day 1990 we have seen an explosion of claims about how environmentally responsible companies are. At both the manufacturing and sales ends, companies continue to jump on the "green marketing" bandwagon. Some of these claims are sincere, others cynical. But at least one thing is certain: the greening of the marketplace is no passing fad.

There are many examples of corporate "green" activities. Xerox is collecting copy cartridges from some machines for recycling. Two large California utilities were the first in the country to announce they would reduce total carbon-dioxide emissions by 20 percent over the next 20 years. Furniture maker Herman Miller eliminated rainforest hardwoods from its line of office chairs. Procter & Gamble has increased the recycled content of many of its packages. Fort Howard introduced 100 percent recycled Green Forest toilet paper. Natural Brew coffee filters are unbleached and contain no dioxins.

How can you tell whether a product is really green? Many products advertised as environmentally sound do not prove so under careful scrutiny. Unfortunately, few standards currently exist for assessing a company's or a product's environmental impact. However, many groups and individuals are working to shed light on these questions and to develop solutions.

The Rainforest Alliance's Smart Wood Program, for example, certifies rainforest woods logged in a manner that sustains the environment. It has developed criteria for certification based on a forestry operation's demonstrated understanding of the local forest ecology, conservation of biological resources, and concern for the well-being of local communities.

On Rainforest Alliance's list of Smart Wood sources, there are two U.S. retailers that sell tropical wood products made *exclusively* of Smart Wood. They are The Plow & Hearth, mail-order retailer of teak outdoor furniture in Orange, Virginia (800-627-1712) and Smith & Hawken, mail-order retailer of outdoor furniture in Javan teak or Honduran cedar, Mill Valley, California (415-383-4415). For more information, call Rainforest Alliance (212-677-1900).

In July 1992, the Federal Trade Commission (FTC) issued guidelines on several environmental terms whose meanings have been unclear to the public and, therefore, often abused by product manufacturers. Though purely voluntary (no penalties if companies don't use them), the guidelines can help you to evaluate supermarket products. Here are some of them.

Degradable, Biodegradable, Photodegradable. Such claims should present solid evidence that the product will indeed break down in landfills. Lack of such evidence got Mobil in trouble when it claimed degradability for Hefty Bags a few years ago.

Ozone-friendly. Though many makers of aerosol and polystyrene foam products trumpet that they are free of ozone-depleting chlorofluorocarbons (CFCs), some have substituted still-harmful ingredients such as trichloroethane or hydrochlorofluorocarbons. Some are using hydrocarbons such as butane that contribute to smog. If you are concerned about harmful propellants, look for simple pump-operated spray containers and call companies using harmful chemicals to register your concerns.

Recyclable. The problem here is that if a container cannot be recycled anywhere near you, it isn't really recyclable. Most recycling facilities, for example, do not process polypropylene, whether it has a "recyclable" mark or not. In general, only containers marked "1" (soft-drink bottles) or "2" (milk and detergent jugs) inside the recycling symbol are frequently recycled, according to *Consumer Reports*. Claims of recyclability should be qualified.

Recycled Content. This label should mean that material used to manufacture a product had been headed for the solid-waste stream. "Post-consumer" waste (actually used by consumers before discarding) is more helpful in the reduction of solid waste than "pre-consumer" waste (mill trimmings, production rejects, etc., long recycled by manufacturers to save money).

Model "minimum content" legislation drafted by 12 states in the

U.S. requires manufacturers to use a varying percentage of post-consumer recycled material in their production processes—within a set timeframe—to produce things like telephone books and newspapers, plastic bags and containers. This increases demand for the recyclable material collected by local governments. Federal government procurement offices spending over $10,000 a year must now purchase, when available, "EPA-preferred" materials and supplies that are recycled or contain recycled material.

Despite such initiatives, however, meaningful recycling—with measurable impact—is still in its infancy in the U.S. The country still has a tremendous problem with the accumulation of solid waste, most of which is packaging.

Germany has led the way in reducing packaging waste, adopting the Packaging Ordinance in 1991 that directed stores to take back all packaging, including boxes, bags, bottles, and cans. When businesses were told they had to comply or pay a deposit of 30 cents on each package, many decided to work together to fulfill the requirements. More than 600 retail, consumer-goods, and packaging companies formed the Dual System: a separate, private organization (other than the public waste-collection operation) to collect, sort, and recycle packaging waste. When this system is introduced throughout the country, Germany expects to recycle at least seven million tons of packaging annually—about half (by volume) of the domestic waste in Germany (see charts, next page).

Already the results are impressive. In 1992, half a million tons less packaging was used than in 1991. Other European governments, including Austria, Belgium, France, and the Netherlands, have introduced regulations similar to the Packaging Ordinance, and expect that a coordinated European Community Directive will result. Meanwhile, American companies with German affiliates, such as Coca-Cola, Kellogg's, and Procter & Gamble, have significantly reduced the packaging of their products for use in Germany. (Information on German environmental efforts comes from Frank J. Sudol, Manager, Division of Engineering & Contract Administration, City of Newark, New Jersey, who recently traveled to Germany.)

The Coalition of Northeastern Governors (CONEG) is working

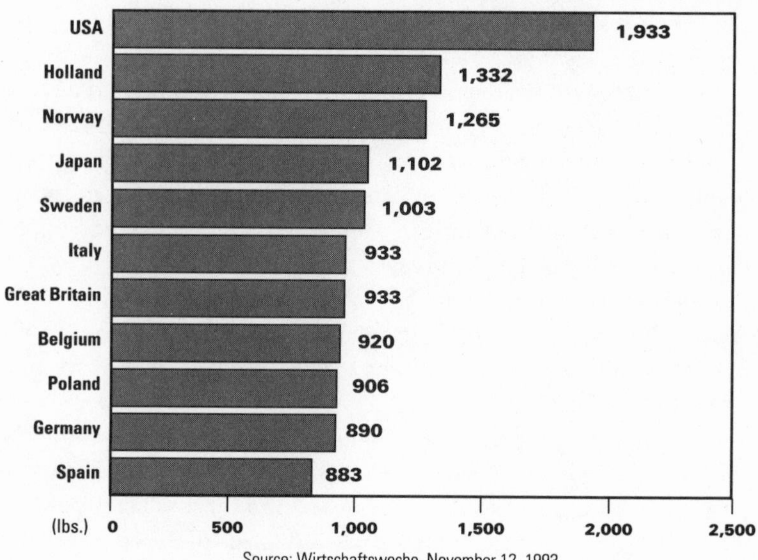

Source: Wirtschaftswoche, November 12, 1993

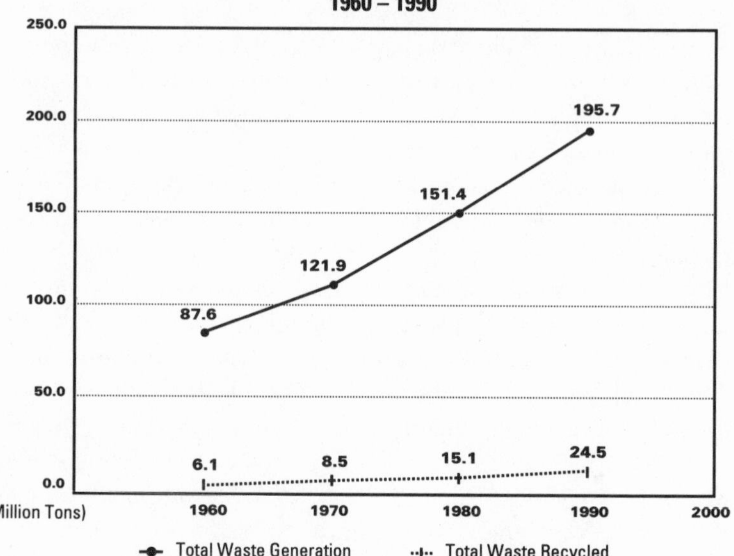

Source: EPA Waste Characterization Report, Franklin Associates, 1992

to make a real dent in U.S. packaging problems and has gone straight to the source. CONEG challenged 256 companies to use more recycled content, enhance recyclability, and cut down or eliminate use of toxic heavy metals in inks. Campbell Soup, Clorox, Gillette, Procter & Gamble, and Scott Paper are among 33 companies that have introduced more environmentally sound packaging as a result. Fourteen states have passed legislation proposed by CONEG to reduce use of heavy metals.

Labeling Helps You Choose

The U.S. has joined the many countries that have voluntary eco-labeling programs, so that environmentally friendly products may carry a validated seal of approval. In 1977, West Germany pioneered the "Blue Angel," the first uniform "Green" seal of approval. This system, which takes into account the use of recycled material or material not harmful to the ozone layer, is used nationally to designate more than 3,600 environmentally preferred products in 64 product categories. A label based on Germany's successful model is being discussed for use throughout the Western European Community. Canada and Japan have adopted a more stringent "cradle-to-grave" scrutiny, using many criteria, for their eco-labeling.

Unlike other countries' programs that are government sponsored, U.S. programs are run by privately operated organizations. The nonprofit Green Seal Inc., based in Washington, D.C., was established as a CEP initiative. Now independent, it is chaired by Denis Hayes (cofounder of Earth Day), who invited well-known environmental and consumer advocates to serve on its board. This organization is the only one working internationally to harmonize standards. Green Seal's standards are set by a scientific advisory board and an Environmental Standards Council, and product claims are verified by Underwriters Laboratories. Companies must pay for testing to prove their products are deserving of the Green Seal, plus an annual licensing fee. Only products that meet Green Seal standards may use the symbol. Green Seal's product scrutiny, called "environmental impact evaluation," focuses on a number of aspects that could be potentially harmful to the environment. By 1994, 48 products were certified, including compact fluorescent lamps made by General Electric (OH) and Lights of America (CA); re-refined engine oil products from Safety-Kleen (Ontario, Canada), and Cato Oil and Grease (OK); water-saving hoses made of recycled tires by Aquapore Moisture Systems, Inc. (AZ); recycled paper products from Mohawk Paper Mills (NY); and water-efficient toilet fixtures made by Clivus Multrum (MA) and Sanitation Equipment (Ontario, Canada). Certification was also awarded to the Clean Air Cab Company (DC) for its fleet of alternative-fueled taxi cabs.

Green Cross is a division of Scientific Certification Systems (SCS), headquartered in Oakland, California. The organization visits manufacturing sites to check out packaging and content claims. Green Cross has certified more than 400 products. Its seals indicate the product is outstanding in a specific area of environmental friendliness, such as whether the item is biodegradable. The organization has said that it intends to do a complete "life-cycle analysis" of products, although this has proved daunting to many. SCS scientists have certified pesticide-free produce and worked with farmers to reduce reliance on toxic pesticides since the mid-eighties.

Moving Toward Green: New Architecture and Building Supplies

If you're an average American, chances are you spend about 80 percent of your time indoors. But that could be damaging to your health, according to a number of reports that have surfaced over the last several years. In some cases, recurring respiratory ills and low productivity have been blamed on "sick office buildings" where air quality was poor. Investigation often showed evidence of inadequate ventilation and/or the presence of chemical emissions from such things as veneered furniture, foam insulation, or carpeting. People with a history of allergies are reported to have moved into their dream homes, only to find they were unable to live in them.

Now, however, it is possible to build—or retrofit—homes and offices in ways that produce healthy interior environments and save in the long run on energy and materials.

CEP talked with architect Bill McDonough, founder of William McDonough Architects, who is busy encouraging others in the building industry to think in terms of the environment, and come up with ideas to make preserving it cost effective. Mr. McDonough and the Rocky Mountain Institute were brought in by the Center for Research Management to lead the environmental consultation for the design team that created Wal-Mart's new Eco-Store in Lawrence, Kansas. Half of the store uses daylighting—high-tech skylights that illuminate the store when the sun shines. They are 55 percent more efficient than ordinary skylights in allowing light to enter without heat. Dimmable fluorescent lights are in place for cloudy days. To save still more energy and energy dollars, the building was converted from steel to wood construction, and only woods from well-managed forests were used. No CFCs were used in either construction or cooling systems. When the building's use as a retail outlet ends, it can be recycled into housing.

"For America's largest store to experiment with this innovative approach," says McDonough, "sends a significant signal to the market. Although the retail world is still completely auto-related, this is a small but important step in the right direction. We still need to look forward to more sensible large-scale planning for our communities." (In 1993, Wal-Mart was opening new stores across the country at the rate of three a week.)

The Colorado-based Rocky Mountain Institute's (RMI) Green Development Services (GDS) program conducts research into the financial and practical implications of environmentally responsive development, and consults with architects and developers to produce more livable and environmentally sound structures. Dianna Lopez Barnett, Senior Research Associate at GDS, not only shared with CEP fascinating glimpses of new developments in "green architecture" but also shed light on which building materials you can use to upgrade your home in an environmentally safe way. (This information is from research done for *A Green Primer on Sustainable Building*, Dianna Lopez Barnett and William Browning, a guide for builders and architects that became available from RMI in spring 1994. Contact RMI at 303-927-3851.)

The Audubon Institute headquarters in New York City is an excellent example of recycling an older building for a new life more gentle to the environment. Designers chose carpets containing no formaldehyde (which many conventional carpets do contain) and paints with no harmful volatile organic compounds (VOCs). (VOCs affect the ozone layer and create a less healthy environment for workers.) All organic waste generated in the building is composted to keep a rooftop garden green and thriving.

New as it is, this innovative approach to building presents some encouraging statistics. According to information gathered by Green Development Services in office buildings constructed or retrofitted using "green" specifications, workers experienced a productivity increase of 7 to 15 percent. Absenteeism dropped 15 to 25 percent. "Green" buildings use one-tenth to one-half the amount of energy and water of conventional buildings. Additional costs incurred in construction, if any, are usually paid back in three years or less.

Case in point: When the British-owned Body Shop set up its new U.S. headquarters in North Carolina, the architect wanted to incorporate environmentally responsive principles, but she was concerned about added costs. However, the paint manufacturer for the project offered to lower his bid by $2,000 so the architect could use costlier non-VOC paints. Why? The manufacturer wanted to have the paints used in a test case. In addition, the contractor said his work crew could breathe easier and work faster if it didn't need frequent "fresh-air" breaks; non-VOC paint is a superior product that covers more completely, requiring fewer coats of paint; and paint without VOCs is nontoxic, so he would have no disposal costs for any leftover paint.

"Green" Construction Materials: New, Old, and Yes, Recycled

By now, all you do-it-yourselfers out there are probably wondering where you can pick up some non-VOC paint! And did you know that most brands of joint compound contain toxic chemicals that are considered cancer causing? According to GDS, many users don't wear masks when sanding joint compound, and it can be harmful to the lungs. Now there is a new kind of joint compound available that is 99 percent free of toxic chemicals. To find out where to buy these and similar products, consult *The Green Pages*. Call 212-779-3365 to order this resource guide ($30) to more than 200 materials and products. Building professionals may wish to subscribe to a newsletter on environmentally sustainable design and construction, the *Environmental Building News*. Call 802-257-7300.

Remember that old-fashioned cork-backed linoleum in your grandmother's kitchen? Still being made from linseed oil, cork, and other benign ingredients, it is a perfect example of an older product that always was environmentally sound.

Builders are seeking ways to recycle old building materials: wood from old structures such as barns is often still strong and usable, as is; even wood salvaged from the ocean can be dried out and used instead of new lumber products.

Homeowners wishing to retrofit their homes (or offices) using environmentally sound principles may want to consult RMI's *Energy Efficient Homes*, published in January 1994 by Brick House Publishers.

Consumer Choices Carry Clout

It's clear that old familiar companies, new entrepreneurs, and the government are responding to consumer and citizen concerns about environmental issues. Below we've provided a list of things you can do individually to help keep up the momentum.

- Reuse containers and products as often as possible.
- Take a mesh, string, or canvas bag to the store for your shopping trips instead of accepting still more plastic bags. For major shopping, fill it with your accumulated paper or plastic bags and reuse them.
- Recycle newspapers, corrugated cardboard, bottles, cans, and whatever other materials your community or municipality collects. The Environmental Protection Agency estimates that 70 percent of all incinerator ash is glass and metals, which we should be recovering.

- Buy fresh ingredients. They are usually more nutritious, tastier, and less enveloped in packaging. Whenever possible, shop at farmers' markets and farm stands. Chances are, the farther food must be shipped, the more synthetic preservatives it will contain—and the more fossil fuel will be used to get it there.
- Start a backyard compost pile to dispose of kitchen scraps. An estimated 20 to 30 percent of household trash disposed of in landfills could be easily converted into useful garden fertilizer through composting.
- Choose personal-care and paper products that have no artificial scent or color, to avoid additives that may be irritating to people with allergies.
- Many shaving creams contain ammonia and ethanol. Look for natural alternatives. Or just use a little soap.
- Look for natural or nontoxic alternatives to household cleaners, paints, garden supplies, building materials, and so on. There are now cleaners available that are free of phosphates, chlorine, and petroleum. Concentrated cleaners are good because they need less packaging. If you read the label of a product you have used, but don't like the content, let the company know. Companies do listen.
- Convince your local supermarket to begin a shelf labeling program that highlights products that are less harmful to the environment. Here are four areas to start with: reusable products; products made from or packaged in recycled material; products containing no toxic ingredients; and organically grown food. Ask the store to set up an advisory board for the program and to invite the participation of community environmental activists.
- Eliminate the use of lawn chemicals. Almost 70 million pounds of potentially hazardous chemicals are applied to American lawns each year. A green, healthy lawn can be maintained with organic fertilizers, nontoxic pest-control techniques, and a little elbow grease. Better yet, replace your lawn with a field of long grasses, wildflowers, or myrtle, and save on water and labor while eliminating the need for chemical treatments.

- Plant trees. Trees turn carbon dioxide into oxygen. Well-placed trees around a house can lower air-conditioning needs by 10 to 50 percent.
- Start or join a community garden. In urban areas, gardens bring communities together and bring a bit of nature into the city.
- Urge your school(s) to provide environmental education. But it should come from an independent source; watch out for corporate curricula. Some are filled with self-serving information.
- Conserve energy. Make sure household equipment and fixtures are maximally efficient in their use of electricity and water. Weatherize your home. See Shopping for Conservation and Energy Savings on page 60.
- Reject disposable products when possible. Use cloth diapers. Buy a pen with a replaceable cartridge or one that is refillable. Use razors with replaceable blades instead of totally disposable ones.
- Avoid products that contain ozone-depleting CFCs, such as cleaning sprays for sewing machines, VCRs, and electronic equipment; aerosol dust removers for cameras; rigid insulation; and foam packaging. Unfortunately, many of these products have no workable substitute currently on the market.
- Leaky car air conditioners are a major source of CFC emissions. If your car has air conditioning, make sure it's well sealed. An increasing number of shops will capture and recycle your car's CFCs.
- Don't buy products made from endangered or overexploited species. Avoid furs, ivory, reptile skin, tortoise shell, and exotic hardwoods such as teak, koa, or zebrawood that aren't harvested sustainably.
- Write to company executives and tell them what you like (or don't like) about their policies.
- Choose brands in this guide made by companies rated "A" or "B" on their environmental stewardship.

Shopping for Better Packaging

Americans love packaging. And the products on supermarket and drugstore shelves reflect that love affair: nearly everything, it seems, is wrapped in something, sometimes a lot of things. Even produce—onions and corn-on-the-cob—sit neatly on a plastic foam tray, encased in clear plastic wrap. Some products have layer upon layer of packaging, for no apparent reason.

Some packaging is important—it prevents tampering and theft, ensures cleanliness, and can be imprinted with helpful information. But a great deal of it is unnecessary and wasteful.

You needn't walk far down any supermarket aisle to find a plastic bowl covered with a plastic lid, contained in a cardboard box, which is shrinkwrapped in yet more plastic. Ironically, some of these overpackaged goods are given awards by the packaging industry for their innovative designs. It is precisely these "innovations" that contribute to our clogged landfills. The average American discards 1,570 pounds of trash each year. Packaging accounts for an estimated 30 percent, or about 470 pounds a year for every man, woman, and child in the country.

The problem isn't just the amount of packaging; it's also the type of materials used. A growing number of products are being wrapped in "composites"—packages containing several layers of materials and adhesives. The components of these boxes cannot always be separated from each other before being thrown away and thus cannot always be recycled. Such packages are likely to end up in landfills, where they may take centuries to break down.

Even when packaging consists of only one type of material, it is often an unrecyclable one. The vast majority of Americans have no means to recycle most types of plastic or polystyrene, or even the kind of coated paperboard used in many product packages. Many manufacturers, attempting to lure environmentally conscious consumers, are labeling their packages "recyclable." That may be technically true: given the right technology and enough financing, the package could be recycled. But for now, glass, aluminum, steel, and corrugated cardboard are the only packaging materials conveniently recyclable.

What about plastic? The good news is that two types of plastic are now viably recyclable: polyethylene terephthalate (PET) plastic, used in soda bottles; and high-density polyethylene (HDPE), used in milk jugs and some shampoo bottles. These may be identified by a plastics-industry coding system stamped on the bottoms of containers. The codes contain a number inside the recycling triangle. The code for PET is #1, for HDPE #2.

Only about 27 percent of PET and 10 percent of HDPE plastic containers were being recycled as of 1992, according to the National Recycling Coalition in Washington, D.C. Many communities still do not have facilities that accept these plastics for recycling. However, only about 4 percent of plastics overall were being recycled, as there is little market for the recycled materials. Hopefully, this situation will change in coming years. But for practical purposes, most plastic packaging remains unrecyclable.

What's the best type of packaging? The best packaging is made from the least amount of material possible, and contains materials you can readily recycle. An aluminum or steel can is one such type of packaging. Even a plastic soda bottle is acceptable if there is a recycling facility in your area that accepts it. Plain boxes made from recycled cardboard are also good. You can identify recycled cardboard easily: the unprinted side of the cardboard is grayish-brown. If it is white, the cardboard is not recycled.

Many companies, including the largest consumer-product firms, are working to reduce or change the type of packaging they use. But for each reduced-packaging product, there seems to be at least one new "convenience" product brimming with packaging. Few, if any, industry or government restrictions are placed on such products, so it will be up to consumers to pressure manufacturers.

Here are things to look for or to avoid:

- Reject packaged produce. Most fruits and vegetables have their own natural "packaging."
- Avoid multimaterial packages such as juice boxes and squeezable plastic containers. They are almost impossible to recycle.
- Look for products packaged in recycled materials or materials that you can readily recycle in your community. For most Americans,

that includes glass, aluminum, steel, and some kinds of cardboard and plastic. Take the empty packages to be recycled.

- Buy the largest-sized package you'll use, to minimize excess packaging.
- Look for concentrated products. They reduce packaging by putting more product in less packaging.
- Look for egg cartons made of paperboard instead of plastic foam.
- Avoid plastic milk containers unless there is a recycling program in your area that accepts them.
- Avoid aerosols. The cans cannot be recycled, and most aerosol products contain propellants that contribute to photochemical smog.
- Let manufacturers and supermarket managers know that you are interested in products packaged in materials that can be recycled in your community. Press supermarkets to provide for recycling on site.
- Urge your community to set up or expand curbside recycling collection and central recycling collection and to actively seek markets for the recyclable materials.
- Bring your own containers and buy in bulk.
- Avoid multiple packages, one inside another.

Shopping for Conservation and Energy Savings

Of all the sources of energy that are now feasible—nuclear, fossil fuels, solar, geothermal, hydroelectric, biomass, wind—energy conservation and improvements in energy efficiency are by far the most sustainable, the cheapest, and the least harmful to workers, neighboring communities, and the environment.

Consider these facts:

- The electric-power industry generates 29 percent of the world's carbon dioxide emissions from fossil fuels, according to the *1994 State of the World Report* (W.W. Norton & Co., 1994) produced by the Worldwatch Institute. The report notes that nearly 40 percent of the world's electricity is supplied by coal-fired plants, which cause major environmental problems like global warming and acid rain.

There are many ways you can contribute to energy conservation:

- Homeowners should take efficiency into account when buying new equipment and fixtures like windows, boilers, furnaces, air conditioners, and insulation. The extra cost for maximum efficiency will often be paid back through savings of fuel costs within a few years.
- Use public transport, ride a bicycle, or walk whenever possible.
- If you must drive to work, join or form a carpool. If you own a car, keep it tuned up and avoid unnecessary idling.
- Recycle. Each recycled aluminum can saves the emission of 0.8 pounds of carbon dioxide.
- Don't overdo air conditioning and heating.
- Consider ordering catalogs from renewable-energy companies like Real Goods Trading Co. (800-762-7325) and Seventh Generation (800-456-1177).
- Use fluorescent lightbulbs. An 18-watt compact fluorescent screw-in bulb is equivalent to a 75-watt incandescent, lasts 10 times as long, saves $40 to $60 over the bulb's lifetime, and prevents the emission of 1,020 pounds of carbon dioxide at the power plant. Three of General Electric's compact fluorescent bulbs are the first to receive certification by Green Seal. They are the 20-watt Electronic Triple Biax CFL and a 20-watt or 15-watt Electronic Double Biax. Other alternatives include Cromolux, full-spectrum incandescent bulbs imported from Finland by Lumiram (914-698-1205); Vita-Lite, made in the U.S. by Duro-Test (800-526-7193); and Marvel, made in the U.S. by Marvel Lighting (800-631-1614). Ask your local hardware store to order these bulbs if they don't have them already.

RATINGS BY COMPANY

COMPANY	COMPANY ABBREV.									EXTRAS
A&P	GAP	A	B	B	B	?	B	A	C	on-site day care
AB Electrolux	ELUXY	?	?	?	?	?	?	?	F	foreign-based company
Alberto-Culver Company	ACV	A	?	B	A	D	D	B	B	Animal testing: non-medical products; increasing TRI
Albertson's, Inc.	ABS	A	F	?	C	D	B	C	C	profile
Allied-Lyons PLC	ALP	B	C	B	D	?	B	?	B	foreign-based company
American Home Products Corporation	AHP	C	F	C	B	B	C	C	A	Animal testing: medical & non-medical products, significant alternative efforts; infant formula
American Stores Company	ASC	A	?	?	C	?	D	B	F	
American Telephone & Telegraph Company (AT&T)	T	B	B	A	B	B	A	B	A	Animal testing: non-medical products; CEP Award — Environment; military contracts; Workplace Principles
Amoco Corporation	AN	C	B	A	C	B	A	C	A	Animal testing: medical & non-medical products, significant alternative efforts; CEDC report; CEP Award — Community; increasing TRI; military contracts; on-site day care
Anheuser-Busch Companies, Inc.★	BUD	C	A	A	B	A	B	A	A	CEDC report
Animal Town	ATOWN	?	?	?	?	?	?	?	F	small company
Apple Computer, Inc.	AAPL	B	B	A	A	D	A	B	C	on-site day care; same-sex partner benefits; Workplace Principles

★ A star denotes an Honor Roll company.

COMPANY	COMPANY ABBREV.	The Environment	Charitable Giving	Community Outreach	Women's Advancement	Minority Advancement	Family	Workplace Issues	Disclosure of Information	EXTRAS
Archer Daniels Midland Company	ADM	D	F	?	D	?	?	D	F	CEDC report; increasing TRI
Aroma Vera	AV	A	F	C	B	B	D	C	C	Small company
AST Research, Inc.	ASTA	?	?	?	F	A	?	?	F	
Atlantic Richfield Company	ARC	D	B	B	A	B	B	C	B	Animal testing: non-medical products; CEDC report
Aveda Corp. H	AVED	A	A	A	A	A	A	A	A	CEP Award — Environment; CERES Principles; profile
Avery Dennison Corporation	AVY	?	?	?	A	?	?	?	F	
Avon Products, Inc. ★	AVP	B	A	A	A	A	A	B	A	CEP Award — EEO; increasing TRI; on-site day care
Ben & Jerry's Homemade, Inc. ★	BJICA	A	A	A	A	B	A	A	A	CERES Principles; CEP Award — Charity; on-site child care; profile; same-sex partner benefits; Workplace Principles
Benetton Group Spa	BTON	?	?	?	?	?	?	?	D	foreign-based company
Black & Decker Corporation	BDK	?	?	?	B	?	?	?	F	increasing TRI; military contracts; nuclear weapons
Body Love Natural Cosmetics	BLN	A	?	A	A	A	B	A	A	Small company
Body Shop, The	BODY	A	?	A	A	B	B	C	A	foreign-based company
Borden, Inc.	BN	C	C	B	A	A	B	B	A	CEDC report
Bristol-Myers Squibb Company	BMY	B	C	B	B	B	B	B	A	Animal testing: medical & non-medical products, significant alternative efforts; infant formula; Workplace Principles

The Environment
Charitable Giving
Community Outreach

Women's Advancement

Minority Advancement

Family

Workplace Issues

Disclosure of Information

★ Honor Roll

For a more detailed explanation, see pages 7–28.

COMPANY	COMPANY ABBREV.									EXTRAS
British Petroleum Company p.l.c.	BP	C	C	A	B	B	A	C	A	Animal testing: non-medical products, significant alternative efforts; CEDC report; foreign-based company; increasing TRI; military contracts; Workplace Principles
Brown-Forman Corporation	BFB	B	?	?	C	?	?	?	F	CEDC report
Brown Group, Inc.	BG	?	A	?	C	?	?	?	F	CEDC report; increasing TRI
Bruno's, Inc.	BRNO	C	?	?	D	?	?	A	D	
Cadbury Schweppes p.l.c.	CADBY	B	?	C	C	?	D	B	C	foreign-based company
Campbell Soup Company	CPB	B	C	B	A	A	A	C	A	Animal testing: non-medical products, significant alternative efforts; CEDC report; on-site child care
Carter Hawley Hale Stores, Inc.	CHH	B	?	C	A	C	C	?	C	
Carter-Wallace, Inc.	CAR	?	?	?	F	?	?	?	F	Animal testing: medical products only; increasing TRI
Chevron Corporation	CHV	F	B	B	B	B	A	B	A	Animal testing: non-medical products, significant alternative efforts; CEDC report; Workplace Principles
Chrysler Corporation	C	B	A	C	D	A	?	?	F	CEDC report; Fair Share; military contracts; on-site child care; Workplace Principles
Church & Dwight Co., Inc.	CHD	A	B	A	C	C	A	A	A	Animal testing: non-medical products, significant alternative efforts; CEP Award — Environment
Clorox Company	CLX	B	B	A	A	A	C	C	A	Animal testing: non-medical products, significant alternative efforts; CEDC report; CEP Award — Community; increasing TRI
Coca-Cola Company	KO	C	B	A	B	A	A	B	A	Workplace Principles

COMPANY	COMPANY ABBREV.	The Environment	Charitable Giving	Community Outreach	Women's Advancement	Minority Advancement	Family	Workplace Issues	Disclosure of Information	EXTRAS
Colgate-Palmolive Company ★	CL	B	B	A	A	B	A	A	A	Animal testing: medical & non-medical products, significant alternative efforts; CEDC report; profile
Compaq Computer Corporation	CPQ	B	C	?	D	?	?	A	C	
ConAgra, Inc.	CAG	C	C	C	C	?	?	F	C	CEDC report; factory farming; profile
Coors Company, Adolph ★	ACCOB	C	A	A	A	B	A	B	A	CEDC report; Fair Share
CPC International Inc.	CPC	C	A	B	A	B	C	A	B	Animal testing: non-medical products, significant alternative efforts; CEDC report; increasing TRI
Dayton Hudson Corporation ★	DH	B	A	A	A	B	B	B	A	CEP Award — Charity; on-site child care
Dell Computer Corporation	DELL	?	?	?	B	B	?	?	F	
Deva Lifewear	DEVA	A	?	?	A	Neutral	A	B	B	small company
Dial Corp.	DL	C	A	B	B	?	F	B	C	CEDC report
Digital Equipment Corporation ★	DEC	A	?	A	A	A	A	B	A	CEP Awards — Community Involvement, Environment; military contracts; profile; Workplace Principles
Dillard Department Stores, Inc.	DDS	?	?	?	C	?	?	?	F	Fair Share
Dole Food Company, Inc.	DOL	B	A	B	C	A	C	C	B	pesticide sterilization suits
Domino's Pizza, Inc.	DOMP	B	?	?	B	B	?	?	C	

 The Environment; Charitable Giving  Community Outreach  Women's Advancement  Minority Advancement  Family  Workplace Issues  Disclosure of Information 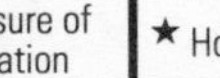 ★ Honor Roll

For a more detailed explanation, see pages 7–28.

COMPANY	COMPANY ABBREV.									EXTRAS
Dow Chemical Company	DOW	C	C	B	B	A	A	B	A	Animal testing: non-medical products, significant alternative efforts; CEDC report; on-site child care; pesticide sterilization suits
DWG Corporation	DWG	?	?	?	B	?	?	?	F	factory farming; increasing TRI
Eastman Kodak Company	EK	C	B	B	B	B	A	B	B	Animal testing: medical and non-medical products, significant alternative efforts; CEDC report; CEP Award — EEO
Ecco Bella	ECC	A	?	C	A	Neutral	C	C	A	Small company
Emily's Toybox	EMTOY	?	?	?	?	?	?	?	F	small company
Esprit de Corp.	ESP	?	?	A	A	A	B	B	C	
Estee Lauder Inc.	EL	B	?	?	A	?	?	?	F	
Exxon Corporation	XON	F	D	B	C	C	A	B	A	Animal testing: non-medical products, significant alternative efforts; C3; CEDC report; increasing TRI; military contracts; on-site child care
Farah Incorporated	FRA	?	?	?	B	A	?	?	F	
Fedders Corporation	FJQ	?	?	?	F	?	?	?	F	
Federated Department Stores, Inc.	FED	?	?	?	A	B	?	?	C	
First Brands Corporation	FBR	C	A	C	F	D	D	B	B	Animal testing: non-medical products, significant alternative efforts; profile
Food Lion, Inc.	FDLNA	?	?	D	D	C	D	F	F	Fair Share; profile
Ford Motor Company	F	C	?	?	D	C	?	?	C	CEDC report

COMPANY	COMPANY ABBREV.	The Environment	Charitable Giving	Community Outreach	Women's Advancement	Minority Advancement	Family	Workplace Issues	Disclosure of Information	EXTRAS
Foster and Gallagher	HSONG	?	?	?	?	?	?	?	F	Small company
Fred Meyer, Inc.	FMY	?	A	A	B	?	?	B	D	
Fuji Photo Film Co. Ltd.	FUJIY	C	?	C	B	C	D	B	C	Animal testing: medical products only; foreign-based company; increasing TRI
Gap, Inc., The	GPS	B	C	A	A	?	B	A	B	
General Electric Company	GE	D	C	B	C	C	B	C	A	C3; CEDC report; military contracts
General Mills, Inc. ★	GIS	B	A	A	A	B	B	A	A	CEDC report; CEP Awards — Charity, EEO, Opportunities for the Disabled; profile; Workplace Principles
General Motors Corporation	GM	D	?	C	C	A	C	C	A	CEDC Report; CERES Principles; Fair Share; military contracts; nuclear weapons
Genesco Inc.	GCO	?	B	C	F	F	?	?	D	CEDC report
Gerber Products	GEB	C	C	?	B	B	?	?	F	CEDC report; increasing TRI; infant formula
Giant Food Inc. ★	GFSA	B	A	B	B	A	B	A	A	
Gillette Company	G	C	C	B	D	D	B	B	A	Animal testing: medical & non-medical products, significant alternative efforts
Gitano Group, Inc.	GIT	?	A	?	F	?	?	?	D	
Grand Metropolitan PLC ★	GMR	C	A	A	B	A	A	B	A	factory farming; foreign-based company

The Environment
Charitable Giving
Community Outreach
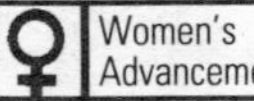
Women's Advancement

Minority Advancement

Family

Workplace Issues

Disclosure of Information
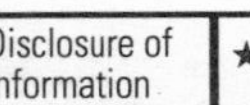
★ Honor Roll

For a more detailed explanation, see pages 7–28.

COMPANY	COMPANY ABBREV.									EXTRAS
Guess Inc.	GUS	?	?	?	?	?	?	?	F	
Hartmarx Corporation	HMX	?	?	?	A	?	?	?	F	
Hasbro, Inc.	HAS	B	B	B	B	?	?	?	D	
Health Valley Natural Foods	HVAL	A	C	C	A	A	B	A	A	
Heinz Company, H.J.	HNZ	B	C	A	B	D	C	A	A	CEDC report; CEP Award — Environment
Helene Curtis Industries, Inc.	HC	A	A	A	B	?	A	B	B	Animal testing: non-medical products
Hershey Foods Corporation	HSY	B	B	A	B	C	A	A	A	CEDC report; increasing TRI; on-site child care
Hewlett Packard Company ★	HWP	B	A	A	B	B	A	A	A	military contracts; profile; nuclear weapons
Honda Motor Co. Ltd.	HMC	?	B	C	A	D	?	B	F	foreign-based company; increasing TRI
Imasco Limited	IMS	?	B	A	B	?	?	?	F	Tobacco; factory farming; Fair Share; foreign-based company
Interco Incorporated	ISS	?	?	?	D	?	?	?	F	
International Business Machines Corporation	IBM	B	A	B	B	B	A	C	B	Animal testing: medical products only; CEP Awards — Employer Responsiveness, Community; Workplace Principles
International Dairy Queen, Inc.	INDQA	B	D	C	B	D	D	C	A	
J. Crew Group Inc.	JC	?	?	?	?	?	?	?	F	
Johnson & Johnson ★	JNJ	B	A	A	A	A	A	A	A	Animal testing: medical products only, significant alternative efforts; CEP Award — Disclosure; on-site child care; profile; Workplace Principles

COMPANY	COMPANY ABBREV.	The Environment	Charitable Giving	Community Outreach	Women's Advancement	Minority Advancement	Family	Workplace Issues	Disclosure of Information	EXTRAS
Johnson & Son, Inc., S.C. ★	SCJ	A	A	A	B	B	A	A	A	Animal testing: non-medical products, significant alternative efforts; CEP Award — environment; on-site child care; profile; Workplace Principles
Kellogg Company ★	K	B	A	A	A	A	A	A	A	Animal testing: non-medical products, significant alternative efforts; CEDC report; CEP Awards — Employer Responsiveness, Disclosure; profile
Kimberly-Clark Corporation	KMB	C	C	B	B	C	B	A	A	Animal testing: non-medical products, significant alternative efforts; CEDC report; tobacco
Kiss My Face	KMF	A	?	A	A	Neutral	A	A	A	Small company
Kroger Company	KR	A	A	B	A	C	D	B	C	Fair Share
L.A. Gear, Inc.	LA	?	?	?	C	?	?	?	F	
Lands' End, Inc.	LE	?	A	C	B	?	B	A	B	
Levi Strauss & Co. ★	LEV	A	B	A	A	A	B	B	A	CEP Award — International Commitment; profile; same-sex partner benefits; Workplace Principles
Limited, Inc., The	LTD	?	?	C	A	?	?	?	F	
Liz Claiborne, Inc.	LIZ	?	F	C	A	?	C	?	F	on-site child care
L'Oreal S.A.	LORA	B	C	B	A	C	C	B	A	foreign-based company
Mars, Inc.	MARS	C	A	B	A	?	?	C	B	

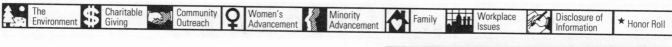

The Environment | Charitable Giving | Community Outreach | Women's Advancement | Minority Advancement | Family | Workplace Issues | Disclosure of Information | ★ Honor Roll

For a more detailed explanation, see pages 7–28.

COMPANY	COMPANY ABBREV.									EXTRAS
Matsushita Electric Industrial Co.	MC	C	?	A	?	?	D	?	C	Fair Share; foreign-based company; increasing TRI; same-sex partner benefits
Mattel, Inc.	MAT	B	D	B	A	B	A	B	A	
May Department Stores Company	MA	?	B	A	B	C	F	C	B	Workplace Principles
Maytag Corporation	MYG	B	A	B	C	D	C	B	A	Workplace Principles
McDonald's Corporation	MCD	B	C	C	B	A	?	?	C	factory farming; Fair Share
MCI Communications Corporation	MCIC	?	F	C	B	A	?	D	F	profile
Mead Corporation	MEA	C	A	B	C	C	D	D	C	CEDC report; Workplace Principles
MEM Company Inc.	MEM	?	?	?	A	?	?	?	D	
Mercantile Stores Company Inc.	MST	?	?	?	F	?	D	D	F	
Minnesota Mining & Manufacturing Company (3M)	MMM	C	B	A	C	B	A	B	A	Animal testing: medical & non-medical products, significant alternative efforts; CEDC report; CEP Award — Environment
Mobil Corporation	MOB	D	C	C	C	C	B	C	A	Animal testing: non-medical products, significant alternative efforts; CEDC report; military contracts; Workplace Principles
Na Na Trading Co.	NA	A	D	C	A	B	?	B	A	Small company
Natural Baby Company, Inc., The	NATB	?	?	C	A	Neutral	A	?	A	small company
Nestle S. A.	NEST	B	?	B	B	B	A	B	B	Animal testing: non-medical products, significant alternative efforts; foreign-based company; infant formula
Neutrogena Corporation	NGNA	?	A	?	C	?	?	?	F	

COMPANY	COMPANY ABBREV.	The Environment	Charitable Giving	Community Outreach	Women's Advancement	Minority Advancement	Family	Workplace Issues	Disclosure of Information	EXTRAS
Newman's Own	NEWO	A	A	A	A	Neutral	C	A	A	100% profit to charity; CEP Award — Charity; small company
Nike, Inc.	NKE	C	C	B	A	D	A	B	A	CEDC report; on-site child care
Nissan Motor Co. Ltd.	NSANY	?	?	C	D	D	?	B	F	foreign-based company; increasing TRI
Nordstrom, Inc. ★	NOBE	B	A	A	A	A	A	C	A	profile
Nova Natural	NOVA	?	?	?	A	Neutral	C	?	A	small company
Olmec	OLMEC	?	?	?	?	?	?	?	F	small company
One World Projects	OWP	?	?	?	?	?	?	?	F	small company
Oshkosh B'Gosh, Inc.	GOSHA	?	?	?	C	?	?	?	F	
Packard Bell Electronics	PCKRD	?	?	?	?	?	?	?	F	
Patagonia, Inc.	LOST	A	A	C	A	C	A	C	A	on-site child care
PepsiCo, Inc.	PEP	B	B	A	A	B	B	B	A	Animal testing: non-medical products; factory farming; increasing TRI
Perdue Farms Inc.	PRDU	?	?	F	?	?	?	F	F	factory farming
Pet Incorporated	PT	C	D	?	B	?	?	?	F	CEDC report; increasing TRI
Pfizer Inc.	PFE	C	B	A	B	C	A	B	A	Animal testing: medical products only, significant alternative efforts; heart valve suits; Workplace Principles

The Environment | Charitable Giving | Community Outreach | Women's Advancement | Minority Advancement | Family | Workplace Issues | Disclosure of Information | ★ Honor Roll

For a more detailed explanation, see pages 7–28.

COMPANY	COMPANY ABBREV.									EXTRAS
Philip Morris Companies, Inc.	MO	D	D	?	A	A	?	?	F	Animal testing: non-medical products; CEDC report; tobacco; increasing TRI; Workplace Principles
Philips' Gloeilampenfabrieken N.V.	PHIL	?	?	?	?	?	?	?	F	foreign-based company; military contracts
Phillips Petroleum Company	P	D	B	B	D	C	A	D	C	CEDC report; military contracts
Phillips-Van Heusen Corporation	PVH	?	?	?	B	?	?	?	F	
Polaroid Corporation	PRD	C	B	A	B	B	A	A	C	CEP Awards — Charity, South Africa; Workplace Principles
Procter & Gamble Company	PG	C	B	A	B	B	A	B	A	Animal testing: medical and non-medical products, significant alternative efforts; CEDC report; CEP Awards — Animal Welfare, Employer Responsiveness; increasing TRI; on-site day care; Workplace Principles
Quaker Oats Company	OAT	B	A	A	B	B	D	?	C	CEDC report; Fair Share
Ralston Purina Company	RAL	C	C	B	B	B	B	C	B	CEDC report; increasing TRI
Raytheon Company	RTN	C	?	B	D	?	?	?	C	CEDC report; military contracts; nuclear weapons
Reebok International Ltd.	RBK	B	C	A	B	B	B	B	A	CEDC report
Revlon, Inc.	REVL	?	?	?	C	?	?	?	F	
Rhino Records, Inc. ★	RHI	B	A	A	A	A	B	B	A	profile; small company
R.H. Macy & Co., Inc.	MACY	?	?	?	?	?	?	?	F	Workplace Principles
RJR Nabisco, Inc.	RN	?	A	C	C	?	?	?	D	Animal testing: non-medical products; CEDC report; tobacco; increasing TRI; Workplace Principles

COMPANY	COMPANY ABBREV.	The Environment	Charitable Giving	Community Outreach	Women's Advancement	Minority Advancement	Family	Workplace Issues	Disclosure of Information	EXTRAS
Royal Dutch/Shell Group of Companies	SCWW-S	C	?	A	D	C	C	C	A	Animal testing: non-medical products, significant alternative efforts; CEDC report; foreign-based company; military contracts; pesticide sterilization suits
Russell Corporation	RML	?	?	B	F	?	?	?	D	increasing TRI
Sara Lee Corporation	SLE	C	B	A	B	B	B	B	A	CEP Award — Charity; on-site child care; tobacco
Schering-Plough Corporation	SGP	B	C	A	B	A	A	B	A	Animal testing: medical products only, significant alternative efforts; on-site child care; Workplace Principles
Seagram Company Ltd.	VO	?	D	?	C	?	?	?	F	foreign-based company; Workplace Principles
Sears, Roebuck & Co.	S	?	A	B	A	C	A	C	B	
Sebastian International, Inc.	SEB	?	?	?	?	?	?	?	F	
Shoney's Inc.	SHN	?	?	?	C	D	?	?	F	
SmithKline Beecham plc	SBH	C	D	C	B	B	A	B	C	Animal testing: medical products only, significant alternative efforts; foreign-based company; Workplace Principles
Snapple Beverage Corporation	SNPL	?	?	?	F	?	?	?	F	
Societe Bic S.A.	BIC	?	?	?	?	?	?	?	F	foreign-based company
Sony Corporation	SNE	B	B	A	B	B	C	B	A	Fair Share; foreign-based company; increasing TRI
Sprint Corporation	FON	B	C	B	A	C	A	C	C	

 The Environment | Charitable Giving  Community Outreach 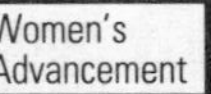 Women's Advancement 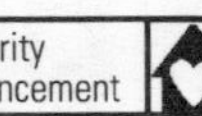 Minority Advancement 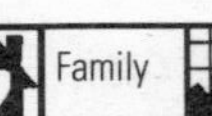 Family  Workplace Issues  Disclosure of Information | ★ Honor Roll

For a more detailed explanation, see pages 7–28.

COMPANY	COMPANY ABBREV.									EXTRAS
Starter Corporation	STA	?	?	?	F	?	?	?	F	
Stonyfield Farm, Inc.	STON	A	?	A	A	Neutral	B	B	A	CEP Award — Environment; small company
Stride-Rite Corporation, The	SRR	B	A	A	A	D	A	B	A	on-site child care
Sun Company, Inc.	SUN	C	?	C	C	C	B	B	A	Animal testing: non-medical products, significant alternative efforts; CEDC report; CERES Principles; increasing TRI; military contracts
Sunshine Biscuits, Inc.	SUNB	?	?	?	?	?	?	?	F	
Tambrands Inc.	TMB	?	?	?	A	?	?	?	F	
Texaco Inc.	TX	F	B	C	F	D	C	C	C	Animal testing: non-medical products; C3; CEDC report; military contracts; profile
Thorn EMI plc	THOR	C	C	?	?	?	?	?	D	foreign-based company; military contracts; nuclear weapons
Threads 4 Life	XCOLS	?	?	?	?	A	?	?	F	
Timberland Company, The	TBL	B	A	A	B	D	D	B	A	CERES Principles
Time Warner Inc.	TWX	B	?	A	B	B	A	C	B	same-sex partner benefits; increasing TRI; Workplace Principles
Tom's of Maine ★	TOM	A	A	A	A	B	A	A	A	CEP Award — Charity; CERES Principles; profile; small company
Toyota Motor Corp.	TOYOY	C	B	A	?	?	B	B	C	foreign-based company; increasing TRI
Tyco Toys, Inc.	TTI	?	?	?	C	?	?	?	F	
Tyson Foods, Inc.	TYSNA	C	?	D	A	B	?	D	D	factory farming; profile

COMPANY	COMPANY ABBREV.	The Environment	Charitable Giving	Community Outreach	Women's Advancement	Minority Advancement	Family	Workplace Issues	Disclosure of Information	EXTRAS
Unilever PLC	UN	B	C	C	F	D	C	B	C	Animal testing: non-medical products, significant alternative efforts; foreign-based company; profile
United Biscuits (Holdings) plc	UBH	?	C	C	D	?	?	?	F	foreign-based company
Unocal Corporation	UCL	D	B	?	C	?	?	?	D	CEDC report
US Shoe Corporation	USR	?	?	?	C	?	?	?	F	
USX Corporation	X	D	?	C	B	C	B	D	A	CEDC report
V.F. Corporation	VFC	?	?	?	B	?	C	?	F	
Vons Companies, Inc.	VON	?	?	A	B	?	?	A	D	
Wal-Mart Stores, Inc.	WMT	A	D	D	F	?	?	?	F	
Warner-Lambert Company ★	WLA	B	B	A	B	A	A	B	A	Animal testing: medical products only; increasing TRI; Workplace Principles
Wendy's International, Inc.	WEN	B	?	?	B	?	?	?	D	factory farming; Fair Share
Whirlpool Corporation	WHR	B	A	A	C	C	B	B	A	
Winn-Dixie Stores, Inc.	WIN	?	C	B	F	F	?	?	D	
Wrigley Jr. Company, Wm.	WWY	C	D	?	D	?	B	?	F	Fair Share
Yamanouchi Pharmaceutical Co. Ltd.	YAMP	?	A	A	?	B	B	A	B	foreign-based company

 The Environment; Charitable Giving  Community Outreach  Women's Advancement  Minority Advancement  Family  Workplace Issues  Disclosure of Information ★ Honor Roll

For a more detailed explanation, see pages 7–28. Ratings by product begin on page 110.

Company Profiles

CEP's Honor Roll Companies

Of the 191 companies rated by CEP in *Shopping for a Better World*, the 20 highlighted in this section earned a grade-point average of 3.5 or higher, taking into account their performances in all eight categories. Companies with an "F" or "?" in any category were not considered (except where a "?" in Charitable Giving indicated losses in two or more years). We have profiled 13 of the highest rated Honor Roll companies. Of course, no company is perfect. But these certainly are companies that deserve a lot of credit, companies whose products you may want on your shopping list, where you might want to work, and whose securities you might like to see in your investment portfolio.

For our Honor Roll, CEP has weighted all categories of social performance equally. Most of our readers tell CEP they see them as roughly equal. Quite a few consumers and activists, however, value one aspect of social performance so highly that a poor grade or an excellent grade in a single category will significantly alter his or her opinion of the company. If you feel especially committed to one issue, you may want to look carefully at a company's specific grade on that issue rather than at whether the company has attained the Honor Roll listings.

In addition to recognizing companies with the strongest overall record on social responsibility, CEP honors those that have excelled in specific areas at our annual America's Corporate Conscience Awards. For a list of the recipients and details on the ceremony, see page 388.

Company profiles can be fascinating and you may want to know more. You'll find the stories for other top-rated companies in the *Better World Investment Guide* (Prentice-Hall, 1991) at your local library.

A CEP SCREEN subscription can provide you with detailed profiles on 400 companies (see page 395).

Honor Roll

(Denoted by a star in the tables.)

Adolph Coors Company
Anheuser-Busch Companies, Inc.
Aveda Corp.
Avon Products, Inc.
Ben & Jerry's Homemade, Inc.
Colgate-Palmolive Company
Dayton Hudson Corporation
Digital Equipment Corporation
General Mills, Inc.
Giant Food Inc.
Grand Metropolitan PLC
Hewlett-Packard Company
Johnson & Johnson
S.C. Johnson & Son, Inc.
Kellogg Company
Levi Strauss & Co.
Nordstrom, Inc.
Rhino Records, Inc.
Tom's of Maine
Warner-Lambert Company

AVEDA CORP.

4000 Pheasant Ridge Drive, Blaine, MN 55449

ABBREVIATION								
AVED	A	A	A	A	A	A	A	A

Aveda develops pure plant products including hair, beauty, skin, and household products made from organically grown plants and flowers using only naturally derived, nonanimal-tested chemicals. In 1992, sales were approximately $50 million (the company is privately held), and the company had about 350 employees.

Environment. Aveda was one of the first corporations to sign the CERES Principles. The company has a comprehensive environmental plan that includes using recycled material in packaging and reclaiming packaging for recycling; recycling in all its office locations; waste reduction at all Aveda manufacturing locations; and environmental-awareness training for employees. Aveda won CEP's America's Corporate Conscience Award for Environmental Stewardship in 1993.

Charity/Community Outreach. Since 1990, Aveda has raised more than $400,000 through its salon-network fundraising campaign.

Aveda contributes 6 percent of its pretax profits each year, predominantly to environmental organizations and programs such as Battered Women Fighting Back. Aveda works with schools on environmental-education programs, and its employees volunteer on food and clothing collections.

Equal Employment Opportunity. Aveda has a strong representation of women and minorities for a company of its size. There are three women on the eight-member board. Sixty-two percent of employees are women, including two of seven corporate officers, and nine of 15 division heads. Three minorities are division heads and one minority is a corporate officer. In the officials and managers category, 48 percent are women and 15 percent minorities. Of the 25 highest-paid officers in the company, 11 are women and five are minorities.

Workplace Issues and Family Benefits. The company's headquarters office reflects health and environmental consciousness, with a cafeteria serving organic foods, exercise facilities, and sunlit workspaces. Child care is provided on site. Aveda had no OSHA or environmental violations in 1992 or 1993.

BEN & JERRY'S HOMEMADE, INC.

Route 100, P.O. Box 240, Waterbury, VT 05676–0240

ABBREVIATION								
BJICA	A	A	A	A	B	A	A	A

Ben & Jerry's makes premium ice cream and frozen yogurt. In 1992, sales were $132 million and the company had 475 employees. Ben & Jerry's won an America's Corporate Conscience Award for Charitable Giving in 1988.

Environment. In 1992, Ben & Jerry's signed the CERES Principles, signaling the company's commitment to recycling, conservation, and source reduction. Packaging is made from recycled paperboard with high post-consumer content. Brochures, pamphlets, and annual reports are printed on recycled paper. The company will replace Freon-based refrigerants and convert to propane fuel for new delivery trucks it acquires as old leases expire. By using Brazil nuts from the rainforest in its popular Rainforest Crunch ice cream, Ben & Jerry's supports the preservation of rainforests.

Charity/Community Outreach. Ben & Jerry's donates an exceptional 7.5 percent of its pretax profits to charity. In 1992, the company donated $917,000 to environmental organizations and programs serving children, families, and disenfranchised groups. Ben & Jerry's encourages employee volunteer efforts. It donates ice cream to many community organizations for special events. "Partnershops" pair up franchises with nonprofit groups: The Partnershop in Harlem is staffed by homeless people and profits go to a homeless shelter, while a Baltimore shop employs and benefits developmentally disabled people.

Equal Employment Opportunity. Women make up about 50 percent of Ben & Jerry's senior managers and professional staff. A woman is Chief Financial Officer and an African-American is Human Resources Director. There is one woman and one minority on the nine-member board. Because of the very low number of minorities in the Vermont population, the company has had to make special efforts to recruit minorities from out of state.

Family Benefits. The company provides up to six weeks of paid leave to all new mothers, including adoptive mothers, and two weeks of paid paternal leave, with up to 10 weeks of unpaid leave for new fathers. On-site child care, phased return to work for new mothers, and flextime are offered. A flexible spending account allows employees to apply pretax dollars to uncovered medical expenses or dependent care. Ben & Jerry's is listed in *Working Mother*'s "100 Best Companies for Working Mothers."

Workplace Issues. At Ben & Jerry's, the highest paid employee cannot earn more than seven times the salary of the lowest paid. Benefits include health and dental coverage, and low-cost coverage for families, including same-sex partners. Some benefits are provided to part-time employees. Ben & Jerry's offers profit sharing, an employee stock ownership program, and a 401(k) matching pension program. The Employee Advisory Group, representing all nonmanagement employees, consults on major new initiatives. Ben & Jerry's has a free fitness center, which helps offset the three free pints of ice cream a day available to employees. Ben & Jerry's is listed in *The 100 Best Companies to Work for in America.*

COLGATE-PALMOLIVE COMPANY
300 Park Avenue, New York, NY 10022

ABBREVIATION								
CL	B	B	A	A	B	A	A	A

Colgate-Palmolive manufactures consumer and household products like toothpaste and soap. Its 1992 revenues were $7 billion. Total employees worldwide were 24,000, of which 7,200 were in the U.S.

Environment. Colgate-Palmolive's Palmolive dishwashing-liquid bottles are made from 50-percent recycled plastic. New fabric-softener refill packages help reduce the amount of plastic going to landfills. "Stand-up" tubes for toothpaste eliminate the need for paper cartons. Colgate-Palmolive reduced energy use at its plants by 30 percent from 1985 to 1990 and its toxic releases by 56 percent from 1988 to 1990.

In 1992, Mexican environmentalists protested Colgate-Palmolive's alleged polluting practices and excessive water consumption, and demanded that the company relocate its factory outside Mexico City. The company is now building a second facility outside Mexico City to alleviate production demand from the city plant.

Charity/Community Outreach. Charitable giving in 1992 was over 1.2 percent of average pretax earnings. Colgate-Palmolive's Oral Health Care Education Program reached more than 20 million youngsters worldwide, at a cost of $6.8 million in 1992. Colgate-Palmolive's CEO chairs the New York City Partnership's Education and Youth Employment Committee, which provides summer jobs, trains teachers, and lobbies for educational reform. Colgate-Palmolive provides financial support to a school in Harlem where employees volunteer as mentors.

Equal Employment Opportunity. Over 17 percent of employees are minorities, including 15 percent of officials and managers. Ten percent of vice presidents, 22 percent of officials and managers, and 41 percent of professional staff are women. Two subsidiaries are headed by African-American men. One minority and two women serve on Colgate-Palmolive's nine-member board. Colgate-Palmolive was included in *The Best Companies for Minorities.*

Family Benefits. Colgate-Palmolive is one of the charter-member companies of the American Business Collaboration for Quality Dependent Care, a 144-company coalition funding facilities for child and elder care. It offers the emergency child-care services of an in-home caregiver to help out when a child is mildly sick or when regular child care is unavailable. Colgate-Palmolive is listed in *Working Mother*'s "100 Best Companies for Working Mothers."

Workplace Issues. Colgate-Palmolive's "You Can Make A Difference" Award celebrates innovative employees. Winners receive $1,000 in stock plus other prizes; 10 to 12 global winners each year are given an additional $2,500 in stock and a week at company headquarters in New York City.

Extras. Colgate-Palmolive's overall use of animals for research increased in 1992 due to testing requirements for a roach pesticide. Its use of animals for other research decreased 42 percent. The company cosponsored development of a successful alternative test that uses fertilized chicken eggs rather than live animals. Colgate-Palmolive is sharing data on this test with other companies and organizations to assist its adoption.

DIGITAL EQUIPMENT CORPORATION

146 Main Street, Maynard, MA 01754–2571

ABBREVIATION								
DEC	A	?	A	A	A	A	B	A

Digital is the world's leader in open client/server solutions from personal computing to integrated worldwide information systems. In 1993, sales were over $14 billion, and the company had 94,200 employees.

Environment. Digital won the 1993 America's Corporate Conscience Award for Environmental Stewardship. Through the Industry Cooperative for Ozone Layer Protection, a joint venture with the EPA and several other manufacturers, Digital shared free of charge a CFC-free technique for cleaning circuit boards. The company offers annual Environmental Excellence Awards to employees who develop creative solutions to environmental problems, and it has conducted internal environmental, health, and safety audits since 1983.

Charity/Community Outreach. Digital's outstanding dedication to community action earned CEP's America's Corporate Conscience Award in 1989. Although recent losses make it impossible to calculate current charitable giving as a percentage of pretax profits, Digital has in the past given 2 percent, mostly in-kind donations of computer equipment. Donations in 1992 included over $2 million in cash and $17 million in kind. Digital has given over $3.5 million to fund AIDS research.

Equal Employment Opportunity. Digital was one of the earliest major U.S. corporations to initiate an affirmative-action program, in 1962. In that year, the company elected a woman director, decades earlier than many other companies. Two minorities and three women are among the corporate officers. Among officials and managers, 26 percent are women and 9 percent minorities.

Family Benefits. Digital offers working parents a number of flexible scheduling options, including part-time work, job sharing, flextime, and work-at-home arrangements. Digital has programs to develop community child-care centers. Other benefits include $2,500 of adoption aid and seminars on work-family issues.

Workplace Issues. In 1988 Digital became the first company to form an office to deal exclusively with AIDS.

Digital introduced its employee stock purchase plan in 1968. The Digital plan allows virtually all U.S. employees to allocate between two and 10 percent of each paycheck to acquire company stock at a 15-percent discount.

In 1986, Digital commissioned the first study on the health effects of exposure to industrial chemicals used in computer manufacturing. The study found a higher incidence of miscarriages among women exposed to such chemicals, prompting further studies. Digital acted quickly to notify workers and relocate pregnant employees.

Extras. In 1992, Digital had $936,000 in contracts with the Department of Defense, providing electronic computers for the Navy and Air Force, but not related to nuclear weapons.

GENERAL MILLS, INC.

#1 General Mills Boulevard, P.O. Box 1113, Minneapolis, MN 55426

ABBREVIATION								
GIS	B	A	A	A	B	B	A	A

General Mills, the world's second-largest cereal maker, also makes other foods and operates Red Lobster, Olive Garden, and China Coast restaurants. The company had 1992 sales of almost $8 billion, and has 110,000 employees worldwide. General Mills has won three America's Corporate Conscience Awards: Equal Employment Opportunity (1990), Opportunities for the Disabled (1988), and Charitable Contributions (1987).

Environment. General Mills uses 50-percent recycled material in all its packaging. By reducing the thickness of the plastic bags in cereal boxes, 500,000 pounds of plastic are saved each year. The company received a citation from the U.S. Public Interest Research Group for excessive packaging of one snack food, but has since reduced the amount of plastic used in its packaging by 21 percent. It has waste-reduction programs in production facilities and offices.

Charity/Community Outreach. In 1993, General Mills' foundation made over $17 million in charitable donations. Total foundation and company giving of $28 million was 3.3 percent of worldwide pretax earnings. Its Volunteer Connection for employees and retirees has placed more than 7,500 people on community projects.

Equal Employment Opportunity. Two women and one minority sit on General Mills' 14-member board. Twenty-eight percent of officials and managers are women and almost 12 percent are minorities. Seventeen percent of senior managers are women and 13 percent are minorities. General Mills was included in *The Best Companies for Minorities.* The two largest General Mills facilities are accessible to the disabled, and the company employs over 1,500 people with disabilities.

Family Benefits. The company provides a range of benefits to its employees, though not all are available companywide. Benefits available to salaried nonunion employees working more than half-time include a dependent-care option as part of flexible benefits, child- and elder-care subsidies, and adoption subsidies. Its insurance program offers long-term care for elderly and disabled family members.

Workplace Issues. General Mills has stock ownership, outplacement training, tuition reimbursement, scholarships for dependents, and fitness/wellness programs. The company is 7 percent unionized, with no strikes in the last five years. The company has had only minor worker-safety citations and has adopted health and safety-training programs. General Mills is one of the companies cited in *The 100 Best Companies to Work for in America.*

HEWLETT-PACKARD COMPANY

3000 Hanover Street, MS 20B, Palo Alto, CA 94304

ABBREVIATION								
HWP	B	A	A	B	B	A	A	A

Hewlett-Packard (H-P) manufactures computers, printers, and other electronic equipment. In 1992, H-P had 56,000 employees and revenues of $16 billion.

Environment. The company had been one of the top users of ozone-depleting chemicals, but eliminated use of CFCs in mid-1993, two years before legally required to do so. H-P computer-component designs facilitate recycling.

Charity/Community Outreach. In 1992, H-P gave over $68 million (including in-kind giving) of equipment valued at over $57 million. H-P encourages employees to make contributions, especially to education, and subsidizes employee contributions of equipment. At many sites, employees develop Community Action Plans identifying the most pressing needs of the area.

Equal Employment Opportunity. Two women are on H-P's board. Among corporate officers and senior executives, 4 percent are women and 6 percent minorities. At the officials and managers level, almost 25 percent are women and over 11 percent minorities. Though few women and minorities are at the level of corporate officers, the company has programs in place to facilitate future advancement, including diversity-awareness training workshops. H-P was recognized for this record in *The Best Companies for Minorities*.

Family Benefits. H-P has developed a unique way to help its working mothers and fathers: it created probably the first on-site public school in the Western U.S. by joining with local officials to open an elementary school at its electronics plant in Santa Rosa, California. The kindergarten-to-second-grade school has 90 students (75 percent of them are children of H-P employees). H-P is on *Working Mother*'s list of "100 Best Companies for Working Mothers."

Workplace Issues. All H-P employees receive a cash profit-sharing bonus of between two and four weeks' pay. The company has offered flextime for over two decades and allows job sharing and reduced work-week arrangements. Recently, several thousand employees have been transferred. But, with a few exceptions that occurred after buying other companies, the company has never resorted to a layoff. Workers are given time to identify a new opportunity within the company, anywhere in the country. Of approximately 2,500 employees whose jobs were excessed in 1989 and 1990, 85 percent were still with H-P in 1993. Salaries and benefits are generous: health insurance 100 percent covered, a stock-purchase plan, and a 401(k) pension plan.

H-P is listed in *The 100 Best Companies to Work for in America*.

Extras. H-P sells electronic components to the Department of Defense. The company reports that these are all off-the-shelf products.

JOHNSON & JOHNSON

One Johnson & Johnson Plaza, New Brunswick, NJ 08933

ABBREVIATION								
JNJ	B	A	A	A	A	A	A	A

Johnson & Johnson (J&J) is the world's largest manufacturer of health-care products. The company operates in 52 countries and distributes its products in almost 100 more. Sales in 1992 were $13.7 billion, and J&J employed 84,900 people.

Environment. J&J has made good progress in reducing its releases of toxic chemicals. As a participant in the Environmental Protection Agency's 33/50 program, J&J was three years early in meeting its goal of halving emissions of certain chemicals. When adjusted for sales, overall toxic releases declined 21 percent between 1988 and 1990. J&J's goal is to use as much recycled material in its packaging as possible, given health and safety requirements, and it has accepted the Coalition of Northeast Governors challenge to reduce packaging. J&J extends its environmental concern to its overseas operations. All U.S. laws are to be followed abroad, J&J does not export wastes, and international operations are monitored for toxic releases.

Charity/Community Outreach. In 1992, J&J donated $35 million in cash to charity, 1.8 percent of its three-year average pretax profits. The company is involved in a number of programs that go beyond donations. For example, the Live for Life School Nurse Program trains school nurses to treat substance abuse; J&J is a leader of New Brunswick Tomorrow, a program trying to revitalize its headquarters city; and J&J teamed with the National Association of Community Health Centers and the National Council of La Raza to develop innovative ways to improve health care for the medically underserved.

Equal Employment Opportunity. J&J is one of very few companies with three women on its board of directors. One corporate officer is a woman, and 30 percent of officials and managers are women. Although there are relatively few minorities in J&J's upper management (one of 15 directors, one of the 25 highest-paid officers), J&J has strong programs to promote diversity. It purchased over $56 million from minority-owned firms in 1992, and has programs to bank with minority-owned banks. J&J was included in *The Best Companies for Minorities*.

Family Benefits. J&J has the highest family-benefits score of any company in CEP's database. Working parents can take advantage of flexible scheduling, on-site day care, and informative company literature. J&J has been on all eight of *Working Mother* magazine's annual "Best Companies for Working Mothers" lists, including two appearances on the "Ten Best" list.

Workplace Issues. J&J earned a place in the 1993 edition of *The 100 Best Companies to Work for in America*, largely because of an atmosphere in which employees are valued and encouraged to be committed to excellence. J&J's benefits package ranks near the top among large companies, and labor relations are generally good.

Extras. J&J has reduced the number of animals used to test cosmetics and personal-care products by 81 percent since 1988. Only 2 percent of the company's animal testing is for consumer products. In 1992, J&J reported it had spent $8.5 million on its own research into alternatives to animal testing, and $225,000 more at outside labs.

In 1991, a federal court ordered J&J to pay $116.3 million to 3M for willfully violating patents on a medical tape, settling a lawsuit begun in 1986.

In 1992, J&J was criticized by a prominent cancer specialist for dramatically raising the price of a drug for worms in sheep when it was discovered that it could fight human colon cancer as well.

S.C. JOHNSON & SON, INC.

1525 Howe Street, Racine, WI 53403

ABBREVIATION								
SCJ	A	A	A	B	B	A	A	A

S.C. Johnson & Son, Inc., produces household-cleaning and other consumer products, including furniture polishes and other cleaners, air fresheners, and insect repellents. The privately held company had 1992 sales of approximately $2.6 billion and 13,500 employees. S. C. Johnson earned CEP's Corporate Conscience Award for Environmental Stewardship in 1994.

Environment. S.C. Johnson has comprehensive environmental policies and management systems to ensure measurement against worldwide goals. Each operation establishes air, water, and solid-waste minimization plans, with annual performance reviews and employee-training programs. The company is working to eliminate the need for wastewater treatment through innovative closed-loop manufacturing and recycling. One plant in Europe closed its wastewater-treatment plant in 1992. The company reduced its toxic releases almost 25 percent from 1989 to 1990.

Charity/Community Outreach. S.C. Johnson gives an average of 5 percent of pretax income each year to charity through direct and foundation giving. Subsidiaries are encouraged to give up to 3 percent of pretax earnings. The company is involved in local education reform, and has an active employee volunteer program. Regular community activities are offered at its in-house theater.

Equal Employment Opportunity. Though no women or minorities sit on the seven-member board, there are three women and two minority corporate officers, and four women division heads. In the officials and managers category, 14 percent are women and 7 percent minorities.

Family Benefits. S.C. Johnson provides up to five months' leave for childbirth, three months' personal leave, adoption aid, on-site child care, flextime, job sharing, and part-time work. Child care includes before- and after-school, holiday, and summer programs. The company resort in northern Wisconsin is used by employees for family vacations. S.C. Johnson is among *Working Mother*'s "100 Best Companies for Working Mothers."

Workplace Issues. S.C. Johnson is one of the few companies to still maintain a no-layoff policy. It offers profit sharing for all employees, contributions to employee savings plans, in-house training, and scholarships for employees' children. An on-site fitness and aquatic center is available in the company's 146-acre private park, which features tennis courts, softball diamonds, a golf driving range, and running trail. The company is included in *The 100 Best Companies to Work for in America*.

KELLOGG COMPANY

P.O. Box 3599, One Kellogg Square, Battle Creek, MI 49016–3599

ABBREVIATION								
K	B	A	A	A	A	A	A	A

Kellogg is the world's leading producer of ready-to-eat cereals, with 17,000 employees worldwide (6,500 in the U.S.) and 1992 sales of over $6 billion. Kellogg has won two America's Corporate Conscience Awards: Responsiveness to Employees (1991) and Disclosure of Information (1988).

Environment. Kellogg has used recycled packaging since the company was formed in 1906. Product packages, cartons, and shipping cases are made from recycled paper. Kellogg has waste-management and recycling programs across the country.

Charity/Community Outreach. The Kellogg Company gave over $10 million in 1992 (about 1.4 percent of pretax income), mostly direct cash giving. It is a major contributor to Second Harvest, the national network of food banks. A job bank provides information on employee volunteer opportunities, and the company provides time for community work. Kellogg has invested nearly $1 billion in its Battle Creek, Michigan, facilities, including $1.5 million in local economic and community development and support to minority businesses.

Equal Employment Opportunity. About 34 percent of Kellogg's employees are women, including 19 percent of officials and managers and three vice presidents. The 14-member board includes two women and two minorities. Seventeen percent of U.S. employees are minorities, including three corporate officers and almost 11 percent of officials and managers. Kellogg's record earned it a place in *The Best Companies for Minorities*.

Family Benefits. Kellogg offers up to three months' paid leave to new mothers and fathers and adoptive parents. Maternity leave provides full salary and benefits. Flextime and job sharing are also available. Referral services for child care, elder care, and disabled-dependents care are available through the employee assistance program.

Workplace Issues. Almost 67 percent of Kellogg's workforce is unionized. There have been no strikes in the last five years. The company has had only minor OSHA violations and has instituted worker-safety programs. Kellogg offers in-house training, tuition reimbursement, an in-house fitness center, health clinics and events, outplacement/retraining, scholarships for dependents, retirement planning, and an employee stock ownership program. Kellogg is listed in *The 100 Best Companies to Work for in America*.

Extras. Animal testing is for nonmedical purposes, measuring the effects of grain-based diets on disease prevention. Kellogg is funding research on alternatives to animal testing.

LEVI STRAUSS & CO.

1155 Battery Street, San Francisco, CA 94111

ABBREVIATION								
LEV	A	B	A	A	A	B	B	A

Levi Strauss & Co., the world's largest clothing maker, won an America's Corporate Conscience Award in 1994 for International Commitment. In 1992, the company had 23,000 employees in the U.S. and sales of $6 billion.

Environment. In an effort to reduce waste generation, Levi Strauss & Co. has adopted worldwide water-effluent standards for company-owned and -operated, as well as contractor, facilities. It has a Global Environmental Committee. Denim fabric scraps are recycled into company stationery.

Charity/Community Outreach. In 1992, Levi Strauss & Co. donated over $9 million (about 1.5 percent of pretax earnings). In 1993, it stopped funding the Boy Scouts because of differences between Boy Scout policies and the company's nondiscrimination policies. In 1991, the Levi Strauss Foundation launched Project Change to improve race and ethnic relations in communities. The company contributes to numerous organizations involved in minority issues.

Equal Employment Opportunity. Three women serve on the board, and four women are corporate officers. Three of the 25 highest-paid employees are minorities. Over 50 percent of officials and managers are women; 36 percent are minorities. The company was included in *The Best Companies for Minorities*. In 1992, Levi Strauss & Co. became the largest American company to cover partners of unmarried employees in its health plan, including same-sex partners.

Family Benefits. The company provides most employee benefits, though not all are offered companywide. The company initiated a work-at-home program in 1991. Its Child Care Fund develops dependent-care resources in plant communities. Levi Strauss & Co. is listed in *Working Mother*'s "100 Best Companies for Working Mothers."

Workplace Issues. Levi Strauss & Co. provides profit sharing, employee stock ownership, and fitness programs for all employees. Workers are covered by life insurance, savings plans, and pension plans. Along with most American garment manufacturers, Levi Strauss & Co. has been criticized for transferring work overseas and laying off U.S. workers. Between 1985 and 1990, 6,000 workers lost their jobs. Levi Strauss & Co. provided more severance benefits than required by law.

International Commitment. Though 75 percent of its manufacturing is in the U.S., the company has extensive operations overseas. Levi Strauss & Co. is at the forefront of concerns over employment and environmental conditions in developing countries. Its Business Partner Terms of Engagement—addressing such issues as child labor, worker health and safety, and environmental standards—establishes guidelines for selection of contractors, suppliers, and countries for contracting. The company conducted audits of over 700 contractors in 60 countries. It dropped 5 percent of its contractors, and convinced 25 percent to make changes. In 1992, the company ended contracts in Myanmar (Burma) because of human-rights abuses. In 1993, Levi Strauss & Co. announced it would not renew contracts in China unless the human-rights situation there improves.

NORDSTROM, INC.

1501 Fifth Avenue, Seattle, WA 98101–1603

ABBREVIATION								
NOBE	B	A	A	A	A	A	C	A

Founded at the turn of the century as a small shoe store, Nordstrom became the biggest independent shoe chain in America by 1960. It has since diversified and is now a large retailer of clothing, shoes, and accessories, still family run. It operates 77 stores in 14 states. In 1992, Nordstrom employed 33,000 people, and had revenues of $3.4 billion.

Environment. Nordstrom has a variety of companywide programs to reduce its environmental impact. Recycling programs extend from the wrap desks to data processing to shipping. Stores have energy- and water-conservation programs, and the company purchases recycled and reusable materials. A full-time corporate environmental coordinator oversees these efforts, and employee committees in each region work to promote environmental awareness in the workplace. An awards program recognizes suppliers who have reduced packaging or otherwise shown concern for conservation efforts.

Charity/Community Outreach. In 1992, Nordstrom gave $3.3 million to charity, 1.6 percent of average pretax profits. Nordstrom encourages its employees to volunteer, and the company participates in a number of community projects, such as a $4.7 million investment in low-income housing in Seattle.

Equal Employment Opportunity. Retailers often employ plenty of women, but not in executive positions. In 1992, Nordstrom had nine women among its top 24 officers. Women also held 73 percent of store-manager positions, and there were two women on the board.

There is one minority on the board and three who are corporate officers. Managers included 678 minorities (roughly 18 percent) in 1992.

Workplace Issues. In 1993, the same year that Nordstrom appeared in *The 100 Best Companies to Work for in America*, the company also settled a lawsuit brought by the United Food and Commercial Workers (UFCW) union. At the heart of the conflict is the way Nordstrom encourages employees to make exceptional efforts to cater to customers. The UFCW suit charged that Nordstrom did not pay employees for some of these exceptional efforts, for example, thank-you notes or personal deliveries. Many employees interviewed by the authors of *The 100 Best* supported the company. Indeed, in 1991 Seattle employees voted overwhelmingly to decertify the UFCW as their bargaining agent.

RHINO RECORDS, INC.

2225 Colorado Avenue, Santa Monica, CA 90404

ABBREVIATION								
RHI	B	A	A	A	A	B	B	A

Rhino Records is a privately held recording and entertainment production, distribution, and marketing company with about 100 employees.

Environment. Because Rhino does not manufacture, its operations have little direct environmental impact. Through the Ban the Box movement, Rhino encouraged the industry's change to a CD packaging format that produces less waste, and is a leader in increasing environmental awareness among consumers. Ban the Box was a coalition of artists and recording-industry executives opposed to the use of long-box packaging of compact discs. The group protested American industry's continued introduction of overpackaged products. Since customers throw away the CD packaging immediately following purchase, Ban the Box called for the adoption of jewel-box packaging to reduce solid wastes. Rhino also spearheaded an environmental-education effort, using its CD packages for environmental messages that reach millions of customers.

Charity/Community Outreach. Rhino contributes 2 percent of pretax profits to community organizations each year. It encourages employees to volunteer by allowing those who give their time to charity work during the year to take Christmas week off with pay. It organizes monthly speakers on social, political, and economic issues.

Equal Employment Opportunity. Rhino has six women and three minorities among its 16 top officers and division heads. Of 15 officials and managers, five are women and three are minorities. Seven women and four minorities are among the 25 highest-paid employees of the company.

Family Benefits. Rhino offers paid parental leave for new mothers and fathers, part-time return to work for new mothers, and work-at-home arrangements. It reimburses adoption expenses and assists community child-care centers.

Workplace Issues. Rhino pays 100 percent of employee medical insurance, and all employees are eligible for its pension plan. The company has had no OSHA violations, and has worksite committees on health and safety.

TOM'S OF MAINE

Railroad Avenue, P.O. Box 710, Kennebunk, ME 04043

ABBREVIATION								
TOM	A	A	A	A	B	A	A	A

Tom's of Maine manufactures natural, cruelty-free health-care products. Tom's won an America's Corporate Conscience Award for Charitable Contributions in 1992. In 1992, sales were $17 million and Tom's had 70 employees.

Environment. Tom's helped the town of Kennebunk expand its recycling program, donating $25,000 for recycling bins so the town could qualify for a state-provided collection truck. In 1991, Tom's recycled its first ton of wastepaper. It was a pioneer in reducing packaging.

Charity/Community Outreach. Including in-kind gifts, in 1992 Tom's gave $129,000—an extraordinary 17 percent of pretax income—mostly to environmental and education groups. The company works with Community Support Services, a nonprofit organization integrating people with disabilities into society. Employees are encouraged to spend 5 percent of company-paid time volunteering.

Equal Employment Opportunity. Tom's has four women and one Native American on its 13-member board, and two women and one African-American among the 25 highest-paid officers of the company. Three women are among the top eight managers of the company, and there are eight women among the 20 officials and managers.

Family Benefits. Tom's offers up to 12 weeks paid maternity and four weeks paid paternity leave, to adoptive parents too. Job sharing, flextime, and work-at-home are available, as are child-care subsidies, and resource and referral services for child care, elder care, and care of disabled family members. Tom's is listed in *Working Mother*'s "100 Best Companies for Working Mothers."

Workplace Issues. Benefits include medical and dental coverage, a suggestion program, fitness/wellness program, and training for career enhancement and personal enrichment. Tom's has had no OSHA violations, and does have ergonomic and safety programs. Tom's has won a number of local "Employer of the Year" awards.

CEP'S X-Rated Companies

Of the 191 consumer companies rated in *Shopping for a Better World* the eight profiled in this section had six or more ratings (not counting "?"s) that yielded a grade-point average of 2.0 or lower.

Of course, no company is entirely without merit. But these are certainly companies whose social record will displease many consumers, whose products you may not want in your shopping cart, where you might be wary of working, and whose securities you might prefer not to see in your investment portfolio.

There are, however, a few caveats. For this X-rated list, we have weighted all categories of social performance equally. Most of our readers tell us this is how they consider them. Quite a few consumers and activists, however, consider one aspect of social performance so important that a grade in a single category will significantly alter his or her opinion of the company. So if you feel more strongly about one issue, you may want to look carefully at each specific grade rather than simply at the number of bottom grades.

Company profiles make interesting reading, and you may want to know more. You'll find the stories for other X-rated companies in the *Better World Investment Guide* (Prentice-Hall, 1991) at your local library.

A CEP SCREEN Research Service Corporate Profiles subscription can provide you with detailed profiles on 400 companies (see page 395).

CEP's X-Rated List

Albertson's, Inc.
ConAgra, Inc.
First Brands Corporation
Food Lion, Inc.
MCI Communications Corporation
Texaco Inc.
Tyson Foods, Inc.
Unilever PLC

ALBERTSON'S, INC.

250 Parkcenter Boulevard, Boise, ID 83726

ABBREVIATION								
ABS	A	F	?	C	D	B	C	C

Albertson's is the nation's sixth-largest food retailer with more than 650 stores in 19 western, midwestern, and southern states. The company employs 71,000 people; sales topped $10 billion in 1992.

Environment. In 1990, Albertson's introduced a line of environmentally preferred paper products. The company asked its 13,000 suppliers to reduce excess packaging and designated an officer responsible for overseeing environmental affairs. Albertson's does not distribute irradiated food, or sell milk from cows treated with bovine growth hormone.

Charity/Community Outreach. In 1992, Albertson's donated a total of $1,425,000 in cash and in-kind giving (less than 0.5 percent of average pretax profits).

Equal Employment Opportunity. In November 1993, Albertson's agreed to pay $29.5 million for lost wages and emotional distress to 20,000 current and former employees in a race- and sex-discrimination case. The suit contended that women at Albertson's stores did not get equal promotional opportunities, training, or desirable shifts and were often placed in sex-segregated jobs. Albertson's settled similar charges in 1989 for $725,000. The company notes that in each case it admitted no wrongdoing and paid substantially less than its anticipated legal fees.

Following the earlier settlement, Albertson's introduced several programs aimed at enhancing promotion opportunities for women and minorities, including job posting and mentoring. In 1992 the company created the position of EEO Specialist to oversee initiatives such as its Management Advisory Program, a mentoring program with a particular eye on women and minorities. The law firm that represented the plaintiffs cited Albertson's "significant steps to consider and promote women and minorities to management positions" as the reason for the firm's willingness to settle early in the litigation.

In 1993, Albertson's promoted a woman to Group Vice President, Employee Development and Communication, one of 16 executive officers of the company. One woman, the widow of the company's founder, serves on its 14-member board. A Native American man is vice president of the Seattle division and is one of 60 corporate officers.

Family Benefits. Unlike many retailers, Albertson's offers a wide range of benefits available at all locations, including parental leave for either parent for six months to a year for biological or adopted children, and flexible work arrangements such as job sharing and flextime.

Workplace Issues. Over 40 percent of Albertson's workforce is represented by collective bargaining agreements. Relations with its primary union, the United Food and Commercial Workers (UFCW), have not been without contention. In 1989, 5,000 grocery clerks and meatcutters struck Albertson's and several other retailers for 25 days before an agreement on a new contract was reached. In 1991, an Albertson's-operated Grocery Warehouse store in Grand Junction, Colorado, locked out 70 UFCW members for five months after contract negotiations failed. The union filed charges with the National Labor Relations Board alleging bad-faith bargaining during the negotiations, though these charges were dismissed by the agency. More recently, in April 1992, the UFCW approved a master agreement with seven retailers, including Albertson's, that covered nearly 70,000 workers. The accord was described by the union as a "decided improvement" over previous contracts. Nevertheless the UFCW continues to rate the company below average in its relations with the union.

CONAGRA, INC.

ConAgra Center, One ConAgra Drive, Omaha, NE 68102–5001

ABBREVIATION								
CAG	C	C	C	C	?	?	F	C

ConAgra is the largest independent food company in the U.S. Sales in 1992 were $21 billion, and ConAgra employed 81,000 people.

Environment. From 1988 to 1990, ConAgra's Toxic Release Inventory totals dropped 16 percent, almost 50 percent when adjusted for sales. As one of the country's largest farming and livestock companies, much of ConAgra's environmental impact stems from pesticides and land-use issues. In September 1991, ConAgra was fined and paid $12,500 for criminal violations of Michigan's pesticide laws. An employee, acting on orders from another employee, had dumped 850 gallons of hazardous chemicals at a grain elevator.

Charity/Community Outreach. In 1992, ConAgra's combined direct and foundation gifts were $5 million, about 1 percent of average pretax profits. Most community involvement is handled locally, with no information collected at headquarters. ConAgra has several programs at headquarters in Omaha, Nebraska, including job training and placement for teenagers and awards to encourage innovative teaching.

Equal Employment Opportunity. There are no women or minorities on ConAgra's 12-person board. Two of 23 corporate officers are women.

Family Benefits. ConAgra reports that these programs are handled locally, and that it has no centralized information.

Workplace Issues. Meat packing is the most dangerous occupation in the U.S., and ConAgra has had a number of problems. The Monfort plant in Grand Island, Nebraska, was hit with $1.1 million in proposed OSHA penalties in 1991, with 107 willful violations. ConAgra contested the penalties. In 1993, Grand Island was again fined after a worker died. Also in 1993, the Monfort plant in St. Joseph, Missouri, was cited for ergonomic violations and failure to properly treat resulting medical conditions. OSHA proposed fines totaling $209,000. These safety problems have led to conflict with some of ConAgra's unions.

Disclosure of Information. ConAgra responded to CEP's questionnaire with some information. But for a number of issues, ConAgra says that it does not collect the data centrally. The company is divided into over 70 operating companies.

FIRST BRANDS CORPORATION

83 Wooster Heights Road, P. O. Box 1911, Danbury, CT 06813–1911

ABBREVIATION								
FBR	C	A	C	F	D	D	B	B

First Brands is a major marketer of household and automotive products, including GLAD plastic wrap and bags, Prestone and STP autocare products, and Simoniz polishes and cleaners. Sales in 1992 were $1 billion, and the company had about 3,700 employees.

Environment. First Brands' Prestone division distributes antifreeze-recycling equipment to automotive service centers, and STP automotive centers recycle used motor oil. First Brands reduced its toxic releases by 17 percent from 1988 to 1990.

In 1991, the Federal Trade Commission found unsubstantiated environmental claims on GLAD degradable trash bags. The company removed or clarified misleading claims. GLAD bags are made thinner to minimize plastic use, and specially designed bags are part of many municipal recycling programs.

Charity/Community Outreach. In 1990, the company made in-kind donations of supplies for community cleanups and Operation Desert Storm worth over 2 percent of pretax earnings ($2.6 million).

First Brands sponsors "GLAD Bag-A-Thons": volunteers in over 100 cities collect litter and recyclables in donated trash bags. In Arkansas and Virginia, First Brands provides job training and work opportunities to unemployed people.

Equal Employment Opportunity. There are no women on the nine-member board, or among corporate officers and division heads. One Hispanic man and one Asian man are division heads of Puerto Rican and Philippine operations, respectively. Eight percent of officials and managers are women and 4 percent minorities.

Workplace Issues. Seventeen percent of the workforce is unionized. There have been no significant work stoppages in the last five years. The company has received some worker-safety citations, but has labor/management committees on safety at all its facilities. First Brands is introducing self-directed work teams, which in many cases eliminate the need for supervisors and enhance productivity, quality, safety, and morale.

Extras. Animal tests, used to determine skin and eye irritancy of automotive products, have decreased from 200 in 1985 to 56 in 1990.

FOOD LION, INC.

P.O. Box 1330, Salisbury, NC 28145–1330

ABBREVIATION								
FDLNA	?	?	D	D	C	D	F	F

Food Lion operates over 1,000 supermarkets primarily in the Southeast and Mid-Atlantic. It had over $7 billion in sales in 1992 and nearly 60,000 employees.

Environment. Food Lion has long recycled cardboard and now collects recyclables from customers. The company has one of the most efficient trucking fleets in the industry and an award-winning energy-management system. Food Lion has no manufacturing operations and so no environmental violations.

Charity/Community Outreach. Most of Food Lion's donations come directly from company directors and officers. In the words of the company, this ensures that customers do not fund contributions through higher prices. Food Lion's efforts to support its communities are limited. The most significant initiative is a dropout prevention program that earned it the North Carolina School-Business Award in 1990. In the early 1980s, a manager was criticized for his United Way involvement, on grounds that it interfered with business activities.

Equal Employment Opportunity. Food Lion has been criticized for its equal-employment record. In 1984, the NAACP targeted 22 companies in the Southeast, including Food Lion, to sign a Fair Share agreement to increase the numbers of minorities in management and do more business with minority-owned businesses. According to the NAACP, Food Lion was the only supermarket chain that would not meet with the NAACP until the NAACP staged a boycott. Food Lion eventually agreed to become part of Fair Share, but the NAACP still questions the position of minorities at Food Lion. The United Food and Commercial Workers (UFCW) found just 29 African-American store managers among 900 stores.

Food Lion recently named the president of a historically black college to its board. According to the UFCW, Food Lion is somewhat more willing to locate stores in inner-city communities than its competitors.

While Food Lion has five women in its senior-management group, there is no female representation on the board or among its corporate vice presidents. Based on the UFCW's survey, fewer than 3 percent of Food Lion store managers are women.

Workplace Issues. Food Lion opposes organized labor and has a confrontational relationship with the UFCW, its primary union. In February 1991, the National Labor Relations Board (NLRB) ordered the company to stop interfering with UFCW attempts to communicate with employees. (The judge also ruled that the union had acted improperly by soliciting within the store.) The UFCW believes that the company fails to share the rewards of its success with rank-and-file employees. Though Food Lion maintains a profit-sharing plan available to all employees, the union has filed a suit charging the company with terminating employees before they become vested in the benefits. The suit also alleges that Food Lion has denied employees COBRA coverage for their health benefits.

In a separate matter, on August 3, 1993, Food Lion settled the largest overtime and child-labor case ever brought by the Department of Labor by agreeing to pay $16.2 million in fines and back pay.

Extras. On November 5, 1992, ABC-TV aired a documentary supporting allegations of unsanitary practices by the company. Two ABC correspondents worked at different Food Lion stores and with hidden cameras recorded similar activities: meat that had passed its "sell by" date was repackaged as fresh; aged ground beef was mixed with new shipments and resold; meat-cutting equipment was improperly maintained. Former Food Lion employees stated that strict performance criteria force store managers to take such actions to achieve financial goals.

MCI COMMUNICATIONS CORPORATION

1801 Pennsylvania Avenue, NW, Washington, DC 20006

ABBREVIATION								
MCIC	?	F	C	B	A	?	D	F

MCI is currently the second-largest long-distance telephone services provider in the U.S., with 1992 sales of $10 billion and 31,000 employees.

Environment. Unlike AT&T, MCI has no manufacturing operations and thus no toxic releases. Bills are printed on recycled paper. For high-volume users, MCI offers billing on CD-ROM; MCI's most active accounts can receive monthly bills of over 10,000 pages.

Charity/Community Outreach. In 1990, MCI made charitable gifts of about $1.1 million, or less than 0.2 percent of its average pretax earnings. The company's community-outreach efforts utilize its communication services. MCI has helped several schools set up evening education-assistance programs where students call in to discuss homework. MCI donates telephone lines and equipment and pays a stipend to the teachers who answer the phones.

Equal Employment Opportunity. In 1993, a woman was named president of MCI's consumer business, becoming the company's highest-ranking female executive. Another woman is among 17 senior vice presidents. Two women and one African-American man are on MCI's 14-member board. Minorities represent 24 percent of total employees, with only 6 percent of these at the executive level and 14 percent in the management pool. MCI's record in this area earned it inclusion in *The Best Companies for Minorities*. In 1988, MCI settled a discrimination case brought by a man who alleged he was fired because of his sexual orientation. MCI made a cash award, and established a policy barring discrimination based on sexual orientation.

Workplace Issues. The Communications Workers of America (CWA) told CEP it considers MCI the most antiunion of the big-three telecommunications firms. The company offers some attractive benefits, including an employee stock ownership plan and a stock purchase plan.

Extras. In 1988, MCI paid customers up to $3.3 million to settle charges that the company billed customers for calls that were not answered. From 1978 to 1985, the problem stemmed from the inadequate access of AT&T's competitors to state-of-the-art exchange technology and to accidental billing errors caused by false signals from exchange centers.

TEXACO INC.

2000 Westchester Avenue, White Plains, NY 10650

ABBREVIATION								
TX	F	B	C	F	D	C	C	C

Texaco, the nation's fourth-largest petrochemical concern, is involved in the worldwide exploration, production, refining, transportation, and marketing of crude oil and its products. In 1992, Texaco had about 38,000 employees and sales of $36.8 billion.

Environment. A series of oil spills and environmental-compliance problems in the early 1990s, along with the severe impact of Texaco's 20-year Ecuadorian operations on the Amazonian environment and the livelihoods of indigenous peoples, combined to put Texaco on CEP's C3 list of America's worst environmental performers.

In 1992, a Texaco affiliate agreed to pay approximately $50 million to 180 Virginia families for damages related to an underground oil leak. This is the single largest settlement of its kind. The subsidiary completely compensated affected homeowners by instituting a property-value protection plan.

In 1993, Texaco was ordered by the EPA under the 1990 Oil Pollution Act to pay an estimated $12 million in cleanup costs and penalties for oil spills at its refineries. The company does have Oil Spill Response Teams to handle cleanups.

In 1992, Texaco was ordered by the EPA to clean up and close all unlined waste pits that could endanger surface water or groundwater quality on Navajo Nation territories in Arizona, New Mexico, and Utah.

Texaco released 21 million pounds of toxic chemicals in 1990, down from 22 million pounds in 1989. Adjusted for sales, Texaco's performance is better than the oil-industry average. Texaco is a member of the EPA's 33/50 voluntary emissions-reduction program, and reduced its aggregate emissions 37 percent from 1988 to 1992.

Charity/Community Outreach. Texaco and the Texaco Foundation contributed a total of over $24 million in 1993 (almost 1.5 percent of average worldwide pretax earnings). Texaco contributed $2 million in 1990 and 1991 to the American Forestry Association's urban tree-planting project. In 1990, Texaco helped launch the National Teacher Training Institute, which trains teachers in 20 sites around the U.S.

Equal Employment Opportunity. Texaco has one woman board member, plus one woman corporate officer and one division head.

Women represent 18 percent, and minorities 9 percent, of officials and managers. One minority serves on its 16-member board.

In 1992, a California jury awarded over $6 million to a woman who sued Texaco for sex discrimination, the largest award ever in such a case. A California Superior Court judge ruled that the damages were excessive and the decision based on insufficient evidence. The case is still under appeal.

Workplace Issues. Texaco participates in OSHA's voluntary STAR Program. It has been recognized for exemplary safety programs, and low injury and lost-workday rates at several facilities.

Extras. In 1991, outside contractors used 2,086 animals in tests of petrochemical products, a 17-percent decrease from the number tested in 1986. Texaco supplies fuel to the U.S. military.

TYSON FOODS, INC.

2210 W. Oaklawn Drive, Springdale, AR 72764

ABBREVIATION								
TYSNA	C	?	D	A	B	?	D	D

Tyson is the world's largest fully integrated producer, processor, and marketer of fresh and frozen poultry-, beef-, pork-, and fish-based food products, and convenience foods. In 1992, Tyson had $4.2 billion in sales and employed 45,000 people.

Environment. Tyson's expenditures on water quality programs ($168 million over 5 years) may have been prompted by a court ruling against the company regarding Clean Water Act violations in Alabama. Tyson is working to reduce its packaging, and redesigned its frozen-dinner package to save over a million pounds of packaging each year.

Charity/Community Outreach. Tyson employees participate in an educational program in Arkansas targeted to kids at risk for dropping out of high school. Tyson also contributes to education through scholarships, and supports the Special Olympics. However, when Tyson took over Holly Farms in 1989, the consolidation forced out many small farmers who were dropped to cut costs.

Equal Employment Opportunity. According to Tyson's annual report, there is one woman among the 15 corporate officers. The one woman on the board is the widow of a Tyson family member. There is one African-American man on the nine-member board.

Workplace Issues. Tyson owns Holly Farms, one of the companies listed on the AFL-CIO's national boycott list of employers with unfair labor practices. The dispute with the Teamsters began in 1989, when Tyson bought Holly Farms. According to the union, Tyson refused to bargain with Teamsters truck drivers, and demanded a pay cut. When 47 of the 200 drivers refused, Tyson fired them. An administrative law judge's ruling found Tyson guilty of unfair labor practices that were "serious, pervasive, numerous and calculated." In 1993, the National Labor Relations Board (NLRB) rejected the company's appeal. Tyson again appealed the case to federal district court in 1994. In a separate case at an Arkansas facility, the NLRB ruled in 1993 that Tyson had illegally directed and controlled a petition drive to decertify the union. The company did not appeal that ruling.

Tyson has a number of programs to combat the ergonomic hazards of the poultry business. In January 1994, two Tyson plants were honored for going one million person-hours without a lost-time accident. According to the company, Tyson's 1993 lost-time injury rate was 2.2 per 100 workers, compared to a poultry-industry average of 11.1. The company offers the Tyson Improvement Program to improve workers' reading and math skills.

UNILEVER PLC

Unilever U.S., Inc., 390 Park Avenue, New York, NY 10022

ABBREVIATION								
UN	B	C	C	F	D	C	B	C

Unilever, jointly owned and based in the Netherlands and the United Kingdom, is a multinational food- and consumer-product conglomerate. This profile pertains to Unilever U.S. operations only, which had 1992 sales of $9 billion and 26,000 employees.

Environment. Unilever is working to reduce its packaging by using lighter-weight materials and introducing concentrated-formula laundry detergents. Some packages contain 25 percent or more recycled paper or plastic content. A Unilever subsidiary developed a label adhesive that dissolves easily in the recycling process. Toxic releases adjusted for sales declined 35 percent from 1988 to 1990, but remain average for the household-products industry. Unilever U.S., however, has problems with toxic releases and Superfund liabilities at two subsidiaries.

Charity/Community Outreach. In 1991, Unilever U.S. contributed $4.6 million (about 0.94 percent of pretax earnings) to charitable organizations, and made donations of food and consumer products worth an additional $1.9 million. Its Lipton subsidiary has a volunteer-recognition program that contributes to organizations where employees volunteer. Lipton also sponsors volunteer fairs in six cities for its employees and for community residents to explore volunteer opportunities.

Equal Employment Opportunity. Women and minorities are poorly represented in senior positions at Unilever. Twelve white men serve on Unilever U.S.'s board. No women and one minority are among the company's 12 corporate officers.

Workplace Issues. Unilever U.S. offers basic medical and pension coverage, profit sharing, and employee skills training, employee-assistance and fitness/wellness programs.

Extras. Unilever continues to test on animals for consumer-product development. It spends over $1 million annually developing non-animal alternatives and supports the Johns Hopkins Center for Alternatives to Animal Testing. Unilever would not divulge the number of animals used currently or in previous years.

RATINGS BY PRODUCT

PRODUCT	PARENT COMPANY									EXTRAS
ALCOHOLIC BEVERAGES										
Absolut Vodka ★	GMR	C	A	A	B	A	A	B	A	factory farming; foreign-based company
Almaden Wines ★	GMR	C	A	A	B	A	A	B	A	factory farming; foreign-based company
Amaretto di Saronno liqueur ★	GMR	C	A	A	B	A	A	B	A	factory farming; foreign-based company
Artic Ice ★	ACCOB	C	A	A	A	B	A	B	A	CEDC report; Fair Share
Bailey's Original Irish Cream Liqueur ★	GMR	C	A	A	B	A	A	B	A	factory farming; foreign-based company
Beefeater	ALP	B	C	B	D	?	B	?	B	foreign-based company
Beringer	NEST	B	?	B	B	B	A	B	B	Animal testing: non-medical products, significant alternative efforts; foreign-based company; infant formula
Black Velvet Canadian Whisky ★	GMR	C	A	A	B	A	A	B	A	factory farming; foreign-based company
Blossom Hill Wines ★	GMR	C	A	A	B	A	A	B	A	factory farming; foreign-based company
Bud ★	BUD	C	A	A	B	A	B	A	A	CEDC report
Budweiser ★	BUD	C	A	A	B	A	B	A	A	CEDC report
Busch ★	BUD	C	A	A	B	A	B	A	A	CEDC report
Carlsberg ★	BUD	C	A	A	B	A	B	A	A	CEDC report

PRODUCT	PARENT COMPANY	The Environment	Charitable Giving	Community Outreach	Women's Advancement	Minority Advancement	Family	Workplace Issues	Disclosure of Information	EXTRAS
Castlemaine ★	ACCOB	C	A	A	A	B	A	B	A	CEDC report; Fair Share
Christian Brothers Brandy ★	GMR	C	A	A	B	A	A	B	A	factory farming; foreign-based company
Cinzano ★	GMR	C	A	A	B	A	A	B	A	factory farming; foreign-based company
Coors ★	ACCOB	C	A	A	A	B	A	B	A	CEDC report; Fair Share
Croft Sherries and Ports ★	GMR	C	A	A	B	A	A	B	A	factory farming; foreign-based company
Dreher Brandy ★	GMR	C	A	A	B	A	A	B	A	factory farming; foreign-based company
Elephant Malt Liquor ★	BUD	C	A	A	B	A	B	A	A	CEDC report
George Killian's Irish Red ★	ACCOB	C	A	A	A	B	A	B	A	CEDC report; Fair Share
Gilbey's ★	GMR	C	A	A	B	A	A	B	A	factory farming; foreign-based company
Grand Marnier ★	GMR	C	A	A	B	A	A	B	A	factory farming; foreign-based company
Inglenook Wines ★	GMR	C	A	A	B	A	A	B	A	factory farming; foreign-based company
J&B ★	GMR	C	A	A	B	A	A	B	A	factory farming; foreign-based company
José Cuervo Tequila ★	GMR	C	A	A	B	A	A	B	A	factory farming; foreign-based company
Keystone ★	ACCOB	C	A	A	A	B	A	B	A	CEDC report; Fair Share

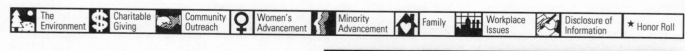

The Environment | Charitable Giving | Community Outreach | Women's Advancement | Minority Advancement | Family | Workplace Issues | Disclosure of Information | ★ Honor Roll

For a more detailed explanation, see pages 7–28.

PRODUCT	PARENT COMPANY		$		♀					EXTRAS
King Cobra ★	BUD	C	A	A	B	A	B	A	A	CEDC report
Lancers ★	GMR	C	A	A	B	A	A	B	A	factory farming; foreign-based company
Le Piat d'Or Wines ★	GMR	C	A	A	B	A	A	B	A	factory farming; foreign-based company
Lite	MO	D	D	?	A	A	?	?	F	Animal testing: non-medical products; CEDC report; tobacco; increasing TRI; Workplace Principles
Lowenbrau	MO	D	D	?	A	A	?	?	F	Animal testing: non-medical products; CEDC report; tobacco; increasing TRI; Workplace Principles
Magnum	MO	D	D	?	A	A	?	?	F	Animal testing: non-medical products; CEDC report; tobacco; increasing TRI; Workplace Principles
Malibu liqueur ★	GMR	C	A	A	B	A	A	B	A	factory farming; foreign-based company
Meister Brau	MO	D	D	?	A	A	?	?	F	Animal testing: non-medical products; CEDC report; tobacco; increasing TRI; Workplace Principles
Metaxa ★	GMR	C	A	A	B	A	A	B	A	factory farming; foreign-based company
Michelob ★	BUD	C	A	A	B	A	B	A	A	CEDC report
Miller	MO	D	D	?	A	A	?	?	F	Animal testing: non-medical products; CEDC report; tobacco; increasing TRI; Workplace Principles
Milwaukee's Best	MO	D	D	?	A	A	?	?	F	Animal testing: non-medical products; CEDC report; tobacco; increasing TRI; Workplace Principles
Munich Oktoberfest	MO	D	D	?	A	A	?	?	F	Animal testing: non-medical products; CEDC report; tobacco; increasing TRI; Workplace Principles

PRODUCT	PARENT COMPANY	The Environment	Charitable Giving	Community Outreach	Women's Advancement	Minority Advancement	Family	Workplace Issues	Disclosure of Information	EXTRAS
Natural Light ★	BUD	C	A	A	B	A	B	A	A	CEDC report
Natural Pilsner ★	BUD	C	A	A	B	A	B	A	A	CEDC report
Popov ★	GMR	C	A	A	B	A	A	B	A	factory farming; foreign-based company
Shulers ★	ACCOB	C	A	A	A	B	A	B	A	CEDC report; Fair Share
Smirnoff Vodka ★	GMR	C	A	A	B	A	A	B	A	factory farming; foreign-based company
Wild Turkey ★	GMR	C	A	A	B	A	A	B	A	factory farming; foreign-based company
Winterfest ★	ACCOB	C	A	A	A	B	A	B	A	CEDC report; Fair Share
Zima Clearmalt ★	ACCOB	C	A	A	A	B	A	B	A	CEDC report; Fair Share
APPLIANCES										
Admiral	MYG	B	A	B	C	D	C	B	A	Workplace Principles
Amana	RTN	C	?	B	D	?	?	?	C	CEDC report; military contracts; nuclear weapons
Estate	WHR	B	A	A	C	C	B	B	A	
GE	GE	D	C	B	C	C	B	C	A	C3; CEDC report; military contracts
Heil	WHR	B	A	A	C	C	B	B	A	

The Environment | Charitable Giving | Community Outreach | Women's Advancement | Minority Advancement | Family | Workplace Issues | Disclosure of Information | ★ Honor Roll

For a more detailed explanation, see pages 7–28.

PRODUCT	PARENT COMPANY									EXTRAS
Hoover	MYG	B	A	B	C	D	C	B	A	Workplace Principles
Hotpoint	GE	D	C	B	C	C	B	C	A	C3; CEDC report; military contracts
Imperial 500	WHR	B	A	A	C	C	B	B	A	
Jenn-Air	MYG	B	A	B	C	D	C	B	A	Workplace Principles
Magic Chef	MYG	B	A	B	C	D	C	B	A	Workplace Principles
Maytag	MYG	B	A	B	C	D	C	B	A	Workplace Principles
Panasonic	MC	C	?	A	?	?	D	?	C	Fair Share; foreign-based company; increasing TRI; same-sex partner benefits
Power Clean	WHR	B	A	A	C	C	B	B	A	
Roper	WHR	B	A	A	C	C	B	B	A	
Serva-Door	WHR	B	A	A	C	C	B	B	A	
Whirlpool	WHR	B	A	A	C	C	B	B	A	
BABY FOODS										
Beech Nut	RAL	C	C	B	B	B	B	C	B	CEDC report; increasing TRI
Enfamil	BMY	B	C	B	B	B	B	B	A	Animal testing: medical & non-medical products, significant alternative efforts; infant formula; Workplace Principles
Gerber	GEB	C	C	?	B	B	?	?	F	CEDC report; increasing TRI; infant formula

PRODUCT	PARENT COMPANY	The Environment	Charitable Giving	Community Outreach	Women's Advancement	Minority Advancement	Family	Workplace Issues	Disclosure of Information	EXTRAS
Metabolic Formulas	BMY	B	C	B	B	B	B	B	A	Animal testing: medical & non-medical products, significant alternative efforts; infant formula; Workplace Principles
Nursoy	AHP	C	F	C	B	B	C	C	A	Animal testing: medical & non-medical products, significant alternative efforts; infant formula
Pregestimil	BMY	B	C	B	B	B	B	B	A	Animal testing: medical & non-medical products, significant alternative efforts; infant formula; Workplace Principles
ProSobee	BMY	B	C	B	B	B	B	B	A	Animal testing: medical & non-medical products, significant alternative efforts; infant formula; Workplace Principles
S-M-A	AHP	C	F	C	B	B	C	C	A	Animal testing: medical & non-medical products, significant alternative efforts; infant formula
BABY NEEDS										
A & D Ointment	SGP	B	C	A	B	A	A	B	A	Animal testing: medical products only, significant alternative efforts; on-site child care; Workplace Principles
Baby Magic ★	CL	B	B	A	A	B	A	A	A	Animal testing: medical & non-medical products, significant alternative efforts; CEDC report; profile
Baby Steps	KMB	C	C	B	B	C	B	A	A	Animal testing: non-medical products, significant alternative efforts; CEDC report; tobacco
Chux ★	JNJ	B	A	A	A	A	A	A	A	Animal testing: medical products only, significant alternative efforts; CEP Award — Disclosure; on-site child care; profile; Workplace Principles

The Environment | Charitable Giving | Community Outreach | Women's Advancement | Minority Advancement | Family | Workplace Issues | Disclosure of Information | ★ Honor Roll

For a more detailed explanation, see pages 7–28.

PRODUCT	PARENT COMPANY									EXTRAS
Desitin	PFE	C	B	A	B	C	A	B	A	Animal testing: medical products only, significant alternative efforts; heart valve suits; Workplace Principles
Diaparene Baby-care Products	EK	C	B	B	B	B	A	B	B	Animal testing: medical and non-medical products, significant alternative efforts; CEDC report; CEP Award — EEO
Gerber	GEB	C	C	?	B	B	?	?	F	CEDC report; increasing TRI; infant formula
Huggies	KMB	C	C	B	B	C	B	A	A	Animal testing: non-medical products, significant alternative efforts; CEDC report; tobacco
Johnson's Baby Powder ★	JNJ	B	A	A	A	A	A	A	A	Animal testing: medical products only, significant alternative efforts; CEP Award — Disclosure; on-site child care; profile; Workplace Principles
Kimbies	KMB	C	C	B	B	C	B	A	A	Animal testing: non-medical products, significant alternative efforts; CEDC report; tobacco
Luvs	PG	C	B	A	B	B	A	B	A	Animal testing: medical and non-medical products, significant alternative efforts; CEDC report; CEP Awards — Animal Welfare, Employer Responsiveness; increasing TRI; on-site day care; Workplace Principles
Pampers	PG	C	B	A	B	B	A	B	A	Animal testing: medical and non-medical products, significant alternative efforts; CEDC report; CEP Awards — Animal Welfare, Employer Responsiveness; increasing TRI; on-site day care; Workplace Principles

PRODUCT	PARENT COMPANY	The Environment	Charitable Giving	Community Outreach	Women's Advancement	Minority Advancement	Family	Workplace Issues	Disclosure of Information	EXTRAS
BAKED GOODS: FRESH & REFRIGERATED										
Aunt Fanny's	PT	C	D	?	B	?	?	?	F	CEDC report; increasing TRI
Biscayne	OAT	B	A	A	B	B	D	?	C	CEDC report; Fair Share
Delacre	CPB	B	C	B	A	A	A	C	A	Animal testing: non-medical products, significant alternative efforts; CEDC report; on-site child care
Entenmann's	MO	D	D	?	A	A	?	?	F	Animal testing: non-medical products; CEDC report; tobacco; increasing TRI; Workplace Principles
Freihofer's	MO	D	D	?	A	A	?	?	F	Animal testing: non-medical products; CEDC report; tobacco; increasing TRI; Workplace Principles
Grands! ★	GMR	C	A	A	B	A	A	B	A	factory farming; foreign-based company
Honey Maid Graham	RN	?	A	C	C	?	?	?	D	Animal testing: non-medical products; CEDC report; tobacco; increasing TRI; Workplace Principles
Hungry Jack ★	GMR	C	A	A	B	A	A	B	A	factory farming; foreign-based company
Pampas	OAT	B	A	A	B	B	D	?	C	CEDC report; Fair Share
Pet-Ritz	PT	C	D	?	B	?	?	?	F	CEDC report; increasing TRI
Roman Meal	PT	C	D	?	B	?	?	?	F	CEDC report; increasing TRI
Tasty	HNZ	B	C	A	B	D	C	A	A	CEDC report; CEP Award — Environment

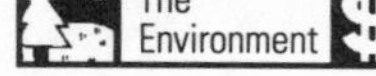

The Environment | Charitable Giving | Community Outreach | Women's Advancement | Minority Advancement | Family | Workplace Issues | Disclosure of Information | ★ Honor Roll

For a more detailed explanation, see pages 7–28.

PRODUCT	PARENT COMPANY									EXTRAS
Winton Bros.	PT	C	D	?	B	?	?	?	F	CEDC report; increasing TRI
BAKED GOODS: FROZEN										
Aunt Jemima	OAT	B	A	A	B	B	D	?	C	CEDC report; Fair Share
Dining Treat	CAG	C	C	C	C	?	?	F	C	CEDC report; factory farming; profile
Donut Shop	CAG	C	C	C	C	?	?	F	C	CEDC report; factory farming; profile
Eggo ★	K	B	A	A	A	A	A	A	A	Animal testing: non-medical products, significant alternative efforts; CEDC report; CEP Awards — Employer Responsiveness, Disclosure; profile
Fruit 'n Creme Delight	CAG	C	C	C	C	?	?	F	C	CEDC report; factory farming; profile
Great Starts	CPB	B	C	B	A	A	A	C	A	Animal testing: non-medical products, significant alternative efforts; CEDC report; on-site child care
Home Bake Shop	CAG	C	C	C	C	?	?	F	C	CEDC report; factory farming; profile
Jiffy	CAG	C	C	C	C	?	?	F	C	CEDC report; factory farming; profile
Lender's Bagels	MO	D	D	?	A	A	?	?	F	Animal testing: non-medical products; CEDC report; tobacco; increasing TRI; Workplace Principles
Light & Healthy	OAT	B	A	A	B	B	D	?	C	CEDC report; Fair Share
Oronoque Orchards	PT	C	D	?	B	?	?	?	F	CEDC report; increasing TRI
Pepperidge Farm	CPB	B	C	B	A	A	A	C	A	Animal testing: non-medical products, significant alternative efforts; CEDC report; on-site child care

PRODUCT	PARENT COMPANY	The Environment	Charitable Giving	Community Outreach	Women's Advancement	Minority Advancement	Family	Workplace Issues	Disclosure of Information	EXTRAS
Sara Lee	SLE	C	B	A	B	B	B	B	A	CEP Award — Charity; on-site child care; tobacco
Toaster Strudel ★	GMR	C	A	A	B	A	A	B	A	factory farming; foreign-based company
Waffle Lovers	OAT	B	A	A	B	B	D	?	C	CEDC report; Fair Share
BAKING MIXES										
Aunt Jemima	OAT	B	A	A	B	B	D	?	C	CEDC report; Fair Share
Betty Crocker ★	GIS	B	A	A	A	B	B	A	A	CEDC report; CEP Awards — Charity, EEO, Opportunities for the Disabled; profile; Workplace Principles
Bisquick ★	GIS	B	A	A	A	B	B	A	A	CEDC report; CEP Awards — Charity, EEO, Opportunities for the Disabled; profile; Workplace Principles
Bundt ★	GMR	C	A	A	B	A	A	B	A	factory farming; foreign-based company
Country Carrot	OAT	B	A	A	B	B	D	?	C	CEDC report; Fair Share
Duncan Hines	PG	C	B	A	B	B	A	B	A	Animal testing: medical and non-medical products, significant alternative efforts; CEDC report; CEP Awards — Animal Welfare, Employer Responsiveness; increasing TRI; on-site day care; Workplace Principles
Flako	OAT	B	A	A	B	B	D	?	C	CEDC report; Fair Share
Gold Medal Pouch Mixes ★	GIS	B	A	A	A	B	B	A	A	CEDC report; CEP Awards — Charity, EEO, Opportunities for the Disabled; profile; Workplace Principles

The Environment | Charitable Giving | Community Outreach | Women's Advancement | Minority Advancement | Family | Workplace Issues | Disclosure of Information | ★ Honor Roll

For a more detailed explanation, see pages 7–28.

PRODUCT	PARENT COMPANY									EXTRAS
Health Valley	HVAL	A	C	C	A	A	B	A	A	
Homestyle	OAT	B	A	A	B	B	D	?	C	CEDC report; Fair Share
Liqui-Dri Foods, Inc.	OAT	B	A	A	B	B	D	?	C	CEDC report; Fair Share
Pennant	UN	B	C	C	F	D	C	B	C	Animal testing: non-medical products, significant alternative efforts; foreign-based company; profile
Pillsbury ★	GMR	C	A	A	B	A	A	B	A	factory farming; foreign-based company
Robin Hood Pouch Mixes ★	GIS	B	A	A	A	B	B	A	A	CEDC report; CEP Awards — Charity, EEO, Opportunities for the Disabled; profile; Workplace Principles
BAKING NEEDS										
Argo	CPC	C	A	B	A	B	C	A	B	Animal testing: non-medical products, significant alternative efforts; CEDC report; increasing TRI
Arm & Hammer	CHD	A	B	A	C	C	A	A	A	Animal testing: non-medical products, significant alternative efforts; CEP Award — Environment
Bakers	MO	D	D	?	A	A	?	?	F	Animal testing: non-medical products; CEDC report; tobacco; increasing TRI; Workplace Principles
Baker's Joy	ACV	A	?	B	A	D	D	B	B	Animal testing: non-medical products; increasing TRI
Calumet	MO	D	D	?	A	A	?	?	F	Animal testing: non-medical products; CEDC report; tobacco; increasing TRI; Workplace Principles
Cookie-ettes	OAT	B	A	A	B	B	D	?	C	CEDC report; Fair Share
Cream Corn Starch	DL	C	A	B	B	?	F	B	C	CEDC report

PRODUCT	PARENT COMPANY	The Environment	Charitable Giving	Community Outreach	Women's Advancement	Minority Advancement	Family	Workplace Issues	Disclosure of Information	EXTRAS
Davis	RN	?	A	C	C	?	?	?	D	Animal testing: non-medical products; CEDC report; tobacco; increasing TRI; Workplace Principles
Frosting Supreme ★	GMR	C	A	A	B	A	A	B	A	factory farming; foreign-based company
Hershey's	HSY	B	B	A	B	C	A	A	A	CEDC report; increasing TRI; on-site child care
Knox	UN	B	C	C	F	D	C	B	C	Animal testing: non-medical products, significant alternative efforts; foreign-based company; profile
PAM	AHP	C	F	C	B	B	C	C	A	Animal testing: medical & non-medical products, significant alternative efforts; infant formula
Sugar Twin	ACV	A	?	B	A	D	D	B	B	Animal testing: non-medical products; increasing TRI
Sure Jell	MO	D	D	?	A	A	?	?	F	Animal testing: non-medical products; CEDC report; tobacco; increasing TRI; Workplace Principles
Toll House Morsels	NEST	B	?	B	B	B	A	B	B	Animal testing: non-medical products, significant alternative efforts; foreign-based company; infant formula
BEANS: CANNED & DRIED										
Beanee-Weenee	OAT	B	A	A	B	B	D	?	C	CEDC report; Fair Share
Jack Rabbit	CAG	C	C	C	C	?	?	F	C	CEDC report; factory farming; profile
Las Palmas	PT	C	D	?	B	?	?	?	F	CEDC report; increasing TRI
Rosarita	CAG	C	C	C	C	?	?	F	C	CEDC report; factory farming; profile

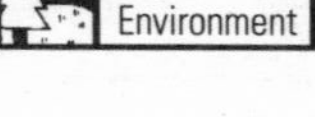

The Environment | Charitable Giving | Community Outreach | Women's Advancement | Minority Advancement | Family | Workplace Issues | Disclosure of Information | ★ Honor Roll

For a more detailed explanation, see pages 7–28.

PRODUCT	PARENT COMPANY									EXTRAS
BEVERAGES										
All Sport	PEP	B	B	A	A	B	B	B	A	Animal testing: non-medical products; factory farming; increasing TRI
Apollinaris	CADBY	B	?	C	C	?	D	B	C	foreign-based company
Ardmore Farms	OAT	B	A	A	B	B	D	?	C	CEDC report; Fair Share
Borden	BN	C	C	B	A	A	B	B	A	CEDC report
Bright & Early	KO	C	B	A	B	A	A	B	A	Workplace Principles
Brookes	CADBY	B	?	C	C	?	D	B	C	foreign-based company
Campbell's	CPB	B	C	B	A	A	A	C	A	Animal testing: non-medical products, significant alternative efforts; CEDC report; on-site child care
Canada Dry	CADBY	B	?	C	C	?	D	B	C	foreign-based company
Citru Sip	OAT	B	A	A	B	B	D	?	C	CEDC report; Fair Share
Coca-Cola	KO	C	B	A	B	A	A	B	A	Workplace Principles
Coco Lopez	BN	C	C	B	A	A	B	B	A	CEDC report
Cottee's	CADBY	B	?	C	C	?	D	B	C	foreign-based company
Country Foods	MO	D	D	?	A	A	?	?	F	Animal testing: non-medical products; CEDC report; tobacco; increasing TRI; Workplace Principles

PRODUCT	PARENT COMPANY	The Environment	Charitable Giving	Community Outreach	Women's Advancement	Minority Advancement	Family	Workplace Issues	Disclosure of Information	EXTRAS
Country Time	MO	D	D	?	A	A	?	?	F	Animal testing: non-medical products; CEDC report; tobacco; increasing TRI; Workplace Principles
Crush	CADBY	B	?	C	C	?	D	B	C	foreign-based company
Crystal Light	MO	D	D	?	A	A	?	?	F	Animal testing: non-medical products; CEDC report; tobacco; increasing TRI; Workplace Principles
Cutter ★	ACCOB	C	A	A	A	B	A	B	A	CEDC report; Fair Share
Diet Sun	MO	D	D	?	A	A	?	?	F	Animal testing: non-medical products; CEDC report; tobacco; increasing TRI; Workplace Principles
Dole	DOL	B	A	B	C	A	C	C	B	pesticide sterilization suits
Fanta	KO	C	B	A	B	A	A	B	A	Workplace Principles
Five Alive	KO	C	B	A	B	A	A	B	A	Workplace Principles
Freestyle	OAT	B	A	A	B	B	D	?	C	CEDC report; Fair Share
Fresca	KO	C	B	A	B	A	A	B	A	Workplace Principles
Fruit Boxes	MO	D	D	?	A	A	?	?	F	Animal testing: non-medical products; CEDC report; tobacco; increasing TRI; Workplace Principles
Gatorade	OAT	B	A	A	B	B	D	?	C	CEDC report; Fair Share

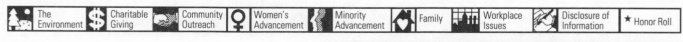

The Environment | Charitable Giving | Community Outreach | Women's Advancement | Minority Advancement | Family | Workplace Issues | Disclosure of Information | ★ Honor Roll

For a more detailed explanation, see pages 7–28.

PRODUCT	PARENT COMPANY									EXTRAS
Hawaiian Punch	PG	C	B	A	B	B	A	B	A	Animal testing: medical and non-medical products, significant alternative efforts; CEDC report; CEP Awards — Animal Welfare, Employer Responsiveness; increasing TRI; on-site day care; Workplace Principles
Health Valley	HVAL	A	C	C	A	A	B	A	A	
Hi-C	KO	C	B	A	B	A	A	B	A	Workplace Principles
Hires	CADBY	B	?	C	C	?	D	B	C	foreign-based company
Juices to Go	KO	C	B	A	B	A	A	B	A	Workplace Principles
Kool-Aid	MO	D	D	?	A	A	?	?	F	Animal testing: non-medical products; CEDC report; tobacco; increasing TRI; Workplace Principles
Light 'n Juicy	KO	C	B	A	B	A	A	B	A	Workplace Principles
Meadow Gold	BN	C	C	B	A	A	B	B	A	CEDC report
Mello Yello	KO	C	B	A	B	A	A	B	A	Workplace Principles
Minute Maid	KO	C	B	A	B	A	A	B	A	Workplace Principles
Mott's	CADBY	B	?	C	C	?	D	B	C	foreign-based company
Mountain Dew	PEP	B	B	A	A	B	B	B	A	Animal testing: non-medical products; factory farming; increasing TRI
Moussy ★	ACCOB	C	A	A	A	B	A	B	A	CEDC report; Fair Share
Mr. Pibb	KO	C	B	A	B	A	A	B	A	Workplace Principles

PRODUCT	PARENT COMPANY	The Environment	Charitable Giving	Community Outreach	Women's Advancement	Minority Advancement	Family	Workplace Issues	Disclosure of Information	EXTRAS
Mug	PEP	B	B	A	A	B	B	B	A	Animal testing: non-medical products; factory farming; increasing TRI
Newman's Own	NEWO	A	A	A	A	Neutral	C	A	A	100% profit to charity; CEP Award — Charity; small company
O'Doul's ★	BUD	C	A	A	B	A	B	A	A	CEDC report
Old Fashioned Root Beer	HVAL	A	C	C	A	A	B	A	A	
Orangeola	HVAL	A	C	C	A	A	B	A	A	
Pepsi Cola	PEP	B	B	A	A	B	B	B	A	Animal testing: non-medical products; factory farming; increasing TRI
Power Ade	KO	C	B	A	B	A	A	B	A	Workplace Principles
Ramblin' Root Beer	KO	C	B	A	B	A	A	B	A	Workplace Principles
ReaLemon/ReaLime	BN	C	C	B	A	A	B	B	A	CEDC report
Saratoga	MO	D	D	?	A	A	?	?	F	Animal testing: non-medical products; CEDC report; tobacco; increasing TRI; Workplace Principles
Schweppes	CADBY	B	?	C	C	?	D	B	C	foreign-based company
Sharp's	MO	D	D	?	A	A	?	?	F	Animal testing: non-medical products; CEDC report; tobacco; increasing TRI; Workplace Principles
Sippin Pak	BN	C	C	B	A	A	B	B	A	CEDC report

The Environment | Charitable Giving | Community Outreach | Women's Advancement | Minority Advancement | Family | Workplace Issues | Disclosure of Information | ★ Honor Roll

For a more detailed explanation, see pages 7–28.

PRODUCT	PARENT COMPANY									EXTRAS
Slice	PEP	B	B	A	A	B	B	B	A	Animal testing: non-medical products; factory farming; increasing TRI
Snapple	SNPL	?	?	?	F	?	?	?	F	
Sprite	KO	C	B	A	B	A	A	B	A	Workplace Principles
Strawberry Falls	MO	D	D	?	A	A	?	?	F	Animal testing: non-medical products; CEDC report; tobacco; increasing TRI; Workplace Principles
Sundrop	CADBY	B	?	C	C	?	D	B	C	foreign-based company
Sunkist	CADBY	B	?	C	C	?	D	B	C	foreign-based company
Sunny Delight	PG	C	B	A	B	B	A	B	A	Animal testing: medical and non-medical products, significant alternative efforts; CEDC report; CEP Awards — Animal Welfare, Employer Responsiveness; increasing TRI; on-site day care; Workplace Principles
Superior	SLE	C	B	A	B	B	B	B	A	CEP Award — Charity; on-site child care; tobacco
Supri	MO	D	D	?	A	A	?	?	F	Animal testing: non-medical products; CEDC report; tobacco; increasing TRI; Workplace Principles
Tab	KO	C	B	A	B	A	A	B	A	Workplace Principles
Tang	MO	D	D	?	A	A	?	?	F	Animal testing: non-medical products; CEDC report; tobacco; increasing TRI; Workplace Principles
Tropi	CAG	C	C	C	C	?	?	F	C	CEDC report; factory farming; profile
Tropicana	VO	?	D	?	C	?	?	?	F	foreign-based company; Workplace Principles
V8	CPB	B	C	B	A	A	A	C	A	Animal testing: non-medical products, significant alternative efforts; CEDC report; on-site child care

PRODUCT	PARENT COMPANY	The Environment	Charitable Giving	Community Outreach	Women's Advancement	Minority Advancement	Family	Workplace Issues	Disclosure of Information	EXTRAS
Wyler's	BN	C	C	B	A	A	B	B	A	CEDC report
BREAD, TOAST & BREAD PRODUCTS										
Arnold	CPC	C	A	B	A	B	C	A	B	Animal testing: non-medical products, significant alternative efforts; CEDC report; increasing TRI
Beefsteak	RAL	C	C	B	B	B	B	C	B	CEDC report; increasing TRI
Boboli	MO	D	D	?	A	A	?	?	F	Animal testing: non-medical products; CEDC report; tobacco; increasing TRI; Workplace Principles
Bran'nola	CPC	C	A	B	A	B	C	A	B	Animal testing: non-medical products, significant alternative efforts; CEDC report; increasing TRI
Bread Du Jour	RAL	C	C	B	B	B	B	C	B	CEDC report; increasing TRI
Brownberry	CPC	C	A	B	A	B	C	A	B	Animal testing: non-medical products, significant alternative efforts; CEDC report; increasing TRI
Corn Flake Crumbs ★	K	B	A	A	A	A	A	A	A	Animal testing: non-medical products, significant alternative efforts; CEDC report; CEP Awards — Employer Responsiveness, Disclosure; profile
Croutettes Stuffing Mix ★	K	B	A	A	A	A	A	A	A	Animal testing: non-medical products, significant alternative efforts; CEDC report; CEP Awards — Employer Responsiveness, Disclosure; profile
Devonsheer	CPC	C	A	B	A	B	C	A	B	Animal testing: non-medical products, significant alternative efforts; CEDC report; increasing TRI

The Environment | Charitable Giving | Community Outreach | Women's Advancement | Minority Advancement | Family | Workplace Issues | Disclosure of Information | ★ Honor Roll

For a more detailed explanation, see pages 7–28.

PRODUCT	PARENT COMPANY									EXTRAS
Elfin Loaves	UBH	?	C	C	D	?	?	?	F	foreign-based company
Good Hearth	RAL	C	C	B	B	B	B	C	B	CEDC report; increasing TRI
Homepride	RAL	C	C	B	B	B	B	C	B	CEDC report; increasing TRI
Levy's	CPC	C	A	B	A	B	C	A	B	Animal testing: non-medical products, significant alternative efforts; CEDC report; increasing TRI
Masa Trigo	OAT	B	A	A	B	B	D	?	C	CEDC report; Fair Share
Oatmeal Goodness	RAL	C	C	B	B	B	B	C	B	CEDC report; increasing TRI
Orowheat	MO	D	D	?	A	A	?	?	F	Animal testing: non-medical products; CEDC report; tobacco; increasing TRI; Workplace Principles
Oven Fry	MO	D	D	?	A	A	?	?	F	Animal testing: non-medical products; CEDC report; tobacco; increasing TRI; Workplace Principles
Pepperidge Farm	CPB	B	C	B	A	A	A	C	A	Animal testing: non-medical products, significant alternative efforts; CEDC report; on-site child care
Sahara	CPC	C	A	B	A	B	C	A	B	Animal testing: non-medical products, significant alternative efforts; CEDC report; increasing TRI
Salad Crispins	CLX	B	B	A	A	A	C	C	A	Animal testing: non-medical products, significant alternative efforts; CEDC report; CEP Award — Community; increasing TRI
Shake 'n Bake	MO	D	D	?	A	A	?	?	F	Animal testing: non-medical products; CEDC report; tobacco; increasing TRI; Workplace Principles

PRODUCT	PARENT COMPANY	The Environment	Charitable Giving	Community Outreach	Women's Advancement	Minority Advancement	Family	Workplace Issues	Disclosure of Information	EXTRAS
Sprouts 7	HVAL	A	C	C	A	A	B	A	A	
Stove Top	MO	D	D	?	A	A	?	?	F	Animal testing: non-medical products; CEDC report; tobacco; increasing TRI; Workplace Principles
Thomas'	CPC	C	A	B	A	B	C	A	B	Animal testing: non-medical products, significant alternative efforts; CEDC report; increasing TRI
Toast-r-Cakes	CPC	C	A	B	A	B	C	A	B	Animal testing: non-medical products, significant alternative efforts; CEDC report; increasing TRI
Wonder	RAL	C	C	B	B	B	B	C	B	CEDC report; increasing TRI
BREAKFAST FOODS										
Downyflake	PT	C	D	?	B	?	?	?	F	CEDC report; increasing TRI
Golden Grits	OAT	B	A	A	B	B	D	?	C	CEDC report; Fair Share
Light n' Lively	MO	D	D	?	A	A	?	?	F	Animal testing: non-medical products; CEDC report; tobacco; increasing TRI; Workplace Principles
Pop Tarts ★	K	B	A	A	A	A	A	A	A	Animal testing: non-medical products, significant alternative efforts; CEDC report; CEP Awards — Employer Responsiveness, Disclosure; profile
Weight Watchers	HNZ	B	C	A	B	D	C	A	A	CEDC report; CEP Award — Environment

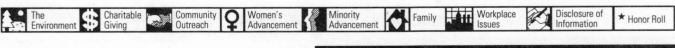

The Environment
Charitable Giving
Community Outreach

Women's Advancement

Minority Advancement

Family

Workplace Issues

Disclosure of Information

★ Honor Roll

For a more detailed explanation, see pages 7–28.

PRODUCT	PARENT COMPANY									EXTRAS
BUTTER										
Breakstone's	MO	D	D	?	A	A	?	?	F	Animal testing: non-medical products; CEDC report; tobacco; increasing TRI; Workplace Principles
Butter Buds	AHP	C	F	C	B	B	C	C	A	Animal testing: medical & non-medical products, significant alternative efforts; infant formula
Molly McButter	ACV	A	?	B	A	D	D	B	B	Animal testing: non-medical products; increasing TRI
CANDY										
3 Musketeers	MARS	C	A	B	A	?	?	C	B	
5th Avenue	HSY	B	B	A	B	C	A	A	A	CEDC report; increasing TRI; on-site child care
Airbons	PT	C	D	?	B	?	?	?	F	CEDC report; increasing TRI
Altoids	CAG	C	C	C	C	?	?	F	C	CEDC report; factory farming; profile
Amazin' Fruit	HSY	B	B	A	B	C	A	A	A	CEDC report; increasing TRI; on-site child care
Baby Ruth	NEST	B	?	B	B	B	A	B	B	Animal testing: non-medical products, significant alternative efforts; foreign-based company; infant formula
Bar None	HSY	B	B	A	B	C	A	A	A	CEDC report; increasing TRI; on-site child care
Bassett's	CADBY	B	?	C	C	?	D	B	C	foreign-based company
Bonkers	RN	?	A	C	C	?	?	?	D	Animal testing: non-medical products; CEDC report; tobacco; increasing TRI; Workplace Principles
Bounty	MARS	C	A	B	A	?	?	C	B	

PRODUCT	PARENT COMPANY									EXTRAS
Breathsavers	HSY	B	B	A	B	C	A	A	A	CEDC report; increasing TRI; on-site child care
Butterfinger	NEST	B	?	B	B	B	A	B	B	Animal testing: non-medical products, significant alternative efforts; foreign-based company; infant formula
Cadbury's	CADBY	B	?	C	C	?	D	B	C	foreign-based company
Campfire	BN	C	C	B	A	A	B	B	A	CEDC report
Caramello	HSY	B	B	A	B	C	A	A	A	CEDC report; increasing TRI; on-site child care
Certs ★	WLA	B	B	A	B	A	A	B	A	Animal testing: medical products only; increasing TRI; Workplace Principles
Charleston Chew! ★	WLA	B	B	A	B	A	A	B	A	Animal testing: medical products only; increasing TRI; Workplace Principles
Clorets ★	WLA	B	B	A	B	A	A	B	A	Animal testing: medical products only; increasing TRI; Workplace Principles
Confeti	MO	D	D	?	A	A	?	?	F	Animal testing: non-medical products; CEDC report; tobacco; increasing TRI; Workplace Principles
Cookies 'n' Mint	HSY	B	B	A	B	C	A	A	A	CEDC report; increasing TRI; on-site child care
Crunch	NEST	B	?	B	B	B	A	B	B	Animal testing: non-medical products, significant alternative efforts; foreign-based company; infant formula
Eagle Brand	BN	C	C	B	A	A	B	B	A	CEDC report

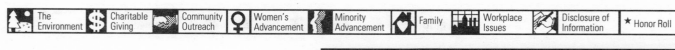

The Environment
Charitable Giving
Community Outreach

Women's Advancement

Minority Advancement

Family

Workplace Issues

Disclosure of Information

★ Honor Roll

For a more detailed explanation, see pages 7–28.

PRODUCT	PARENT COMPANY									EXTRAS
Eclairs	CADBY	B	?	C	C	?	D	B	C	foreign-based company
Fairhill	PT	C	D	?	B	?	?	?	F	CEDC report; increasing TRI
Flick-ettes	OAT	B	A	A	B	B	D	?	C	CEDC report; Fair Share
FunYuns	PEP	B	B	A	A	B	B	B	A	Animal testing: non-medical products; factory farming; increasing TRI
Godiva	CPB	B	C	B	A	A	A	C	A	Animal testing: non-medical products, significant alternative efforts; CEDC report; on-site child care
Golden Almond	HSY	B	B	A	B	C	A	A	A	CEDC report; increasing TRI; on-site child care
Hershey's	HSY	B	B	A	B	C	A	A	A	CEDC report; increasing TRI; on-site child care
Junior Mints ★	WLA	B	B	A	B	A	A	B	A	Animal testing: medical products only; increasing TRI; Workplace Principles
Kisses	HSY	B	B	A	B	C	A	A	A	CEDC report; increasing TRI; on-site child care
Kit Kat	HSY	B	B	A	B	C	A	A	A	CEDC report; increasing TRI; on-site child care
Krackel	HSY	B	B	A	B	C	A	A	A	CEDC report; increasing TRI; on-site child care
Kraft	MO	D	D	?	A	A	?	?	F	Animal testing: non-medical products; CEDC report; tobacco; increasing TRI; Workplace Principles
Life Savers	RN	?	A	C	C	?	?	?	D	Animal testing: non-medical products; CEDC report; tobacco; increasing TRI; Workplace Principles
M & M's	MARS	C	A	B	A	?	?	C	B	
Mars	MARS	C	A	B	A	?	?	C	B	

PRODUCT	PARENT COMPANY	The Environment	Charitable Giving	Community Outreach	Women's Advancement	Minority Advancement	Family	Workplace Issues	Disclosure of Information	EXTRAS
Mellow	MO	D	D	?	A	A	?	?	F	Animal testing: non-medical products; CEDC report; tobacco; increasing TRI; Workplace Principles
Milky Way	MARS	C	A	B	A	?	?	C	B	
Mr. Goodbar	HSY	B	B	A	B	C	A	A	A	CEDC report; increasing TRI; on-site child care
Nibs	HSY	B	B	A	B	C	A	A	A	CEDC report; increasing TRI; on-site child care
Now and Later	RN	?	A	C	C	?	?	?	D	Animal testing: non-medical products; CEDC report; tobacco; increasing TRI; Workplace Principles
P.B. Max	MARS	C	A	B	A	?	?	C	B	
Pascall	CADBY	B	?	C	C	?	D	B	C	foreign-based company
Peter Paul Almond Joy	HSY	B	B	A	B	C	A	A	A	CEDC report; increasing TRI; on-site child care
Peter Paul Mounds	HSY	B	B	A	B	C	A	A	A	CEDC report; increasing TRI; on-site child care
Planters	RN	?	A	C	C	?	?	?	D	Animal testing: non-medical products; CEDC report; tobacco; increasing TRI; Workplace Principles
Pom Poms ★	WLA	B	B	A	B	A	A	B	A	Animal testing: medical products only; increasing TRI; Workplace Principles
Pop Rocks	MO	D	D	?	A	A	?	?	F	Animal testing: non-medical products; CEDC report; tobacco; increasing TRI; Workplace Principles

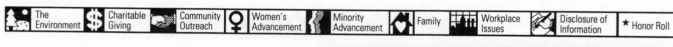

The Environment | Charitable Giving | Community Outreach | Women's Advancement | Minority Advancement | Family | Workplace Issues | Disclosure of Information | ★ Honor Roll

For a more detailed explanation, see pages 7–28.

PRODUCT	PARENT COMPANY									EXTRAS
Queen Anne	HSY	B	B	A	B	C	A	A	A	CEDC report; increasing TRI; on-site child care
Rainforest Chew ★	BJICA	A	A	A	A	B	A	A	A	CERES Principles; CEP Award — Charity; on-site child care; profile; same-sex partner benefits; Workplace Principles
Red Tulip	CADBY	B	?	C	C	?	D	B	C	foreign-based company
Reese's	HSY	B	B	A	B	C	A	A	A	CEDC report; increasing TRI; on-site child care
Rolo	HSY	B	B	A	B	C	A	A	A	CEDC report; increasing TRI; on-site child care
Sharps	CADBY	B	?	C	C	?	D	B	C	foreign-based company
Skittles	MARS	C	A	B	A	?	?	C	B	
Skor	HSY	B	B	A	B	C	A	A	A	CEDC report; increasing TRI; on-site child care
Snickers	MARS	C	A	B	A	?	?	C	B	
Special Dark	HSY	B	B	A	B	C	A	A	A	CEDC report; increasing TRI; on-site child care
Starburst	MARS	C	A	B	A	?	?	C	B	
Sugar Babies ★	WLA	B	B	A	B	A	A	B	A	Animal testing: medical products only; increasing TRI; Workplace Principles
Sugar Daddy ★	WLA	B	B	A	B	A	A	B	A	Animal testing: medical products only; increasing TRI; Workplace Principles
Symphony	HSY	B	B	A	B	C	A	A	A	CEDC report; increasing TRI; on-site child care
Toblerone	MO	D	D	?	A	A	?	?	F	Animal testing: non-medical products; CEDC report; tobacco; increasing TRI; Workplace Principles

PRODUCT	PARENT COMPANY	The Environment	Charitable Giving	Community Outreach	Women's Advancement	Minority Advancement	Family	Workplace Issues	Disclosure of Information	EXTRAS
Trebor	CADBY	B	?	C	C	?	D	B	C	foreign-based company
Truffel	CADBY	B	?	C	C	?	D	B	C	foreign-based company
Twix	MARS	C	A	B	A	?	?	C	B	
Twizzlers	HSY	B	B	A	B	C	A	A	A	CEDC report; increasing TRI; on-site child care
Whatchamacallit	HSY	B	B	A	B	C	A	A	A	CEDC report; increasing TRI; on-site child care
Whirligigs	RN	?	A	C	C	?	?	?	D	Animal testing: non-medical products; CEDC report; tobacco; increasing TRI; Workplace Principles
Whitman's Chocolates	PT	C	D	?	B	?	?	?	F	CEDC report; increasing TRI
Y&S	HSY	B	B	A	B	C	A	A	A	CEDC report; increasing TRI; on-site child care
York Peppermint Patties	HSY	B	B	A	B	C	A	A	A	CEDC report; increasing TRI; on-site child care
CARS										
Acura	HMC	?	B	C	A	D	?	B	F	foreign-based company; increasing TRI
Buick	GM	D	?	C	C	A	C	C	A	CEDC Report; CERES Principles; Fair Share; military contracts; nuclear weapons
Cadillac	GM	D	?	C	C	A	C	C	A	CEDC Report; CERES Principles; Fair Share; military contracts; nuclear weapons

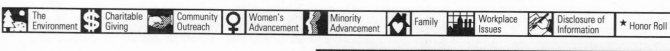

The Environment
Charitable Giving
Community Outreach

Women's Advancement

Minority Advancement

Family

Workplace Issues
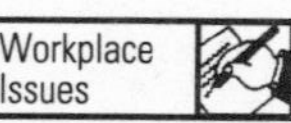

Disclosure of Information
★ Honor Roll

For a more detailed explanation, see pages 7–28.

PRODUCT	PARENT COMPANY									EXTRAS
Chevrolet	GM	D	?	C	C	A	C	C	A	CEDC Report; CERES Principles; Fair Share; military contracts; nuclear weapons
Chrysler	C	B	A	C	D	A	?	?	F	CEDC report; Fair Share; military contracts; on-site child care; Workplace Principles
Dodge	C	B	A	C	D	A	?	?	F	CEDC report; Fair Share; military contracts; on-site child care; Workplace Principles
Eagle	C	B	A	C	D	A	?	?	F	CEDC report; Fair Share; military contracts; on-site child care; Workplace Principles
Ford	F	C	?	?	D	C	?	?	C	CEDC report
GMC	GM	D	?	C	C	A	C	C	A	CEDC Report; CERES Principles; Fair Share; military contracts; nuclear weapons
Geo	GM	D	?	C	C	A	C	C	A	CEDC Report; CERES Principles; Fair Share; military contracts; nuclear weapons
Honda	HMC	?	B	C	A	D	?	B	F	foreign-based company; increasing TRI
Infiniti	NSANY	?	?	C	D	D	?	B	F	foreign-based company; increasing TRI
Jaguar	F	C	?	?	D	C	?	?	C	CEDC report
Jeep	C	B	A	C	D	A	?	?	F	CEDC report; Fair Share; military contracts; on-site child care; Workplace Principles
Lexus	TOYOY	C	B	A	?	?	B	B	C	foreign-based company; increasing TRI
Lincoln	F	C	?	?	D	C	?	?	C	CEDC report
Mercury	F	C	?	?	D	C	?	?	C	CEDC report

PRODUCT	PARENT COMPANY	The Environment	Charitable Giving	Community Outreach	Women's Advancement	Minority Advancement	Family	Workplace Issues	Disclosure of Information	EXTRAS
Nissan	NSANY	?	?	C	D	D	?	B	F	foreign-based company; increasing TRI
Oldsmobile	GM	D	?	C	C	A	C	C	A	CEDC Report; CERES Principles; Fair Share; military contracts; nuclear weapons
Plymouth	C	B	A	C	D	A	?	?	F	CEDC report; Fair Share; military contracts; on-site child care; Workplace Principles
Pontiac	GM	D	?	C	C	A	C	C	A	CEDC Report; CERES Principles; Fair Share; military contracts; nuclear weapons
Saab	GM	D	?	C	C	A	C	C	A	CEDC Report; CERES Principles; Fair Share; military contracts; nuclear weapons
Saturn	GM	D	?	C	C	A	C	C	A	CEDC Report; CERES Principles; Fair Share; military contracts; nuclear weapons
Toyota	TOYOY	C	B	A	?	?	B	B	C	foreign-based company; increasing TRI
CATALOG										
Beyond Buttondowns	LE	?	A	C	B	?	B	A	B	
Lands' End clothing	LE	?	A	C	B	?	B	A	B	
Natural Baby Company	NATB	?	?	C	A	Neutral	A	?	A	small company
Shaklee	YAMP	?	A	A	?	B	B	A	B	foreign-based company

The Environment | Charitable Giving | Community Outreach | Women's Advancement | Minority Advancement | Family | Workplace Issues | Disclosure of Information | ★ Honor Roll

For a more detailed explanation, see pages 7–28.

PRODUCT	PARENT COMPANY									EXTRAS
CEREAL										
All-Bran ★	K	B	A	A	A	A	A	A	A	Animal testing: non-medical products, significant alternative efforts; CEDC report; CEP Awards — Employer Responsiveness, Disclosure; profile
Almond Delight	RAL	C	C	B	B	B	B	C	B	CEDC report; increasing TRI
Alpha-Bits	MO	D	D	?	A	A	?	?	F	Animal testing: non-medical products; CEDC report; tobacco; increasing TRI; Workplace Principles
Amaranth Crunch	HVAL	A	C	C	A	A	B	A	A	
Apple Jacks ★	K	B	A	A	A	A	A	A	A	Animal testing: non-medical products, significant alternative efforts; CEDC report; CEP Awards — Employer Responsiveness, Disclosure; profile
Apple Raisin Crisp ★	K	B	A	A	A	A	A	A	A	Animal testing: non-medical products, significant alternative efforts; CEDC report; CEP Awards — Employer Responsiveness, Disclosure; profile
Basic 4 ★	GIS	B	A	A	A	B	B	A	A	CEDC report; CEP Awards — Charity, EEO, Opportunities for the Disabled; profile; Workplace Principles
Boo Berry ★	GIS	B	A	A	A	B	B	A	A	CEDC report; CEP Awards — Charity, EEO, Opportunities for the Disabled; profile; Workplace Principles
Bran Buds ★	K	B	A	A	A	A	A	A	A	Animal testing: non-medical products, significant alternative efforts; CEDC report; CEP Awards — Employer Responsiveness, Disclosure; profile
Bran Chex	RAL	C	C	B	B	B	B	C	B	CEDC report; increasing TRI
Bran News	RAL	C	C	B	B	B	B	C	B	CEDC report; increasing TRI

PRODUCT	PARENT COMPANY	The Environment	Charitable Giving	Community Outreach	Women's Advancement	Minority Advancement	Family	Workplace Issues	Disclosure of Information	EXTRAS
Breakfast on the Run	RAL	C	C	B	B	B	B	C	B	CEDC report; increasing TRI
Buckeye	OAT	B	A	A	B	B	D	?	C	CEDC report; Fair Share
Bunuelitos ★	GIS	B	A	A	A	B	B	A	A	CEDC report; CEP Awards — Charity, EEO, Opportunities for the Disabled; profile; Workplace Principles
Cap'n Crunch	OAT	B	A	A	B	B	D	?	C	CEDC report; Fair Share
Cheerios ★	GIS	B	A	A	A	B	B	A	A	CEDC report; CEP Awards — Charity, EEO, Opportunities for the Disabled; profile; Workplace Principles
Chex	RAL	C	C	B	B	B	B	C	B	CEDC report; increasing TRI
Chris Crunch	RAL	C	C	B	B	B	B	C	B	CEDC report; increasing TRI
Cinnamon Mini Buns ★	K	B	A	A	A	A	A	A	A	Animal testing: non-medical products, significant alternative efforts; CEDC report; CEP Awards — Employer Responsiveness, Disclosure; profile
Cinnamon Toast Crunch ★	GIS	B	A	A	A	B	B	A	A	CEDC report; CEP Awards — Charity, EEO, Opportunities for the Disabled; profile; Workplace Principles
Cinnamon Treats	RN	?	A	C	C	?	?	?	D	Animal testing: non-medical products; CEDC report; tobacco; increasing TRI; Workplace Principles
Circus Rings	RAL	C	C	B	B	B	B	C	B	CEDC report; increasing TRI
Clusters ★	GIS	B	A	A	A	B	B	A	A	CEDC report; CEP Awards — Charity, EEO, Opportunities for the Disabled; profile; Workplace Principles

The Environment
Charitable Giving

Community Outreach
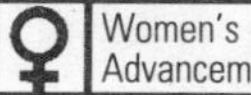
Women's Advancement

Minority Advancement

Family

Workplace Issues

Disclosure of Information
★ Honor Roll

For a more detailed explanation, see pages 7–28.

PRODUCT	PARENT COMPANY									EXTRAS
Cocoa Krispies ★	K	B	A	A	A	A	A	A	A	Animal testing: non-medical products, significant alternative efforts; CEDC report; CEP Awards — Employer Responsiveness, Disclosure; profile
Cocoa Puffs ★	GIS	B	A	A	A	B	B	A	A	CEDC report; CEP Awards — Charity, EEO, Opportunities for the Disabled; profile; Workplace Principles
Common Sense Oat Bran ★	K	B	A	A	A	A	A	A	A	Animal testing: non-medical products, significant alternative efforts; CEDC report; CEP Awards — Employer Responsiveness, Disclosure; profile
Complete Bran Flakes ★	K	B	A	A	A	A	A	A	A	Animal testing: non-medical products, significant alternative efforts; CEDC report; CEP Awards — Employer Responsiveness, Disclosure; profile
Cookie Crisp	RAL	C	C	B	B	B	B	C	B	CEDC report; increasing TRI
Corn Chex	RAL	C	C	B	B	B	B	C	B	CEDC report; increasing TRI
Corn Flakes ★	K	B	A	A	A	A	A	A	A	Animal testing: non-medical products, significant alternative efforts; CEDC report; CEP Awards — Employer Responsiveness, Disclosure; profile
Corn Pops ★	K	B	A	A	A	A	A	A	A	Animal testing: non-medical products, significant alternative efforts; CEDC report; CEP Awards — Employer Responsiveness, Disclosure; profile
Corn Squares	OAT	B	A	A	B	B	D	?	C	CEDC report; Fair Share
Count Chocula ★	GIS	B	A	A	A	B	B	A	A	CEDC report; CEP Awards — Charity, EEO, Opportunities for the Disabled; profile; Workplace Principles
Country Corn Flakes ★	GIS	B	A	A	A	B	B	A	A	CEDC report; CEP Awards — Charity, EEO, Opportunities for the Disabled; profile; Workplace Principles

PRODUCT	PARENT COMPANY	The Environment	Charitable Giving	Community Outreach	Women's Advancement	Minority Advancement	Family	Workplace Issues	Disclosure of Information	EXTRAS
Crackels	OAT	B	A	A	B	B	D	?	C	CEDC report; Fair Share
Cracker Jack	RAL	C	C	B	B	B	B	C	B	CEDC report; increasing TRI
Cracklin' Oat Bran ★	K	B	A	A	A	A	A	A	A	Animal testing: non-medical products, significant alternative efforts; CEDC report; CEP Awards — Employer Responsiveness, Disclosure; profile
Cream of Rice	RN	?	A	C	C	?	?	?	D	Animal testing: non-medical products; CEDC report; tobacco; increasing TRI; Workplace Principles
Cream of Rye	CAG	C	C	C	C	?	?	F	C	CEDC report; factory farming; profile
Cream of Wheat	RN	?	A	C	C	?	?	?	D	Animal testing: non-medical products; CEDC report; tobacco; increasing TRI; Workplace Principles
Cremerie Triple Cream	MO	D	D	?	A	A	?	?	F	Animal testing: non-medical products; CEDC report; tobacco; increasing TRI; Workplace Principles
Crispix ★	K	B	A	A	A	A	A	A	A	Animal testing: non-medical products, significant alternative efforts; CEDC report; CEP Awards — Employer Responsiveness, Disclosure; profile
Crispy Wheats 'n Raisins ★	GIS	B	A	A	A	B	B	A	A	CEDC report; CEP Awards — Charity, EEO, Opportunities for the Disabled; profile; Workplace Principles
Crunch Berries	OAT	B	A	A	B	B	D	?	C	CEDC report; Fair Share
Dinersaurs	RAL	C	C	B	B	B	B	C	B	CEDC report; increasing TRI

The Environment | Charitable Giving | Community Outreach | Women's Advancement | Minority Advancement | Family | Workplace Issues | Disclosure of Information | ★ Honor Roll

For a more detailed explanation, see pages 7–28.

PRODUCT	PARENT COMPANY		$		♀					EXTRAS
Dinky Donuts	RAL	C	C	B	B	B	B	C	B	CEDC report; increasing TRI
Double Chex	RAL	C	C	B	B	B	B	C	B	CEDC report; increasing TRI
Double Dip Crunch ★	K	B	A	A	A	A	A	A	A	Animal testing: non-medical products, significant alternative efforts; CEDC report; CEP Awards — Employer Responsiveness, Disclosure; profile
Farina ★	GMR	C	A	A	B	A	A	B	A	factory farming; foreign-based company
Fiber 7	HVAL	A	C	C	A	A	B	A	A	
Fiber One ★	GIS	B	A	A	A	B	B	A	A	CEDC report; CEP Awards — Charity, EEO, Opportunities for the Disabled; profile; Workplace Principles
Fingos ★	GIS	B	A	A	A	B	B	A	A	CEDC report; CEP Awards — Charity, EEO, Opportunities for the Disabled; profile; Workplace Principles
Flakes O' Bran	HVAL	A	C	C	A	A	B	A	A	
Fortune Cookie Crunch	OAT	B	A	A	B	B	D	?	C	CEDC report; Fair Share
FrankenBerry ★	GIS	B	A	A	A	B	B	A	A	CEDC report; CEP Awards — Charity, EEO, Opportunities for the Disabled; profile; Workplace Principles
Freakies	RAL	C	C	B	B	B	B	C	B	CEDC report; increasing TRI
Froot Loops ★	K	B	A	A	A	A	A	A	A	Animal testing: non-medical products, significant alternative efforts; CEDC report; CEP Awards — Employer Responsiveness, Disclosure; profile
Frosted Bran ★	K	B	A	A	A	A	A	A	A	Animal testing: non-medical products, significant alternative efforts; CEDC report; CEP Awards — Employer Responsiveness, Disclosure; profile

PRODUCT	PARENT COMPANY	The Environment	Charitable Giving	Community Outreach	Women's Advancement	Minority Advancement	Family	Workplace Issues	Disclosure of Information	EXTRAS
Frosted Flakes ★	K	B	A	A	A	A	A	A	A	Animal testing: non-medical products, significant alternative efforts; CEDC report; CEP Awards — Employer Responsiveness, Disclosure; profile
Frosted Krispies ★	K	B	A	A	A	A	A	A	A	Animal testing: non-medical products, significant alternative efforts; CEDC report; CEP Awards — Employer Responsiveness, Disclosure; profile
Frosted Mini-Wheats ★	K	B	A	A	A	A	A	A	A	Animal testing: non-medical products, significant alternative efforts; CEDC report; CEP Awards — Employer Responsiveness, Disclosure; profile
Frosted Rice Chex Juniors	RAL	C	C	B	B	B	B	C	B	CEDC report; increasing TRI
Frosted Rice Krinkles	MO	D	D	?	A	A	?	?	F	Animal testing: non-medical products; CEDC report; tobacco; increasing TRI; Workplace Principles
Frosted Wheat Squares	RN	?	A	C	C	?	?	?	D	Animal testing: non-medical products; CEDC report; tobacco; increasing TRI; Workplace Principles
Fruit & Cream	OAT	B	A	A	B	B	D	?	C	CEDC report; Fair Share
Fruit & Fibre	MO	D	D	?	A	A	?	?	F	Animal testing: non-medical products; CEDC report; tobacco; increasing TRI; Workplace Principles
Fruit & Fitness	HVAL	A	C	C	A	A	B	A	A	
Fruit Islands	RAL	C	C	B	B	B	B	C	B	CEDC report; increasing TRI
Fruit Lites	HVAL	A	C	C	A	A	B	A	A	

The Environment | Charitable Giving | Community Outreach | Women's Advancement | Minority Advancement | Family | Workplace Issues | Disclosure of Information | ★ Honor Roll

For a more detailed explanation, see pages 7–28.

PRODUCT	PARENT COMPANY									EXTRAS
Fruitful Bran ★	K	B	A	A	A	A	A	A	A	Animal testing: non-medical products, significant alternative efforts; CEDC report; CEP Awards — Employer Responsiveness, Disclosure; profile
Fruity Marshmallow Krispies ★	K	B	A	A	A	A	A	A	A	Animal testing: non-medical products, significant alternative efforts; CEDC report; CEP Awards — Employer Responsiveness, Disclosure; profile
Golden Crisp	MO	D	D	?	A	A	?	?	F	Animal testing: non-medical products; CEDC report; tobacco; increasing TRI; Workplace Principles
Golden Grahams ★	GIS	B	A	A	A	B	B	A	A	CEDC report; CEP Awards — Charity, EEO, Opportunities for the Disabled; profile; Workplace Principles
Good Things in the Middle	OAT	B	A	A	B	B	D	?	C	CEDC report; Fair Share
Good n' Hot	OAT	B	A	A	B	B	D	?	C	CEDC report; Fair Share
Grape-Nuts	MO	D	D	?	A	A	?	?	F	Animal testing: non-medical products; CEDC report; tobacco; increasing TRI; Workplace Principles
Harvest Bounty	OAT	B	A	A	B	B	D	?	C	CEDC report; Fair Share
Harvest Crunch	OAT	B	A	A	B	B	D	?	C	CEDC report; Fair Share
Health Valley	HVAL	A	C	C	A	A	B	A	A	
Healthy Crunch	HVAL	A	C	C	A	A	B	A	A	
Healthy O	HVAL	A	C	C	A	A	B	A	A	
Heartland	PT	C	D	?	B	?	?	?	F	CEDC report; increasing TRI
Honey Bran	RAL	C	C	B	B	B	B	C	B	CEDC report; increasing TRI

PRODUCT	PARENT COMPANY	The Environment	Charitable Giving	Community Outreach	Women's Advancement	Minority Advancement	Family	Workplace Issues	Disclosure of Information	EXTRAS
Honey Bunches of Oats	MO	D	D	?	A	A	?	?	F	Animal testing: non-medical products; CEDC report; tobacco; increasing TRI; Workplace Principles
Honeycomb	MO	D	D	?	A	A	?	?	F	Animal testing: non-medical products; CEDC report; tobacco; increasing TRI; Workplace Principles
Honey Nut Cheerios ★	GIS	B	A	A	A	B	B	A	A	CEDC report; CEP Awards — Charity, EEO, Opportunities for the Disabled; profile; Workplace Principles
Honey Nut Crunch	MO	D	D	?	A	A	?	?	F	Animal testing: non-medical products; CEDC report; tobacco; increasing TRI; Workplace Principles
Horizon	MO	D	D	?	A	A	?	?	F	Animal testing: non-medical products; CEDC report; tobacco; increasing TRI; Workplace Principles
Imperial	OAT	B	A	A	B	B	D	?	C	CEDC report; Fair Share
Just Right ★	K	B	A	A	A	A	A	A	A	Animal testing: non-medical products, significant alternative efforts; CEDC report; CEP Awards — Employer Responsiveness, Disclosure; profile
Kenmei Rice Bran ★	K	B	A	A	A	A	A	A	A	Animal testing: non-medical products, significant alternative efforts; CEDC report; CEP Awards — Employer Responsiveness, Disclosure; profile
King Vitamin	OAT	B	A	A	B	B	D	?	C	CEDC report; Fair Share
Kix ★	GIS	B	A	A	A	B	B	A	A	CEDC report; CEP Awards — Charity, EEO, Opportunities for the Disabled; profile; Workplace Principles

The Environment | Charitable Giving | Community Outreach | Women's Advancement | Minority Advancement | Family | Workplace Issues | Disclosure of Information | ★ Honor Roll

For a more detailed explanation, see pages 7–28.

PRODUCT	PARENT COMPANY									EXTRAS
Kretschmer Wheat Germ	OAT	B	A	A	B	B	D	?	C	CEDC report; Fair Share
Life	OAT	B	A	A	B	B	D	?	C	CEDC report; Fair Share
Lucky Charms ★	GIS	B	A	A	A	B	B	A	A	CEDC report; CEP Awards — Charity, EEO, Opportunities for the Disabled; profile; Workplace Principles
Maypo Oatmeal	AHP	C	F	C	B	B	C	C	A	Animal testing: medical & non-medical products, significant alternative efforts; infant formula
Morning Funnies	RAL	C	C	B	B	B	B	C	B	CEDC report; increasing TRI
Mother's Rolled Oats	OAT	B	A	A	B	B	D	?	C	CEDC report; Fair Share
Muesli	RAL	C	C	B	B	B	B	C	B	CEDC report; increasing TRI
Mueslix ★	K	B	A	A	A	A	A	A	A	Animal testing: non-medical products, significant alternative efforts; CEDC report; CEP Awards — Employer Responsiveness, Disclosure; profile
Nabisco Raisin Bran	RN	?	A	C	C	?	?	?	D	Animal testing: non-medical products; CEDC report; tobacco; increasing TRI; Workplace Principles
Nintendo Cereals	RAL	C	C	B	B	B	B	C	B	CEDC report; increasing TRI
Nut & Honey Crunch ★	K	B	A	A	A	A	A	A	A	Animal testing: non-medical products, significant alternative efforts; CEDC report; CEP Awards — Employer Responsiveness, Disclosure; profile
Nutri-Grain ★	K	B	A	A	A	A	A	A	A	Animal testing: non-medical products, significant alternative efforts; CEDC report; CEP Awards — Employer Responsiveness, Disclosure; profile
Nuttin'	RAL	C	C	B	B	B	B	C	B	CEDC report; increasing TRI

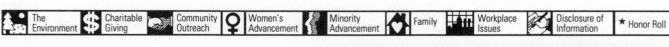

PRODUCT	PARENT COMPANY	The Environment	Charitable Giving	Community Outreach	Women's Advancement	Minority Advancement	Family	Workplace Issues	Disclosure of Information	EXTRAS
Oat Bran Options	RAL	C	C	B	B	B	B	C	B	CEDC report; increasing TRI
Oat Bran O's	HVAL	A	C	C	A	A	B	A	A	
Oat Chex	RAL	C	C	B	B	B	B	C	B	CEDC report; increasing TRI
Oat Cups	OAT	B	A	A	B	B	D	?	C	CEDC report; Fair Share
Oat Squares	OAT	B	A	A	B	B	D	?	C	CEDC report; Fair Share
Oatbake ★	K	B	A	A	A	A	A	A	A	Animal testing: non-medical products, significant alternative efforts; CEDC report; CEP Awards — Employer Responsiveness, Disclosure; profile
Oatmeal Crisp ★	GIS	B	A	A	A	B	B	A	A	CEDC report; CEP Awards — Charity, EEO, Opportunities for the Disabled; profile; Workplace Principles
Oh's	OAT	B	A	A	B	B	D	?	C	CEDC report; Fair Share
Orangeola	HVAL	A	C	C	A	A	B	A	A	
Orchard Bran	RAL	C	C	B	B	B	B	C	B	CEDC report; increasing TRI
Pebbles	MO	D	D	?	A	A	?	?	F	Animal testing: non-medical products; CEDC report; tobacco; increasing TRI; Workplace Principles
Post Grape Nuts	MO	D	D	?	A	A	?	?	F	Animal testing: non-medical products; CEDC report; tobacco; increasing TRI; Workplace Principles

The Environment | Charitable Giving | Community Outreach | Women's Advancement | Minority Advancement | Family | Workplace Issues | Disclosure of Information | ★ Honor Roll

For a more detailed explanation, see pages 7–28.

PRODUCT	PARENT COMPANY									EXTRAS
Post Great Grains	MO	D	D	?	A	A	?	?	F	Animal testing: non-medical products; CEDC report; tobacco; increasing TRI; Workplace Principles
Post Raisin Bran	MO	D	D	?	A	A	?	?	F	Animal testing: non-medical products; CEDC report; tobacco; increasing TRI; Workplace Principles
Pritikin	OAT	B	A	A	B	B	D	?	C	CEDC report; Fair Share
Product 19 ★	K	B	A	A	A	A	A	A	A	Animal testing: non-medical products, significant alternative efforts; CEDC report; CEP Awards — Employer Responsiveness, Disclosure; profile
Punch Crunch	OAT	B	A	A	B	B	D	?	C	CEDC report; Fair Share
Quaker	OAT	B	A	A	B	B	D	?	C	CEDC report; Fair Share
Quisp	OAT	B	A	A	B	B	D	?	C	CEDC report; Fair Share
Raisin Bran ★	K	B	A	A	A	A	A	A	A	Animal testing: non-medical products, significant alternative efforts; CEDC report; CEP Awards — Employer Responsiveness, Disclosure; profile
Raisin Life	OAT	B	A	A	B	B	D	?	C	CEDC report; Fair Share
Raisin Nut Bran ★	GIS	B	A	A	A	B	B	A	A	CEDC report; CEP Awards — Charity, EEO, Opportunities for the Disabled; profile; Workplace Principles
Ralston	RAL	C	C	B	B	B	B	C	B	CEDC report; increasing TRI
Real	HVAL	A	C	C	A	A	B	A	A	
Rice Bran Options	RAL	C	C	B	B	B	B	C	B	CEDC report; increasing TRI
Rice Chex	RAL	C	C	B	B	B	B	C	B	CEDC report; increasing TRI

PRODUCT	PARENT COMPANY	The Environment	Charitable Giving	Community Outreach	Women's Advancement	Minority Advancement	Family	Workplace Issues	Disclosure of Information	EXTRAS
Rice Krispies ★	K	B	A	A	A	A	A	A	A	Animal testing: non-medical products, significant alternative efforts; CEDC report; CEP Awards — Employer Responsiveness, Disclosure; profile
Rice Squares	OAT	B	A	A	B	B	D	?	C	CEDC report; Fair Share
Ripple Crisp ★	GIS	B	A	A	A	B	B	A	A	CEDC report; CEP Awards — Charity, EEO, Opportunities for the Disabled; profile; Workplace Principles
Shredded Wheat	RN	?	A	C	C	?	?	?	D	Animal testing: non-medical products; CEDC report; tobacco; increasing TRI; Workplace Principles
Smacks ★	K	B	A	A	A	A	A	A	A	Animal testing: non-medical products, significant alternative efforts; CEDC report; CEP Awards — Employer Responsiveness, Disclosure; profile
Special K ★	K	B	A	A	A	A	A	A	A	Animal testing: non-medical products, significant alternative efforts; CEDC report; CEP Awards — Employer Responsiveness, Disclosure; profile
Sprinkle Spangles ★	GIS	B	A	A	A	B	B	A	A	CEDC report; CEP Awards — Charity, EEO, Opportunities for the Disabled; profile; Workplace Principles
Squares ★	K	B	A	A	A	A	A	A	A	Animal testing: non-medical products, significant alternative efforts; CEDC report; CEP Awards — Employer Responsiveness, Disclosure; profile
Sun Country	OAT	B	A	A	B	B	D	?	C	CEDC report; Fair Share
Sunflakes	RAL	C	C	B	B	B	B	C	B	CEDC report; increasing TRI

The Environment | Charitable Giving |  Community Outreach |  Women's Advancement |  Minority Advancement |  Family |  Workplace Issues |  Disclosure of Information | ★ Honor Roll

For a more detailed explanation, see pages 7–28.

PRODUCT	PARENT COMPANY									EXTRAS
Sunmaid	RAL	C	C	B	B	B	B	C	B	CEDC report; increasing TRI
Super Golden Crisp	MO	D	D	?	A	A	?	?	F	Animal testing: non-medical products; CEDC report; tobacco; increasing TRI; Workplace Principles
Swiss Breakfast	HVAL	A	C	C	A	A	B	A	A	
Tasteeos	RAL	C	C	B	B	B	B	C	B	CEDC report; increasing TRI
Toasties	MO	D	D	?	A	A	?	?	F	Animal testing: non-medical products; CEDC report; tobacco; increasing TRI; Workplace Principles
Total ★	GIS	B	A	A	A	B	B	A	A	CEDC report; CEP Awards — Charity, EEO, Opportunities for the Disabled; profile; Workplace Principles
Triples ★	GIS	B	A	A	A	B	B	A	A	CEDC report; CEP Awards — Charity, EEO, Opportunities for the Disabled; profile; Workplace Principles
Trix ★	GIS	B	A	A	A	B	B	A	A	CEDC report; CEP Awards — Charity, EEO, Opportunities for the Disabled; profile; Workplace Principles
Waffelos	RAL	C	C	B	B	B	B	C	B	CEDC report; increasing TRI
Wheat Chex	RAL	C	C	B	B	B	B	C	B	CEDC report; increasing TRI
Wheatena	AHP	C	F	C	B	B	C	C	A	Animal testing: medical & non-medical products, significant alternative efforts; infant formula
Wheat Honeys	RN	?	A	C	C	?	?	?	D	Animal testing: non-medical products; CEDC report; tobacco; increasing TRI; Workplace Principles
Wheaties ★	GIS	B	A	A	A	B	B	A	A	CEDC report; CEP Awards — Charity, EEO, Opportunities for the Disabled; profile; Workplace Principles

PRODUCT	PARENT COMPANY	The Environment	Charitable Giving	Community Outreach	Women's Advancement	Minority Advancement	Family	Workplace Issues	Disclosure of Information	EXTRAS
Wheat Squares	OAT	B	A	A	B	B	D	?	C	CEDC report; Fair Share
CHEESE										
Aerofil	CAG	C	C	C	C	?	?	F	C	CEDC report; factory farming; profile
Borden	BN	C	C	B	A	A	B	B	A	CEDC report
Butterfly	CAG	C	C	C	C	?	?	F	C	CEDC report; factory farming; profile
Casino	MO	D	D	?	A	A	?	?	F	Animal testing: non-medical products; CEDC report; tobacco; increasing TRI; Workplace Principles
Cheese Whip	MO	D	D	?	A	A	?	?	F	Animal testing: non-medical products; CEDC report; tobacco; increasing TRI; Workplace Principles
Cheez Whiz	MO	D	D	?	A	A	?	?	F	Animal testing: non-medical products; CEDC report; tobacco; increasing TRI; Workplace Principles
Churny	MO	D	D	?	A	A	?	?	F	Animal testing: non-medical products; CEDC report; tobacco; increasing TRI; Workplace Principles
Coon	MO	D	D	?	A	A	?	?	F	Animal testing: non-medical products; CEDC report; tobacco; increasing TRI; Workplace Principles
Country Crock	UN	B	C	C	F	D	C	B	C	Animal testing: non-medical products, significant alternative efforts; foreign-based company; profile
County Line	CAG	C	C	C	C	?	?	F	C	CEDC report; factory farming; profile

★ Honor Roll

For a more detailed explanation, see pages 7–28.

PRODUCT	PARENT COMPANY									EXTRAS
Cracker Barrel	MO	D	D	?	A	A	?	?	F	Animal testing: non-medical products; CEDC report; tobacco; increasing TRI; Workplace Principles
Fisher	BN	C	C	B	A	A	B	B	A	CEDC report
Goldbrick	CAG	C	C	C	C	?	?	F	C	CEDC report; factory farming; profile
Healthy Choice	CAG	C	C	C	C	?	?	F	C	CEDC report; factory farming; profile
Jersey Maid	MO	D	D	?	A	A	?	?	F	Animal testing: non-medical products; CEDC report; tobacco; increasing TRI; Workplace Principles
Knudsen	MO	D	D	?	A	A	?	?	F	Animal testing: non-medical products; CEDC report; tobacco; increasing TRI; Workplace Principles
Kraft	MO	D	D	?	A	A	?	?	F	Animal testing: non-medical products; CEDC report; tobacco; increasing TRI; Workplace Principles
Lily Lake	CAG	C	C	C	C	?	?	F	C	CEDC report; factory farming; profile
Maman Luise	MO	D	D	?	A	A	?	?	F	Animal testing: non-medical products; CEDC report; tobacco; increasing TRI; Workplace Principles
Meadow Gold	BN	C	C	B	A	A	B	B	A	CEDC report
New Dimensions	CAG	C	C	C	C	?	?	F	C	CEDC report; factory farming; profile
Paul Jean Barnett	MO	D	D	?	A	A	?	?	F	Animal testing: non-medical products; CEDC report; tobacco; increasing TRI; Workplace Principles
Pauly	CAG	C	C	C	C	?	?	F	C	CEDC report; factory farming; profile
Philadelphia Cream Cheese	MO	D	D	?	A	A	?	?	F	Animal testing: non-medical products; CEDC report; tobacco; increasing TRI; Workplace Principles

PRODUCT	PARENT COMPANY	The Environment	Charitable Giving	Community Outreach	Women's Advancement	Minority Advancement	Family	Workplace Issues	Disclosure of Information	EXTRAS
Polly-O	MO	D	D	?	A	A	?	?	F	Animal testing: non-medical products; CEDC report; tobacco; increasing TRI; Workplace Principles
Red Rooster	MO	D	D	?	A	A	?	?	F	Animal testing: non-medical products; CEDC report; tobacco; increasing TRI; Workplace Principles
Temp Tee	MO	D	D	?	A	A	?	?	F	Animal testing: non-medical products; CEDC report; tobacco; increasing TRI; Workplace Principles
Velveeta	MO	D	D	?	A	A	?	?	F	Animal testing: non-medical products; CEDC report; tobacco; increasing TRI; Workplace Principles
CHICKEN: CANNED & REFRIGERATED										
Butcher's Best	TYSNA	C	?	D	A	B	?	D	D	factory farming; profile
Butterball	CAG	C	C	C	C	?	?	F	C	CEDC report; factory farming; profile
Buttermilk/Battergold	TYSNA	C	?	D	A	B	?	D	D	factory farming; profile
Chicken Originals	TYSNA	C	?	D	A	B	?	D	D	factory farming; profile
Chicken Rondelets	TYSNA	C	?	D	A	B	?	D	D	factory farming; profile
Chick'n Chunks	TYSNA	C	?	D	A	B	?	D	D	factory farming; profile
Chick'n Dippers	TYSNA	C	?	D	A	B	?	D	D	factory farming; profile
Chick'n Quick	TYSNA	C	?	D	A	B	?	D	D	factory farming; profile

The Environment | Charitable Giving | Community Outreach | Women's Advancement | Minority Advancement | Family | Workplace Issues | Disclosure of Information | ★ Honor Roll

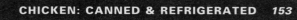

For a more detailed explanation, see pages 7–28.

PRODUCT	PARENT COMPANY									EXTRAS
Chill Chick	CAG	C	C	C	C	?	?	F	C	CEDC report; factory farming; profile
Country Fresh	TYSNA	C	?	D	A	B	?	D	D	factory farming; profile
Country Pride	CAG	C	C	C	C	?	?	F	C	CEDC report; factory farming; profile
Crispy Light	TYSNA	C	?	D	A	B	?	D	D	factory farming; profile
Delecta-ray	TYSNA	C	?	D	A	B	?	D	D	factory farming; profile
Deli Ready	TYSNA	C	?	D	A	B	?	D	D	factory farming; profile
Drumettes	CAG	C	C	C	C	?	?	F	C	CEDC report; factory farming; profile
Dutch Frye	TYSNA	C	?	D	A	B	?	D	D	factory farming; profile
Family Recipe	TYSNA	C	?	D	A	B	?	D	D	factory farming; profile
Flings	TYSNA	C	?	D	A	B	?	D	D	factory farming; profile
Flyers	TYSNA	C	?	D	A	B	?	D	D	factory farming; profile
Golden Farms	CAG	C	C	C	C	?	?	F	C	CEDC report; factory farming; profile
Gold Leaf	TYSNA	C	?	D	A	B	?	D	D	factory farming; profile
Hayden House	TYSNA	C	?	D	A	B	?	D	D	factory farming; profile
Holly Farms	TYSNA	C	?	D	A	B	?	D	D	factory farming; profile
Homestyle	TYSNA	C	?	D	A	B	?	D	D	factory farming; profile

PRODUCT	PARENT COMPANY	The Environment	Charitable Giving	Community Outreach	Women's Advancement	Minority Advancement	Family	Workplace Issues	Disclosure of Information	EXTRAS
Honey Stung	TYSNA	C	?	D	A	B	?	D	D	factory farming; profile
Mr. Turkey	SLE	C	B	A	B	B	B	B	A	CEP Award — Charity; on-site child care; tobacco
Ocoma	TYSNA	C	?	D	A	B	?	D	D	factory farming; profile
Oven Express	TYSNA	C	?	D	A	B	?	D	D	factory farming; profile
Shorgood	CAG	C	C	C	C	?	?	F	C	CEDC report; factory farming; profile
Tyson	TYSNA	C	?	D	A	B	?	D	D	factory farming; profile
Weaver	TYSNA	C	?	D	A	B	?	D	D	factory farming; profile
Wilkes Poultry Farms	TYSNA	C	?	D	A	B	?	D	D	factory farming; profile
Wingettes	CAG	C	C	C	C	?	?	F	C	CEDC report; factory farming; profile
Zesty Wings	TYSNA	C	?	D	A	B	?	D	D	factory farming; profile
CLEANSERS & SPONGES FOR HOUSEHOLD USE										
Ajax ★	CL	B	B	A	A	B	A	A	A	Animal testing: medical & non-medical products, significant alternative efforts; CEDC report; profile
Arm & Hammer	CHD	A	B	A	C	C	A	A	A	Animal testing: non-medical products, significant alternative efforts; CEP Award — Environment

The Environment | Charitable Giving | Community Outreach | Women's Advancement | Minority Advancement | Family | Workplace Issues | Disclosure of Information | ★ Honor Roll

For a more detailed explanation, see pages 7–28.

PRODUCT	PARENT COMPANY									EXTRAS
Armstrong Cleaner ★	SCJ	A	A	A	B	B	A	A	A	Animal testing: non-medical products, significant alternative efforts; CEP Award — Environment; on-site child care; profile; Workplace Principles
Avon ★	AVP	B	A	A	A	A	A	B	A	CEP Award — EEO; increasing TRI; on-site day care
Bathroom Duck ★	SCJ	A	A	A	B	B	A	A	A	Animal testing: non-medical products, significant alternative efforts; CEP Award — Environment; on-site child care; profile; Workplace Principles
Bo-Peep	DL	C	A	B	B	?	F	B	C	CEDC report
Brillo	DL	C	A	B	B	?	F	B	C	CEDC report
Brite ★	SCJ	A	A	A	B	B	A	A	A	Animal testing: non-medical products, significant alternative efforts; CEP Award — Environment; on-site child care; profile; Workplace Principles
Bruce	DL	C	A	B	B	?	F	B	C	CEDC report
Cameo	DL	C	A	B	B	?	F	B	C	CEDC report
Carpet Science ★	SCJ	A	A	A	B	B	A	A	A	Animal testing: non-medical products, significant alternative efforts; CEP Award — Environment; on-site child care; profile; Workplace Principles
Cascade	PG	C	B	A	B	B	A	B	A	Animal testing: medical and non-medical products, significant alternative efforts; CEDC report; CEP Awards — Animal Welfare, Employer Responsiveness; increasing TRI; on-site day care; Workplace Principles
Clean-Safe	AHP	C	F	C	B	B	C	C	A	Animal testing: medical & non-medical products, significant alternative efforts; infant formula

PRODUCT	PARENT COMPANY	The Environment	Charitable Giving	Community Outreach	Women's Advancement	Minority Advancement	Family	Workplace Issues	Disclosure of Information	EXTRAS
Clorox Clean-Up	CLX	B	B	A	A	A	C	C	A	Animal testing: non-medical products, significant alternative efforts; CEDC report; CEP Award—Community; increasing TRI
Comet	PG	C	B	A	B	B	A	B	A	Animal testing: medical and non-medical products, significant alternative efforts; CEDC report; CEP Awards — Animal Welfare, Employer Responsiveness; increasing TRI; on-site day care; Workplace Principles
Crystal White ★	CL	B	B	A	A	B	A	A	A	Animal testing: medical & non-medical products, significant alternative efforts; CEDC report; profile
Dawn	PG	C	B	A	B	B	A	B	A	Animal testing: medical and non-medical products, significant alternative efforts; CEDC report; CEP Awards — Animal Welfare, Employer Responsiveness; increasing TRI; on-site day care; Workplace Principles
Direct	EK	C	B	B	B	B	A	B	B	Animal testing: medical and non-medical products, significant alternative efforts; CEDC report; CEP Award — EEO
Dobie	DL	C	A	B	B	?	F	B	C	CEDC report
Dow Bathroom Cleaner	DOW	C	C	B	B	A	A	B	A	Animal testing: non-medical products, significant alternative efforts; CEDC report; on-site child care; pesticide sterilization suits
Drano ★	SCJ	A	A	A	B	B	A	A	A	Animal testing: non-medical products, significant alternative efforts; CEP Award — Environment; on-site child care; profile; Workplace Principles

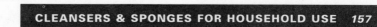

 The Environment; Charitable Giving; Community Outreach
 Women's Advancement
 Minority Advancement

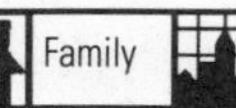 Family

 Workplace Issues
 Disclosure of Information
★ Honor Roll

For a more detailed explanation, see pages 7–28.

PRODUCT	PARENT COMPANY									EXTRAS
Dry Breezes	AHP	C	F	C	B	B	C	C	A	Animal testing: medical & non-medical products, significant alternative efforts; infant formula
Duster Plus ★	SCJ	A	A	A	B	B	A	A	A	Animal testing: non-medical products, significant alternative efforts; CEP Award — Environment; on-site child care; profile; Workplace Principles
Endust	SLE	C	B	A	B	B	B	B	A	CEP Award — Charity; on-site child care; tobacco
Ever Fresh	BN	C	C	B	A	A	B	B	A	CEDC report
Fabuloso ★	CL	B	B	A	A	B	A	A	A	Animal testing: medical & non-medical products, significant alternative efforts; CEDC report; profile
Fantastik	DOW	C	C	B	B	A	A	B	A	Animal testing: non-medical products, significant alternative efforts; CEDC report; on-site child care; pesticide sterilization suits
Favor ★	SCJ	A	A	A	B	B	A	A	A	Animal testing: non-medical products, significant alternative efforts; CEP Award — Environment; on-site child care; profile; Workplace Principles
Fine Wood ★	SCJ	A	A	A	B	B	A	A	A	Animal testing: non-medical products, significant alternative efforts; CEP Award — Environment; on-site child care; profile; Workplace Principles
Formby	EK	C	B	B	B	B	A	B	B	Animal testing: medical and non-medical products, significant alternative efforts; CEDC report; CEP Award — EEO
Formula 409	CLX	B	B	A	A	A	C	C	A	Animal testing: non-medical products, significant alternative efforts; CEDC report; CEP Award — Community; increasing TRI

PRODUCT	PARENT COMPANY	The Environment	Charitable Giving	Community Outreach	Women's Advancement	Minority Advancement	Family	Workplace Issues	Disclosure of Information	EXTRAS
Future ★	SCJ	A	A	A	B	B	A	A	A	Animal testing: non-medical products, significant alternative efforts; CEP Award — Environment; on-site child care; profile; Workplace Principles
Glade ★	SCJ	A	A	A	B	B	A	A	A	Animal testing: non-medical products, significant alternative efforts; CEP Award — Environment; on-site child care; profile; Workplace Principles
Glass Mates glass cleaning wipes	EK	C	B	B	B	B	A	B	B	Animal testing: medical and non-medical products, significant alternative efforts; CEDC report; CEP Award — EEO
Glass Plus	DOW	C	C	B	B	A	A	B	A	Animal testing: non-medical products, significant alternative efforts; CEDC report; on-site child care; pesticide sterilization suits
Glo-Coat ★	SCJ	A	A	A	B	B	A	A	A	Animal testing: non-medical products, significant alternative efforts; CEP Award — Environment; on-site child care; profile; Workplace Principles
Glory ★	SCJ	A	A	A	B	B	A	A	A	Animal testing: non-medical products, significant alternative efforts; CEP Award — Environment; on-site child care; profile; Workplace Principles
Grease Relief	DOW	C	C	B	B	A	A	B	A	Animal testing: non-medical products, significant alternative efforts; CEDC report; on-site child care; pesticide sterilization suits
Great Scents	DL	C	A	B	B	?	F	B	C	CEDC report

The Environment | Charitable Giving | Community Outreach | Women's Advancement | Minority Advancement | Family | Workplace Issues | Disclosure of Information | ★ Honor Roll

For a more detailed explanation, see pages 7–28.

PRODUCT	PARENT COMPANY									EXTRAS
Handi Wipes ★	CL	B	B	A	A	B	A	A	A	Animal testing: medical & non-medical products, significant alternative efforts; CEDC report; profile
Ivory Liquid	PG	C	B	A	B	B	A	B	A	Animal testing: medical and non-medical products, significant alternative efforts; CEDC report; CEP Awards — Animal Welfare, Employer Responsiveness; increasing TRI; on-site day care; Workplace Principles
Joy	PG	C	B	A	B	B	A	B	A	Animal testing: medical and non-medical products, significant alternative efforts; CEDC report; CEP Awards — Animal Welfare, Employer Responsiveness; increasing TRI; on-site day care; Workplace Principles
Jubilee ★	SCJ	A	A	A	B	B	A	A	A	Animal testing: non-medical products, significant alternative efforts; CEP Award — Environment; on-site child care; profile; Workplace Principles
Klean 'n Shine ★	SCJ	A	A	A	B	B	A	A	A	Animal testing: non-medical products, significant alternative efforts; CEP Award — Environment; on-site child care; profile; Workplace Principles
Klear ★	SCJ	A	A	A	B	B	A	A	A	Animal testing: non-medical products, significant alternative efforts; CEP Award — Environment; on-site child care; profile; Workplace Principles
Kleen Guard	ACV	A	?	B	A	D	D	B	B	Animal testing: non-medical products; increasing TRI
Lestoil	PG	C	B	A	B	B	A	B	A	Animal testing: medical and non-medical products, significant alternative efforts; CEDC report; CEP Awards — Animal Welfare, Employer Responsiveness; increasing TRI; on-site day care; Workplace Principles
Liquid-Plumr	CLX	B	B	A	A	A	C	C	A	Animal testing: non-medical products, significant alternative efforts; CEDC report; CEP Award — Community; increasing TRI

PRODUCT	PARENT COMPANY	The Environment	Charitable Giving	Community Outreach	Women's Advancement	Minority Advancement	Family	Workplace Issues	Disclosure of Information	EXTRAS
Love My Carpet	EK	C	B	B	B	B	A	B	B	Animal testing: medical and non-medical products, significant alternative efforts; CEDC report; CEP Award — EEO
Lysoform	UN	B	C	C	F	D	C	B	C	Animal testing: non-medical products, significant alternative efforts; foreign-based company; profile
Lysol	EK	C	B	B	B	B	A	B	B	Animal testing: medical and non-medical products, significant alternative efforts; CEDC report; CEP Award — EEO
Minwax	EK	C	B	B	B	B	A	B	B	Animal testing: medical and non-medical products, significant alternative efforts; CEDC report; CEP Award — EEO
Mop & Glow	EK	C	B	B	B	B	A	B	B	Animal testing: medical and non-medical products, significant alternative efforts; CEDC report; CEP Award — EEO
Mr. Bathroom	AHP	C	F	C	B	B	C	C	A	Animal testing: medical & non-medical products, significant alternative efforts; infant formula
Mr. Clean	PG	C	B	A	B	B	A	B	A	Animal testing: medical and non-medical products, significant alternative efforts; CEDC report; CEP Awards — Animal Welfare, Employer Responsiveness; increasing TRI; on-site day care; Workplace Principles
Murphy's Oil Soap ★	CL	B	B	A	A	B	A	A	A	Animal testing: medical & non-medical products, significant alternative efforts; CEDC report; profile

The Environment | Charitable Giving | Community Outreach | Women's Advancement | Minority Advancement | Family | Workplace Issues | Disclosure of Information | ★ Honor Roll

For a more detailed explanation, see pages 7–28.

PRODUCT	PARENT COMPANY									EXTRAS
O-Cel-O	MMM	C	B	A	C	B	A	B	A	Animal testing: medical & non-medical products, significant alternative efforts; CEDC report; CEP Award — Environment
Once Overs	KMB	C	C	B	B	C	B	A	A	Animal testing: non-medical products, significant alternative efforts; CEDC report; tobacco
Parson's	DL	C	A	B	B	?	F	B	C	CEDC report
Perk	EK	C	B	B	B	B	A	B	B	Animal testing: medical and non-medical products, significant alternative efforts; CEDC report; CEP Award — EEO
Pine-Sol	CLX	B	B	A	A	A	C	C	A	Animal testing: non-medical products, significant alternative efforts; CEDC report; CEP Award — Community; increasing TRI
Pledge ★	SCJ	A	A	A	B	B	A	A	A	Animal testing: non-medical products, significant alternative efforts; CEP Award — Environment; on-site child care; profile; Workplace Principles
Radiant	AHP	C	F	C	B	B	C	C	A	Animal testing: medical & non-medical products, significant alternative efforts; infant formula
Resolve	EK	C	B	B	B	B	A	B	B	Animal testing: medical and non-medical products, significant alternative efforts; CEDC report; CEP Award — EEO
Sani Drain	AHP	C	F	C	B	B	C	C	A	Animal testing: medical & non-medical products, significant alternative efforts; infant formula
Scotch-Brite	MMM	C	B	A	C	B	A	B	A	Animal testing: medical & non-medical products, significant alternative efforts; CEDC report; CEP Award — Environment
Sno Bowl	DL	C	A	B	B	?	F	B	C	CEDC report

PRODUCT	PARENT COMPANY	The Environment	Charitable Giving	Community Outreach	Women's Advancement	Minority Advancement	Family	Workplace Issues	Disclosure of Information	EXTRAS
Sno Drops	DL	C	A	B	B	?	F	B	C	CEDC report
Soft Scrub	CLX	B	B	A	A	A	C	C	A	Animal testing: non-medical products, significant alternative efforts; CEDC report; CEP Award — Community; increasing TRI
S.O.S.	CLX	B	B	A	A	A	C	C	A	Animal testing: non-medical products, significant alternative efforts; CEDC report; CEP Award — Community; increasing TRI
Spic & Span	PG	C	B	A	B	B	A	B	A	Animal testing: medical and non-medical products, significant alternative efforts; CEDC report; CEP Awards — Animal Welfare, Employer Responsiveness; increasing TRI; on-site day care; Workplace Principles
Step Saver ★	SCJ	A	A	A	B	B	A	A	A	Animal testing: non-medical products, significant alternative efforts; CEP Award — Environment; on-site child care; profile; Workplace Principles
Sun Light	UN	B	C	C	F	D	C	B	C	Animal testing: non-medical products, significant alternative efforts; foreign-based company; profile
Supreme	DL	C	A	B	B	?	F	B	C	CEDC report
Tackle	CLX	B	B	A	A	A	C	C	A	Animal testing: non-medical products, significant alternative efforts; CEDC report; CEP Award — Community; increasing TRI
Tilex	CLX	B	B	A	A	A	C	C	A	Animal testing: non-medical products, significant alternative efforts; CEDC report; CEP Award — Community; increasing TRI

The Environment | Charitable Giving | Community Outreach |  Women's Advancement |  Minority Advancement |  Family |  Workplace Issues |    Disclosure of Information | ★ Honor Roll

For a more detailed explanation, see pages 7–28.

PRODUCT	PARENT COMPANY									EXTRAS
Toilet Duck *	SCJ	A	A	A	B	B	A	A	A	Animal testing: non-medical products, significant alternative efforts; CEP Award — Environment; on-site child care; profile; Workplace Principles
Top Job	PG	C	B	A	B	B	A	B	A	Animal testing: medical and non-medical products, significant alternative efforts; CEDC report; CEP Awards — Animal Welfare, Employer Responsiveness; increasing TRI; on-site day care; Workplace Principles
Tough Act	DOW	C	C	B	B	A	A	B	A	Animal testing: non-medical products, significant alternative efforts; CEDC report; on-site child care; pesticide sterilization suits
Tuffy	CLX	B	B	A	A	A	C	C	A	Animal testing: non-medical products, significant alternative efforts; CEDC report; CEP Award — Community; increasing TRI
Vanish *	SCJ	A	A	A	B	B	A	A	A	Animal testing: non-medical products, significant alternative efforts; CEP Award — Environment; on-site child care; profile; Workplace Principles
Windex *	SCJ	A	A	A	B	B	A	A	A	Animal testing: non-medical products, significant alternative efforts; CEP Award — Environment; on-site child care; profile; Workplace Principles
CLOTHES										
Aris	SLE	C	B	A	B	B	B	B	A	CEP Award — Charity; on-site child care; tobacco
Baby Gap	GPS	B	C	A	A	?	B	A	B	
Bali	SLE	C	B	A	B	B	B	B	A	CEP Award — Charity; on-site child care; tobacco

PRODUCT	PARENT COMPANY	The Environment	Charitable Giving	Community Outreach	Women's Advancement	Minority Advancement	Family	Workplace Issues	Disclosure of Information	EXTRAS
Brittania ★	LEV	A	B	A	A	A	B	B	A	CEP Award — International Commitment; profile; same-sex partner benefits; Workplace Principles
Champion	SLE	C	B	A	B	B	B	B	A	CEP Award — Charity; on-site child care; tobacco
Crazy Horse	LIZ	?	F	C	A	?	C	?	F	on-site child care
Deva Lifewear	DEVA	A	?	?	A	Neutral	A	B	B	small company
Dockers ★	LEV	A	B	A	A	A	B	B	A	CEP Award — International Commitment; profile; same-sex partner benefits; Workplace Principles
Domani	GCO	?	B	C	F	F	?	?	D	CEDC report
Elisabeth	LIZ	?	F	C	A	?	C	?	F	on-site child care
Ellesse	RBK	B	C	A	B	B	B	B	A	CEDC report
Esprit	ESP	?	?	A	A	A	B	B	C	
Gap, The	GPS	B	C	A	A	?	B	A	B	
Gapkids	GPS	B	C	A	A	?	B	A	B	
Gerber	GEB	C	C	?	B	B	?	?	F	CEDC report; increasing TRI; infant formula
Grays by Gary Wasserman	GCO	?	B	C	F	F	?	?	D	CEDC report
Greif	GCO	?	B	C	F	F	?	?	D	CEDC report

The Environment · Charitable Giving · Community Outreach · Women's Advancement ·  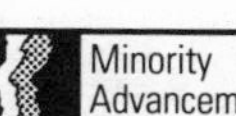 Minority Advancement ·  Family ·  Workplace Issues · 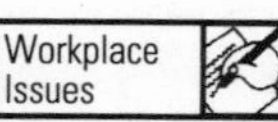  Disclosure of Information · ★ Honor Roll

For a more detailed explanation, see pages 7–28.

PRODUCT	PARENT COMPANY									EXTRAS
Hanes	SLE	C	B	A	B	B	B	B	A	CEP Award — Charity; on-site child care; tobacco
Kilgour French & Stanbury	GCO	?	B	C	F	F	?	?	D	CEDC report
L'Eggs	SLE	C	B	A	B	B	B	B	A	CEP Award — Charity; on-site child care; tobacco
Levi ★	LEV	A	B	A	A	A	B	B	A	CEP Award — International Commitment; profile; same-sex partner benefits; Workplace Principles
Liz Claiborne	LIZ	?	F	C	A	?	C	?	F	on-site child care
Liz Claiborne Collections	LIZ	?	F	C	A	?	C	?	F	on-site child care
Lizsport	LIZ	?	F	C	A	?	C	?	F	on-site child care
Lizwear	LIZ	?	F	C	A	?	C	?	F	on-site child care
Mondo di Marcos	GCO	?	B	C	F	F	?	?	D	CEDC report
Na Na clothing	NA	A	D	C	A	B	?	B	A	Small company
Nike	NKE	C	C	B	A	D	A	B	A	CEDC report; on-site child care
Patagonia	LOST	A	A	C	A	C	A	C	A	on-site child care
Perry Ellis	GCO	?	B	C	F	F	?	?	D	CEDC report
Polo	GCO	?	B	C	F	F	?	?	D	CEDC report
Reebok	RBK	B	C	A	B	B	B	B	A	CEDC report
Russ	LIZ	?	F	C	A	?	C	?	F	on-site child care
Susie Tompkins	ESP	?	?	A	A	A	B	B	C	

PRODUCT	PARENT COMPANY	The Environment	Charitable Giving	Community Outreach	Women's Advancement	Minority Advancement	Family	Workplace Issues	Disclosure of Information	EXTRAS
Timberland	TBL	B	A	A	B	D	D	B	A	CERES Principles
Villager, The	LIZ	?	F	C	A	?	C	?	F	on-site child care
Weebok	RBK	B	C	A	B	B	B	B	A	CEDC report
Weltware	NA	A	D	C	A	B	?	B	A	Small company
CLOTHING STORES										
Bacon's	MST	?	?	?	F	?	D	D	F	
Banana Republic	GPS	B	C	A	A	?	B	A	B	
Broadway, The	CHH	B	?	C	A	C	C	?	C	
Broadway Southwest, The	CHH	B	?	C	A	C	C	?	C	
Castner-Knott	MST	?	?	?	F	?	D	D	F	
Dayton's ★	DH	B	A	A	A	B	B	B	A	CEP Award — Charity; on-site child care
De Lendrecie's Department Store	MST	?	?	?	F	?	D	D	F	
Emporium	CHH	B	?	C	A	C	C	?	C	
Filene's	MA	?	B	A	B	C	F	C	B	Workplace Principles
Foley's	MA	?	B	A	B	C	F	C	B	Workplace Principles

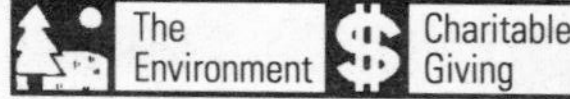
The Environment

Charitable Giving

Community Outreach

Women's Advancement
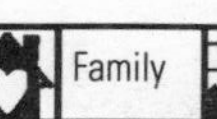
Minority Advancement

Family

Workplace Issues

Disclosure of Information
★ Honor Roll

For a more detailed explanation, see pages 7–28.

PRODUCT	PARENT COMPANY									EXTRAS
Gap, The	GPS	B	C	A	A	?	B	A	B	
Gayfer's	MST	?	?	?	F	?	D	D	F	
Glass Block	MST	?	?	?	F	?	D	D	F	
Hardy	GCO	?	B	C	F	F	?	?	D	CEDC report
Hecht's	MA	?	B	A	B	C	F	C	B	Workplace Principles
Hennessy	MST	?	?	?	F	?	D	D	F	
Hudson's ★	DH	B	A	A	A	B	B	B	A	CEP Award — Charity; on-site child care
J B White & Co.	MST	?	?	?	F	?	D	D	F	
Jones Store Co.	MST	?	?	?	F	?	D	D	F	
Joslins Dry Goods	MST	?	?	?	F	?	D	D	F	
Kaufman's	MA	?	B	A	B	C	F	C	B	Workplace Principles
Lion Dry Goods	MST	?	?	?	F	?	D	D	F	
Lord & Taylor	MA	?	B	A	B	C	F	C	B	Workplace Principles
Mc Alpin's	MST	?	?	?	F	?	D	D	F	
Maison Blanche	MST	?	?	?	F	?	D	D	F	
Marshall Field's ★	DH	B	A	A	A	B	B	B	A	CEP Award — Charity; on-site child care
May Department Stores	MA	?	B	A	B	C	F	C	B	Workplace Principles

PRODUCT	PARENT COMPANY	The Environment	Charitable Giving	Community Outreach	Women's Advancement	Minority Advancement	Family	Workplace Issues	Disclosure of Information	EXTRAS
Mercantile	MST	?	?	?	F	?	D	D	F	
Mervyn's ★	DH	B	A	A	A	B	B	B	A	CEP Award — Charity; on-site child care
Nordstrom ★	NOBE	B	A	A	A	A	A	C	A	profile
Robinsons	MA	?	B	A	B	C	F	C	B	Workplace Principles
Root's	MST	?	?	?	F	?	D	D	F	
Sam's Club	WMT	A	D	D	F	?	?	?	F	
Sears	S	?	A	B	A	C	A	C	B	
Structure	LTD	?	?	C	A	?	?	?	F	
Target ★	DH	B	A	A	A	B	B	B	A	CEP Award — Charity; on-site child care
Timberland	TBL	B	A	A	B	D	D	B	A	CERES Principles
Victoria's Secret	LTD	?	?	C	A	?	?	?	F	
Wal-Mart	WMT	A	D	D	F	?	?	?	F	
Weinstocks	CHH	B	?	C	A	C	C	?	C	
COCOA & MILK MODIFIERS										
Alba	HNZ	B	C	A	B	D	C	A	A	CEDC report; CEP Award — Environment

The Environment | Charitable Giving | Community Outreach | Women's Advancement | Minority Advancement | Family | Workplace Issues | Disclosure of Information | ★ Honor Roll

For a more detailed explanation, see pages 7–28.

PRODUCT	PARENT COMPANY		$							EXTRAS
Choc-O-Rich	OAT	B	A	A	B	B	D	?	C	CEDC report; Fair Share
Hershey's	HSY	B	B	A	B	C	A	A	A	CEDC report; increasing TRI; on-site child care
Swiss Miss	CAG	C	C	C	C	?	?	F	C	CEDC report; factory farming; profile
Weight Watchers	HNZ	B	C	A	B	D	C	A	A	CEDC report; CEP Award — Environment
COFFEE & TEA										
All Seasons	CADBY	B	?	C	C	?	D	B	C	foreign-based company
Brim	MO	D	D	?	A	A	?	?	F	Animal testing: non-medical products; CEDC report; tobacco; increasing TRI; Workplace Principles
Bustelo	ALP	B	C	B	D	?	B	?	B	foreign-based company
Continental Coffee	OAT	B	A	A	B	B	D	?	C	CEDC report; Fair Share
Douwe Egberts	SLE	C	B	A	B	B	B	B	A	CEP Award — Charity; on-site child care; tobacco
Eight O'Clock	GAP	A	B	B	B	?	B	A	C	on-site day care
Favorite	OAT	B	A	A	B	B	D	?	C	CEDC report; Fair Share
Folgers	PG	C	B	A	B	B	A	B	A	Animal testing: medical and non-medical products, significant alternative efforts; CEDC report; CEP Awards — Animal Welfare, Employer Responsiveness; increasing TRI; on-site day care; Workplace Principles
Fruit Tea	MO	D	D	?	A	A	?	?	F	Animal testing: non-medical products; CEDC report; tobacco; increasing TRI; Workplace Principles

PRODUCT	PARENT COMPANY	The Environment	Charitable Giving	Community Outreach	Women's Advancement	Minority Advancement	Family	Workplace Issues	Disclosure of Information	EXTRAS
General Foods International Coffee	MO	D	D	?	A	A	?	?	F	Animal testing: non-medical products; CEDC report; tobacco; increasing TRI; Workplace Principles
Gevalia	MO	D	D	?	A	A	?	?	F	Animal testing: non-medical products; CEDC report; tobacco; increasing TRI; Workplace Principles
Hag	MO	D	D	?	A	A	?	?	F	Animal testing: non-medical products; CEDC report; tobacco; increasing TRI; Workplace Principles
Hills Brothers	NEST	B	?	B	B	B	A	B	B	Animal testing: non-medical products, significant alternative efforts; foreign-based company; infant formula
Instea	OAT	B	A	A	B	B	D	?	C	CEDC report; Fair Share
Kava	BN	C	C	B	A	A	B	B	A	CEDC report
Lipton	UN	B	C	C	F	D	C	B	C	Animal testing: non-medical products, significant alternative efforts; foreign-based company; profile
Lyons	ALP	B	C	B	D	?	B	?	B	foreign-based company
Maison du Cafe	SLE	C	B	A	B	B	B	B	A	CEP Award — Charity; on-site child care; tobacco
Martinson	ALP	B	C	B	D	?	B	?	B	foreign-based company
Master Blend	MO	D	D	?	A	A	?	?	F	Animal testing: non-medical products; CEDC report; tobacco; increasing TRI; Workplace Principles
Maxim	MO	D	D	?	A	A	?	?	F	Animal testing: non-medical products; CEDC report; tobacco; increasing TRI; Workplace Principles

 The Environment, Charitable Giving  Community Outreach  Women's Advancement  Minority Advancement  Family  Workplace Issues  Disclosure of Information  ★ Honor Roll

For a more detailed explanation, see pages 7–28.

PRODUCT	PARENT COMPANY									EXTRAS
Maxwell House	MO	D	D	?	A	A	?	?	F	Animal testing: non-medical products; CEDC report; tobacco; increasing TRI; Workplace Principles
Medaglia D'Oro	ALP	B	C	B	D	?	B	?	B	foreign-based company
Nescafe	NEST	B	?	B	B	B	A	B	B	Animal testing: non-medical products, significant alternative efforts; foreign-based company; infant formula
Nestea	NEST	B	?	B	B	B	A	B	B	Animal testing: non-medical products, significant alternative efforts; foreign-based company; infant formula
Postum	MO	D	D	?	A	A	?	?	F	Animal testing: non-medical products; CEDC report; tobacco; increasing TRI; Workplace Principles
Sanka	MO	D	D	?	A	A	?	?	F	Animal testing: non-medical products; CEDC report; tobacco; increasing TRI; Workplace Principles
Savarin	ALP	B	C	B	D	?	B	?	B	foreign-based company
Superior	SLE	C	B	A	B	B	B	B	A	CEP Award — Charity; on-site child care; tobacco
Taster's Choice	NEST	B	?	B	B	B	A	B	B	Animal testing: non-medical products, significant alternative efforts; foreign-based company; infant formula
Tender Leaf	PG	C	B	A	B	B	A	B	A	Animal testing: medical and non-medical products, significant alternative efforts; CEDC report; CEP Awards — Animal Welfare, Employer Responsiveness; increasing TRI; on-site day care; Workplace Principles
Tetley	ALP	B	C	B	D	?	B	?	B	foreign-based company
W-B	OAT	B	A	A	B	B	D	?	C	CEDC report; Fair Share
Windsor	OAT	B	A	A	B	B	D	?	C	CEDC report; Fair Share

PRODUCT	PARENT COMPANY	The Environment	Charitable Giving	Community Outreach	Women's Advancement	Minority Advancement	Family	Workplace Issues	Disclosure of Information	EXTRAS
World's Best	OAT	B	A	A	B	B	D	?	C	CEDC report; Fair Share
Yuban	MO	D	D	?	A	A	?	?	F	Animal testing: non-medical products; CEDC report; tobacco; increasing TRI; Workplace Principles
COMPACT DISCS/AUDIOTAPES										
Atlantic Records	TWX	B	?	A	B	B	A	C	B	same-sex partner benefits; increasing TRI; Workplace Principles
CBS	SNE	B	B	A	B	B	C	B	A	Fair Share; foreign-based company; increasing TRI
Columbia Records	SNE	B	B	A	B	B	C	B	A	Fair Share; foreign-based company; increasing TRI
DGC Records	MC	C	?	A	?	?	D	?	C	Fair Share; foreign-based company; increasing TRI; same-sex partner benefits
Elektra Records	TWX	B	?	A	B	B	A	C	B	same-sex partner benefits; increasing TRI; Workplace Principles
Epic Records	SNE	B	B	A	B	B	C	B	A	Fair Share; foreign-based company; increasing TRI
Geffen Records	MC	C	?	A	?	?	D	?	C	Fair Share; foreign-based company; increasing TRI; same-sex partner benefits
MCA Records	MC	C	?	A	?	?	D	?	C	Fair Share; foreign-based company; increasing TRI; same-sex partner benefits
Portrait	SNE	B	B	A	B	B	C	B	A	Fair Share; foreign-based company; increasing TRI

The Environment | Charitable Giving | Community Outreach | Women's Advancement | Minority Advancement | Family | Workplace Issues | Disclosure of Information | ★ Honor Roll

For a more detailed explanation, see pages 7–28.

PRODUCT	PARENT COMPANY									EXTRAS
Rhino Records ★	RHI	B	A	A	A	A	B	B	A	profile; small company
Virgin	SNE	B	B	A	B	B	C	B	A	Fair Share; foreign-based company; increasing TRI
WTG	SNE	B	B	A	B	B	C	B	A	Fair Share; foreign-based company; increasing TRI
Warner Bros. Records	TWX	B	?	A	B	B	A	C	B	same-sex partner benefits; increasing TRI; Workplace Principles
World Beat ★	RHI	B	A	A	A	A	B	B	A	profile; small company
COMPUTERS										
Apple	AAPL	B	B	A	A	D	A	B	C	on-site day care; same-sex partner benefits; Workplace Principles
AT&T	T	B	B	A	B	B	A	B	A	Animal testing: non-medical products; CEP Award — Environment; military contracts; Workplace Principles
Compaq	CPQ	B	C	?	D	?	?	A	C	
Digital ★	DEC	A	?	A	A	A	A	B	A	CEP Awards — Community Involvement, Environment; military contracts; profile; Workplace Principles
HP ★	HWP	B	A	A	B	B	A	A	A	military contracts; profile; nuclear weapons
IBM	IBM	B	A	B	B	B	A	C	B	Animal testing: medical products only; CEP Awards — Employer Responsiveness, Community; Workplace Principles
Macintosh	AAPL	B	B	A	A	D	A	B	C	on-site day care; same-sex partner benefits; Workplace Principles

PRODUCT	PARENT COMPANY	The Environment	Charitable Giving	Community Outreach	Women's Advancement	Minority Advancement	Family	Workplace Issues	Disclosure of Information	EXTRAS
CONDIMENTS										
57	HNZ	B	C	A	B	D	C	A	A	CEDC report; CEP Award — Environment
A.1. Steak Sauce	RN	?	A	C	C	?	?	?	D	Animal testing: non-medical products; CEDC report; tobacco; increasing TRI; Workplace Principles
Bama	BN	C	C	B	A	A	B	B	A	CEDC report
Best Foods	CPC	C	A	B	A	B	C	A	B	Animal testing: non-medical products, significant alternative efforts; CEDC report; increasing TRI
Diablo	AHP	C	F	C	B	B	C	C	A	Animal testing: medical & non-medical products, significant alternative efforts; infant formula
Grey Poupon	RN	?	A	C	C	?	?	?	D	Animal testing: non-medical products; CEDC report; tobacco; increasing TRI; Workplace Principles
Gulden's Mustard	AHP	C	F	C	B	B	C	C	A	Animal testing: medical & non-medical products, significant alternative efforts; infant formula
Health Valley	HVAL	A	C	C	A	A	B	A	A	
Heinz	HNZ	B	C	A	B	D	C	A	A	CEDC report; CEP Award — Environment
Hellmann's	CPC	C	A	B	A	B	C	A	B	Animal testing: non-medical products, significant alternative efforts; CEDC report; increasing TRI
Hunt's	CAG	C	C	C	C	?	?	F	C	CEDC report; factory farming; profile

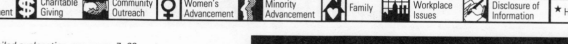

The Environment | Charitable Giving | Community Outreach | Women's Advancement | Minority Advancement | Family | Workplace Issues | Disclosure of Information | ★ Honor Roll

For a more detailed explanation, see pages 7–28.

PRODUCT	PARENT COMPANY									EXTRAS
Kraft	MO	D	D	?	A	A	?	?	F	Animal testing: non-medical products; CEDC report; tobacco; increasing TRI; Workplace Principles
Miracle Whip	MO	D	D	?	A	A	?	?	F	Animal testing: non-medical products; CEDC report; tobacco; increasing TRI; Workplace Principles
Pritikin	OAT	B	A	A	B	B	D	?	C	CEDC report; Fair Share
Regina	RN	?	A	C	C	?	?	?	D	Animal testing: non-medical products; CEDC report; tobacco; increasing TRI; Workplace Principles
Sa-Son	PT	C	D	?	B	?	?	?	F	CEDC report; increasing TRI
Washington	AHP	C	F	C	B	B	C	C	A	Animal testing: medical & non-medical products, significant alternative efforts; infant formula
COOKIES										
Almost Home	RN	?	A	C	C	?	?	?	D	Animal testing: non-medical products; CEDC report; tobacco; increasing TRI; Workplace Principles
Amaranth Cookies	HVAL	A	C	C	A	A	B	A	A	
Animal Snaps	HVAL	A	C	C	A	A	B	A	A	
Apple Crisp	RN	?	A	C	C	?	?	?	D	Animal testing: non-medical products; CEDC report; tobacco; increasing TRI; Workplace Principles
Baker's Bonus	RN	?	A	C	C	?	?	?	D	Animal testing: non-medical products; CEDC report; tobacco; increasing TRI; Workplace Principles
Biscos	RN	?	A	C	C	?	?	?	D	Animal testing: non-medical products; CEDC report; tobacco; increasing TRI; Workplace Principles

PRODUCT	PARENT COMPANY	The Environment	Charitable Giving	Community Outreach	Women's Advancement	Minority Advancement	Family	Workplace Issues	Disclosure of Information	EXTRAS
Bite Size	UBH	?	C	C	D	?	?	?	F	foreign-based company
Brink	ALP	B	C	B	D	?	B	?	B	foreign-based company
Brown Edge Wafers	RN	?	A	C	C	?	?	?	D	Animal testing: non-medical products; CEDC report; tobacco; increasing TRI; Workplace Principles
Bugs Bunny Graham Cookies	RN	?	A	C	C	?	?	?	D	Animal testing: non-medical products; CEDC report; tobacco; increasing TRI; Workplace Principles
Cameo Creme Sandwich	RN	?	A	C	C	?	?	?	D	Animal testing: non-medical products; CEDC report; tobacco; increasing TRI; Workplace Principles
Chips Ahoy	RN	?	A	C	C	?	?	?	D	Animal testing: non-medical products; CEDC report; tobacco; increasing TRI; Workplace Principles
Chocolate Chip Snaps	RN	?	A	C	C	?	?	?	D	Animal testing: non-medical products; CEDC report; tobacco; increasing TRI; Workplace Principles
Chocolate Grahams	RN	?	A	C	C	?	?	?	D	Animal testing: non-medical products; CEDC report; tobacco; increasing TRI; Workplace Principles
Chocolate Snaps	RN	?	A	C	C	?	?	?	D	Animal testing: non-medical products; CEDC report; tobacco; increasing TRI; Workplace Principles
Cookie Break	RN	?	A	C	C	?	?	?	D	Animal testing: non-medical products; CEDC report; tobacco; increasing TRI; Workplace Principles
Cookies 'n' Fudge	RN	?	A	C	C	?	?	?	D	Animal testing: non-medical products; CEDC report; tobacco; increasing TRI; Workplace Principles

The Environment  Charitable Giving | Community Outreach | Women's Advancement | Minority Advancement | Family | Workplace Issues | Disclosure of Information | ★ Honor Roll

For a more detailed explanation, see pages 7–28.

PRODUCT	PARENT COMPANY									EXTRAS
Crunchy Cubs	RAL	C	C	B	B	B	B	C	B	CEDC report; increasing TRI
Devil's Food Cakes	RN	?	A	C	C	?	?	?	D	Animal testing: non-medical products; CEDC report; tobacco; increasing TRI; Workplace Principles
Dixie Bell	RAL	C	C	B	B	B	B	C	B	CEDC report; increasing TRI
Elfin Delights	UBH	?	C	C	D	?	?	?	F	foreign-based company
Elfkins	UBH	?	C	C	D	?	?	?	F	foreign-based company
E.L. Fudge	UBH	?	C	C	D	?	?	?	F	foreign-based company
Famous Chocolate Wafers	RN	?	A	C	C	?	?	?	D	Animal testing: non-medical products; CEDC report; tobacco; increasing TRI; Workplace Principles
Fiber Jumbos	HVAL	A	C	C	A	A	B	A	A	
Fig Newtons	RN	?	A	C	C	?	?	?	D	Animal testing: non-medical products; CEDC report; tobacco; increasing TRI; Workplace Principles
Fruit & Fitness	HVAL	A	C	C	A	A	B	A	A	
Fruit Centers	HVAL	A	C	C	A	A	B	A	A	
Fruit Jumbos	HVAL	A	C	C	A	A	B	A	A	
Giggles	RN	?	A	C	C	?	?	?	D	Animal testing: non-medical products; CEDC report; tobacco; increasing TRI; Workplace Principles
Grandma's	PEP	B	B	A	A	B	B	B	A	Animal testing: non-medical products; factory farming; increasing TRI

PRODUCT	PARENT COMPANY	The Environment	Charitable Giving	Community Outreach	Women's Advancement	Minority Advancement	Family	Workplace Issues	Disclosure of Information	EXTRAS
Haust	ALP	B	C	B	D	?	B	?	B	foreign-based company
Health Valley	HVAL	A	C	C	A	A	B	A	A	
Healthy Grahams	HVAL	A	C	C	A	A	B	A	A	
Heyday	RN	?	A	C	C	?	?	?	D	Animal testing: non-medical products; CEDC report; tobacco; increasing TRI; Workplace Principles
Honey Graham	UBH	?	C	C	D	?	?	?	F	foreign-based company
Honey Jumbos	HVAL	A	C	C	A	A	B	A	A	
Iced Animals	UBH	?	C	C	D	?	?	?	F	foreign-based company
Ideal	RN	?	A	C	C	?	?	?	D	Animal testing: non-medical products; CEDC report; tobacco; increasing TRI; Workplace Principles
Keebler	UBH	?	C	C	D	?	?	?	F	foreign-based company
Lorna Doone	RN	?	A	C	C	?	?	?	D	Animal testing: non-medical products; CEDC report; tobacco; increasing TRI; Workplace Principles
Magic Middles	UBH	?	C	C	D	?	?	?	F	foreign-based company
Maryland Cookies	ALP	B	C	B	D	?	B	?	B	foreign-based company
Mayfair	RN	?	A	C	C	?	?	?	D	Animal testing: non-medical products; CEDC report; tobacco; increasing TRI; Workplace Principles

The Environment | Charitable Giving | Community Outreach | Women's Advancement

Minority Advancement
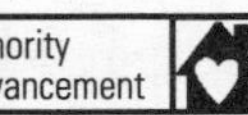
Family

Workplace Issues

Disclosure of Information | ★ Honor Roll

For a more detailed explanation, see pages 7–28.

PRODUCT	PARENT COMPANY									EXTRAS
Mini Middle	UBH	?	C	C	D	?	?	?	F	foreign-based company
Newtons	RN	?	A	C	C	?	?	?	D	Animal testing: non-medical products; CEDC report; tobacco; increasing TRI; Workplace Principles
Nilla wafers	RN	?	A	C	C	?	?	?	D	Animal testing: non-medical products; CEDC report; tobacco; increasing TRI; Workplace Principles
Nutter Butter	RN	?	A	C	C	?	?	?	D	Animal testing: non-medical products; CEDC report; tobacco; increasing TRI; Workplace Principles
Old Fashion Ginger Snaps	RN	?	A	C	C	?	?	?	D	Animal testing: non-medical products; CEDC report; tobacco; increasing TRI; Workplace Principles
Oreos	RN	?	A	C	C	?	?	?	D	Animal testing: non-medical products; CEDC report; tobacco; increasing TRI; Workplace Principles
Peak Freans	RN	?	A	C	C	?	?	?	D	Animal testing: non-medical products; CEDC report; tobacco; increasing TRI; Workplace Principles
Pecan Sandies	UBH	?	C	C	D	?	?	?	F	foreign-based company
Pecan Supreme	RN	?	A	C	C	?	?	?	D	Animal testing: non-medical products; CEDC report; tobacco; increasing TRI; Workplace Principles
Pepperidge Farm	CPB	B	C	B	A	A	A	C	A	Animal testing: non-medical products, significant alternative efforts; CEDC report; on-site child care
Pinwheels	RN	?	A	C	C	?	?	?	D	Animal testing: non-medical products; CEDC report; tobacco; increasing TRI; Workplace Principles
Rich 'n Chewy	PEP	B	B	A	A	B	B	B	A	Animal testing: non-medical products; factory farming; increasing TRI

PRODUCT	PARENT COMPANY	The Environment	Charitable Giving	Community Outreach	Women's Advancement	Minority Advancement	Family	Workplace Issues	Disclosure of Information	EXTRAS
Snackwell's Cookies	RN	?	A	C	C	?	?	?	D	Animal testing: non-medical products; CEDC report; tobacco; increasing TRI; Workplace Principles
Social Tea	RN	?	A	C	C	?	?	?	D	Animal testing: non-medical products; CEDC report; tobacco; increasing TRI; Workplace Principles
Soft Batch	UBH	?	C	C	D	?	?	?	F	foreign-based company
Stella D'oro	RN	?	A	C	C	?	?	?	D	Animal testing: non-medical products; CEDC report; tobacco; increasing TRI; Workplace Principles
Teddy Grahams	RN	?	A	C	C	?	?	?	D	Animal testing: non-medical products; CEDC report; tobacco; increasing TRI; Workplace Principles
T.G. Bearwich	RN	?	A	C	C	?	?	?	D	Animal testing: non-medical products; CEDC report; tobacco; increasing TRI; Workplace Principles
CRACKERS										
7-Grain Stone Wheat	HVAL	A	C	C	A	A	B	A	A	
American Classic	RN	?	A	C	C	?	?	?	D	Animal testing: non-medical products; CEDC report; tobacco; increasing TRI; Workplace Principles
Barnum's Animals	RN	?	A	C	C	?	?	?	D	Animal testing: non-medical products; CEDC report; tobacco; increasing TRI; Workplace Principles
Better Cheddars	RN	?	A	C	C	?	?	?	D	Animal testing: non-medical products; CEDC report; tobacco; increasing TRI; Workplace Principles

The Environment | Charitable Giving | Community Outreach | Women's Advancement | Minority Advancement | Family | Workplace Issues | Disclosure of Information | ★ Honor Roll

For a more detailed explanation, see pages 7–28.

PRODUCT	PARENT COMPANY									EXTRAS
Better Cheeses	RN	?	A	C	C	?	?	?	D	Animal testing: non-medical products; CEDC report; tobacco; increasing TRI; Workplace Principles
Carr's	UBH	?	C	C	D	?	?	?	F	foreign-based company
C.C. Ricers	UBH	?	C	C	D	?	?	?	F	foreign-based company
Chacho's	UBH	?	C	C	D	?	?	?	F	foreign-based company
Cheddar Wedges	RN	?	A	C	C	?	?	?	D	Animal testing: non-medical products; CEDC report; tobacco; increasing TRI; Workplace Principles
Cheese Nips	RN	?	A	C	C	?	?	?	D	Animal testing: non-medical products; CEDC report; tobacco; increasing TRI; Workplace Principles
Cheese Tid-Bits	RN	?	A	C	C	?	?	?	D	Animal testing: non-medical products; CEDC report; tobacco; increasing TRI; Workplace Principles
Cheese Wheels	HVAL	A	C	C	A	A	B	A	A	
Chico-San	HNZ	B	C	A	B	D	C	A	A	CEDC report; CEP Award — Environment
Club Crackers	UBH	?	C	C	D	?	?	?	F	foreign-based company
Comet	RN	?	A	C	C	?	?	?	D	Animal testing: non-medical products; CEDC report; tobacco; increasing TRI; Workplace Principles
Crazy	OAT	B	A	A	B	B	D	?	C	CEDC report; Fair Share
Cris Bix	OAT	B	A	A	B	B	D	?	C	CEDC report; Fair Share
Crown Pilot	RN	?	A	C	C	?	?	?	D	Animal testing: non-medical products; CEDC report; tobacco; increasing TRI; Workplace Principles

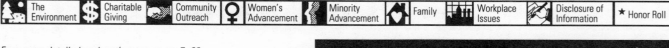

PRODUCT	PARENT COMPANY									EXTRAS
Entertainers	RN	?	A	C	C	?	?	?	D	Animal testing: non-medical products; CEDC report; tobacco; increasing TRI; Workplace Principles
Fat Free Organic Whole Wheat	HVAL	A	C	C	A	A	B	A	A	
Garden Crisps	RN	?	A	C	C	?	?	?	D	Animal testing: non-medical products; CEDC report; tobacco; increasing TRI; Workplace Principles
Graham Crackers	RN	?	A	C	C	?	?	?	D	Animal testing: non-medical products; CEDC report; tobacco; increasing TRI; Workplace Principles
Harvest Crisps	RN	?	A	C	C	?	?	?	D	Animal testing: non-medical products; CEDC report; tobacco; increasing TRI; Workplace Principles
Health Valley	HVAL	A	C	C	A	A	B	A	A	
Honey Graham Crackers	HVAL	A	C	C	A	A	B	A	A	
Honey Maid	RN	?	A	C	C	?	?	?	D	Animal testing: non-medical products; CEDC report; tobacco; increasing TRI; Workplace Principles
Keebler	UBH	?	C	C	D	?	?	?	F	foreign-based company
Low Salt Club	UBH	?	C	C	D	?	?	?	F	foreign-based company
Munch'Ems	UBH	?	C	C	D	?	?	?	F	foreign-based company
Nips	RN	?	A	C	C	?	?	?	D	Animal testing: non-medical products; CEDC report; tobacco; increasing TRI; Workplace Principles

 The Environment  Charitable Giving Community Outreach 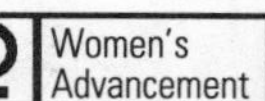 Women's Advancement 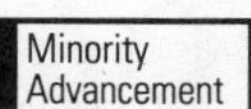 Minority Advancement  Family  Workplace Issues  Disclosure of Information ★ Honor Roll

For a more detailed explanation, see pages 7–28.

PRODUCT	PARENT COMPANY									EXTRAS
Oat Thins	RN	?	A	C	C	?	?	?	D	Animal testing: non-medical products; CEDC report; tobacco; increasing TRI; Workplace Principles
Oysterettes	RN	?	A	C	C	?	?	?	D	Animal testing: non-medical products; CEDC report; tobacco; increasing TRI; Workplace Principles
Pepperidge Farm	CPB	B	C	B	A	A	A	C	A	Animal testing: non-medical products, significant alternative efforts; CEDC report; on-site child care
Premium	RN	?	A	C	C	?	?	?	D	Animal testing: non-medical products; CEDC report; tobacco; increasing TRI; Workplace Principles
Pretzel	UBH	?	C	C	D	?	?	?	F	foreign-based company
Ralston Stax	RAL	C	C	B	B	B	B	C	B	CEDC report; increasing TRI
Red Oval Farms	RN	?	A	C	C	?	?	?	D	Animal testing: non-medical products; CEDC report; tobacco; increasing TRI; Workplace Principles
Ritz	RN	?	A	C	C	?	?	?	D	Animal testing: non-medical products; CEDC report; tobacco; increasing TRI; Workplace Principles
Ry-Brot	OAT	B	A	A	B	B	D	?	C	CEDC report; Fair Share
Rykrisp	RAL	C	C	B	B	B	B	C	B	CEDC report; increasing TRI
Snackwell's	RN	?	A	C	C	?	?	?	D	Animal testing: non-medical products; CEDC report; tobacco; increasing TRI; Workplace Principles
Snorkels Fun Crackers	RN	?	A	C	C	?	?	?	D	Animal testing: non-medical products; CEDC report; tobacco; increasing TRI; Workplace Principles
Sociables	RN	?	A	C	C	?	?	?	D	Animal testing: non-medical products; CEDC report; tobacco; increasing TRI; Workplace Principles

PRODUCT	PARENT COMPANY	The Environment	Charitable Giving	Community Outreach	Women's Advancement	Minority Advancement	Family	Workplace Issues	Disclosure of Information	EXTRAS
Stoned Wheat Crackers	HVAL	A	C	C	A	A	B	A	A	
Swiss Cheese	RN	?	A	C	C	?	?	?	D	Animal testing: non-medical products; CEDC report; tobacco; increasing TRI; Workplace Principles
Time Treat	OAT	B	A	A	B	B	D	?	C	CEDC report; Fair Share
Town House	UBH	?	C	C	D	?	?	?	F	foreign-based company
Triscuit	RN	?	A	C	C	?	?	?	D	Animal testing: non-medical products; CEDC report; tobacco; increasing TRI; Workplace Principles
Twigs	RN	?	A	C	C	?	?	?	D	Animal testing: non-medical products; CEDC report; tobacco; increasing TRI; Workplace Principles
Uneeda	RN	?	A	C	C	?	?	?	D	Animal testing: non-medical products; CEDC report; tobacco; increasing TRI; Workplace Principles
Vegetable Thins	RN	?	A	C	C	?	?	?	D	Animal testing: non-medical products; CEDC report; tobacco; increasing TRI; Workplace Principles
Waverly	RN	?	A	C	C	?	?	?	D	Animal testing: non-medical products; CEDC report; tobacco; increasing TRI; Workplace Principles
Wheatables	UBH	?	C	C	D	?	?	?	F	foreign-based company
Wheatcone	OAT	B	A	A	B	B	D	?	C	CEDC report; Fair Share
Wheat Thins	RN	?	A	C	C	?	?	?	D	Animal testing: non-medical products; CEDC report; tobacco; increasing TRI; Workplace Principles

The Environment | Charitable Giving | Community Outreach | Women's Advancement | Minority Advancement | Family | Workplace Issues | Disclosure of Information | ★ Honor Roll

For a more detailed explanation, see pages 7–28.

PRODUCT	PARENT COMPANY									EXTRAS
Wheatstone	RAL	C	C	B	B	B	B	C	B	CEDC report; increasing TRI
Wheatsworth	RN	?	A	C	C	?	?	?	D	Animal testing: non-medical products; CEDC report; tobacco; increasing TRI; Workplace Principles
Zesta	UBH	?	C	C	D	?	?	?	F	foreign-based company
Zings	RN	?	A	C	C	?	?	?	D	Animal testing: non-medical products; CEDC report; tobacco; increasing TRI; Workplace Principles
DEODORANTS										
5 Day	SBH	C	D	C	B	B	A	B	C	Animal testing: medical products only, significant alternative efforts; foreign-based company; Workplace Principles
Avon ★	AVP	B	A	A	A	A	A	B	A	CEP Award — EEO; increasing TRI; on-site day care
Ban	BMY	B	C	B	B	B	B	B	A	Animal testing: medical & non-medical products, significant alternative efforts; infant formula; Workplace Principles
Barbasol	PFE	C	B	A	B	C	A	B	A	Animal testing: medical products only, significant alternative efforts; heart valve suits; Workplace Principles
Cashmere Bouquet ★	CL	B	B	A	A	B	A	A	A	Animal testing: medical & non-medical products, significant alternative efforts; CEDC report; profile
Consort Deodorant	ACV	A	?	B	A	D	D	B	B	Animal testing: non-medical products; increasing TRI
Degree	HC	A	A	A	B	?	A	B	B	Animal testing: non-medical products
Dry Idea	G	C	C	B	D	D	B	B	A	Animal testing: medical & non-medical products, significant alternative efforts

PRODUCT	PARENT COMPANY	The Environment	Charitable Giving	Community Outreach	Women's Advancement	Minority Advancement	Family	Workplace Issues	Disclosure of Information	EXTRAS
E.S.P.	SBH	C	D	C	B	B	A	B	C	Animal testing: medical products only, significant alternative efforts; foreign-based company; profile; Workplace Principles
Faberge	UN	B	C	C	F	D	C	B	C	Animal testing: non-medical products, significant alternative efforts; foreign-based company; profile
Foot Guard	G	C	C	B	D	D	B	B	A	Animal testing: medical & non-medical products, significant alternative efforts
Gillette	G	C	C	B	D	D	B	B	A	Animal testing: medical & non-medical products, significant alternative efforts
Irish Spring ★	CL	B	B	A	A	B	A	A	A	Animal testing: medical & non-medical products, significant alternative efforts; CEDC report; profile
Mennen ★	CL	B	B	A	A	B	A	A	A	Animal testing: medical & non-medical products, significant alternative efforts; CEDC report; profile
Mum	BMY	B	C	B	B	B	B	B	A	Animal testing: medical & non-medical products, significant alternative efforts; infant formula; Workplace Principles
Natrel	G	C	C	B	D	D	B	B	A	Animal testing: medical & non-medical products, significant alternative efforts
Old Spice	PG	C	B	A	B	B	A	B	A	Animal testing: medical and non-medical products, significant alternative efforts; CEDC report; CEP Awards — Animal Welfare, Employer Responsiveness; increasing TRI; on-site day care; Workplace Principles
Right Guard	G	C	C	B	D	D	B	B	A	Animal testing: medical & non-medical products, significant alternative efforts

The Environment | Charitable Giving | Community Outreach | Women's Advancement |  Minority Advancement | Family | Workplace Issues | Disclosure of Information | ★ Honor Roll

For a more detailed explanation, see pages 7–28.

PRODUCT	PARENT COMPANY									EXTRAS
Secret	PG	C	B	A	B	B	A	B	A	Animal testing: medical and non-medical products, significant alternative efforts; CEDC report; CEP Awards — Animal Welfare, Employer Responsiveness; increasing TRI; on-site day care; Workplace Principles
Soft & Dri	G	C	C	B	D	D	B	B	A	Animal testing: medical & non-medical products, significant alternative efforts
Suave	HC	A	A	A	B	?	A	B	B	Animal testing: non-medical products
Sure	PG	C	B	A	B	B	A	B	A	Animal testing: medical and non-medical products, significant alternative efforts; CEDC report; CEP Awards — Animal Welfare, Employer Responsiveness; increasing TRI; on-site day care; Workplace Principles
Teen Spirit ★	CL	B	B	A	A	B	A	A	A	Animal testing: medical & non-medical products, significant alternative efforts; CEDC report; profile
Tom's of Maine ★	TOM	A	A	A	A	B	A	A	A	CEP Award — Charity; CERES Principles; profile; small company
Tussy	EK	C	B	B	B	B	A	B	B	Animal testing: medical and non-medical products, significant alternative efforts; CEDC report; CEP Award — EEO
Yodora	SBH	C	D	C	B	B	A	B	C	Animal testing: medical products only, significant alternative efforts; foreign-based company; profile; Workplace Principles
DESSERTS: REFRIGERATED & FROZEN										
Ambrosia	CPC	C	A	B	A	B	C	A	B	Animal testing: non-medical products, significant alternative efforts; CEDC report; increasing TRI

PRODUCT	PARENT COMPANY	The Environment	Charitable Giving	Community Outreach	Women's Advancement	Minority Advancement	Family	Workplace Issues	Disclosure of Information	EXTRAS
Ben & Jerry's ★	BJICA	A	A	A	A	B	A	A	A	CERES Principles; CEP Award — Charity; on-site child care; profile; same-sex partner benefits; Workplace Principles
Birds	MO	D	D	?	A	A	?	?	F	Animal testing: non-medical products; CEDC report; tobacco; increasing TRI; Workplace Principles
Borden	BN	C	C	B	A	A	B	B	A	CEDC report
Breyer's	MO	D	D	?	A	A	?	?	F	Animal testing: non-medical products; CEDC report; tobacco; increasing TRI; Workplace Principles
Columbo Frozen Yogurt ★	GIS	B	A	A	A	B	B	A	A	CEDC report; CEP Awards — Charity, EEO, Opportunities for the Disabled; profile; Workplace Principles
Cool Whip	MO	D	D	?	A	A	?	?	F	Animal testing: non-medical products; CEDC report; tobacco; increasing TRI; Workplace Principles
Clover Farms	MO	D	D	?	A	A	?	?	F	Animal testing: non-medical products; CEDC report; tobacco; increasing TRI; Workplace Principles
D-Zerta	MO	D	D	?	A	A	?	?	F	Animal testing: non-medical products; CEDC report; tobacco; increasing TRI; Workplace Principles
Dove	MARS	C	A	B	A	?	?	C	B	
Dream Whip	MO	D	D	?	A	A	?	?	F	Animal testing: non-medical products; CEDC report; tobacco; increasing TRI; Workplace Principles
Drumstick	NEST	B	?	B	B	B	A	B	B	Animal testing: non-medical products, significant alternative efforts; foreign-based company; infant formula

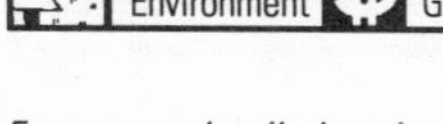
The Environment
Charitable Giving
Community Outreach
Women's Advancement
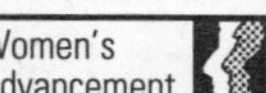
Minority Advancement
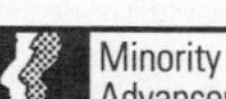
Family

Workplace Issues

Disclosure of Information

★ Honor Roll

For a more detailed explanation, see pages 7–28.

PRODUCT	PARENT COMPANY									EXTRAS
Eagle Brand	BN	C	C	B	A	A	B	B	A	CEDC report
Foremost	MO	D	D	?	A	A	?	?	F	Animal testing: non-medical products; CEDC report; tobacco; increasing TRI; Workplace Principles
Fruit-Line	UN	B	C	C	F	D	C	B	C	Animal testing: non-medical products, significant alternative efforts; foreign-based company; profile
Frusen Gladje	MO	D	D	?	A	A	?	?	F	Animal testing: non-medical products; CEDC report; tobacco; increasing TRI; Workplace Principles
Gold Bond	UN	B	C	C	F	D	C	B	C	Animal testing: non-medical products, significant alternative efforts; foreign-based company; profile
Good Humor	UN	B	C	C	F	D	C	B	C	Animal testing: non-medical products, significant alternative efforts; foreign-based company; profile
Haagen-Dazs ★	GMR	C	A	A	B	A	A	B	A	factory farming; foreign-based company
Handi-Snacks	MO	D	D	?	A	A	?	?	F	Animal testing: non-medical products; CEDC report; tobacco; increasing TRI; Workplace Principles
Healthy Choice	CAG	C	C	C	C	?	?	F	C	CEDC report; factory farming; profile
Hershey's Free	HSY	B	B	A	B	C	A	A	A	CEDC report; increasing TRI; on-site child care
Hunt's Snack Pack	CAG	C	C	C	C	?	?	F	C	CEDC report; factory farming; profile
Jell-O	MO	D	D	?	A	A	?	?	F	Animal testing: non-medical products; CEDC report; tobacco; increasing TRI; Workplace Principles
Jells-Best	OAT	B	A	A	B	B	D	?	C	CEDC report; Fair Share
Lyons	ALP	B	C	B	D	?	B	?	B	foreign-based company

PRODUCT	PARENT COMPANY	The Environment	Charitable Giving	Community Outreach	Women's Advancement	Minority Advancement	Family	Workplace Issues	Disclosure of Information	EXTRAS
Meadow Gold	BN	C	C	B	A	A	B	B	A	CEDC report
Minimilk	UN	B	C	C	F	D	C	B	C	Animal testing: non-medical products, significant alternative efforts; foreign-based company; profile
Minute Tapioca	MO	D	D	?	A	A	?	?	F	Animal testing: non-medical products; CEDC report; tobacco; increasing TRI; Workplace Principles
My*T*Fine	RN	?	A	C	C	?	?	?	D	Animal testing: non-medical products; CEDC report; tobacco; increasing TRI; Workplace Principles
Nice 'n Light	MO	D	D	?	A	A	?	?	F	Animal testing: non-medical products; CEDC report; tobacco; increasing TRI; Workplace Principles
Nutrifil	CAG	C	C	C	C	?	?	F	C	CEDC report; factory farming; profile
Peace Pops ★	BJICA	A	A	A	A	B	A	A	A	CERES Principles; CEP Award — Charity; on-site child care; profile; same-sex partner benefits; Workplace Principles
Pet	PT	C	D	?	B	?	?	?	F	CEDC report; increasing TRI
Pet Whip	PT	C	D	?	B	?	?	?	F	CEDC report; increasing TRI
Pet-ritz	PT	C	D	?	B	?	?	?	F	CEDC report; increasing TRI
Polar B'ar	MO	D	D	?	A	A	?	?	F	Animal testing: non-medical products; CEDC report; tobacco; increasing TRI; Workplace Principles
Reddi-Wip	CAG	C	C	C	C	?	?	F	C	CEDC report; factory farming; profile

The Environment | Charitable Giving | Community Outreach | Women's Advancement | Minority Advancement | Family | Workplace Issues | Disclosure of Information | ★ Honor Roll

For a more detailed explanation, see pages 7–28.

PRODUCT	PARENT COMPANY									EXTRAS
Richardson	OAT	B	A	A	B	B	D	?	C	CEDC report; Fair Share
Richardson & Robbins	PT	C	D	?	B	?	?	?	F	CEDC report; increasing TRI
Royal	RN	?	A	C	C	?	?	?	D	Animal testing: non-medical products; CEDC report; tobacco; increasing TRI; Workplace Principles
R.W. Snyder Foods	OAT	B	A	A	B	B	D	?	C	CEDC report; Fair Share
Sealtest	MO	D	D	?	A	A	?	?	F	Animal testing: non-medical products; CEDC report; tobacco; increasing TRI; Workplace Principles
Stater Bros.	MO	D	D	?	A	A	?	?	F	Animal testing: non-medical products; CEDC report; tobacco; increasing TRI; Workplace Principles
Untoppables	OAT	B	A	A	B	B	D	?	C	CEDC report; Fair Share
Weight Watchers	HNZ	B	C	A	B	D	C	A	A	CEDC report; CEP Award — Environment
DIETARY SUPPLEMENTS										
Avail	SBH	C	D	C	B	B	A	B	C	Animal testing: medical products only, significant alternative efforts; foreign-based company; Workplace Principles
Citric Plus	SBH	C	D	C	B	B	A	B	C	Animal testing: medical products only, significant alternative efforts; foreign-based company; Workplace Principles
Eskatrol	SBH	C	D	C	B	B	A	B	C	Animal testing: medical products only, significant alternative efforts; foreign-based company; Workplace Principles
Fastin	SBH	C	D	C	B	B	A	B	C	Animal testing: medical products only, significant alternative efforts; foreign-based company; Workplace Principles

PRODUCT	PARENT COMPANY	The Environment	Charitable Giving	Community Outreach	Women's Advancement	Minority Advancement	Family	Workplace Issues	Disclosure of Information	EXTRAS
Femiron	SBH	C	D	C	B	B	A	B	C	Animal testing: medical products only, significant alternative efforts; foreign-based company; Workplace Principles
Geritol	SBH	C	D	C	B	B	A	B	C	Animal testing: medical products only, significant alternative efforts; foreign-based company; Workplace Principles
Melozets	SBH	C	D	C	B	B	A	B	C	Animal testing: medical products only, significant alternative efforts; foreign-based company; Workplace Principles
Myadec ★	WLA	B	B	A	B	A	A	B	A	Animal testing: medical products only; increasing TRI; Workplace Principles
Nutrament	BMY	B	C	B	B	B	B	B	A	Animal testing: medical & non-medical products, significant alternative efforts; infant formula; Workplace Principles
Nutramigen	BMY	B	C	B	B	B	B	B	A	Animal testing: medical & non-medical products, significant alternative efforts; infant formula; Workplace Principles
Popeye	SBH	C	D	C	B	B	A	B	C	Animal testing: medical products only, significant alternative efforts; foreign-based company; Workplace Principles
Scott's Emulsion	SBH	C	D	C	B	B	A	B	C	Animal testing: medical products only, significant alternative efforts; foreign-based company; Workplace Principles
Sustagen	BMY	B	C	B	B	B	B	B	A	Animal testing: medical & non-medical products, significant alternative efforts; infant formula; Workplace Principles
Theragran	BMY	B	C	B	B	B	B	B	A	Animal testing: medical & non-medical products, significant alternative efforts; infant formula; Workplace Principles

The Environment | Charitable Giving | Community Outreach | Women's Advancement | Minority Advancement | Family | Workplace Issues | Disclosure of Information | ★ Honor Roll

For a more detailed explanation, see pages 7–28.

PRODUCT	PARENT COMPANY									EXTRAS
FAMILY PLANNING										
E.P.T. ★	WLA	B	B	A	B	A	A	B	A	Animal testing: medical products only; increasing TRI; Workplace Principles
Today Sponge	AHP	C	F	C	B	B	C	C	A	Animal testing: medical & non-medical products, significant alternative efforts; infant formula
FAST FOOD										
Baskin Robbins 31	ALP	B	C	B	D	?	B	?	B	foreign-based company
Burger King ★	GMR	C	A	A	B	A	A	B	A	factory farming; foreign-based company
Dairy Queen	INDQA	B	D	C	B	D	D	C	A	
Domino's Pizza	DOMP	B	?	?	B	B	?	?	C	
Dunkin Donuts	ALP	B	C	B	D	?	B	?	B	foreign-based company
Golden Skillet	INDQA	B	D	C	B	D	D	C	A	
Hardee's	IMS	?	B	A	B	?	?	?	F	tobacco; factory farming; Fair Share; foreign-based company
Karmelkorn	INDQA	B	D	C	B	D	D	C	A	
KFC	PEP	B	B	A	A	B	B	B	A	Animal testing: non-medical products; factory farming; increasing TRI
McDonald's	MCD	B	C	C	B	A	?	?	C	factory farming; Fair Share
Mister Donut	ALP	B	C	B	D	?	B	?	B	foreign-based company

PRODUCT	PARENT COMPANY	The Environment	Charitable Giving	Community Outreach	Women's Advancement	Minority Advancement	Family	Workplace Issues	Disclosure of Information	EXTRAS
Orange Julius	INDQA	B	D	C	B	D	D	C	A	
Pizza Hut	PEP	B	B	A	A	B	B	B	A	Animal testing: non-medical products; factory farming; increasing TRI
Roy Rogers	IMS	?	B	A	B	?	?	?	F	tobacco; factory farming; Fair Share; foreign-based company
Taco Bell	PEP	B	B	A	A	B	B	B	A	Animal testing: non-medical products; factory farming; increasing TRI
FEMININE HYGIENE										
Always	PG	C	B	A	B	B	A	B	A	Animal testing: medical and non-medical products, significant alternative efforts; CEDC report; CEP Awards — Animal Welfare, Employer Responsiveness; increasing TRI; on-site day care; Workplace Principles
Anyday	KMB	C	C	B	B	C	B	A	A	Animal testing: non-medical products, significant alternative efforts; CEDC report; tobacco
Assure ★	JNJ	B	A	A	A	A	A	A	A	Animal testing: medical products only, significant alternative efforts; CEP Award — Disclosure; on-site child care; profile; Workplace Principles
Carefree ★	JNJ	B	A	A	A	A	A	A	A	Animal testing: medical products only, significant alternative efforts; CEP Award — Disclosure; on-site child care; profile; Workplace Principles
Comfort-Design	KMB	C	C	B	B	C	B	A	A	Animal testing: non-medical products, significant alternative efforts; CEDC report; tobacco

The Environment | Charitable Giving | Community Outreach | Women's Advancement | Minority Advancement | Family | Workplace Issues | Disclosure of Information | ★ Honor Roll

For a more detailed explanation, see pages 7–28.

PRODUCT	PARENT COMPANY		$		♀					EXTRAS
FDS	ACV	A	?	B	A	D	D	B	B	Animal testing: non-medical products; increasing TRI
FemCare	SGP	B	C	A	B	A	A	B	A	Animal testing: medical products only, significant alternative efforts; on-site child care; Workplace Principles
Fems	KMB	C	C	B	B	C	B	A	A	Animal testing: non-medical products, significant alternative efforts; CEDC report; tobacco
Free & Easy	KMB	C	C	B	B	C	B	A	A	Animal testing: non-medical products, significant alternative efforts; CEDC report; tobacco
Freshguard	KMB	C	C	B	B	C	B	A	A	Animal testing: non-medical products, significant alternative efforts; CEDC report; tobacco
Gyne-Moistrin	SGP	B	C	A	B	A	A	B	A	Animal testing: medical products only, significant alternative efforts; on-site child care; Workplace Principles
Kotex	KMB	C	C	B	B	C	B	A	A	Animal testing: non-medical products, significant alternative efforts; CEDC report; tobacco
Lightdays	KMB	C	C	B	B	C	B	A	A	Animal testing: non-medical products, significant alternative efforts; CEDC report; tobacco
Massengill	SBH	C	D	C	B	B	A	B	C	Animal testing: medical products only, significant alternative efforts; foreign-based company; Workplace Principles
Modess *	JNJ	B	A	A	A	A	A	A	A	Animal testing: medical products only, significant alternative efforts; CEP Award — Disclosure; on-site child care; profile; Workplace Principles
New Freedom	KMB	C	C	B	B	C	B	A	A	Animal testing: non-medical products, significant alternative efforts; CEDC report; tobacco

PRODUCT	PARENT COMPANY	The Environment	Charitable Giving	Community Outreach	Women's Advancement	Minority Advancement	Family	Workplace Issues	Disclosure of Information	EXTRAS
Novaera	KMB	C	C	B	B	C	B	A	A	Animal testing: non-medical products, significant alternative efforts; CEDC report; tobacco
o.b. ★	JNJ	B	A	A	A	A	A	A	A	Animal testing: medical products only, significant alternative efforts; CEP Award — Disclosure; on-site child care; profile; Workplace Principles
Overnites	KMB	C	C	B	B	C	B	A	A	Animal testing: non-medical products, significant alternative efforts; CEDC report; tobacco
Playtex	SLE	C	B	A	B	B	B	B	A	CEP Award — Charity; on-site child care; tobacco
Poise	KMB	C	C	B	B	C	B	A	A	Animal testing: non-medical products, significant alternative efforts; CEDC report; tobacco
Profile	KMB	C	C	B	B	C	B	A	A	Animal testing: non-medical products, significant alternative efforts; CEDC report; tobacco
Replens ★	WLA	B	B	A	B	A	A	B	A	Animal testing: medical products only; increasing TRI; Workplace Principles
Security	KMB	C	C	B	B	C	B	A	A	Animal testing: non-medical products, significant alternative efforts; CEDC report; tobacco
Silhouettes ★	JNJ	B	A	A	A	A	A	A	A	Animal testing: medical products only, significant alternative efforts; CEP Award — Disclosure; on-site child care; profile; Workplace Principles
Simplique	KMB	C	C	B	B	C	B	A	A	Animal testing: non-medical products, significant alternative efforts; CEDC report; tobacco

The Environment · Charitable Giving · Community Outreach

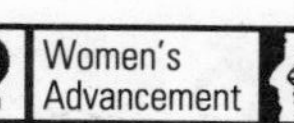
Women's Advancement

Minority Advancement

Family

Workplace Issues

Disclosure of Information

★ Honor Roll

For a more detailed explanation, see pages 7–28.

PRODUCT	PARENT COMPANY									EXTRAS
Stayfree *	JNJ	B	A	A	A	A	A	A	A	Animal testing: medical products only, significant alternative efforts; CEP Award — Disclosure; on-site child care; profile; Workplace Principles
Sure & Natural *	JNJ	B	A	A	A	A	A	A	A	Animal testing: medical products only, significant alternative efforts; CEP Award — Disclosure; on-site child care; profile; Workplace Principles
Thin Super	KMB	C	C	B	B	C	B	A	A	Animal testing: non-medical products, significant alternative efforts; CEDC report; tobacco
Tru-Fit	KMB	C	C	B	B	C	B	A	A	Animal testing: non-medical products, significant alternative efforts; CEDC report; tobacco
Wrap Around	KMB	C	C	B	B	C	B	A	A	Animal testing: non-medical products, significant alternative efforts; CEDC report; tobacco
Zonite	SBH	C	D	C	B	B	A	B	C	Animal testing: medical products only, significant alternative efforts; foreign-based company; Workplace Principles
FILM										
Fuji	FUJIY	C	?	C	B	C	D	B	C	Animal testing: medical products only; foreign-based company; increasing TRI
Kodak	EK	C	B	B	B	B	A	B	B	Animal testing: medical and non-medical products, significant alternative efforts; CEDC report; CEP Award — EEO
One Film	PRD	C	B	A	B	B	A	A	C	CEP Awards — Charity, South Africa; Workplace Principles
Polachrome	PRD	C	B	A	B	B	A	A	C	CEP Awards — Charity, South Africa; Workplace Principles

PRODUCT	PARENT COMPANY	The Environment	Charitable Giving	Community Outreach	Women's Advancement	Minority Advancement	Family	Workplace Issues	Disclosure of Information	EXTRAS
Polacolor	PRD	C	B	A	B	B	A	A	C	CEP Awards — Charity, South Africa; Workplace Principles
Polagraph	PRD	C	B	A	B	B	A	A	C	CEP Awards — Charity, South Africa; Workplace Principles
Polapan	PRD	C	B	A	B	B	A	A	C	CEP Awards — Charity, South Africa; Workplace Principles
Polaroid	PRD	C	B	A	B	B	A	A	C	CEP Awards — Charity, South Africa; Workplace Principles
Superchrome	PRD	C	B	A	B	B	A	A	C	CEP Awards — Charity, South Africa; Workplace Principles
Super-color	PRD	C	B	A	B	B	A	A	C	CEP Awards — Charity, South Africa; Workplace Principles
FIRST AID										
Band-Aid ★	JNJ	B	A	A	A	A	A	A	A	Animal testing: medical products only, significant alternative efforts; CEP Award — Disclosure; on-site child care; profile; Workplace Principles
B.F.I.	SBH	C	D	C	B	B	A	B	C	Animal testing: medical products only, significant alternative efforts; foreign-based company; Workplace Principles
Campho-Phenique	EK	C	B	B	B	B	A	B	B	Animal testing: medical and non-medical products, significant alternative efforts; CEDC report; CEP Award — EEO
Coach Sports Tape & Elastic Bandages ★	JNJ	B	A	A	A	A	A	A	A	Animal testing: medical products only, significant alternative efforts; CEP Award — Disclosure; on-site child care; profile; Workplace Principles

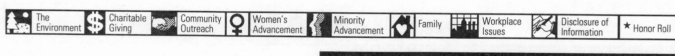

The Environment · Charitable Giving · Community Outreach · Women's Advancement
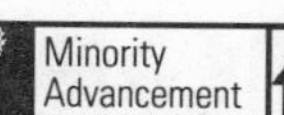

Minority Advancement

Family

Workplace Issues

Disclosure of Information · ★ Honor Roll

For a more detailed explanation, see pages 7–28.

PRODUCT	PARENT COMPANY									EXTRAS
Johnson & Johnson ★	JNJ	B	A	A	A	A	A	A	A	Animal testing: medical products only, significant alternative efforts; CEP Award — Disclosure; on-site child care; profile; Workplace Principles
Micropore	MMM	C	B	A	C	B	A	B	A	Animal testing: medical & non-medical products, significant alternative efforts; CEDC report; CEP Award — Environment
Off! ★	SCJ	A	A	A	B	B	A	A	A	Animal testing: non-medical products, significant alternative efforts; CEP Award — Environment; on-site child care; profile; Workplace Principles
Rhuli ★	SCJ	A	A	A	B	B	A	A	A	Animal testing: non-medical products, significant alternative efforts; CEP Award — Environment; on-site child care; profile; Workplace Principles
Ridsect	SLE	C	B	A	B	B	B	B	A	CEP Award — Charity; on-site child care; tobacco
Solarcaine	SGP	B	C	A	B	A	A	B	A	Animal testing: medical products only, significant alternative efforts; on-site child care; Workplace Principles
ST-37	SBH	C	D	C	B	B	A	B	C	Animal testing: medical products only, significant alternative efforts; foreign-based company; Workplace Principles
FISH: CANNED & REFRIGERATED										
American Original	BN	C	C	B	A	A	B	B	A	CEDC report
Blue Surf	BN	C	C	B	A	A	B	B	A	CEDC report

PRODUCT	PARENT COMPANY	The Environment	Charitable Giving	Community Outreach	Women's Advancement	Minority Advancement	Family	Workplace Issues	Disclosure of Information	EXTRAS
Cutcher	BN	C	C	B	A	A	B	B	A	CEDC report
Doxsee	BN	C	C	B	A	A	B	B	A	CEDC report
Harris	BN	C	C	B	A	A	B	B	A	CEDC report
Louis Kemp	MO	D	D	?	A	A	?	?	F	Animal testing: non-medical products; CEDC report; tobacco; increasing TRI; Workplace Principles
Ocean Fresh	BN	C	C	B	A	A	B	B	A	CEDC report
Orleans	BN	C	C	B	A	A	B	B	A	CEDC report
Singleton	CAG	C	C	C	C	?	?	F	C	CEDC report; factory farming; profile
Snow's	BN	C	C	B	A	A	B	B	A	CEDC report
StarKist	HNZ	B	C	A	B	D	C	A	A	CEDC report; CEP Award — Environment
Sweepstakes Jack	HNZ	B	C	A	B	D	C	A	A	CEDC report; CEP Award — Environment
FLOUR										
Action	ADM	D	F	?	D	?	?	D	F	CEDC report; increasing TRI
Amapola	CAG	C	C	C	C	?	?	F	C	CEDC report; factory farming; profile

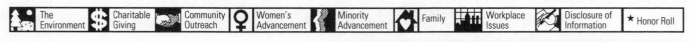

The Environment
Charitable Giving
Community Outreach

Women's Advancement

Minority Advancement

Family

Workplace Issues

Disclosure of Information

★ Honor Roll

For a more detailed explanation, see pages 7–28.

PRODUCT	PARENT COMPANY									EXTRAS
Ardex 550	ADM	D	F	?	D	?	?	D	F	CEDC report; increasing TRI
Bakemaster	ADM	D	F	?	D	?	?	D	F	CEDC report; increasing TRI
Commander	ADM	D	F	?	D	?	?	D	F	CEDC report; increasing TRI
ConAgra America Beauty High Ratio	CAG	C	C	C	C	?	?	F	C	CEDC report; factory farming; profile
ConAgra Stone Ground Whole Wheat Flour	CAG	C	C	C	C	?	?	F	C	CEDC report; factory farming; profile
Cream Loaf	ADM	D	F	?	D	?	?	D	F	CEDC report; increasing TRI
Empress	ADM	D	F	?	D	?	?	D	F	CEDC report; increasing TRI
Freedom	ADM	D	F	?	D	?	?	D	F	CEDC report; increasing TRI
Gigantic	ADM	D	F	?	D	?	?	D	F	CEDC report; increasing TRI
Gold Medal ★	GIS	B	A	A	A	B	B	A	A	CEDC report; CEP Awards — Charity, EEO, Opportunities for the Disabled; profile; Workplace Principles
Great Caesar	ADM	D	F	?	D	?	?	D	F	CEDC report; increasing TRI
Husky	ADM	D	F	?	D	?	?	D	F	CEDC report; increasing TRI
King Midas	CAG	C	C	C	C	?	?	F	C	CEDC report; factory farming; profile
La Pina ★	GIS	B	A	A	A	B	B	A	A	CEDC report; CEP Awards — Charity, EEO, Opportunities for the Disabled; profile; Workplace Principles

PRODUCT	PARENT COMPANY	The Environment	Charitable Giving	Community Outreach	Women's Advancement	Minority Advancement	Family	Workplace Issues	Disclosure of Information	EXTRAS
Larabees Best	ADM	D	F	?	D	?	?	D	F	CEDC report; increasing TRI
Maplesota	ADM	D	F	?	D	?	?	D	F	CEDC report; increasing TRI
Minneapolis Best	ADM	D	F	?	D	?	?	D	F	CEDC report; increasing TRI
Miss Minneapolis	ADM	D	F	?	D	?	?	D	F	CEDC report; increasing TRI
Mother's Best	CAG	C	C	C	C	?	?	F	C	CEDC report; factory farming; profile
Myti Strong	ADM	D	F	?	D	?	?	D	F	CEDC report; increasing TRI
NW Special	ADM	D	F	?	D	?	?	D	F	CEDC report; increasing TRI
Quaker	OAT	B	A	A	B	B	D	?	C	CEDC report; Fair Share
Red Band ★	GIS	B	A	A	A	B	B	A	A	CEDC report; CEP Awards — Charity, EEO, Opportunities for the Disabled; profile; Workplace Principles
Schumacher	OAT	B	A	A	B	B	D	?	C	CEDC report; Fair Share
Softasilk ★	GIS	B	A	A	A	B	B	A	A	CEDC report; CEP Awards — Charity, EEO, Opportunities for the Disabled; profile; Workplace Principles
Southern Supreme	CAG	C	C	C	C	?	?	F	C	CEDC report; factory farming; profile
Spartan	ADM	D	F	?	D	?	?	D	F	CEDC report; increasing TRI

The Environment
Charitable Giving
Community Outreach
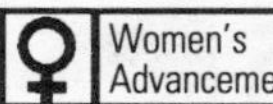
Women's Advancement

Minority Advancement

Family

Workplace Issues

Disclosure of Information
★ Honor Roll

For a more detailed explanation, see pages 7–28.

PRODUCT	PARENT COMPANY		$		♀					EXTRAS
Ster-o-pro	OAT	B	A	A	B	B	D	?	C	CEDC report; Fair Share
Strongheart	ADM	D	F	?	D	?	?	D	F	CEDC report; increasing TRI
Sunfed	ADM	D	F	?	D	?	?	D	F	CEDC report; increasing TRI
Sunloaf	ADM	D	F	?	D	?	?	D	F	CEDC report; increasing TRI
Wondra ★	GIS	B	A	A	A	B	B	A	A	CEDC report; CEP Awards — Charity, EEO, Opportunities for the Disabled; profile; Workplace Principles
FOOTWEAR										
Boks	RBK	B	C	A	B	B	B	B	A	CEDC report
Boot Factory	GCO	?	B	C	F	F	?	?	D	CEDC report
Champion	SRR	B	A	A	A	D	A	B	A	on-site child care
Code West	GCO	?	B	C	F	F	?	?	D	CEDC report
Cole Haan	NKE	C	C	B	A	D	A	B	A	CEDC report; on-site child care
Creepers	NA	A	D	C	A	B	?	B	A	Small company
Doc Martens	NA	A	D	C	A	B	?	B	A	Small company
Dockers	GCO	?	B	C	F	F	?	?	D	CEDC report
Edwards	SRR	B	A	A	A	D	A	B	A	on-site child care
Firstie	SRR	B	A	A	A	D	A	B	A	on-site child care

PRODUCT	PARENT COMPANY	The Environment	Charitable Giving	Community Outreach	Women's Advancement	Minority Advancement	Family	Workplace Issues	Disclosure of Information	EXTRAS
Gapshoes	GPS	B	C	A	A	?	B	A	B	
Grasshoppers	SRR	B	A	A	A	D	A	B	A	on-site child care
Jarmon	GCO	?	B	C	F	F	?	?	D	CEDC report
Johnston & Murphy	GCO	?	B	C	F	F	?	?	D	CEDC report
Keds	SRR	B	A	A	A	D	A	B	A	on-site child care
Kid's University	GCO	?	B	C	F	F	?	?	D	CEDC report
Laredo	GCO	?	B	C	F	F	?	?	D	CEDC report
Mitre	GCO	?	B	C	F	F	?	?	D	CEDC report
Na Na	NA	A	D	C	A	B	?	B	A	Small company
Nautica	GCO	?	B	C	F	F	?	?	D	CEDC report
Nike	NKE	C	C	B	A	D	A	B	A	CEDC report; on-site child care
PayLess Shoe Source	MA	?	B	A	B	C	F	C	B	Workplace Principles
Pro-Keds	SRR	B	A	A	A	D	A	B	A	on-site child care
Reebok	RBK	B	C	A	B	B	B	B	A	CEDC report
Rockport	RBK	B	C	A	B	B	B	B	A	CEDC report

For a more detailed explanation, see pages 7–28.

PRODUCT	PARENT COMPANY									EXTRAS
Sperry Top-Sider	SRR	B	A	A	A	D	A	B	A	on-site child care
Street Hot	GCO	?	B	C	F	F	?	?	D	CEDC report
Stride-Rite	SRR	B	A	A	A	D	A	B	A	on-site child care
Timberland	TBL	B	A	A	B	D	D	B	A	CERES Principles
Toddler University	GCO	?	B	C	F	F	?	?	D	CEDC report
Utility	NA	A	D	C	A	B	?	B	A	Small company
Weebok	RBK	B	C	A	B	B	B	B	A	CEDC report
Zips	SRR	B	A	A	A	D	A	B	A	on-site child care
FRUIT: CANNED, DRIED, FRESH & FROZEN										
Bird's Eye	MO	D	D	?	A	A	?	?	F	Animal testing: non-medical products; CEDC report; tobacco; increasing TRI; Workplace Principles
Dole	DOL	B	A	B	C	A	C	C	B	pesticide sterilization suits
McMillin	PT	C	D	?	B	?	?	?	F	CEDC report; increasing TRI
GAS/OIL										
76	UCL	D	B	?	C	?	?	?	D	CEDC report
Amoco	AN	C	B	A	C	B	A	C	A	Animal testing: medical & non-medical products, significant alternative efforts; CEDC report; CEP Award — Community; increasing TRI; military contracts; on-site day care

PRODUCT	PARENT COMPANY	The Environment	Charitable Giving	Community Outreach	Women's Advancement	Minority Advancement	Family	Workplace Issues	Disclosure of Information	EXTRAS
ARCO	ARC	D	B	B	A	B	B	C	B	Animal testing: non-medical products; CEDC report
BP America	BP	C	C	A	B	B	A	C	A	Animal testing: non-medical products, significant alternative efforts; CEDC report; foreign-based company; increasing TRI; military contracts; Workplace Principles
Chevron	CHV	F	B	B	B	B	A	B	A	Animal testing: non-medical products, significant alternative efforts; CEDC report; Workplace Principles
Exxon	XON	F	D	B	C	C	A	B	A	Animal testing: non-medical products, significant alternative efforts; C3; CEDC report; increasing TRI; military contracts; on-site child care
Marathon	X	D	?	C	B	C	B	D	A	CEDC report
Mobil	MOB	D	C	C	C	C	B	C	A	Animal testing: non-medical products, significant alternative efforts; CEDC report; military contracts; Workplace Principles
Phillips 66	P	D	B	B	D	C	A	D	C	CEDC report; military contracts
Shell	SCWW-S	C	?	A	D	C	C	C	A	Animal testing: non-medical products, significant alternative efforts; CEDC report; foreign-based company; military contracts; pesticide sterilization suits
Sunoco	SUN	C	?	C	C	C	B	B	A	Animal testing: non-medical products, significant alternative efforts; CEDC report; CERES Principles; increasing TRI; military contracts
Texaco	TX	F	B	C	F	D	C	C	C	Animal testing: non-medical products; C3; CEDC report; military contracts; profile

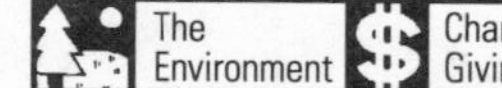
The Environment
Charitable Giving

Community Outreach
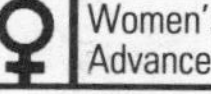
Women's Advancement

Minority Advancement

Family

Workplace Issues

Disclosure of Information

★ Honor Roll

For a more detailed explanation, see pages 7–28.

PRODUCT	PARENT COMPANY									EXTRAS
GUM										
Beechnut	CADBY	B	?	C	C	?	D	B	C	foreign-based company
Big Red	WWY	C	D	?	D	?	B	?	F	Fair Share
Bubble Yum	RN	?	A	C	C	?	?	?	D	Animal testing: non-medical products; CEDC report; tobacco; increasing TRI; Workplace Principles
Bubblicious ★	WLA	B	B	A	B	A	A	B	A	Animal testing: medical products only; increasing TRI; Workplace Principles
Carefree	RN	?	A	C	C	?	?	?	D	Animal testing: non-medical products; CEDC report; tobacco; increasing TRI; Workplace Principles
Chiclets ★	WLA	B	B	A	B	A	A	B	A	Animal testing: medical products only; increasing TRI; Workplace Principles
Cinn*A*Burst ★	WLA	B	B	A	B	A	A	B	A	Animal testing: medical products only; increasing TRI; Workplace Principles
Clorets ★	WLA	B	B	A	B	A	A	B	A	Animal testing: medical products only; increasing TRI; Workplace Principles
Dentyne ★	WLA	B	B	A	B	A	A	B	A	Animal testing: medical products only; increasing TRI; Workplace Principles
Doublemint	WWY	C	D	?	D	?	B	?	F	Fair Share
Extra Sugarfree Gum	WWY	C	D	?	D	?	B	?	F	Fair Share
Freedent	WWY	C	D	?	D	?	B	?	F	Fair Share

PRODUCT	PARENT COMPANY	The Environment	Charitable Giving	Community Outreach	Women's Advancement	Minority Advancement	Family	Workplace Issues	Disclosure of Information	EXTRAS
Freshen-Up ★	WLA	B	B	A	B	A	A	B	A	Animal testing: medical products only; increasing TRI; Workplace Principles
Juicy Fruit	WWY	C	D	?	D	?	B	?	F	Fair Share
Trident ★	WLA	B	B	A	B	A	A	B	A	Animal testing: medical products only; increasing TRI; Workplace Principles
Wrigley's Spearmint	WWY	C	D	?	D	?	B	?	F	Fair Share
JAMS, JELLIES & FRUIT SPREADS										
Bama	BN	C	C	B	A	A	B	B	A	CEDC report
Health Valley	HVAL	A	C	C	A	A	B	A	A	
Home Brands	CAG	C	C	C	C	?	?	F	C	CEDC report; factory farming; profile
Whole Earth	HVAL	A	C	C	A	A	B	A	A	
LAUNDRY SUPPLIES										
All	UN	B	C	C	F	D	C	B	C	Animal testing: non-medical products, significant alternative efforts; foreign-based company; profile
Arm & Hammer	CHD	A	B	A	C	C	A	A	A	Animal testing: non-medical products, significant alternative efforts; CEP Award — Environment
Blu White	DL	C	A	B	B	?	F	B	C	CEDC report

The Environment | Charitable Giving | Community Outreach | Women's Advancement | Minority Advancement | Family | Workplace Issues | Disclosure of Information | ★ Honor Roll

For a more detailed explanation, see pages 7–28.

PRODUCT	PARENT COMPANY									EXTRAS
Bold	PG	C	B	A	B	B	A	B	A	Animal testing: medical and non-medical products, significant alternative efforts; CEDC report; CEP Awards — Animal Welfare, Employer Responsiveness; increasing TRI; on-site day care; Workplace Principles
Borateem	DL	C	A	B	B	?	F	B	C	CEDC report
Borax	DL	C	A	B	B	?	F	B	C	CEDC report
Bounce	PG	C	B	A	B	B	A	B	A	Animal testing: medical and non-medical products, significant alternative efforts; CEDC report; CEP Awards — Animal Welfare, Employer Responsiveness; increasing TRI; on-site day care; Workplace Principles
Cheer	PG	C	B	A	B	B	A	B	A	Animal testing: medical and non-medical products, significant alternative efforts; CEDC report; CEP Awards — Animal Welfare, Employer Responsiveness; increasing TRI; on-site day care; Workplace Principles
Cling Free	SBH	C	D	C	B	B	A	B	C	Animal testing: medical products only, significant alternative efforts; foreign-based company; Workplace Principles
Clorox	CLX	B	B	A	A	A	C	C	A	Animal testing: non-medical products, significant alternative efforts; CEDC report; CEP Award — Community; increasing TRI
Clorox 2	CLX	B	B	A	A	A	C	C	A	Animal testing: non-medical products, significant alternative efforts; CEDC report; CEP Award — Community; increasing TRI
Cold Power ★	CL	B	B	A	A	B	A	A	A	Animal testing: medical & non-medical products, significant alternative efforts; CEDC report; profile
Command	KMB	C	C	B	B	C	B	A	A	Animal testing: non-medical products, significant alternative efforts; CEDC report; tobacco

PRODUCT	PARENT COMPANY	The Environment	Charitable Giving	Community Outreach	Women's Advancement	Minority Advancement	Family	Workplace Issues	Disclosure of Information	EXTRAS
Dash	PG	C	B	A	B	B	A	B	A	Animal testing: medical and non-medical products, significant alternative efforts; CEDC report; CEP Awards — Animal Welfare, Employer Responsiveness; increasing TRI; on-site day care; Workplace Principles
Delicare	SBH	C	D	C	B	B	A	B	C	Animal testing: medical products only, significant alternative efforts; foreign-based company; Workplace Principles
Derma-Safe	AHP	C	F	C	B	B	C	C	A	Animal testing: medical & non-medical products, significant alternative efforts; infant formula
Downy	PG	C	B	A	B	B	A	B	A	Animal testing: medical and non-medical products, significant alternative efforts; CEDC report; CEP Awards — Animal Welfare, Employer Responsiveness; increasing TRI; on-site day care; Workplace Principles
Dreft	PG	C	B	A	B	B	A	B	A	Animal testing: medical and non-medical products, significant alternative efforts; CEDC report; CEP Awards — Animal Welfare, Employer Responsiveness; increasing TRI; on-site day care; Workplace Principles
Dutch	DL	C	A	B	B	?	F	B	C	CEDC report
Dynamo ★	CL	B	B	A	A	B	A	A	A	Animal testing: medical & non-medical products, significant alternative efforts; CEDC report; profile
Era	PG	C	B	A	B	B	A	B	A	Animal testing: medical and non-medical products, significant alternative efforts; CEDC report; CEP Awards — Animal Welfare, Employer Responsiveness; increasing TRI; on-site day care; Workplace Principles

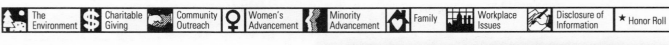

The Environment | Charitable Giving | Community Outreach | Women's Advancement | Minority Advancement | Family | Workplace Issues | Disclosure of Information | ★ Honor Roll

For a more detailed explanation, see pages 7–28.

PRODUCT	PARENT COMPANY									EXTRAS
Fab ★	CL	B	B	A	A	B	A	A	A	Animal testing: medical & non-medical products, significant alternative efforts; CEDC report; profile
Fels	DL	C	A	B	B	?	F	B	C	CEDC report
Final Touch	UN	B	C	C	F	D	C	B	C	Animal testing: non-medical products, significant alternative efforts; foreign-based company; profile
Fresh Start ★	CL	B	B	A	A	B	A	A	A	Animal testing: medical & non-medical products, significant alternative efforts; CEDC report; profile
Gain	PG	C	B	A	B	B	A	B	A	Animal testing: medical and non-medical products, significant alternative efforts; CEDC report; CEP Awards — Animal Welfare, Employer Responsiveness; increasing TRI; on-site day care; Workplace Principles
Ivory Snow	PG	C	B	A	B	B	A	B	A	Animal testing: medical and non-medical products, significant alternative efforts; CEDC report; CEP Awards — Animal Welfare, Employer Responsiveness; increasing TRI; on-site day care; Workplace Principles
Magic	DL	C	A	B	B	?	F	B	C	CEDC report
Niagara	CPC	C	A	B	A	B	C	A	B	Animal testing: non-medical products, significant alternative efforts; CEDC report; increasing TRI
Octagon ★	CL	B	B	A	A	B	A	A	A	Animal testing: medical & non-medical products, significant alternative efforts; CEDC report; profile
Oxydol	PG	C	B	A	B	B	A	B	A	Animal testing: medical and non-medical products, significant alternative efforts; CEDC report; CEP Awards — Animal Welfare, Employer Responsiveness; increasing TRI; on-site day care; Workplace Principles

PRODUCT	PARENT COMPANY	The Environment	Charitable Giving	Community Outreach	Women's Advancement	Minority Advancement	Family	Workplace Issues	Disclosure of Information	EXTRAS
Punch ★	CL	B	B	A	A	B	A	A	A	Animal testing: medical & non-medical products, significant alternative efforts; CEDC report; profile
Purex	DL	C	A	B	B	?	F	B	C	CEDC report
Shout ★	SCJ	A	A	A	B	B	A	A	A	Animal testing: non-medical products, significant alternative efforts; CEP Award — Environment; on-site child care; profile; Workplace Principles
Snuggle	UN	B	C	C	F	D	C	B	C	Animal testing: non-medical products, significant alternative efforts; foreign-based company; profile
Solo	PG	C	B	A	B	B	A	B	A	Animal testing: medical and non-medical products, significant alternative efforts; CEDC report; CEP Awards — Animal Welfare, Employer Responsiveness; increasing TRI; on-site day care; Workplace Principles
Spray'n Starch	DOW	C	C	B	B	A	A	B	A	Animal testing: non-medical products, significant alternative efforts; CEDC report; on-site child care; pesticide sterilization suits
Spray'n Wash	DOW	C	C	B	B	A	A	B	A	Animal testing: non-medical products, significant alternative efforts; CEDC report; on-site child care; pesticide sterilization suits
Sta-Puf	DL	C	A	B	B	?	F	B	C	CEDC report
Stain-Out	CLX	B	B	A	A	A	C	C	A	Animal testing: non-medical products, significant alternative efforts; CEDC report; CEP Award — Community; increasing TRI
Static Guard	ACV	A	?	B	A	D	D	B	B	Animal testing: non-medical products; increasing TRI

The Environment | Charitable Giving | Community Outreach | Women's Advancement | Minority Advancement | Family | Workplace Issues | Disclosure of Information | ★ Honor Roll

For a more detailed explanation, see pages 7–28.

PRODUCT	PARENT COMPANY									EXTRAS
Surf	UN	B	C	C	F	D	C	B	C	Animal testing: non-medical products, significant alternative efforts; foreign-based company; profile
Texize	DOW	C	C	B	B	A	A	B	A	Animal testing: non-medical products, significant alternative efforts; CEDC report; on-site child care; pesticide sterilization suits
Tide	PG	C	B	A	B	B	A	B	A	Animal testing: medical and non-medical products, significant alternative efforts; CEDC report; CEP Awards — Animal Welfare, Employer Responsiveness; increasing TRI; on-site day care; Workplace Principles
Trend	DL	C	A	B	B	?	F	B	C	CEDC report
Vano	DL	C	A	B	B	?	F	B	C	CEDC report
Vivid	DOW	C	C	B	B	A	A	B	A	Animal testing: non-medical products, significant alternative efforts; CEDC report; on-site child care; pesticide sterilization suits
Wisk	UN	B	C	C	F	D	C	B	C	Animal testing: non-medical products, significant alternative efforts; foreign-based company; profile
Yes	DOW	C	C	B	B	A	A	B	A	Animal testing: non-medical products, significant alternative efforts; CEDC report; on-site child care; pesticide sterilization suits
MARGARINE										
Baker's Blend	RN	?	A	C	C	?	?	?	D	Animal testing: non-medical products; CEDC report; tobacco; increasing TRI; Workplace Principles
Better than Butter	RN	?	A	C	C	?	?	?	D	Animal testing: non-medical products; CEDC report; tobacco; increasing TRI; Workplace Principles

PRODUCT	PARENT COMPANY	The Environment	Charitable Giving	Community Outreach	Women's Advancement	Minority Advancement	Family	Workplace Issues	Disclosure of Information	EXTRAS
Blue Bonnet	RN	?	A	C	C	?	?	?	D	Animal testing: non-medical products; CEDC report; tobacco; increasing TRI; Workplace Principles
Canola Choice	RN	?	A	C	C	?	?	?	D	Animal testing: non-medical products; CEDC report; tobacco; increasing TRI; Workplace Principles
Chiffon	MO	D	D	?	A	A	?	?	F	Animal testing: non-medical products; CEDC report; tobacco; increasing TRI; Workplace Principles
Countryside Spread	MO	D	D	?	A	A	?	?	F	Animal testing: non-medical products; CEDC report; tobacco; increasing TRI; Workplace Principles
Good Luck	UN	B	C	C	F	D	C	B	C	Animal testing: non-medical products, significant alternative efforts; foreign-based company; profile
I Can't Believe It's Not Butter	UN	B	C	C	F	D	C	B	C	Animal testing: non-medical products, significant alternative efforts; foreign-based company; profile
Imperial	UN	B	C	C	F	D	C	B	C	Animal testing: non-medical products, significant alternative efforts; foreign-based company; profile
Mazola	CPC	C	A	B	A	B	C	A	B	Animal testing: non-medical products, significant alternative efforts; CEDC report; increasing TRI
Move Over Butter	RN	?	A	C	C	?	?	?	D	Animal testing: non-medical products; CEDC report; tobacco; increasing TRI; Workplace Principles
Parkay	MO	D	D	?	A	A	?	?	F	Animal testing: non-medical products; CEDC report; tobacco; increasing TRI; Workplace Principles

The Environment | Charitable Giving | Community Outreach | Women's Advancement | Minority Advancement | Family | Workplace Issues | Disclosure of Information | ★ Honor Roll

For a more detailed explanation, see pages 7–28.

PRODUCT	PARENT COMPANY									EXTRAS
Promise	UN	B	C	C	F	D	C	B	C	Animal testing: non-medical products, significant alternative efforts; foreign-based company; profile
Shedd's Spread	UN	B	C	C	F	D	C	B	C	Animal testing: non-medical products, significant alternative efforts; foreign-based company; profile
Sun Valley	UN	B	C	C	F	D	C	B	C	Animal testing: non-medical products, significant alternative efforts; foreign-based company; profile
Touch Of Butter	MO	D	D	?	A	A	?	?	F	Animal testing: non-medical products; CEDC report; tobacco; increasing TRI; Workplace Principles
MEAT: CANNED & REFRIGERATED										
Armour	CAG	C	C	C	C	?	?	F	C	CEDC report; factory farming; profile
Armour Star	DL	C	A	B	B	?	F	B	C	CEDC report
Ball Park	SLE	C	B	A	B	B	B	B	A	CEP Award — Charity; on-site child care; tobacco
Blue Ribbon Beef	CAG	C	C	C	C	?	?	F	C	CEDC report; factory farming; profile
Breakfast Strips	CAG	C	C	C	C	?	?	F	C	CEDC report; factory farming; profile
Brookfield	CAG	C	C	C	C	?	?	F	C	CEDC report; factory farming; profile
Brown 'n' Serve	CAG	C	C	C	C	?	?	F	C	CEDC report; factory farming; profile
Bryan	SLE	C	B	A	B	B	B	B	A	CEP Award — Charity; on-site child care; tobacco
Bun Length	MO	D	D	?	A	A	?	?	F	Animal testing: non-medical products; CEDC report; tobacco; increasing TRI; Workplace Principles

PRODUCT	PARENT COMPANY	The Environment	Charitable Giving	Community Outreach	Women's Advancement	Minority Advancement	Family	Workplace Issues	Disclosure of Information	EXTRAS
Cook's	CAG	C	C	C	C	?	?	F	C	CEDC report; factory farming; profile
Country Skillet	CAG	C	C	C	C	?	?	F	C	CEDC report; factory farming; profile
Decker	CAG	C	C	C	C	?	?	F	C	CEDC report; factory farming; profile
Eckrich	CAG	C	C	C	C	?	?	F	C	CEDC report; factory farming; profile
Gold Leaf	TYSNA	C	?	D	A	B	?	D	D	factory farming; profile
Great Grillin's	OAT	B	A	A	B	B	D	?	C	CEDC report; Fair Share
Healthy Balance	CAG	C	C	C	C	?	?	F	C	CEDC report; factory farming; profile
Healthy Choice	CAG	C	C	C	C	?	?	F	C	CEDC report; factory farming; profile
Hillshire Farm	SLE	C	B	A	B	B	B	B	A	CEP Award — Charity; on-site child care; tobacco
Holly Farms	TYSNA	C	?	D	A	B	?	D	D	factory farming; profile
Hygrade	SLE	C	B	A	B	B	B	B	A	CEP Award — Charity; on-site child care; tobacco
Jimmy Dean	SLE	C	B	A	B	B	B	B	A	CEP Award — Charity; on-site child care; tobacco
Kahn's	SLE	C	B	A	B	B	B	B	A	CEP Award — Charity; on-site child care; tobacco
Lean'N Crisp	ADM	D	F	?	D	?	?	D	F	CEDC report; increasing TRI
Libby's	NEST	B	?	B	B	B	A	B	B	Animal testing: non-medical products, significant alternative efforts; foreign-based company; infant formula

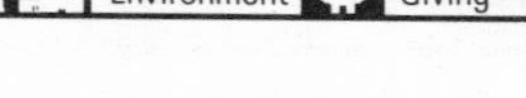

The Environment | Charitable Giving | Community Outreach | Women's Advancement | Minority Advancement | Family | Workplace Issues | Disclosure of Information | ★ Honor Roll

For a more detailed explanation, see pages 7–28.

PRODUCT	PARENT COMPANY									EXTRAS
Longmont	CAG	C	C	C	C	?	?	F	C	CEDC report; factory farming; profile
Louis Rich	MO	D	D	?	A	A	?	?	F	Animal testing: non-medical products; CEDC report; tobacco; increasing TRI; Workplace Principles
Monfort	CAG	C	C	C	C	?	?	F	C	CEDC report; factory farming; profile
None Such	BN	C	C	B	A	A	B	B	A	CEDC report
Oscar Mayer	MO	D	D	?	A	A	?	?	F	Animal testing: non-medical products; CEDC report; tobacco; increasing TRI; Workplace Principles
Sizzlean	CAG	C	C	C	C	?	?	F	C	CEDC report; factory farming; profile
Surrey Farm	CAG	C	C	C	C	?	?	F	C	CEDC report; factory farming; profile
Swift Premium	CAG	C	C	C	C	?	?	F	C	CEDC report; factory farming; profile
Turkey Selects	CAG	C	C	C	C	?	?	F	C	CEDC report; factory farming; profile
MILK: CANNED & POWDERED										
Borden	BN	C	C	B	A	A	B	B	A	CEDC report
Carousel	MO	D	D	?	A	A	?	?	F	Animal testing: non-medical products; CEDC report; tobacco; increasing TRI; Workplace Principles
Coffee-mate	NEST	B	?	B	B	B	A	B	B	Animal testing: non-medical products, significant alternative efforts; foreign-based company; infant formula
Coffeetwin	MO	D	D	?	A	A	?	?	F	Animal testing: non-medical products; CEDC report; tobacco; increasing TRI; Workplace Principles
Cremora	BN	C	C	B	A	A	B	B	A	CEDC report

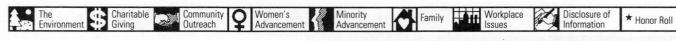

PRODUCT	PARENT COMPANY	The Environment	Charitable Giving	Community Outreach	Women's Advancement	Minority Advancement	Family	Workplace Issues	Disclosure of Information	EXTRAS
Dairymate	PT	C	D	?	B	?	?	?	F	CEDC report; increasing TRI
Dime Brand	BN	C	C	B	A	A	B	B	A	CEDC report
Eagle Brand	BN	C	C	B	A	A	B	B	A	CEDC report
Fabulite	OAT	B	A	A	B	B	D	?	C	CEDC report; Fair Share
Golden Key	PT	C	D	?	B	?	?	?	F	CEDC report; increasing TRI
Hershey's Chocolate Milk	HSY	B	B	A	B	C	A	A	A	CEDC report; increasing TRI; on-site child care
Ice Milk	HNZ	B	C	A	B	D	C	A	A	CEDC report; CEP Award — Environment
Klim	BN	C	C	B	A	A	B	B	A	CEDC report
Magnolia Brand	BN	C	C	B	A	A	B	B	A	CEDC report
Meadow Gold	BN	C	C	B	A	A	B	B	A	CEDC report
Mil-Lait	CAG	C	C	C	C	?	?	F	C	CEDC report; factory farming; profile
N-Rich	CAG	C	C	C	C	?	?	F	C	CEDC report; factory farming; profile
Party Time	MO	D	D	?	A	A	?	?	F	Animal testing: non-medical products; CEDC report; tobacco; increasing TRI; Workplace Principles
Pet	PT	C	D	?	B	?	?	?	F	CEDC report; increasing TRI

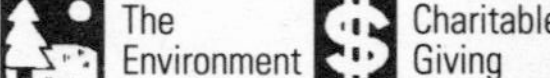 The Environment  Charitable Giving  Community Outreach  Women's Advancement  Minority Advancement 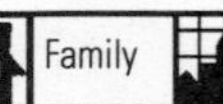 Family  Workplace Issues  Disclosure of Information  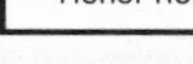 ★ Honor Roll

For a more detailed explanation, see pages 7–28.

PRODUCT	PARENT COMPANY									EXTRAS
Sanalac	CAG	C	C	C	C	?	?	F	C	CEDC report; factory farming; profile
Sego	PT	C	D	?	B	?	?	?	F	CEDC report; increasing TRI
Star Brand	BN	C	C	B	A	A	B	B	A	CEDC report
OFFICE/SCHOOL SUPPLIES										
Block Busters	MEA	C	A	B	C	C	D	D	C	CEDC report; Workplace Principles
Cambridge	MEA	C	A	B	C	C	D	D	C	CEDC report; Workplace Principles
Chieftain	KMB	C	C	B	B	C	B	A	A	Animal testing: non-medical products, significant alternative efforts; CEDC report; tobacco
Classic	KMB	C	C	B	B	C	B	A	A	Animal testing: non-medical products, significant alternative efforts; CEDC report; tobacco
Classifiler, The	MEA	C	A	B	C	C	D	D	C	CEDC report; Workplace Principles
Class Mate	MEA	C	A	B	C	C	D	D	C	CEDC report; Workplace Principles
Clipmate	MEA	C	A	B	C	C	D	D	C	CEDC report; Workplace Principles
Data Center	MEA	C	A	B	C	C	D	D	C	CEDC report; Workplace Principles
Data Files	MEA	C	A	B	C	C	D	D	C	CEDC report; Workplace Principles
Design-a-Cover	MEA	C	A	B	C	C	D	D	C	CEDC report; Workplace Principles
Elmer's	BN	C	C	B	A	A	B	B	A	CEDC report
Envelok	MEA	C	A	B	C	C	D	D	C	CEDC report; Workplace Principles

PRODUCT	PARENT COMPANY	The Environment	Charitable Giving	Community Outreach	Women's Advancement	Minority Advancement	Family	Workplace Issues	Disclosure of Information	EXTRAS
Five Star	MEA	C	A	B	C	C	D	D	C	CEDC report; Workplace Principles
Flapper	MEA	C	A	B	C	C	D	D	C	CEDC report; Workplace Principles
Flex 3	MEA	C	A	B	C	C	D	D	C	CEDC report; Workplace Principles
Gillette	G	C	C	B	D	D	B	B	A	Animal testing: medical & non-medical products, significant alternative efforts
Glare Care	MEA	C	A	B	C	C	D	D	C	CEDC report; Workplace Principles
Gripper Edge	MEA	C	A	B	C	C	D	D	C	CEDC report; Workplace Principles
Hytone	MEA	C	A	B	C	C	D	D	C	CEDC report; Workplace Principles
In Line	MEA	C	A	B	C	C	D	D	C	CEDC report; Workplace Principles
Kimberly	KMB	C	C	B	B	C	B	A	A	Animal testing: non-medical products, significant alternative efforts; CEDC report; tobacco
Krazy Glue	BN	C	C	B	A	A	B	B	A	CEDC report
Kwik Clip	MEA	C	A	B	C	C	D	D	C	CEDC report; Workplace Principles
Mead	MEA	C	A	B	C	C	D	D	C	CEDC report; Workplace Principles
Moistrite	MEA	C	A	B	C	C	D	D	C	CEDC report; Workplace Principles
Old Council Tree	KMB	C	C	B	B	C	B	A	A	Animal testing: non-medical products, significant alternative efforts; CEDC report; tobacco

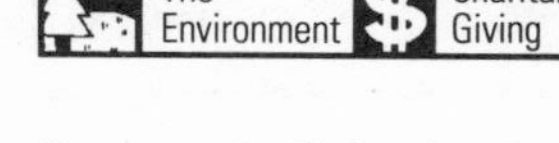

The Environment | Charitable Giving | Community Outreach | Women's Advancement | Minority Advancement | Family | Workplace Issues | Disclosure of Information | ★ Honor Roll

For a more detailed explanation, see pages 7–28.

PRODUCT	PARENT COMPANY									EXTRAS
Organizer	MEA	C	A	B	C	C	D	D	C	CEDC report; Workplace Principles
Pinchless	MEA	C	A	B	C	C	D	D	C	CEDC report; Workplace Principles
Post-It	MMM	C	B	A	C	B	A	B	A	Animal testing: medical & non-medical products, significant alternative efforts; CEDC report; CEP Award — Environment
Pressit Sealit	MEA	C	A	B	C	C	D	D	C	CEDC report; Workplace Principles
Protector	MEA	C	A	B	C	C	D	D	C	CEDC report; Workplace Principles
Regency	MEA	C	A	B	C	C	D	D	C	CEDC report; Workplace Principles
Runa/Tab	MEA	C	A	B	C	C	D	D	C	CEDC report; Workplace Principles
Scotch	MMM	C	B	A	C	B	A	B	A	Animal testing: medical & non-medical products, significant alternative efforts; CEDC report; CEP Award — Environment
Scribe	KMB	C	C	B	B	C	B	A	A	Animal testing: non-medical products, significant alternative efforts; CEDC report; tobacco
Slide Ring	MEA	C	A	B	C	C	D	D	C	CEDC report; Workplace Principles
Smart Shopper	MEA	C	A	B	C	C	D	D	C	CEDC report; Workplace Principles
Spell-Write	MEA	C	A	B	C	C	D	D	C	CEDC report; Workplace Principles
Square Deal	MEA	C	A	B	C	C	D	D	C	CEDC report; Workplace Principles
Super Shades	MEA	C	A	B	C	C	D	D	C	CEDC report; Workplace Principles
Texoprint	KMB	C	C	B	B	C	B	A	A	Animal testing: non-medical products, significant alternative efforts; CEDC report; tobacco

PRODUCT	PARENT COMPANY	The Environment	Charitable Giving	Community Outreach	Women's Advancement	Minority Advancement	Family	Workplace Issues	Disclosure of Information	EXTRAS
OVER-THE-COUNTER REMEDIES										
4-Way Nasal Spray	BMY	B	C	B	B	B	B	B	A	Animal testing: medical & non-medical products, significant alternative efforts; infant formula; Workplace Principles
Advil	AHP	C	F	C	B	B	C	C	A	Animal testing: medical & non-medical products, significant alternative efforts; infant formula
Afrin	SGP	B	C	A	B	A	A	B	A	Animal testing: medical products only, significant alternative efforts; on-site child care; Workplace Principles
Anacin	AHP	C	F	C	B	B	C	C	A	Animal testing: medical & non-medical products, significant alternative efforts; infant formula
Anbesol	AHP	C	F	C	B	B	C	C	A	Animal testing: medical & non-medical products, significant alternative efforts; infant formula
Anusol ★	WLA	B	B	A	B	A	A	B	A	Animal testing: medical products only; increasing TRI; Workplace Principles
Aroma Vera	AV	A	F	C	B	B	D	C	C	Small company
Attends	PG	C	B	A	B	B	A	B	A	Animal testing: medical and non-medical products, significant alternative efforts; CEDC report; CEP Awards — Animal Welfare, Employer Responsiveness; increasing TRI; on-site day care; Workplace Principles
Backache	BMY	B	C	B	B	B	B	B	A	Animal testing: medical & non-medical products, significant alternative efforts; infant formula; Workplace Principles

 The Environment, Charitable Giving, Community Outreach 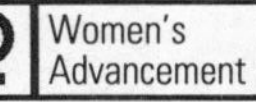 Women's Advancement  Minority Advancement  Family   Workplace Issues   Disclosure of Information ★ Honor Roll

For a more detailed explanation, see pages 7–28.

PRODUCT	PARENT COMPANY									EXTRAS
Bayer	EK	C	B	B	B	B	A	B	B	Animal testing: medical and non-medical products, significant alternative efforts; CEDC report; CEP Award — EEO
Ben-Gay	PFE	C	B	A	B	C	A	B	A	Animal testing: medical products only, significant alternative efforts; heart valve suits; Workplace Principles
Benadryl ★	WLA	B	B	A	B	A	A	B	A	Animal testing: medical products only; increasing TRI; Workplace Principles
Benylin ★	WLA	B	B	A	B	A	A	B	A	Animal testing: medical products only; increasing TRI; Workplace Principles
Bonine	PFE	C	B	A	B	C	A	B	A	Animal testing: medical products only, significant alternative efforts; heart valve suits; Workplace Principles
Bufferin	BMY	B	C	B	B	B	B	B	A	Animal testing: medical & non-medical products, significant alternative efforts; infant formula; Workplace Principles
Caladryl ★	WLA	B	B	A	B	A	A	B	A	Animal testing: medical products only; increasing TRI; Workplace Principles
Cepastat	DOW	C	C	B	B	A	A	B	A	Animal testing: non-medical products, significant alternative efforts; CEDC report; on-site child care; pesticide sterilization suits
Chlor-Trimeton	SGP	B	C	A	B	A	A	B	A	Animal testing: medical products only, significant alternative efforts; on-site child care; Workplace Principles
Citrucel	DOW	C	C	B	B	A	A	B	A	Animal testing: non-medical products, significant alternative efforts; CEDC report; on-site child care; pesticide sterilization suits
Colace	BMY	B	C	B	B	B	B	B	A	Animal testing: medical & non-medical products, significant alternative efforts; infant formula; Workplace Principles

PRODUCT	PARENT COMPANY	The Environment	Charitable Giving	Community Outreach	Women's Advancement	Minority Advancement	Family	Workplace Issues	Disclosure of Information	EXTRAS
Comtrex	BMY	B	C	B	B	B	B	B	A	Animal testing: medical & non-medical products, significant alternative efforts; infant formula; Workplace Principles
Congestac	SBH	C	D	C	B	B	A	B	C	Animal testing: medical products only, significant alternative efforts; foreign-based company; Workplace Principles
Coricidin	SGP	B	C	A	B	A	A	B	A	Animal testing: medical products only, significant alternative efforts; on-site child care; Workplace Principles
Correctol	SGP	B	C	A	B	A	A	B	A	Animal testing: medical products only, significant alternative efforts; on-site child care; Workplace Principles
De Witt's	CHD	A	B	A	C	C	A	A	A	Animal testing: non-medical products, significant alternative efforts; CEP Award — Environment
Denol	CHD	A	B	A	C	C	A	A	A	Animal testing: non-medical products, significant alternative efforts; CEP Award — Environment
DI-GEL	SGP	B	C	A	B	A	A	B	A	Animal testing: medical products only, significant alternative efforts; on-site child care; Workplace Principles
Dimetapp	AHP	C	F	C	B	B	C	C	A	Animal testing: medical & non-medical products, significant alternative efforts; infant formula
Dristan	AHP	C	F	C	B	B	C	C	A	Animal testing: medical & non-medical products, significant alternative efforts; infant formula
Drixoral	SGP	B	C	A	B	A	A	B	A	Animal testing: medical products only, significant alternative efforts; on-site child care; Workplace Principles

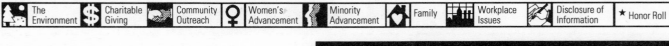

The Environment | Charitable Giving | Community Outreach | Women's Advancement | Minority Advancement | Family | Workplace Issues | Disclosure of Information | ★ Honor Roll

For a more detailed explanation, see pages 7–28.

PRODUCT	PARENT COMPANY									EXTRAS
Duration	SGP	B	C	A	B	A	A	B	A	Animal testing: medical products only, significant alternative efforts; on-site child care; Workplace Principles
Excedrin	BMY	B	C	B	B	B	B	B	A	Animal testing: medical & non-medical products, significant alternative efforts; infant formula; Workplace Principles
Feen-A-Mint	SGP	B	C	A	B	A	A	B	A	Animal testing: medical products only, significant alternative efforts; on-site child care; Workplace Principles
Formula 44	PG	C	B	A	B	B	A	B	A	Animal testing: medical and non-medical products, significant alternative efforts; CEDC report; CEP Awards — Animal Welfare, Employer Responsiveness; increasing TRI; on-site day care; Workplace Principles
Gyne-Lotrimin	SGP	B	C	A	B	A	A	B	A	Animal testing: medical products only, significant alternative efforts; on-site child care; Workplace Principles
Haley's M/O laxative	EK	C	B	B	B	B	A	B	B	Animal testing: medical and non-medical products, significant alternative efforts; CEDC report; CEP Award — EEO
Halls ★	WLA	B	B	A	B	A	A	B	A	Animal testing: medical products only; increasing TRI; Workplace Principles
Heet	AHP	C	F	C	B	B	C	C	A	Animal testing: medical & non-medical products, significant alternative efforts; infant formula
Helps	HSY	B	B	A	B	C	A	A	A	CEDC report; increasing TRI; on-site child care
Hold	SBH	C	D	C	B	B	A	B	C	Animal testing: medical products only, significant alternative efforts; foreign-based company; Workplace Principles
Imodium A-D ★	JNJ	B	A	A	A	A	A	A	A	Animal testing: medical products only, significant alternative efforts; CEP Award — Disclosure; on-site child care; profile; Workplace Principles

PRODUCT	PARENT COMPANY	The Environment	Charitable Giving	Community Outreach	Women's Advancement	Minority Advancement	Family	Workplace Issues	Disclosure of Information	EXTRAS
Liquiprin	SBH	C	D	C	B	B	A	B	C	Animal testing: medical products only, significant alternative efforts; foreign-based company; Workplace Principles
Luden's	HSY	B	B	A	B	C	A	A	A	CEDC report; increasing TRI; on-site child care
Medipren ★	JNJ	B	A	A	A	A	A	A	A	Animal testing: medical products only, significant alternative efforts; CEP Award — Disclosure; on-site child care; profile; Workplace Principles
Metamucil	PG	C	B	A	B	B	A	B	A	Animal testing: medical and non-medical products, significant alternative efforts; CEDC report; CEP Awards — Animal Welfare, Employer Responsiveness; increasing TRI; on-site day care; Workplace Principles
Midol	EK	C	B	B	B	B	A	B	B	Animal testing: medical and non-medical products, significant alternative efforts; CEDC report; CEP Award — EEO
Mineral Ice	BMY	B	C	B	B	B	B	B	A	Animal testing: medical & non-medical products, significant alternative efforts; infant formula; Workplace Principles
Momentum	AHP	C	F	C	B	B	C	C	A	Animal testing: medical & non-medical products, significant alternative efforts; infant formula
Mylanta ★	JNJ	B	A	A	A	A	A	A	A	Animal testing: medical products only, significant alternative efforts; CEP Award — Disclosure; on-site child care; profile; Workplace Principles
Nature's Remedy	SBH	C	D	C	B	B	A	B	C	Animal testing: medical products only, significant alternative efforts; foreign-based company; Workplace Principles

The Environment | Charitable Giving | Community Outreach |  Women's Advancement | Minority Advancement | Family | Workplace Issues | Disclosure of Information | ★ Honor Roll

For a more detailed explanation, see pages 7–28.

PRODUCT	PARENT COMPANY									EXTRAS
Neo-synephrine	EK	C	B	B	B	B	A	B	B	Animal testing: medical and non-medical products, significant alternative efforts; CEDC report; CEP Award — EEO
N'ice	SBH	C	D	C	B	B	A	B	C	Animal testing: medical products only, significant alternative efforts; foreign-based company; Workplace Principles
Novahistine	DOW	C	C	B	B	A	A	B	A	Animal testing: non-medical products, significant alternative efforts; CEDC report; on-site child care; pesticide sterilization suits
Nuprin	BMY	B	C	B	B	B	B	B	A	Animal testing: medical & non-medical products, significant alternative efforts; infant formula; Workplace Principles
Nyquil	PG	C	B	A	B	B	A	B	A	Animal testing: medical and non-medical products, significant alternative efforts; CEDC report; CEP Awards — Animal Welfare, Employer Responsiveness; increasing TRI; on-site day care; Workplace Principles
Ocuclear	SGP	B	C	A	B	A	A	B	A	Animal testing: medical products only, significant alternative efforts; on-site child care; Workplace Principles
Panadol	EK	C	B	B	B	B	A	B	B	Animal testing: medical and non-medical products, significant alternative efforts; CEDC report; CEP Award — EEO
Pepto-Bismol	PG	C	B	A	B	B	A	B	A	Animal testing: medical and non-medical products, significant alternative efforts; CEDC report; CEP Awards — Animal Welfare, Employer Responsiveness; increasing TRI; on-site day care; Workplace Principles
Percogesic	PG	C	B	A	B	B	A	B	A	Animal testing: medical and non-medical products, significant alternative efforts; CEDC report; CEP Awards — Animal Welfare, Employer Responsiveness; increasing TRI; on-site day care; Workplace Principles

PRODUCT	PARENT COMPANY	The Environment	Charitable Giving	Community Outreach	Women's Advancement	Minority Advancement	Family	Workplace Issues	Disclosure of Information	EXTRAS
Peri-Colace	BMY	B	C	B	B	B	B	B	A	Animal testing: medical & non-medical products, significant alternative efforts; infant formula; Workplace Principles
Phillips Milk of Magnesia	EK	C	B	B	B	B	A	B	B	Animal testing: medical and non-medical products, significant alternative efforts; CEDC report; CEP Award — EEO
Preparation H	AHP	C	F	C	B	B	C	C	A	Animal testing: medical & non-medical products, significant alternative efforts; infant formula
Primatene	AHP	C	F	C	B	B	C	C	A	Animal testing: medical & non-medical products, significant alternative efforts; infant formula
Rid	PFE	C	B	A	B	C	A	B	A	Animal testing: medical products only, significant alternative efforts; heart valve suits; Workplace Principles
Robitussin	AHP	C	F	C	B	B	C	C	A	Animal testing: medical & non-medical products, significant alternative efforts; infant formula
Rolaids ★	WLA	B	B	A	B	A	A	B	A	Animal testing: medical products only; increasing TRI; Workplace Principles
St. Joseph's	SGP	B	C	A	B	A	A	B	A	Animal testing: medical products only, significant alternative efforts; on-site child care; Workplace Principles
Serenity ★	JNJ	B	A	A	A	A	A	A	A	Animal testing: medical products only, significant alternative efforts; CEP Award — Disclosure; on-site child care; profile; Workplace Principles
Sine-Aid ★	JNJ	B	A	A	A	A	A	A	A	Animal testing: medical products only, significant alternative efforts; CEP Award — Disclosure; on-site child care; profile; Workplace Principles

The Environment | Charitable Giving | Community Outreach | Women's Advancement | Minority Advancement | Family | Workplace Issues | Disclosure of Information | ★ Honor Roll

For a more detailed explanation, see pages 7–28.

PRODUCT	PARENT COMPANY									EXTRAS
Sinutab ★	WLA	B	B	A	B	A	A	B	A	Animal testing: medical products only; increasing TRI; Workplace Principles
Sportsgel	PFE	C	B	A	B	C	A	B	A	Animal testing: medical products only, significant alternative efforts; heart valve suits; Workplace Principles
Sucrets	SBH	C	D	C	B	B	A	B	C	Animal testing: medical products only, significant alternative efforts; foreign-based company; Workplace Principles
Trendar	AHP	C	F	C	B	B	C	C	A	Animal testing: medical & non-medical products, significant alternative efforts; infant formula
Tucks ★	WLA	B	B	A	B	A	A	B	A	Animal testing: medical products only; increasing TRI; Workplace Principles
Tums	SBH	C	D	C	B	B	A	B	C	Animal testing: medical products only, significant alternative efforts; foreign-based company; Workplace Principles
Tylenol ★	JNJ	B	A	A	A	A	A	A	A	Animal testing: medical products only, significant alternative efforts; CEP Award — Disclosure; on-site child care; profile; Workplace Principles
Unisom Dual Relief	PFE	C	B	A	B	C	A	B	A	Animal testing: medical products only, significant alternative efforts; heart valve suits; Workplace Principles
Vanquish	EK	C	B	B	B	B	A	B	B	Animal testing: medical and non-medical products, significant alternative efforts; CEDC report; CEP Award — EEO
Vicks	PG	C	B	A	B	B	A	B	A	Animal testing: medical and non-medical products, significant alternative efforts; CEDC report; CEP Awards — Animal Welfare, Employer Responsiveness; increasing TRI; on-site day care; Workplace Principles

PRODUCT	PARENT COMPANY	The Environment	Charitable Giving	Community Outreach	Women's Advancement	Minority Advancement	Family	Workplace Issues	Disclosure of Information	EXTRAS
Visine	PFE	C	B	A	B	C	A	B	A	Animal testing: medical products only, significant alternative efforts; heart valve suits; Workplace Principles
Vital Eyes	SBH	C	D	C	B	B	A	B	C	Animal testing: medical products only, significant alternative efforts; foreign-based company; Workplace Principles
PAPER & PLASTIC PRODUCTS										
Avert	KMB	C	C	B	B	C	B	A	A	Animal testing: non-medical products, significant alternative efforts; CEDC report; tobacco
Baggies	MOB	D	C	C	C	C	B	C	A	Animal testing: non-medical products, significant alternative efforts; CEDC report; military contracts; Workplace Principles
Banner	PG	C	B	A	B	B	A	B	A	Animal testing: medical and non-medical products, significant alternative efforts; CEDC report; CEP Awards — Animal Welfare, Employer Responsiveness; increasing TRI; on-site day care; Workplace Principles
Basic	KMB	C	C	B	B	C	B	A	A	Animal testing: non-medical products, significant alternative efforts; CEDC report; tobacco
Bounty	PG	C	B	A	B	B	A	B	A	Animal testing: medical and non-medical products, significant alternative efforts; CEDC report; CEP Awards — Animal Welfare, Employer Responsiveness; increasing TRI; on-site day care; Workplace Principles
Boutique	KMB	C	C	B	B	C	B	A	A	Animal testing: non-medical products, significant alternative efforts; CEDC report; tobacco

The Environment | Charitable Giving | Community Outreach | Women's Advancement |  Minority Advancement |  Family |  Workplace Issues |  Disclosure of Information | ★ Honor Roll

For a more detailed explanation, see pages 7–28.

PRODUCT	PARENT COMPANY		$							EXTRAS
Bundle Pack	KMB	C	C	B	B	C	B	A	A	Animal testing: non-medical products, significant alternative efforts; CEDC report; tobacco
Casuals	KMB	C	C	B	B	C	B	A	A	Animal testing: non-medical products, significant alternative efforts; CEDC report; tobacco
Charmin	PG	C	B	A	B	B	A	B	A	Animal testing: medical and non-medical products, significant alternative efforts; CEDC report; CEP Awards — Animal Welfare, Employer Responsiveness; increasing TRI; on-site day care; Workplace Principles
Chubs	EK	C	B	B	B	B	A	B	B	Animal testing: medical and non-medical products, significant alternative efforts; CEDC report; CEP Award — EEO
Cinch Sak	MOB	D	C	C	C	C	B	C	A	Animal testing: non-medical products, significant alternative efforts; CEDC report; military contracts; Workplace Principles
Clout	KMB	C	C	B	B	C	B	A	A	Animal testing: non-medical products, significant alternative efforts; CEDC report; tobacco
Dawn	KMB	C	C	B	B	C	B	A	A	Animal testing: non-medical products, significant alternative efforts; CEDC report; tobacco
Delsey	KMB	C	C	B	B	C	B	A	A	Animal testing: non-medical products, significant alternative efforts; CEDC report; tobacco
Depend	KMB	C	C	B	B	C	B	A	A	Animal testing: non-medical products, significant alternative efforts; CEDC report; tobacco
Glad	FBR	C	A	C	F	D	D	B	B	Animal testing: non-medical products, significant alternative efforts; profile

PRODUCT	PARENT COMPANY	The Environment	Charitable Giving	Community Outreach	Women's Advancement	Minority Advancement	Family	Workplace Issues	Disclosure of Information	EXTRAS
Handi-Wrap	DOW	C	C	B	B	A	A	B	A	Animal testing: non-medical products, significant alternative efforts; CEDC report; on-site child care; pesticide sterilization suits
Hefty	MOB	D	C	C	C	C	B	C	A	Animal testing: non-medical products, significant alternative efforts; CEDC report; military contracts; Workplace Principles
Hi-Count	KMB	C	C	B	B	C	B	A	A	Animal testing: non-medical products, significant alternative efforts; CEDC report; tobacco
Hi-Dri	KMB	C	C	B	B	C	B	A	A	Animal testing: non-medical products, significant alternative efforts; CEDC report; tobacco
Himolene	FBR	C	A	C	F	D	D	B	B	Animal testing: non-medical products, significant alternative efforts; profile
Holiday	MOB	D	C	C	C	C	B	C	A	Animal testing: non-medical products, significant alternative efforts; CEDC report; military contracts; Workplace Principles
Kaydry	KMB	C	C	B	B	C	B	A	A	Animal testing: non-medical products, significant alternative efforts; CEDC report; tobacco
Kleenex	KMB	C	C	B	B	C	B	A	A	Animal testing: non-medical products, significant alternative efforts; CEDC report; tobacco
Kordite	MOB	D	C	C	C	C	B	C	A	Animal testing: non-medical products, significant alternative efforts; CEDC report; military contracts; Workplace Principles
Little Travelers	KMB	C	C	B	B	C	B	A	A	Animal testing: non-medical products, significant alternative efforts; CEDC report; tobacco

The Environment
Charitable Giving

Community Outreach
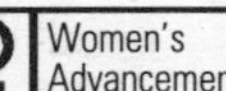
Women's Advancement

Minority Advancement

Family

Workplace Issues

Disclosure of Information
★ Honor Roll

For a more detailed explanation, see pages 7–28.

PRODUCT	PARENT COMPANY									EXTRAS
Man Size	KMB	C	C	B	B	C	B	A	A	Animal testing: non-medical products, significant alternative efforts; CEDC report; tobacco
Mead	MEA	C	A	B	C	C	D	D	C	CEDC report; Workplace Principles
Montag	MEA	C	A	B	C	C	D	D	C	CEDC report; Workplace Principles
Popee	KMB	C	C	B	B	C	B	A	A	Animal testing: non-medical products, significant alternative efforts; CEDC report; tobacco
Post-It	MMM	C	B	A	C	B	A	B	A	Animal testing: medical & non-medical products, significant alternative efforts; CEDC report; CEP Award — Environment
Puffs	PG	C	B	A	B	B	A	B	A	Animal testing: medical and non-medical products, significant alternative efforts; CEDC report; CEP Awards — Animal Welfare, Employer Responsiveness; increasing TRI; on-site day care; Workplace Principles
Roar	KMB	C	C	B	B	C	B	A	A	Animal testing: non-medical products, significant alternative efforts; CEDC report; tobacco
Saran Wrap	DOW	C	C	B	B	A	A	B	A	Animal testing: non-medical products, significant alternative efforts; CEDC report; on-site child care; pesticide sterilization suits
Softique	KMB	C	C	B	B	C	B	A	A	Animal testing: non-medical products, significant alternative efforts; CEDC report; tobacco
Steel-Sak	MOB	D	C	C	C	C	B	C	A	Animal testing: non-medical products, significant alternative efforts; CEDC report; military contracts; Workplace Principles
Summit	PG	C	B	A	B	B	A	B	A	Animal testing: medical and non-medical products, significant alternative efforts; CEDC report; CEP Awards — Animal Welfare, Employer Responsiveness; increasing TRI; on-site day care; Workplace Principles

PRODUCT	PARENT COMPANY	The Environment	Charitable Giving	Community Outreach	Women's Advancement	Minority Advancement	Family	Workplace Issues	Disclosure of Information	EXTRAS
Super Weight	MOB	D	C	C	C	C	B	C	A	Animal testing: non-medical products, significant alternative efforts; CEDC report; military contracts; Workplace Principles
Surpass	KMB	C	C	B	B	C	B	A	A	Animal testing: non-medical products, significant alternative efforts; CEDC report; tobacco
Teri	KMB	C	C	B	B	C	B	A	A	Animal testing: non-medical products, significant alternative efforts; CEDC report; tobacco
Thick & Thirsty	KMB	C	C	B	B	C	B	A	A	Animal testing: non-medical products, significant alternative efforts; CEDC report; tobacco
Trapper	MEA	C	A	B	C	C	D	D	C	CEDC report; Workplace Principles
Veldown	KMB	C	C	B	B	C	B	A	A	Animal testing: non-medical products, significant alternative efforts; CEDC report; tobacco
Versatowel	KMB	C	C	B	B	C	B	A	A	Animal testing: non-medical products, significant alternative efforts; CEDC report; tobacco
Vogue	KMB	C	C	B	B	C	B	A	A	Animal testing: non-medical products, significant alternative efforts; CEDC report; tobacco
Wash 'N Dry ★	CL	B	B	A	A	B	A	A	A	Animal testing: medical & non-medical products, significant alternative efforts; CEDC report; profile
Wet Ones	EK	C	B	B	B	B	A	B	B	Animal testing: medical and non-medical products, significant alternative efforts; CEDC report; CEP Award — EEO

The Environment | Charitable Giving | Community Outreach | Women's Advancement | Minority Advancement | Family | Workplace Issues | Disclosure of Information | ★ Honor Roll

For a more detailed explanation, see pages 7–28.

PRODUCT	PARENT COMPANY									EXTRAS
Wondersoft	KMB	C	C	B	B	C	B	A	A	Animal testing: non-medical products, significant alternative efforts; CEDC report; tobacco
Ziploc	DOW	C	C	B	B	A	A	B	A	Animal testing: non-medical products, significant alternative efforts; CEDC report; on-site child care; pesticide sterilization suits
PASTA										
ABC-123	AHP	C	F	C	B	B	C	C	A	Animal testing: medical & non-medical products, significant alternative efforts; infant formula
Albadoro	BN	C	C	B	A	A	B	B	A	CEDC report
American Beauty	HSY	B	B	A	B	C	A	A	A	CEDC report; increasing TRI; on-site child care
Anthony's	BN	C	C	B	A	A	B	B	A	CEDC report
Beef-O-Getti	AHP	C	F	C	B	B	C	C	A	Animal testing: medical & non-medical products, significant alternative efforts; infant formula
Beefaroni	AHP	C	F	C	B	B	C	C	A	Animal testing: medical & non-medical products, significant alternative efforts; infant formula
Best Bet	OAT	B	A	A	B	B	D	?	C	CEDC report; Fair Share
Bravo	BN	C	C	B	A	A	B	B	A	CEDC report
Contadina	NEST	B	?	B	B	B	A	B	B	Animal testing: non-medical products, significant alternative efforts; foreign-based company; infant formula
Creamette	BN	C	C	B	A	A	B	B	A	CEDC report
Cupatini	OAT	B	A	A	B	B	D	?	C	CEDC report; Fair Share

PRODUCT	PARENT COMPANY	The Environment	Charitable Giving	Community Outreach	Women's Advancement	Minority Advancement	Family	Workplace Issues	Disclosure of Information	EXTRAS
Delmonico	HSY	B	B	A	B	C	A	A	A	CEDC report; increasing TRI; on-site child care
Di Giorno	MO	D	D	?	A	A	?	?	F	Animal testing: non-medical products; CEDC report; tobacco; increasing TRI; Workplace Principles
Dutch Maid	BN	C	C	B	A	A	B	B	A	CEDC report
Fancy Cut	OAT	B	A	A	B	B	D	?	C	CEDC report; Fair Share
Fiberoni	BN	C	C	B	A	A	B	B	A	CEDC report
Franco-American	CPB	B	C	B	A	A	A	C	A	Animal testing: non-medical products, significant alternative efforts; CEDC report; on-site child care
Gioia	BN	C	C	B	A	A	B	B	A	CEDC report
Globe A-1	BN	C	C	B	A	A	B	B	A	CEDC report
Gooch Foods	ADM	D	F	?	D	?	?	D	F	CEDC report; increasing TRI
Goodman's	BN	C	C	B	A	A	B	B	A	CEDC report
Health Valley	HVAL	A	C	C	A	A	B	A	A	
Healthy Ribbons	HSY	B	B	A	B	C	A	A	A	CEDC report; increasing TRI; on-site child care
Jiffies	OAT	B	A	A	B	B	D	?	C	CEDC report; Fair Share
La Rosa	ADM	D	F	?	D	?	?	D	F	CEDC report; increasing TRI

The Environment | Charitable Giving | Community Outreach | Women's Advancement | Minority Advancement | Family | Workplace Issues | Disclosure of Information | ★ Honor Roll

For a more detailed explanation, see pages 7–28.

PRODUCT	PARENT COMPANY		$							EXTRAS
Light 'N Fluffy	HSY	B	B	A	B	C	A	A	A	CEDC report; increasing TRI; on-site child care
Luxury	BN	C	C	B	A	A	B	B	A	CEDC report
Mama Leone	AHP	C	F	C	B	B	C	C	A	Animal testing: medical & non-medical products, significant alternative efforts; infant formula
Manchu	OAT	B	A	A	B	B	D	?	C	CEDC report; Fair Share
Merlino's	BN	C	C	B	A	A	B	B	A	CEDC report
Mini Bites	AHP	C	F	C	B	B	C	C	A	Animal testing: medical & non-medical products, significant alternative efforts; infant formula
Mrs. Grass	BN	C	C	B	A	A	B	B	A	CEDC report
Mueller's	CPC	C	A	B	A	B	C	A	B	Animal testing: non-medical products, significant alternative efforts; CEDC report; increasing TRI
Napolina	CPC	C	A	B	A	B	C	A	B	Animal testing: non-medical products, significant alternative efforts; CEDC report; increasing TRI
Never-Stik	OAT	B	A	A	B	B	D	?	C	CEDC report; Fair Share
New Mill	BN	C	C	B	A	A	B	B	A	CEDC report
Noodle Roni	OAT	B	A	A	B	B	D	?	C	CEDC report; Fair Share
Pastamania	HSY	B	B	A	B	C	A	A	A	CEDC report; increasing TRI; on-site child care
Pennsylvania Dutch	BN	C	C	B	A	A	B	B	A	CEDC report
Perfection	HSY	B	B	A	B	C	A	A	A	CEDC report; increasing TRI; on-site child care

PRODUCT	PARENT COMPANY	The Environment	Charitable Giving	Community Outreach	Women's Advancement	Minority Advancement	Family	Workplace Issues	Disclosure of Information	EXTRAS
Eternity	UN	B	C	C	F	D	C	B	C	Animal testing: non-medical products, significant alternative efforts; foreign-based company; profile
Giorgio Armani	LORA	B	C	B	A	C	C	B	A	foreign-based company
Gloria Vanderbilt	LORA	B	C	B	A	C	C	B	A	foreign-based company
Guy Laroche	LORA	B	C	B	A	C	C	B	A	foreign-based company
Hero	UN	B	C	C	F	D	C	B	C	Animal testing: non-medical products, significant alternative efforts; foreign-based company; profile
Hugo Boss	PG	C	B	A	B	B	A	B	A	Animal testing: medical and non-medical products, significant alternative efforts; CEDC report; CEP Awards — Animal Welfare, Employer Responsiveness; increasing TRI; on-site day care; Workplace Principles
Imari ★	AVP	B	A	A	A	A	A	B	A	CEP Award — EEO; increasing TRI; on-site day care
Incognito	PG	C	B	A	B	B	A	B	A	Animal testing: medical and non-medical products, significant alternative efforts; CEDC report; CEP Awards — Animal Welfare, Employer Responsiveness; increasing TRI; on-site day care; Workplace Principles
Laura Biagiotti-Roma	PG	C	B	A	B	B	A	B	A	Animal testing: medical and non-medical products, significant alternative efforts; CEDC report; CEP Awards — Animal Welfare, Employer Responsiveness; increasing TRI; on-site day care; Workplace Principles
le Jardin	PG	C	B	A	B	B	A	B	A	Animal testing: medical and non-medical products, significant alternative efforts; CEDC report; CEP Awards — Animal Welfare, Employer Responsiveness; increasing TRI; on-site day care; Workplace Principles

PRODUCT	PARENT COMPANY	The Environment	Charitable Giving	Community Outreach	Women's Advancement	Minority Advancement	Family	Workplace Issues	Disclosure of Information	EXTRAS
Prince	BN	C	C	B	A	A	B	B	A	CEDC report
Procino-Rossi (P&R)	HSY	B	B	A	B	C	A	A	A	CEDC report; increasing TRI; on-site child care
Protini	OAT	B	A	A	B	B	D	?	C	CEDC report; Fair Share
R&F	BN	C	C	B	A	A	B	B	A	CEDC report
Red Cross	BN	C	C	B	A	A	B	B	A	CEDC report
Roller Coasters	AHP	C	F	C	B	B	C	C	A	Animal testing: medical & non-medical products, significant alternative efforts; infant formula
Ronco	BN	C	C	B	A	A	B	B	A	CEDC report
Ronzoni	HSY	B	B	A	B	C	A	A	A	CEDC report; increasing TRI; on-site child care
Russo	ADM	D	F	?	D	?	?	D	F	CEDC report; increasing TRI
San Giorgio	HSY	B	B	A	B	C	A	A	A	CEDC report; increasing TRI; on-site child care
Skinner	HSY	B	B	A	B	C	A	A	A	CEDC report; increasing TRI; on-site child care
Spun Gold	OAT	B	A	A	B	B	D	?	C	CEDC report; Fair Share
Superoni	BN	C	C	B	A	A	B	B	A	CEDC report
Suzy Wan	MO	D	D	?	A	A	?	?	F	Animal testing: non-medical products; CEDC report; tobacco; increasing TRI; Workplace Principles

 The Environment · Charitable Giving  Community Outreach  Women's Advancement 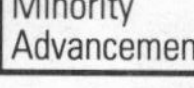 Minority Advancement  Family  Workplace Issues  Disclosure of Information · ★ Honor Roll

For a more detailed explanation, see pages 7–28.

PRODUCT	PARENT COMPANY									EXTRAS
Tenderoni	OAT	B	A	A	B	B	D	?	C	CEDC report; Fair Share
Tenderthin	OAT	B	A	A	B	B	D	?	C	CEDC report; Fair Share
Vimco	BN	C	C	B	A	A	B	B	A	CEDC report
Zooroni	AHP	C	F	C	B	B	C	C	A	Animal testing: medical & non-medical products, significant alternative efforts; infant formula
PEANUT BUTTER & OTHER SPREADS										
Bama	BN	C	C	B	A	A	B	B	A	CEDC report
Jif	PG	C	B	A	B	B	A	B	A	Animal testing: medical and non-medical products, significant alternative efforts; CEDC report; CEP Awards — Animal Welfare, Employer Responsiveness; increasing TRI; on-site day care; Workplace Principles
Laura Scudder's	BN	C	C	B	A	A	B	B	A	CEDC report
Marmite	CPC	C	A	B	A	B	C	A	B	Animal testing: non-medical products, significant alternative efforts; CEDC report; increasing TRI
Ox-Heart	OAT	B	A	A	B	B	D	?	C	CEDC report; Fair Share
Peter Pan	CAG	C	C	C	C	?	?	F	C	CEDC report; factory farming; profile
Skippy	CPC	C	A	B	A	B	C	A	B	Animal testing: non-medical products, significant alternative efforts; CEDC report; increasing TRI
Squirrel	CPC	C	A	B	A	B	C	A	B	Animal testing: non-medical products, significant alternative efforts; CEDC report; increasing TRI

PRODUCT	PARENT COMPANY									EXTRAS
Super Krunch	MO	D	D	?	A	A	?	?	F	Animal testing: non-medical products; CEDC report; tobacco; increasing TRI; Workplace Principles
Tinker Bell	CAG	C	C	C	C	?	?	F	C	CEDC report; factory farming; profile
PERFUMES & COLOGNES										
Anais Anais	LORA	B	C	B	A	C	C	B	A	foreign-based company
Aqua Velva	SBH	C	D	C	B	B	A	B	C	Animal testing: medical products only, significant alternative efforts; foreign-based company; Workplace Principles
Aroma Oil	BLN	A	?	A	A	A	B	A	A	Small company
Avon ★	AVP	B	A	A	A	A	A	B	A	CEP Award — EEO; increasing TRI; on-site day care
Body Shop	BODY	A	?	A	A	B	B	C	A	foreign-based company
Brut 33	UN	B	C	C	F	D	C	B	C	Animal testing: non-medical products, significant alternative efforts; foreign-based company; profile
Cacharel	LORA	B	C	B	A	C	C	B	A	foreign-based company
California	PG	C	B	A	B	B	A	B	A	Animal testing: medical and non-medical products, significant alternative efforts; CEDC report; CEP A[illegible] Animal Welfare, Employer Resp[illegible] on-site day care[illegible]
Elizabeth Arden	UN	B	C	C	F	D	[illegible]	[illegible]	[illegible]	[illegible]

PRODUCT	PARENT COMPANY	The Environment	Charitable Giving	Community Outreach	Women's Advancement	Minority Advancement	Family	Workplace Issues	Disclosure of Information	EXTRAS
Mesmerize ★	AVP	B	A	A	A	A	A	B	A	CEP Award — EEO; increasing TRI; on-site day care
Navy	PG	C	B	A	B	B	A	B	A	Animal testing: medical and non-medical products, significant alternative efforts; CEDC report; CEP Awards — Animal Welfare, Employer Responsiveness; increasing TRI; on-site day care; Workplace Principles
Obsession	UN	B	C	C	F	D	C	B	C	Animal testing: non-medical products, significant alternative efforts; foreign-based company; profile
Old Spice	PG	C	B	A	B	B	A	B	A	Animal testing: medical and non-medical products, significant alternative efforts; CEDC report; CEP Awards — Animal Welfare, Employer Responsiveness; increasing TRI; on-site day care; Workplace Principles
Paloma Picasso	LORA	B	C	B	A	C	C	B	A	foreign-based company
Ralph Lauren	LORA	B	C	B	A	C	C	B	A	foreign-based company
Redken ★	CL	B	B	A	A	B	A	A	A	Animal testing: medical & non-medical products, significant alternative efforts; CEDC report; profile
Toujours Moi	PG	C	B	A	B	B	A	B	A	Animal testing: medical and non-medical products, significant alternative efforts; CEDC report; CEP Awards — Animal Welfare, Employer Responsiveness; increasing TRI; on-site day care; Workplace Principles
Venezia	PG	C	B	A	B	B	A	B	A	Animal testing: medical and non-medical products, significant alternative efforts; CEDC report; CEP Awards — Animal Welfare, Employer Responsiveness; increasing TRI; on-site day care; Workplace Principles

The Environment | Charitable Giving | Community Outreach | Women's Advancement |  Minority Advancement |  Family | Workplace Issues | Disclosure of Information | ★ Honor Roll

For a more detailed explanation, see pages 7–28.

PRODUCT	PARENT COMPANY									EXTRAS
Whisper Of Musk	SBH	C	D	C	B	B	A	B	C	Animal testing: medical products only, significant alternative efforts; foreign-based company; Workplace Principles
PERSONAL CARE & COSMETICS										
Acnomel	SBH	C	D	C	B	B	A	B	C	Animal testing: medical products only, significant alternative efforts; foreign-based company; Workplace Principles
Adidas	SBH	C	D	C	B	B	A	B	C	Animal testing: medical products only, significant alternative efforts; foreign-based company; Workplace Principles
Afta Skin Conditioner ★	CL	B	B	A	A	B	A	A	A	Animal testing: medical & non-medical products, significant alternative efforts; CEDC report; profile
Aftate	SGP	B	C	A	B	A	A	B	A	Animal testing: medical products only, significant alternative efforts; on-site child care; Workplace Principles
Air-Pillo	SGP	B	C	A	B	A	A	B	A	Animal testing: medical products only, significant alternative efforts; on-site child care; Workplace Principles
Albolene	SBH	C	D	C	B	B	A	B	C	Animal testing: medical products only, significant alternative efforts; foreign-based company; Workplace Principles
Amazing Grains	BLN	A	?	A	A	A	B	A	A	Small company
Ammens	BMY	B	C	B	B	B	B	B	A	Animal testing: medical & non-medical products, significant alternative efforts; infant formula; Workplace Principles
Anew ★	AVP	B	A	A	A	A	A	B	A	CEP Award — EEO; increasing TRI; on-site day care

PRODUCT	PARENT COMPANY	The Environment	Charitable Giving	Community Outreach	Women's Advancement	Minority Advancement	Family	Workplace Issues	Disclosure of Information	EXTRAS
Anti-Itch ★	SCJ	A	A	A	B	B	A	A	A	Animal testing: non-medical products, significant alternative efforts; CEP Award — Environment; on-site child care; profile; Workplace Principles
Aqua Care	SBH	C	D	C	B	B	A	B	C	Animal testing: medical products only, significant alternative efforts; foreign-based company; Workplace Principles
Aqua Velva	SBH	C	D	C	B	B	A	B	C	Animal testing: medical products only, significant alternative efforts; foreign-based company; Workplace Principles
Arch Supports	SGP	B	C	A	B	A	A	B	A	Animal testing: medical products only, significant alternative efforts; on-site child care; Workplace Principles
Aroma Lotion	BLN	A	?	A	A	A	B	A	A	Small company
Aroma Oil	BLN	A	?	A	A	A	B	A	A	Small company
Aroma Vera	AV	A	F	C	B	B	D	C	C	Small company
Atra	G	C	C	B	D	D	B	B	A	Animal testing: medical & non-medical products, significant alternative efforts
Aveda ★	AVED	A	A	A	A	A	A	A	A	CEP Award — Environment; CERES principles; profile
Aveeno ★	SCJ	A	A	A	B	B	A	A	A	Animal testing: non-medical products, significant alternative efforts; CEP Award — Environment; on-site child care; profile; Workplace Principles
Avon ★	AVP	B	A	A	A	A	A	B	A	CEP Award — EEO; increasing TRI; on-site day care

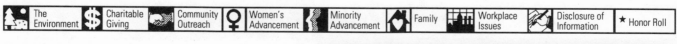

The Environment | Charitable Giving | Community Outreach | Women's Advancement | Minority Advancement | Family | Workplace Issues | Disclosure of Information | ★ Honor Roll

For a more detailed explanation, see pages 7–28.

PRODUCT	PARENT COMPANY									EXTRAS
Avon Color ★	AVP	B	A	A	A	A	A	B	A	CEP Award — EEO; increasing TRI; on-site day care
Back Guard	SGP	B	C	A	B	A	A	B	A	Animal testing: medical products only, significant alternative efforts; on-site child care; Workplace Principles
Bain de Soleil	PG	C	B	A	B	B	A	B	A	Animal testing: medical and non-medical products, significant alternative efforts; CEDC report; CEP Awards — Animal Welfare, Employer Responsiveness; increasing TRI; on-site day care; Workplace Principles
Balm Barr ★	CL	B	B	A	A	B	A	A	A	Animal testing: medical & non-medical products, significant alternative efforts; CEDC report; profile
Barbasol	PFE	C	B	A	B	C	A	B	A	Animal testing: medical products only, significant alternative efforts; heart valve suits; Workplace Principles
Benadryl ★	WLA	B	B	A	B	A	A	B	A	Animal testing: medical products only; increasing TRI; Workplace Principles
Biotherm	LORA	B	C	B	A	C	C	B	A	foreign-based company
Body Shop	BODY	A	?	A	A	B	B	C	A	foreign-based company
Boraxo	DL	C	A	B	B	?	F	B	C	CEDC report
Brut 33	UN	B	C	C	F	D	C	B	C	Animal testing: non-medical products, significant alternative efforts; foreign-based company; profile
Buf Puf	MMM	C	B	A	C	B	A	B	A	Animal testing: medical & non-medical products, significant alternative efforts; CEDC report; CEP Award — Environment
Calgon	SBH	C	D	C	B	B	A	B	C	Animal testing: medical products only, significant alternative efforts; foreign-based company; Workplace Principles

PRODUCT	PARENT COMPANY	The Environment	Charitable Giving	Community Outreach	Women's Advancement	Minority Advancement	Family	Workplace Issues	Disclosure of Information	EXTRAS
Calvin Klein	UN	B	C	C	F	D	C	B	C	Animal testing: non-medical products, significant alternative efforts; foreign-based company; profile
Camay	PG	C	B	A	B	B	A	B	A	Animal testing: medical and non-medical products, significant alternative efforts; CEDC report; CEP Awards — Animal Welfare, Employer Responsiveness; increasing TRI; on-site day care; Workplace Principles
Canterbury Collection	DL	C	A	B	B	?	F	B	C	CEDC report
Caress	UN	B	C	C	F	D	C	B	C	Animal testing: non-medical products, significant alternative efforts; foreign-based company; profile
Caribee	UN	B	C	C	F	D	C	B	C	Animal testing: non-medical products, significant alternative efforts; foreign-based company; profile
Cashmere Bouquet ★	CL	B	B	A	A	B	A	A	A	Animal testing: medical & non-medical products, significant alternative efforts; CEDC report; profile
Chapstick	AHP	C	F	C	B	B	C	C	A	Animal testing: medical & non-medical products, significant alternative efforts; infant formula
Clarion	PG	C	B	A	B	B	A	B	A	Animal testing: medical and non-medical products, significant alternative efforts; CEDC report; CEP Awards — Animal Welfare, Employer Responsiveness; increasing TRI; on-site day care; Workplace Principles
Clean & Clear ★	JNJ	B	A	A	A	A	A	A	A	Animal testing: medical products only, significant alternative efforts; CEP Award — Disclosure; on-site child care; profile; Workplace Principles

The Environment Charitable Giving

Community Outreach Women's Advancement

Minority Advancement

Family

Workplace Issues

Disclosure of Information ★ Honor Roll

For a more detailed explanation, see pages 7–28.

PRODUCT	PARENT COMPANY									EXTRAS
Clear Away	SGP	B	C	A	B	A	A	B	A	Animal testing: medical products only, significant alternative efforts; on-site child care; Workplace Principles
Clearasil	PG	C	B	A	B	B	A	B	A	Animal testing: medical and non-medical products, significant alternative efforts; CEDC report; CEP Awards — Animal Welfare, Employer Responsiveness; increasing TRI; on-site day care; Workplace Principles
Clear By Design	SBH	C	D	C	B	B	A	B	C	Animal testing: medical products only, significant alternative efforts; foreign-based company; Workplace Principles
Clearstick	PG	C	B	A	B	B	A	B	A	Animal testing: medical and non-medical products, significant alternative efforts; CEDC report; CEP Awards — Animal Welfare, Employer Responsiveness; increasing TRI; on-site day care; Workplace Principles
Coast	PG	C	B	A	B	B	A	B	A	Animal testing: medical and non-medical products, significant alternative efforts; CEDC report; CEP Awards — Animal Welfare, Employer Responsiveness; increasing TRI; on-site day care; Workplace Principles
Colgate ★	CL	B	B	A	A	B	A	A	A	Animal testing: medical & non-medical products, significant alternative efforts; CEDC report; profile
Complex 15	SGP	B	C	A	B	A	A	B	A	Animal testing: medical products only, significant alternative efforts; on-site child care; Workplace Principles
Compound W	AHP	C	F	C	B	B	C	C	A	Animal testing: medical & non-medical products, significant alternative efforts; infant formula
Conti	SBH	C	D	C	B	B	A	B	C	Animal testing: medical products only, significant alternative efforts; foreign-based company; Workplace Principles
Cool Coconut	SBH	C	D	C	B	B	A	B	C	Animal testing: medical products only, significant alternative efforts; foreign-based company; Workplace Principles

PRODUCT	PARENT COMPANY	The Environment	Charitable Giving	Community Outreach	Women's Advancement	Minority Advancement	Family	Workplace Issues	Disclosure of Information	EXTRAS
Coppertone	SGP	B	C	A	B	A	A	B	A	Animal testing: medical products only, significant alternative efforts; on-site child care; Workplace Principles
Cover Girl	PG	C	B	A	B	B	A	B	A	Animal testing: medical and non-medical products, significant alternative efforts; CEDC report; CEP Awards — Animal Welfare, Employer Responsiveness; increasing TRI; on-site day care; Workplace Principles
Crystal Radiance	AV	A	F	C	B	B	D	C	C	Small company
Cutex	UN	B	C	C	F	D	C	B	C	Animal testing: non-medical products, significant alternative efforts; foreign-based company; profile
Daily Revival ★	AVP	B	A	A	A	A	A	B	A	CEP Award — EEO; increasing TRI; on-site day care
Dermassage ★	CL	B	B	A	A	B	A	A	A	Animal testing: medical & non-medical products, significant alternative efforts; CEDC report; profile
Dial	DL	C	A	B	B	?	F	B	C	CEDC report
Dorothy Gray	EK	C	B	B	B	B	A	B	B	Animal testing: medical and non-medical products, significant alternative efforts; CEDC report; CEP Award — EEO
Dove	UN	B	C	C	F	D	C	B	C	Animal testing: non-medical products, significant alternative efforts; foreign-based company; profile
Dr. Scholl	SGP	B	C	A	B	A	A	B	A	Animal testing: medical products only, significant alternative efforts; on-site child care; Workplace Principles
Drakkar Noir	LORA	B	C	B	A	C	C	B	A	foreign-based company

The Environment | Charitable Giving | Community Outreach | Women's Advancement | Minority Advancement | Family | Workplace Issues | Disclosure of Information | ★ Honor Roll

For a more detailed explanation, see pages 7–28.

PRODUCT	PARENT COMPANY		$							EXTRAS
Dry & Clear	AHP	C	F	C	B	B	C	C	A	Animal testing: medical & non-medical products, significant alternative efforts; infant formula
Duo	SBH	C	D	C	B	B	A	B	C	Animal testing: medical products only, significant alternative efforts; foreign-based company; Workplace Principles
DuoFilm Liquid	SGP	B	C	A	B	A	A	B	A	Animal testing: medical products only, significant alternative efforts; on-site child care; Workplace Principles
DuoPlant	SGP	B	C	A	B	A	A	B	A	Animal testing: medical products only, significant alternative efforts; on-site child care; Workplace Principles
DuoPlant Gel	SGP	B	C	A	B	A	A	B	A	Animal testing: medical products only, significant alternative efforts; on-site child care; Workplace Principles
Duofilm	SGP	B	C	A	B	A	A	B	A	Animal testing: medical products only, significant alternative efforts; on-site child care; Workplace Principles
Ecco Bella	ECC	A	?	C	A	Neutral	C	C	A	Small company
Edge ★	SCJ	A	A	A	B	B	A	A	A	Animal testing: non-medical products, significant alternative efforts; CEP Award — Environment; on-site child care; profile; Workplace Principles
Elizabeth Arden	UN	B	C	C	F	D	C	B	C	Animal testing: non-medical products, significant alternative efforts; foreign-based company; profile
Esoterica	SBH	C	D	C	B	B	A	B	C	Animal testing: medical products only, significant alternative efforts; foreign-based company; Workplace Principles
Flic	G	C	C	B	D	D	B	B	A	Animal testing: medical & non-medical products, significant alternative efforts
Foamy	G	C	C	B	D	D	B	B	A	Animal testing: medical & non-medical products, significant alternative efforts

PRODUCT	PARENT COMPANY	The Environment	Charitable Giving	Community Outreach	Women's Advancement	Minority Advancement	Family	Workplace Issues	Disclosure of Information	EXTRAS
Fostex	BMY	B	C	B	B	B	B	B	A	Animal testing: medical & non-medical products, significant alternative efforts; infant formula; Workplace Principles
Gillette	G	C	C	B	D	D	B	B	A	Animal testing: medical & non-medical products, significant alternative efforts
Good News!	G	C	C	B	D	D	B	B	A	Animal testing: medical & non-medical products, significant alternative efforts
Handsdown	KMB	C	C	B	B	C	B	A	A	Animal testing: non-medical products, significant alternative efforts; CEDC report; tobacco
Hawk After Shave ★	CL	B	B	A	A	B	A	A	A	Animal testing: medical & non-medical products, significant alternative efforts; CEDC report; profile
Herbal Facial Steams	BLN	A	?	A	A	A	B	A	A	Small company
Hidden Comfort	SGP	B	C	A	B	A	A	B	A	Animal testing: medical products only, significant alternative efforts; on-site child care; Workplace Principles
Irish Spring ★	CL	B	B	A	A	B	A	A	A	Animal testing: medical & non-medical products, significant alternative efforts; CEDC report; profile
Ivory	PG	C	B	A	B	B	A	B	A	Animal testing: medical and non-medical products, significant alternative efforts; CEDC report; CEP Awards — Animal Welfare, Employer Responsiveness; increasing TRI; on-site day care; Workplace Principles
Jafra	G	C	C	B	D	D	B	B	A	Animal testing: medical & non-medical products, significant alternative efforts

The Environment | Charitable Giving | Community Outreach | Women's Advancement | Minority Advancement | Family | Workplace Issues | Disclosure of Information | ★ Honor Roll

For a more detailed explanation, see pages 7–28.

PRODUCT	PARENT COMPANY									EXTRAS
Johnson's Baby Powder ★	JNJ	B	A	A	A	A	A	A	A	Animal testing: medical products only, significant alternative efforts; CEP Award — Disclosure; on-site child care; profile; Workplace Principles
Johnson's Swabs ★	JNJ	B	A	A	A	A	A	A	A	Animal testing: medical products only, significant alternative efforts; CEP Award — Disclosure; on-site child care; profile; Workplace Principles
Juniper Tonic Massage Oil	BLN	A	?	A	A	A	B	A	A	Small company
Keri Lotion	BMY	B	C	B	B	B	B	B	A	Animal testing: medical & non-medical products, significant alternative efforts; infant formula; Workplace Principles
Kirk	PG	C	B	A	B	B	A	B	A	Animal testing: medical and non-medical products, significant alternative efforts; CEDC report; CEP Awards — Animal Welfare, Employer Responsiveness; increasing TRI; on-site day care; Workplace Principles
Kiss My Face	KMF	A	?	A	A	Neutral	A	A	A	Small company
Lady Esther	SBH	C	D	C	B	B	A	B	C	Animal testing: medical products only, significant alternative efforts; foreign-based company; Workplace Principles
Lancaster	SBH	C	D	C	B	B	A	B	C	Animal testing: medical products only, significant alternative efforts; foreign-based company; Workplace Principles
Lancome	LORA	B	C	B	A	C	C	B	A	foreign-based company
Lather Shave ★	CL	B	B	A	A	B	A	A	A	Animal testing: medical & non-medical products, significant alternative efforts; CEDC report; profile
Lava	PG	C	B	A	B	B	A	B	A	Animal testing: medical and non-medical products, significant alternative efforts; CEDC report; CEP Awards — Animal Welfare, Employer Responsiveness; increasing TRI; on-site day care; Workplace Principles

PRODUCT	PARENT COMPANY	The Environment	Charitable Giving	Community Outreach	Women's Advancement	Minority Advancement	Family	Workplace Issues	Disclosure of Information	EXTRAS
Lectric Shave	SBH	C	D	C	B	B	A	B	C	Animal testing: medical products only, significant alternative efforts; foreign-based company; Workplace Principles
Lever 2000	UN	B	C	C	F	D	C	B	C	Animal testing: non-medical products, significant alternative efforts; foreign-based company; profile
L'Oreal	LORA	B	C	B	A	C	C	B	A	foreign-based company
Lotrimin AF	SGP	B	C	A	B	A	A	B	A	Animal testing: medical products only, significant alternative efforts; on-site child care; Workplace Principles
Love Mitts	BLN	A	?	A	A	A	B	A	A	Small company
Lubriderm ★	WLA	B	B	A	B	A	A	B	A	Animal testing: medical products only; increasing TRI; Workplace Principles
Luron Pink	DL	C	A	B	B	?	F	B	C	CEDC report
Lux	UN	B	C	C	F	D	C	B	C	Animal testing: non-medical products, significant alternative efforts; foreign-based company; profile
Max Factor	PG	C	B	A	B	B	A	B	A	Animal testing: medical and non-medical products, significant alternative efforts; CEDC report; CEP Awards — Animal Welfare, Employer Responsiveness; increasing TRI; on-site day care; Workplace Principles
Millionaire After Shave ★	CL	B	B	A	A	B	A	A	A	Animal testing: medical & non-medical products, significant alternative efforts; CEDC report; profile
Moisturel	BMY	B	C	B	B	B	B	B	A	Animal testing: medical & non-medical products, significant alternative efforts; infant formula; Workplace Principles

The Environment | Charitable Giving | Community Outreach | Women's Advancement | Minority Advancement | Family | Workplace Issues | Disclosure of Information | ★ Honor Roll

For a more detailed explanation, see pages 7–28.

PRODUCT	PARENT COMPANY									EXTRAS
Moisture Therapy ★	AVP	B	A	A	A	A	A	B	A	CEP Award — EEO; increasing TRI; on-site day care
Noxzema	PG	C	B	A	B	B	A	B	A	Animal testing: medical and non-medical products, significant alternative efforts; CEDC report; CEP Awards — Animal Welfare, Employer Responsiveness; increasing TRI; on-site day care; Workplace Principles
Oil of Olay	PG	C	B	A	B	B	A	B	A	Animal testing: medical and non-medical products, significant alternative efforts; CEDC report; CEP Awards — Animal Welfare, Employer Responsiveness; increasing TRI; on-site day care; Workplace Principles
Or Bleu	SBH	C	D	C	B	B	A	B	C	Animal testing: medical products only, significant alternative efforts; foreign-based company; Workplace Principles
Oxy	SBH	C	D	C	B	B	A	B	C	Animal testing: medical products only, significant alternative efforts; foreign-based company; Workplace Principles
Pacquin	PFE	C	B	A	B	C	A	B	A	Animal testing: medical products only, significant alternative efforts; heart valve suits; Workplace Principles
Pageant ★	AVP	B	A	A	A	A	A	B	A	CEP Award — EEO; increasing TRI; on-site day care
Palme D'Or	SBH	C	D	C	B	B	A	B	C	Animal testing: medical products only, significant alternative efforts; foreign-based company; Workplace Principles
Palmolive ★	CL	B	B	A	A	B	A	A	A	Animal testing: medical & non-medical products, significant alternative efforts; CEDC report; profile
Personal Touch ★	WLA	B	B	A	B	A	A	B	A	Animal testing: medical products only; increasing TRI; Workplace Principles
PHiso-Derm	EK	C	B	B	B	B	A	B	B	Animal testing: medical and non-medical products, significant alternative efforts; CEDC report; CEP Award — EEO

PRODUCT	PARENT COMPANY	The Environment	Charitable Giving	Community Outreach	Women's Advancement	Minority Advancement	Family	Workplace Issues	Disclosure of Information	EXTRAS
Pond's	UN	B	C	C	F	D	C	B	C	Animal testing: non-medical products, significant alternative efforts; foreign-based company; profile
PreSun	BMY	B	C	B	B	B	B	B	A	Animal testing: medical & non-medical products, significant alternative efforts; infant formula; Workplace Principles
Protector ★	WLA	B	B	A	B	A	A	B	A	Animal testing: medical products only; increasing TRI; Workplace Principles
Pure & Natural	DL	C	A	B	B	?	F	B	C	CEDC report
Q-Tips	UN	B	C	C	F	D	C	B	C	Animal testing: non-medical products, significant alternative efforts; foreign-based company; profile
Redken ★	CL	B	B	A	A	B	A	A	A	Animal testing: medical & non-medical products, significant alternative efforts; CEDC report; profile
Rimmel	UN	B	C	C	F	D	C	B	C	Animal testing: non-medical products, significant alternative efforts; foreign-based company; profile
Rose Milk	SBH	C	D	C	B	B	A	B	C	Animal testing: medical products only, significant alternative efforts; foreign-based company; Workplace Principles
Safeguard	PG	C	B	A	B	B	A	B	A	Animal testing: medical and non-medical products, significant alternative efforts; CEDC report; CEP Awards — Animal Welfare, Employer Responsiveness; increasing TRI; on-site day care; Workplace Principles
Schick ★	WLA	B	B	A	B	A	A	B	A	Animal testing: medical products only; increasing TRI; Workplace Principles

The Environment
Charitable Giving

Community Outreach

Women's Advancement

Minority Advancement

Family

Workplace Issues

Disclosure of Information
★ Honor Roll

For a more detailed explanation, see pages 7–28.

PRODUCT	PARENT COMPANY									EXTRAS
Sea Breeze	BMY	B	C	B	B	B	B	B	A	Animal testing: medical & non-medical products, significant alternative efforts; infant formula; Workplace Principles
Shade	SGP	B	C	A	B	A	A	B	A	Animal testing: medical products only, significant alternative efforts; on-site child care; Workplace Principles
Shaklee	YAMP	?	A	A	?	B	B	A	B	foreign-based company
Shield	UN	B	C	C	F	D	C	B	C	Animal testing: non-medical products, significant alternative efforts; foreign-based company; profile
Skin Bracer ★	CL	B	B	A	A	B	A	A	A	Animal testing: medical & non-medical products, significant alternative efforts; CEDC report; profile
Skin-So-Soft ★	AVP	B	A	A	A	A	A	B	A	CEP Award — EEO; increasing TRI; on-site day care
Slim Twin ★	WLA	B	B	A	B	A	A	B	A	Animal testing: medical products only; increasing TRI; Workplace Principles
Smooth Touch	SGP	B	C	A	B	A	A	B	A	Animal testing: medical products only, significant alternative efforts; on-site child care; Workplace Principles
Sof Comfort	SGP	B	C	A	B	A	A	B	A	Animal testing: medical products only, significant alternative efforts; on-site child care; Workplace Principles
Soft Sense ★	SCJ	A	A	A	B	B	A	A	A	Animal testing: non-medical products, significant alternative efforts; CEP Award — Environment; on-site child care; profile; Workplace Principles
Softsoap ★	CL	B	B	A	A	B	A	A	A	Animal testing: medical & non-medical products, significant alternative efforts; CEDC report; profile
Solarcaine	SGP	B	C	A	B	A	A	B	A	Animal testing: medical products only, significant alternative efforts; on-site child care; Workplace Principles

PRODUCT	PARENT COMPANY	The Environment	Charitable Giving	Community Outreach	Women's Advancement	Minority Advancement	Family	Workplace Issues	Disclosure of Information	EXTRAS
Spirit	DL	C	A	B	B	?	F	B	C	CEDC report
Sports Cushion	SGP	B	C	A	B	A	A	B	A	Animal testing: medical products only, significant alternative efforts; on-site child care; Workplace Principles
Stri-Dex	EK	C	B	B	B	B	A	B	B	Animal testing: medical and non-medical products, significant alternative efforts; CEDC report; CEP Award — EEO
Suave	HC	A	A	A	B	?	A	B	B	Animal testing: non-medical products
Sundown ★	JNJ	B	A	A	A	A	A	A	A	Animal testing: medical products only, significant alternative efforts; CEP Award — Disclosure; on-site child care; profile; Workplace Principles
Super II ★	WLA	B	B	A	B	A	A	B	A	Animal testing: medical products only; increasing TRI; Workplace Principles
Tenderface	SBH	C	D	C	B	B	A	B	C	Animal testing: medical products only, significant alternative efforts; foreign-based company; Workplace Principles
Tinactin	SGP	B	C	A	B	A	A	B	A	Animal testing: medical products only, significant alternative efforts; on-site child care; Workplace Principles
Tom's of Maine ★	TOM	A	A	A	A	B	A	A	A	CEP Award — Charity; CERES Principles; profile; small company
Tone	DL	C	A	B	B	?	F	B	C	CEDC report
Trac II	G	C	C	B	D	D	B	B	A	Animal testing: medical & non-medical products, significant alternative efforts

The Environment | Charitable Giving | Community Outreach | Women's Advancement | Minority Advancement | Family | Workplace Issues | Disclosure of Information | ★ Honor Roll

For a more detailed explanation, see pages 7–28.

PRODUCT	PARENT COMPANY									EXTRAS
Tracer/FX ★	WLA	B	B	A	B	A	A	B	A	Animal testing: medical products only; increasing TRI; Workplace Principles
Tranquil Moments ★	AVP	B	A	A	A	A	A	B	A	CEP Award — EEO; increasing TRI; on-site day care
Tritin	SGP	B	C	A	B	A	A	B	A	Animal testing: medical products only, significant alternative efforts; on-site child care; Workplace Principles
Tropical Blend	SGP	B	C	A	B	A	A	B	A	Animal testing: medical products only, significant alternative efforts; on-site child care; Workplace Principles
Ultrex ★	WLA	B	B	A	B	A	A	B	A	Animal testing: medical products only; increasing TRI; Workplace Principles
Vaseline	UN	B	C	C	F	D	C	B	C	Animal testing: non-medical products, significant alternative efforts; foreign-based company; profile
Vel ★	CL	B	B	A	A	B	A	A	A	Animal testing: medical & non-medical products, significant alternative efforts; CEDC report; profile
Village Bath ★	CL	B	B	A	A	B	A	A	A	Animal testing: medical & non-medical products, significant alternative efforts; CEDC report; profile
Warm-Eze	SGP	B	C	A	B	A	A	B	A	Animal testing: medical products only, significant alternative efforts; on-site child care; Workplace Principles
Water Babies	SGP	B	C	A	B	A	A	B	A	Animal testing: medical products only, significant alternative efforts; on-site child care; Workplace Principles
Wilkinson Sword ★	WLA	B	B	A	B	A	A	B	A	Animal testing: medical products only; increasing TRI; Workplace Principles
Williams	SBH	C	D	C	B	B	A	B	C	Animal testing: medical products only, significant alternative efforts; foreign-based company; Workplace Principles

PRODUCT	PARENT COMPANY	The Environment	Charitable Giving	Community Outreach	Women's Advancement	Minority Advancement	Family	Workplace Issues	Disclosure of Information	EXTRAS
Work Day	SGP	B	C	A	B	A	A	B	A	Animal testing: medical products only, significant alternative efforts; on-site child care; Workplace Principles
Youth Garde	AHP	C	F	C	B	B	C	C	A	Animal testing: medical & non-medical products, significant alternative efforts; infant formula
Zest	PG	C	B	A	B	B	A	B	A	Animal testing: medical and non-medical products, significant alternative efforts; CEDC report; CEP Awards — Animal Welfare, Employer Responsiveness; increasing TRI; on-site day care; Workplace Principles
PET FOOD & PET PRODUCTS										
100	RAL	C	C	B	B	B	B	C	B	CEDC report; increasing TRI
9 Lives	HNZ	B	C	A	B	D	C	A	A	CEDC report; CEP Award — Environment
Alley Kat	RAL	C	C	B	B	B	B	C	B	CEDC report; increasing TRI
All Tender	OAT	B	A	A	B	B	D	?	C	CEDC report; Fair Share
All the Fixin's	OAT	B	A	A	B	B	D	?	C	CEDC report; Fair Share
Alpo ★	GMR	C	A	A	B	A	A	B	A	factory farming; foreign-based company
Amore	HNZ	B	C	A	B	D	C	A	A	CEDC report; CEP Award — Environment
ANF	CAG	C	C	C	C	?	?	F	C	CEDC report; factory farming; profile

The Environment | Charitable Giving | Community Outreach | Women's Advancement | Minority Advancement | Family | Workplace Issues | Disclosure of Information | ★ Honor Roll

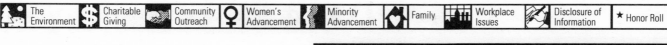

For a more detailed explanation, see pages 7–28.

PRODUCT	PARENT COMPANY									EXTRAS
Arm & Hammer	CHD	A	B	A	C	C	A	A	A	Animal testing: non-medical products, significant alternative efforts; CEP Award — Environment
Bansect	CAG	C	C	C	C	?	?	F	C	CEDC report; factory farming; profile
Barrington Farms	OAT	B	A	A	B	B	D	?	C	CEDC report; Fair Share
Beggin' Strips	RAL	C	C	B	B	B	B	C	B	CEDC report; increasing TRI
Blends	RAL	C	C	B	B	B	B	C	B	CEDC report; increasing TRI
Blue Mountain ★	GMR	C	A	A	B	A	A	B	A	factory farming; foreign-based company
Bone Appetit	RAL	C	C	B	B	B	B	C	B	CEDC report; increasing TRI
Bonkers	CAG	C	C	C	C	?	?	F	C	CEDC report; factory farming; profile
Bonz	RAL	C	C	B	B	B	B	C	B	CEDC report; increasing TRI
Burger'n Bones	OAT	B	A	A	B	B	D	?	C	CEDC report; Fair Share
Butcher Bones	RN	?	A	C	C	?	?	?	D	Animal testing: non-medical products; CEDC report; tobacco; increasing TRI; Workplace Principles
Butcher Brand ★	GMR	C	A	A	B	A	A	B	A	factory farming; foreign-based company
Butcher Cuts	OAT	B	A	A	B	B	D	?	C	CEDC report; Fair Share
Butcher's Blend	RAL	C	C	B	B	B	B	C	B	CEDC report; increasing TRI
Cano	HNZ	B	C	A	B	D	C	A	A	CEDC report; CEP Award — Environment
Cat Chow	RAL	C	C	B	B	B	B	C	B	CEDC report; increasing TRI

PRODUCT	PARENT COMPANY									EXTRAS
Cat Kitchen	OAT	B	A	A	B	B	D	?	C	CEDC report; Fair Share
Cat Menu	RAL	C	C	B	B	B	B	C	B	CEDC report; increasing TRI
Catviar	RAL	C	C	B	B	B	B	C	B	CEDC report; increasing TRI
Cheesedawgs	RAL	C	C	B	B	B	B	C	B	CEDC report; increasing TRI
Chewy Morsels	RAL	C	C	B	B	B	B	C	B	CEDC report; increasing TRI
Chuck Wagon	RAL	C	C	B	B	B	B	C	B	CEDC report; increasing TRI
Chunky 'n Tender	OAT	B	A	A	B	B	D	?	C	CEDC report; Fair Share
Control	CLX	B	B	A	A	A	C	C	A	Animal testing: non-medical products, significant alternative efforts; CEDC report; CEP Award — Community; increasing TRI
Country Blend	RAL	C	C	B	B	B	B	C	B	CEDC report; increasing TRI
Country Dog	OAT	B	A	A	B	B	D	?	C	CEDC report; Fair Share
Course	OAT	B	A	A	B	B	D	?	C	CEDC report; Fair Share
Crunch 'n Burger	OAT	B	A	A	B	B	D	?	C	CEDC report; Fair Share
Crunch 'n Chew	OAT	B	A	A	B	B	D	?	C	CEDC report; Fair Share
Cycle	OAT	B	A	A	B	B	D	?	C	CEDC report; Fair Share

    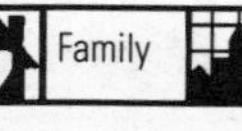    

The Environment | Charitable Giving | Community Outreach | Women's Advancement | Minority Advancement | Family | Workplace Issues | Disclosure of Information | ★ Honor Roll

For a more detailed explanation, see pages 7–28.

PRODUCT	PARENT COMPANY									EXTRAS
Dairy Dinner	RAL	C	C	B	B	B	B	C	B	CEDC report; increasing TRI
Dealer's Pride	RAL	C	C	B	B	B	B	C	B	CEDC report; increasing TRI
Deli	HNZ	B	C	A	B	D	C	A	A	CEDC report; CEP Award — Environment
Dinner Bag	OAT	B	A	A	B	B	D	?	C	CEDC report; Fair Share
Dinner Mix	RAL	C	C	B	B	B	B	C	B	CEDC report; increasing TRI
Dinner Rounds	HNZ	B	C	A	B	D	C	A	A	CEDC report; CEP Award — Environment
Dinnertime	HNZ	B	C	A	B	D	C	A	A	CEDC report; CEP Award — Environment
Dog Chow	RAL	C	C	B	B	B	B	C	B	CEDC report; increasing TRI
Doglovers Farm	HNZ	B	C	A	B	D	C	A	A	CEDC report; CEP Award — Environment
Dog's Choice	OAT	B	A	A	B	B	D	?	C	CEDC report; Fair Share
Dr. Ballards	RN	?	A	C	C	?	?	?	D	Animal testing: non-medical products; CEDC report; tobacco; increasing TRI; Workplace Principles
Encore	RAL	C	C	B	B	B	B	C	B	CEDC report; increasing TRI
Ever Clean	FBR	C	A	C	F	D	D	B	B	Animal testing: non-medical products, significant alternative efforts; profile
Fancy Feast	NEST	B	?	B	B	B	A	B	B	Animal testing: non-medical products, significant alternative efforts; foreign-based company; infant formula
Felobits	SBH	C	D	C	B	B	A	B	C	Animal testing: medical products only, significant alternative efforts; foreign-based company; Workplace Principles

PRODUCT	PARENT COMPANY	The Environment	Charitable Giving	Community Outreach	Women's Advancement	Minority Advancement	Family	Workplace Issues	Disclosure of Information	EXTRAS
Field Master	RAL	C	C	B	B	B	B	C	B	CEDC report; increasing TRI
Field 'n Farm	RAL	C	C	B	B	B	B	C	B	CEDC report; increasing TRI
Filaribits	SBH	C	D	C	B	B	A	B	C	Animal testing: medical products only, significant alternative efforts; foreign-based company; Workplace Principles
Finicky Bits	HNZ	B	C	A	B	D	C	A	A	CEDC report; CEP Award — Environment
Fisherman's Platter	OAT	B	A	A	B	B	D	?	C	CEDC report; Fair Share
Fishets	HNZ	B	C	A	B	D	C	A	A	CEDC report; CEP Award — Environment
Fit & Trim	RAL	C	C	B	B	B	B	C	B	CEDC report; increasing TRI
Flavor Snack	RN	?	A	C	C	?	?	?	D	Animal testing: non-medical products; CEDC report; tobacco; increasing TRI; Workplace Principles
Freckles	ADM	D	F	?	D	?	?	D	F	CEDC report; increasing TRI
Fresh Choice	OAT	B	A	A	B	B	D	?	C	CEDC report; Fair Share
Fresh Step	CLX	B	B	A	A	A	C	C	A	Animal testing: non-medical products, significant alternative efforts; CEDC report; CEP Award — Community; increasing TRI
Frisbee Flying Dog Treats	OAT	B	A	A	B	B	D	?	C	CEDC report; Fair Share
Friskies	NEST	B	?	B	B	B	A	B	B	Animal testing: non-medical products, significant alternative efforts; foreign-based company; infant formula

The Environment | Charitable Giving | Community Outreach | Women's Advancement | Minority Advancement | Family | Workplace Issues | Disclosure of Information | ★ Honor Roll

For a more detailed explanation, see pages 7–28.

PRODUCT	PARENT COMPANY									EXTRAS
Fulfill	RAL	C	C	B	B	B	B	C	B	CEDC report; increasing TRI
Full Course	OAT	B	A	A	B	B	D	?	C	CEDC report; Fair Share
Fur-so-fresh	CAG	C	C	C	C	?	?	F	C	CEDC report; factory farming; profile
Gaines	OAT	B	A	A	B	B	D	?	C	CEDC report; Fair Share
Geisler	CAG	C	C	C	C	?	?	F	C	CEDC report; factory farming; profile
Glamour Puss	HNZ	B	C	A	B	D	C	A	A	CEDC report; CEP Award — Environment
Good Mews	RAL	C	C	B	B	B	B	C	B	CEDC report; increasing TRI
Goody Two Chews	RAL	C	C	B	B	B	B	C	B	CEDC report; increasing TRI
Gravy Train	OAT	B	A	A	B	B	D	?	C	CEDC report; Fair Share
Great Eats	OAT	B	A	A	B	B	D	?	C	CEDC report; Fair Share
Grille Style	OAT	B	A	A	B	B	D	?	C	CEDC report; Fair Share
Growth	RAL	C	C	B	B	B	B	C	B	CEDC report; increasing TRI
Grrravy	RAL	C	C	B	B	B	B	C	B	CEDC report; increasing TRI
Hale & Hearty	OAT	B	A	A	B	B	D	?	C	CEDC report; Fair Share
Happy Cat	RAL	C	C	B	B	B	B	C	B	CEDC report; increasing TRI
Happy Dog	RAL	C	C	B	B	B	B	C	B	CEDC report; increasing TRI
Happy Kitten	RAL	C	C	B	B	B	B	C	B	CEDC report; increasing TRI

PRODUCT	PARENT COMPANY	The Environment	Charitable Giving	Community Outreach	Women's Advancement	Minority Advancement	Family	Workplace Issues	Disclosure of Information	EXTRAS
Hearty Chews	RAL	C	C	B	B	B	B	C	B	CEDC report; increasing TRI
Hearty Dinners	HNZ	B	C	A	B	D	C	A	A	CEDC report; CEP Award — Environment
Hero	RAL	C	C	B	B	B	B	C	B	CEDC report; increasing TRI
High Protein	RAL	C	C	B	B	B	B	C	B	CEDC report; increasing TRI
High Stakes	OAT	B	A	A	B	B	D	?	C	CEDC report; Fair Share
Hill's ★	CL	B	B	A	A	B	A	A	A	Animal testing: medical & non-medical products, significant alternative efforts; CEDC report; profile
Holiday ★	CL	B	B	A	A	B	A	A	A	Animal testing: medical & non-medical products, significant alternative efforts; CEDC report; profile
Hunger Stopper	OAT	B	A	A	B	B	D	?	C	CEDC report; Fair Share
Instinct	OAT	B	A	A	B	B	D	?	C	CEDC report; Fair Share
Jerky	HNZ	B	C	A	B	D	C	A	A	CEDC report; CEP Award — Environment
Jerky Strips	RN	?	A	C	C	?	?	?	D	Animal testing: non-medical products; CEDC report; tobacco; increasing TRI; Workplace Principles
Jim Dandy ★	GMR	C	A	A	B	A	A	B	A	factory farming; foreign-based company
Kal Kan	MARS	C	A	B	A	?	?	C	B	
Katfish Pickins	RAL	C	C	B	B	B	B	C	B	CEDC report; increasing TRI

The Environment | Charitable Giving | Community Outreach | Women's Advancement | Minority Advancement | Family | Workplace Issues | Disclosure of Information | ★ Honor Roll

For a more detailed explanation, see pages 7–28.

PRODUCT	PARENT COMPANY									EXTRAS
Ken-L	OAT	B	A	A	B	B	D	?	C	CEDC report; Fair Share
Kennel Club	OAT	B	A	A	B	B	D	?	C	CEDC report; Fair Share
Kibbles	RAL	C	C	B	B	B	B	C	B	CEDC report; increasing TRI
Kibbles 'N Bits	OAT	B	A	A	B	B	D	?	C	CEDC report; Fair Share
Kit-e-ration	OAT	B	A	A	B	B	D	?	C	CEDC report; Fair Share
Kit 'N Kaboodle	RAL	C	C	B	B	B	B	C	B	CEDC report; increasing TRI
Kitten Chow	RAL	C	C	B	B	B	B	C	B	CEDC report; increasing TRI
Kitty's Gourmet Feast	OAT	B	A	A	B	B	D	?	C	CEDC report; Fair Share
Kozy Kitten	HNZ	B	C	A	B	D	C	A	A	CEDC report; CEP Award — Environment
Kozy Kritter	HNZ	B	C	A	B	D	C	A	A	CEDC report; CEP Award — Environment
Litter Green	CLX	B	B	A	A	A	C	C	A	Animal testing: non-medical products, significant alternative efforts; CEDC report; CEP Award — Community; increasing TRI
Little Big Meal	RAL	C	C	B	B	B	B	C	B	CEDC report; increasing TRI
Little Critter	CAG	C	C	C	C	?	?	F	C	CEDC report; factory farming; profile
Love Me Tender	OAT	B	A	A	B	B	D	?	C	CEDC report; Fair Share
Lovin' Spoonfuls	RAL	C	C	B	B	B	B	C	B	CEDC report; increasing TRI
Lucky Dog	RAL	C	C	B	B	B	B	C	B	CEDC report; increasing TRI

PRODUCT	PARENT COMPANY									EXTRAS
Main Dish	OAT	B	A	A	B	B	D	?	C	CEDC report; Fair Share
Mainstay	RAL	C	C	B	B	B	B	C	B	CEDC report; increasing TRI
Marathon ★	GMR	C	A	A	B	A	A	B	A	factory farming; foreign-based company
Maverick	RAL	C	C	B	B	B	B	C	B	CEDC report; increasing TRI
Meal Maker	RAL	C	C	B	B	B	B	C	B	CEDC report; increasing TRI
Mealtime	MARS	C	A	B	A	?	?	C	B	
Meaty Bone	HNZ	B	C	A	B	D	C	A	A	CEDC report; CEP Award — Environment
Meow Mix	RAL	C	C	B	B	B	B	C	B	CEDC report; increasing TRI
Milk-Bone	RN	?	A	C	C	?	?	?	D	Animal testing: non-medical products; CEDC report; tobacco; increasing TRI; Workplace Principles
Moist & Chunky	RAL	C	C	B	B	B	B	C	B	CEDC report; increasing TRI
Moist & Meaty	RAL	C	C	B	B	B	B	C	B	CEDC report; increasing TRI
Moist Meals	OAT	B	A	A	B	B	D	?	C	CEDC report; Fair Share
Moist N Beefy	OAT	B	A	A	B	B	D	?	C	CEDC report; Fair Share
MPS Chunks	MARS	C	A	B	A	?	?	C	B	

The Environment | Charitable Giving | Community Outreach | Women's Advancement | Minority Advancement | Family | Workplace Issues | Disclosure of Information | ★ Honor Roll

For a more detailed explanation, see pages 7–28.

PRODUCT	PARENT COMPANY		$		♀					EXTRAS
Mycodex	SBH	C	D	C	B	B	A	B	C	Animal testing: medical products only, significant alternative efforts; foreign-based company; Workplace Principles
Nature's Course	RAL	C	C	B	B	B	B	C	B	CEDC report; increasing TRI
Norden Labs	SBH	C	D	C	B	B	A	B	C	Animal testing: medical products only, significant alternative efforts; foreign-based company; Workplace Principles
Nutrivance	RAL	C	C	B	B	B	B	C	B	CEDC report; increasing TRI
Occo	ADM	D	F	?	D	?	?	D	F	CEDC report; increasing TRI
Ocean Blend	RAL	C	C	B	B	B	B	C	B	CEDC report; increasing TRI
O.N.E.	RAL	C	C	B	B	B	B	C	B	CEDC report; increasing TRI
Original Blend	RAL	C	C	B	B	B	B	C	B	CEDC report; increasing TRI
Pedigree	MARS	C	A	B	A	?	?	C	B	
Pet Tabs	SBH	C	D	C	B	B	A	B	C	Animal testing: medical products only, significant alternative efforts; foreign-based company; Workplace Principles
Pick-A-Pouch	RAL	C	C	B	B	B	B	C	B	CEDC report; increasing TRI
Poultry Platter	OAT	B	A	A	B	B	D	?	C	CEDC report; Fair Share
Pounce	OAT	B	A	A	B	B	D	?	C	CEDC report; Fair Share
Praise	RAL	C	C	B	B	B	B	C	B	CEDC report; increasing TRI
Prescription Diet ★	CL	B	B	A	A	B	A	A	A	Animal testing: medical & non-medical products, significant alternative efforts; CEDC report; profile

PRODUCT	PARENT COMPANY	The Environment	Charitable Giving	Community Outreach	Women's Advancement	Minority Advancement	Family	Workplace Issues	Disclosure of Information	EXTRAS
Prime	RAL	C	C	B	B	B	B	C	B	CEDC report; increasing TRI
Prime Platter	OAT	B	A	A	B	B	D	?	C	CEDC report; Fair Share
Pro Plan	RAL	C	C	B	B	B	B	C	B	CEDC report; increasing TRI
Pup-Peroni	OAT	B	A	A	B	B	D	?	C	CEDC report; Fair Share
Puppy Choice	OAT	B	A	A	B	B	D	?	C	CEDC report; Fair Share
Puppy Chow	RAL	C	C	B	B	B	B	C	B	CEDC report; increasing TRI
Puppy Pieces	HNZ	B	C	A	B	D	C	A	A	CEDC report; CEP Award — Environment
Purina	RAL	C	C	B	B	B	B	C	B	CEDC report; increasing TRI
Puss 'N Boots	OAT	B	A	A	B	B	D	?	C	CEDC report; Fair Share
Quota	OAT	B	A	A	B	B	D	?	C	CEDC report; Fair Share
Rally	OAT	B	A	A	B	B	D	?	C	CEDC report; Fair Share
Recipe	HNZ	B	C	A	B	D	C	A	A	CEDC report; CEP Award — Environment
Reward	HNZ	B	C	A	B	D	C	A	A	CEDC report; CEP Award — Environment
Rival	CAG	C	C	C	C	?	?	F	C	CEDC report; factory farming; profile
Rosco	HNZ	B	C	A	B	D	C	A	A	CEDC report; CEP Award — Environment

The Environment | Charitable Giving | Community Outreach | Women's Advancement | Minority Advancement | Family | Workplace Issues | Disclosure of Information | ★ Honor Roll

For a more detailed explanation, see pages 7–28.

PRODUCT	PARENT COMPANY									EXTRAS
Savor	RAL	C	C	B	B	B	B	C	B	CEDC report; increasing TRI
Science Diet ★	CL	B	B	A	A	B	A	A	A	Animal testing: medical & non-medical products, significant alternative efforts; CEDC report; profile
Scoop Away	FBR	C	A	C	F	D	D	B	B	Animal testing: non-medical products, significant alternative efforts; profile
Scoop Fresh	CLX	B	B	A	A	A	C	C	A	Animal testing: non-medical products, significant alternative efforts; CEDC report; CEP Award — Community; increasing TRI
Sea Dog	RAL	C	C	B	B	B	B	C	B	CEDC report; increasing TRI
Sea Nip	RAL	C	C	B	B	B	B	C	B	CEDC report; increasing TRI
Security	CAG	C	C	C	C	?	?	F	C	CEDC report; factory farming; profile
Select Blend	OAT	B	A	A	B	B	D	?	C	CEDC report; Fair Share
Sergeants	CAG	C	C	C	C	?	?	F	C	CEDC report; factory farming; profile
Sheba	MARS	C	A	B	A	?	?	C	B	
Short Ribz	RAL	C	C	B	B	B	B	C	B	CEDC report; increasing TRI
Shurchoice	OAT	B	A	A	B	B	D	?	C	CEDC report; Fair Share
Sixth Sense	OAT	B	A	A	B	B	D	?	C	CEDC report; Fair Share
Skip	CAG	C	C	C	C	?	?	F	C	CEDC report; factory farming; profile
Skippy	HNZ	B	C	A	B	D	C	A	A	CEDC report; CEP Award — Environment

PRODUCT	PARENT COMPANY	The Environment	Charitable Giving	Community Outreach	Women's Advancement	Minority Advancement	Family	Workplace Issues	Disclosure of Information	EXTRAS
Smart Cat	RAL	C	C	B	B	B	B	C	B	CEDC report; increasing TRI
Smorgasburger	OAT	B	A	A	B	B	D	?	C	CEDC report; Fair Share
Snausages	OAT	B	A	A	B	B	D	?	C	CEDC report; Fair Share
Snoopy	CAG	C	C	C	C	?	?	F	C	CEDC report; factory farming; profile
Songberry	RAL	C	C	B	B	B	B	C	B	CEDC report; increasing TRI
Special Care	RAL	C	C	B	B	B	B	C	B	CEDC report; increasing TRI
Special Cuts	OAT	B	A	A	B	B	D	?	C	CEDC report; Fair Share
Special Dinners	RAL	C	C	B	B	B	B	C	B	CEDC report; increasing TRI
Sturdy	HNZ	B	C	A	B	D	C	A	A	CEDC report; CEP Award — Environment
Super Supper	HNZ	B	C	A	B	D	C	A	A	CEDC report; CEP Award — Environment
Sure Shot	CAG	C	C	C	C	?	?	F	C	CEDC report; factory farming; profile
T-Bone	OAT	B	A	A	B	B	D	?	C	CEDC report; Fair Share
Tender Chops	OAT	B	A	A	B	B	D	?	C	CEDC report; Fair Share
Tender Chunks	OAT	B	A	A	B	B	D	?	C	CEDC report; Fair Share
Tender Meals	HNZ	B	C	A	B	D	C	A	A	CEDC report; CEP Award — Environment

For a more detailed explanation, see pages 7–28.

PRODUCT	PARENT COMPANY									EXTRAS
Tender Meaty Chunx	OAT	B	A	A	B	B	D	?	C	CEDC report; Fair Share
Tender Vittles	RAL	C	C	B	B	B	B	C	B	CEDC report; increasing TRI
Thrive	RAL	C	C	B	B	B	B	C	B	CEDC report; increasing TRI
Tiger Food	OAT	B	A	A	B	B	D	?	C	CEDC report; Fair Share
Tiger Treats	OAT	B	A	A	B	B	D	?	C	CEDC report; Fair Share
Top Choice	OAT	B	A	A	B	B	D	?	C	CEDC report; Fair Share
Top Secret	RAL	C	C	B	B	B	B	C	B	CEDC report; increasing TRI
Unique	RAL	C	C	B	B	B	B	C	B	CEDC report; increasing TRI
Variety Menu	RAL	C	C	B	B	B	B	C	B	CEDC report; increasing TRI
Waggles	RAL	C	C	B	B	B	B	C	B	CEDC report; increasing TRI
Wellington	HNZ	B	C	A	B	D	C	A	A	CEDC report; CEP Award — Environment
Western Grille	OAT	B	A	A	B	B	D	?	C	CEDC report; Fair Share
Whiskas	MARS	C	A	B	A	?	?	C	B	
Whisker Lickin's	RAL	C	C	B	B	B	B	C	B	CEDC report; increasing TRI
Worm-away	CAG	C	C	C	C	?	?	F	C	CEDC report; factory farming; profile
PICKLES & RELISHES										
Claussen	MO	D	D	?	A	A	?	?	F	Animal testing: non-medical products; CEDC report; tobacco; increasing TRI; Workplace Principles

PRODUCT	PARENT COMPANY	The Environment	Charitable Giving	Community Outreach	Women's Advancement	Minority Advancement	Family	Workplace Issues	Disclosure of Information	EXTRAS
Early California	CPB	B	C	B	A	A	A	C	A	Animal testing: non-medical products, significant alternative efforts; CEDC report; on-site child care
Kraft Horseradish	MO	D	D	?	A	A	?	?	F	Animal testing: non-medical products; CEDC report; tobacco; increasing TRI; Workplace Principles
Vlasic	CPB	B	C	B	A	A	A	C	A	Animal testing: non-medical products, significant alternative efforts; CEDC report; on-site child care
POTATOES										
Homestyle Potatoes ★	GIS	B	A	A	A	B	B	A	A	CEDC report; CEP Awards — Charity, EEO, Opportunities for the Disabled; profile; Workplace Principles
Potato Casseroles ★	GIS	B	A	A	A	B	B	A	A	CEDC report; CEP Awards — Charity, EEO, Opportunities for the Disabled; profile; Workplace Principles
Potato Express ★	GIS	B	A	A	A	B	B	A	A	CEDC report; CEP Awards — Charity, EEO, Opportunities for the Disabled; profile; Workplace Principles
Special Recipe	HNZ	B	C	A	B	D	C	A	A	CEDC report; CEP Award — Environment
Twice Baked Potatoes ★	GIS	B	A	A	A	B	B	A	A	CEDC report; CEP Awards — Charity, EEO, Opportunities for the Disabled; profile; Workplace Principles
POTATOES: FROZEN										
Act II French Fries	CAG	C	C	C	C	?	?	F	C	CEDC report; factory farming; profile
Crispy Browns	CAG	C	C	C	C	?	?	F	C	CEDC report; factory farming; profile

The Environment
Charitable Giving

Community Outreach

Women's Advancement

Minority Advancement

Family

Workplace Issues
Disclosure of Information
★ Honor Roll

For a more detailed explanation, see pages 7–28.

PRODUCT	PARENT COMPANY									EXTRAS
Garden Gourmet ★	GMR	C	A	A	B	A	A	B	A	factory farming; foreign-based company
Lamb-Weston	CAG	C	C	C	C	?	?	F	C	CEDC report; factory farming; profile
Ore-Ida	HNZ	B	C	A	B	D	C	A	A	CEDC report; CEP Award — Environment
Tiny Taters	MO	D	D	?	A	A	?	?	F	Animal testing: non-medical products; CEDC report; tobacco; increasing TRI; Workplace Principles
PREPARED FOODS										
Appian Way	DL	C	A	B	B	?	F	B	C	CEDC report
Award	CAG	C	C	C	C	?	?	F	C	CEDC report; factory farming; profile
B & M	PT	C	D	?	B	?	?	?	F	CEDC report; increasing TRI
Campbell's	CPB	B	C	B	A	A	A	C	A	Animal testing: non-medical products, significant alternative efforts; CEDC report; on-site child care
Chef Boyardee	AHP	C	F	C	B	B	C	C	A	Animal testing: medical & non-medical products, significant alternative efforts; infant formula
Chicken Helper ★	GIS	B	A	A	A	B	B	A	A	CEDC report; CEP Awards — Charity, EEO, Opportunities for the Disabled; profile; Workplace Principles
Cook Off	AHP	C	F	C	B	B	C	C	A	Animal testing: medical & non-medical products, significant alternative efforts; infant formula
Country Store	BN	C	C	B	A	A	B	B	A	CEDC report
Country Style	AHP	C	F	C	B	B	C	C	A	Animal testing: medical & non-medical products, significant alternative efforts; infant formula

PRODUCT	PARENT COMPANY	The Environment	Charitable Giving	Community Outreach	Women's Advancement	Minority Advancement	Family	Workplace Issues	Disclosure of Information	EXTRAS
Dennison's	AHP	C	F	C	B	B	C	C	A	Animal testing: medical & non-medical products, significant alternative efforts; infant formula
Festive Dinner	PT	C	D	?	B	?	?	?	F	CEDC report; increasing TRI
Franco-American	CPB	B	C	B	A	A	A	C	A	Animal testing: non-medical products, significant alternative efforts; CEDC report; on-site child care
Gebhardt	CAG	C	C	C	C	?	?	F	C	CEDC report; factory farming; profile
Hamburger Fixin's	CAG	C	C	C	C	?	?	F	C	CEDC report; factory farming; profile
Hamburger Helper ★	GIS	B	A	A	A	B	B	A	A	CEDC report; CEP Awards — Charity, EEO, Opportunities for the Disabled; profile; Workplace Principles
Health Valley	HVAL	A	C	C	A	A	B	A	A	
Heinz	HNZ	B	C	A	B	D	C	A	A	CEDC report; CEP Award — Environment
Iron Kettle	AHP	C	F	C	B	B	C	C	A	Animal testing: medical & non-medical products, significant alternative efforts; infant formula
Knorr Instant Potatoes	CPC	C	A	B	A	B	C	A	B	Animal testing: non-medical products, signifcant alternative efforts; CEDC report; increasing TRI
Kraft	MO	D	D	?	A	A	?	?	F	Animal testing: non-medical products; CEDC report; tobacco; increasing TRI; Workplace Principles
La Choy	CAG	C	C	C	C	?	?	F	C	CEDC report; factory farming; profile

The Environment | Charitable Giving | Community Outreach | Women's Advancement | Minority Advancement | Family | Workplace Issues | Disclosure of Information | ★ Honor Roll

For a more detailed explanation, see pages 7–28.

PRODUCT	PARENT COMPANY									EXTRAS
Lunch Bucket	DL	C	A	B	B	?	F	B	C	CEDC report
Macaroni & Cheese	MO	D	D	?	A	A	?	?	F	Animal testing: non-medical products; CEDC report; tobacco; increasing TRI; Workplace Principles
Main Street	CAG	C	C	C	C	?	?	F	C	CEDC report; factory farming; profile
Northern States	CAG	C	C	C	C	?	?	F	C	CEDC report; factory farming; profile
Old El Paso	PT	C	D	?	B	?	?	?	F	CEDC report; increasing TRI
Ortega	RN	?	A	C	C	?	?	?	D	Animal testing: non-medical products; CEDC report; tobacco; increasing TRI; Workplace Principles
Pancho Villa	PT	C	D	?	B	?	?	?	F	CEDC report; increasing TRI
Pillsbury ★	GMR	C	A	A	B	A	A	B	A	factory farming; foreign-based company
Pizza Pockets	CAG	C	C	C	C	?	?	F	C	CEDC report; factory farming; profile
Potato Buds ★	GIS	B	A	A	A	B	B	A	A	CEDC report; CEP Awards — Charity, EEO, Opportunities for the Disabled; profile; Workplace Principles
Recipe Sauces ★	GIS	B	A	A	A	B	B	A	A	CEDC report; CEP Awards — Charity, EEO, Opportunities for the Disabled; profile; Workplace Principles
Suddenly Salad ★	GIS	B	A	A	A	B	B	A	A	CEDC report; CEP Awards — Charity, EEO, Opportunities for the Disabled; profile; Workplace Principles
Tuna Helper ★	GIS	B	A	A	A	B	B	A	A	CEDC report; CEP Awards — Charity, EEO, Opportunities for the Disabled; profile; Workplace Principles
Van Camp's	OAT	B	A	A	B	B	D	?	C	CEDC report; Fair Share

PRODUCT	PARENT COMPANY	The Environment	Charitable Giving	Community Outreach	Women's Advancement	Minority Advancement	Family	Workplace Issues	Disclosure of Information	EXTRAS
Velveeta Shells & Cheese	MO	D	D	?	A	A	?	?	F	Animal testing: non-medical products; CEDC report; tobacco; increasing TRI; Workplace Principles
Wolf	OAT	B	A	A	B	B	D	?	C	CEDC report; Fair Share
World's Fare	CAG	C	C	C	C	?	?	F	C	CEDC report; factory farming; profile
PREPARED FOODS: FROZEN										
A La Carte	MO	D	D	?	A	A	?	?	F	Animal testing: non-medical products; CEDC report; tobacco; increasing TRI; Workplace Principles
Abbondanza	OAT	B	A	A	B	B	D	?	C	CEDC report; Fair Share
Applause	MO	D	D	?	A	A	?	?	F	Animal testing: non-medical products; CEDC report; tobacco; increasing TRI; Workplace Principles
Armour Classics	CAG	C	C	C	C	?	?	F	C	CEDC report; factory farming; profile
Aunt Jemima	OAT	B	A	A	B	B	D	?	C	CEDC report; Fair Share
Banquet	CAG	C	C	C	C	?	?	F	C	CEDC report; factory farming; profile
Bluebox	MO	D	D	?	A	A	?	?	F	Animal testing: non-medical products; CEDC report; tobacco; increasing TRI; Workplace Principles
Budget Gourmet	MO	D	D	?	A	A	?	?	F	Animal testing: non-medical products; CEDC report; tobacco; increasing TRI; Workplace Principles
Cajun Cookin'	PT	C	D	?	B	?	?	?	F	CEDC report; increasing TRI

The Environment | Charitable Giving | Community Outreach | Women's Advancement | Minority Advancement | Family | Workplace Issues | Disclosure of Information | ★ Honor Roll

For a more detailed explanation, see pages 7–28.

PRODUCT	PARENT COMPANY									EXTRAS
Celeste	OAT	B	A	A	B	B	D	?	C	CEDC report; Fair Share
Chun King	CAG	C	C	C	C	?	?	F	C	CEDC report; factory farming; profile
Classic ★	GMR	C	A	A	B	A	A	B	A	factory farming; foreign-based company
Country Table	CAG	C	C	C	C	?	?	F	C	CEDC report; factory farming; profile
Culinova	MO	D	D	?	A	A	?	?	F	Animal testing: non-medical products; CEDC report; tobacco; increasing TRI; Workplace Principles
Dining In	CAG	C	C	C	C	?	?	F	C	CEDC report; factory farming; profile
Dining Treat	CAG	C	C	C	C	?	?	F	C	CEDC report; factory farming; profile
Entree Express	CAG	C	C	C	C	?	?	F	C	CEDC report; factory farming; profile
Extra Helpings	CAG	C	C	C	C	?	?	F	C	CEDC report; factory farming; profile
Family Favorites	CAG	C	C	C	C	?	?	F	C	CEDC report; factory farming; profile
Family Kitchen	RN	?	A	C	C	?	?	?	D	Animal testing: non-medical products; CEDC report; tobacco; increasing TRI; Workplace Principles
Fresh Creations	MO	D	D	?	A	A	?	?	F	Animal testing: non-medical products; CEDC report; tobacco; increasing TRI; Workplace Principles
Gorton's ★	GIS	B	A	A	A	B	B	A	A	CEDC report; CEP Awards — Charity, EEO, Opportunities for the Disabled; profile; Workplace Principles
Gourmet, The	MO	D	D	?	A	A	?	?	F	Animal testing: non-medical products; CEDC report; tobacco; increasing TRI; Workplace Principles
Hasty Hearth	CAG	C	C	C	C	?	?	F	C	CEDC report; factory farming; profile

PRODUCT	PARENT COMPANY	The Environment	Charitable Giving	Community Outreach	Women's Advancement	Minority Advancement	Family	Workplace Issues	Disclosure of Information	EXTRAS
Healthy Choice	CAG	C	C	C	C	?	?	F	C	CEDC report; factory farming; profile
Homestyle	OAT	B	A	A	B	B	D	?	C	CEDC report; Fair Share
Hot Bites	CAG	C	C	C	C	?	?	F	C	CEDC report; factory farming; profile
Hot 'n Spicy	CAG	C	C	C	C	?	?	F	C	CEDC report; factory farming; profile
Jeno's ★	GMR	C	A	A	B	A	A	B	A	factory farming; foreign-based company
Jiffy	CAG	C	C	C	C	?	?	F	C	CEDC report; factory farming; profile
Lean Cuisine	NEST	B	?	B	B	B	A	B	B	Animal testing: non-medical products, significant alternative efforts; foreign-based company; infant formula
Le Menu	CPB	B	C	B	A	A	A	C	A	Animal testing: non-medical products, significant alternative efforts; CEDC report; on-site child care
Morton	CAG	C	C	C	C	?	?	F	C	CEDC report; factory farming; profile
Mrs. Paul's	CPB	B	C	B	A	A	A	C	A	Animal testing: non-medical products, significant alternative efforts; CEDC report; on-site child care
Old American	TYSNA	C	?	D	A	B	?	D	D	factory farming; profile
Ovenstuffs	OAT	B	A	A	B	B	D	?	C	CEDC report; Fair Share
Pappalo's Frozen Pizza ★	GMR	C	A	A	B	A	A	B	A	factory farming; foreign-based company
Pasta Accents ★	GMR	C	A	A	B	A	A	B	A	factory farming; foreign-based company

The Environment | Charitable Giving | Community Outreach | Women's Advancement | Minority Advancement | Family | Workplace Issues | Disclosure of Information | ★ Honor Roll

For a more detailed explanation, see pages 7–28.

PRODUCT	PARENT COMPANY									EXTRAS
Patio	CAG	C	C	C	C	?	?	F	C	CEDC report; factory farming; profile
Patti Jean	TYSNA	C	?	D	A	B	?	D	D	factory farming; profile
Pepperidge Farm	CPB	B	C	B	A	A	A	C	A	Animal testing: non-medical products, significant alternative efforts; CEDC report; on-site child care
Smart Ones	HNZ	B	C	A	B	D	C	A	A	CEDC report; CEP Award — Environment
Steak-Umm	HNZ	B	C	A	B	D	C	A	A	CEDC report; CEP Award — Environment
Stouffer's	NEST	B	?	B	B	B	A	B	B	Animal testing: non-medical products, significant alternative efforts; foreign-based company; infant formula
Swanson	CPB	B	C	B	A	A	A	C	A	Animal testing: non-medical products, significant alternative efforts; CEDC report; on-site child care
Taste O' Sea	CAG	C	C	C	C	?	?	F	C	CEDC report; factory farming; profile
Tombstone	MO	D	D	?	A	A	?	?	F	Animal testing: non-medical products; CEDC report; tobacco; increasing TRI; Workplace Principles
Weight Watchers	HNZ	B	C	A	B	D	C	A	A	CEDC report; CEP Award — Environment
RICE & RICE DISHES										
Country Inn	MARS	C	A	B	A	?	?	C	B	
Golden Grain	OAT	B	A	A	B	B	D	?	C	CEDC report; Fair Share
Minute Rice	MO	D	D	?	A	A	?	?	F	Animal testing: non-medical products; CEDC report; tobacco; increasing TRI; Workplace Principles
Pantry Express ★	GMR	C	A	A	B	A	A	B	A	factory farming; foreign-based company

PRODUCT	PARENT COMPANY	The Environment	Charitable Giving	Community Outreach	Women's Advancement	Minority Advancement	Family	Workplace Issues	Disclosure of Information	EXTRAS
Pillsbury ★	GMR	C	A	A	B	A	A	B	A	factory farming; foreign-based company
Pritikin	OAT	B	A	A	B	B	D	?	C	CEDC report; Fair Share
Rice-A-Roni	OAT	B	A	A	B	B	D	?	C	CEDC report; Fair Share
Savory Classics	OAT	B	A	A	B	B	D	?	C	CEDC report; Fair Share
Uncle Ben's	MARS	C	A	B	A	?	?	C	B	
SALAD DRESSINGS										
Bennett's	BN	C	C	B	A	A	B	B	A	CEDC report
Catalina	MO	D	D	?	A	A	?	?	F	Animal testing: non-medical products; CEDC report; tobacco; increasing TRI; Workplace Principles
Classic Herb	MO	D	D	?	A	A	?	?	F	Animal testing: non-medical products; CEDC report; tobacco; increasing TRI; Workplace Principles
Conzelo	MO	D	D	?	A	A	?	?	F	Animal testing: non-medical products; CEDC report; tobacco; increasing TRI; Workplace Principles
Good Seasons	MO	D	D	?	A	A	?	?	F	Animal testing: non-medical products; CEDC report; tobacco; increasing TRI; Workplace Principles
Hidden Valley Ranch	CLX	B	B	A	A	A	C	C	A	Animal testing: non-medical products, significant alternative efforts; CEDC report; CEP Award — Community; increasing TRI

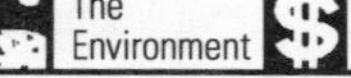 The Environment  Charitable Giving  Community Outreach  Women's Advancement  Minority Advancement 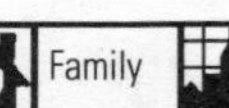 Family  Workplace Issues  Disclosure of Information ★ Honor Roll

For a more detailed explanation, see pages 7–28.

PRODUCT	PARENT COMPANY		$							EXTRAS
Kraft	MO	D	D	?	A	A	?	?	F	Animal testing: non-medical products; CEDC report; tobacco; increasing TRI; Workplace Principles
Marie's	CPB	B	C	B	A	A	A	C	A	Animal testing: non-medical products, significant alternative efforts; CEDC report; on-site child care
Newman's Own	NEWO	A	A	A	A	Neutral	C	A	A	100% profit to charity; CEP Award — Charity; Small company
Salad Life	HVAL	A	C	C	A	A	B	A	A	
Seven Seas	MO	D	D	?	A	A	?	?	F	Animal testing: non-medical products; CEDC report; tobacco; increasing TRI; Workplace Principles
Thousand Island	MO	D	D	?	A	A	?	?	F	Animal testing: non-medical products; CEDC report; tobacco; increasing TRI; Workplace Principles
Weight Watchers	HNZ	B	C	A	B	D	C	A	A	CEDC report; CEP Award — Environment
Wishbone	UN	B	C	C	F	D	C	B	C	Animal testing: non-medical products, significant alternative efforts; foreign-based company; profile
SALT, SEASONINGS & SPICES										
Ac'cent	PT	C	D	?	B	?	?	?	F	CEDC report; increasing TRI
ADOBO	UN	B	C	C	F	D	C	B	C	Animal testing: non-medical products, significant alternative efforts; foreign-based company; profile
Adolph's Meat Tenderizer	UN	B	C	C	F	D	C	B	C	Animal testing: non-medical products, significant alternative efforts; foreign-based company; profile
All Purpose	HVAL	A	C	C	A	A	B	A	A	

PRODUCT	PARENT COMPANY	The Environment	Charitable Giving	Community Outreach	Women's Advancement	Minority Advancement	Family	Workplace Issues	Disclosure of Information	EXTRAS
Bac'os ★	GIS	B	A	A	A	B	B	A	A	CEDC report; CEP Awards — Charity, EEO, Opportunities for the Disabled; profile; Workplace Principles
El Molino	BN	C	C	B	A	A	B	B	A	CEDC report
Hollywood	PT	C	D	?	B	?	?	?	F	CEDC report; increasing TRI
Instead-of-Salt	HVAL	A	C	C	A	A	B	A	A	
Lawry's	UN	B	C	C	F	D	C	B	C	Animal testing: non-medical products, significant alternative efforts; foreign-based company; profile
Makin' Cajun	MO	D	D	?	A	A	?	?	F	Animal testing: non-medical products; CEDC report; tobacco; increasing TRI; Workplace Principles
Mrs. Dash	ACV	A	?	B	A	D	D	B	B	Animal testing: non-medical products; increasing TRI
No Salt	SBH	C	D	C	B	B	A	B	C	Animal testing: medical products only, significant alternative efforts; foreign-based company; Workplace Principles
Papa Dash Lite Salt Blends	ACV	A	?	B	A	D	D	B	B	Animal testing: non-medical products; increasing TRI
Sausage Seasoning	ADM	D	F	?	D	?	?	D	F	CEDC report; increasing TRI
SAUCES & GRAVY										
Albadoro	BN	C	C	B	A	A	B	B	A	CEDC report
Aunt Millie's	BN	C	C	B	A	A	B	B	A	CEDC report

The Environment | Charitable Giving | Community Outreach | Women's Advancement | Minority Advancement | Family | Workplace Issues | Disclosure of Information | ★ Honor Roll

For a more detailed explanation, see pages 7–28.

PRODUCT	PARENT COMPANY									EXTRAS
Bull's Eye	MO	D	D	?	A	A	?	?	F	Animal testing: non-medical products; CEDC report; tobacco; increasing TRI; Workplace Principles
Butcher's Choice	OAT	B	A	A	B	B	D	?	C	CEDC report; Fair Share
Catch-Up	HVAL	A	C	C	A	A	B	A	A	
Classico	BN	C	C	B	A	A	B	B	A	CEDC report
Compliment	PT	C	D	?	B	?	?	?	F	CEDC report; increasing TRI
Contadina	NEST	B	?	B	B	B	A	B	B	Animal testing: non-medical products, significant alternative efforts; foreign-based company; infant formula
Fiesta Santa Fe	PT	C	D	?	B	?	?	?	F	CEDC report; increasing TRI
Healthy Choice	CAG	C	C	C	C	?	?	F	C	CEDC report; factory farming; profile
Healthy Request	CPB	B	C	B	A	A	A	C	A	Animal testing: non-medical products, significant alternative efforts; CEDC report; on-site child care
Home Style	HNZ	B	C	A	B	D	C	A	A	CEDC report; CEP Award — Environment
Hunt's	CAG	C	C	C	C	?	?	F	C	CEDC report; factory farming; profile
K.C. Masterpiece	CLX	B	B	A	A	A	C	C	A	Animal testing: non-medical products, significant alternative efforts; CEDC report; CEP Award — Community; increasing TRI
Kitchen Bouquet	CLX	B	B	A	A	A	C	C	A	Animal testing: non-medical products, significant alternative efforts; CEDC report; CEP Award — Community; increasing TRI

PRODUCT	PARENT COMPANY	The Environment	Charitable Giving	Community Outreach	Women's Advancement	Minority Advancement	Family	Workplace Issues	Disclosure of Information	EXTRAS
Knorr	CPC	C	A	B	A	B	C	A	B	Animal testing: non-medical products, significant alternative efforts; CEDC report; increasing TRI
La Croix	CPB	B	C	B	A	A	A	C	A	Animal testing: non-medical products, significant alternative efforts; CEDC report; on-site child care
Magic Touch	CAG	C	C	C	C	?	?	F	C	CEDC report; factory farming; profile
Manwich	CAG	C	C	C	C	?	?	F	C	CEDC report; factory farming; profile
Mexican Way	OAT	B	A	A	B	B	D	?	C	CEDC report; Fair Share
Milani 1890	ACV	A	?	B	A	D	D	B	B	Animal testing: non-medical products; increasing TRI
Newman's Own	NEWO	A	A	A	A	Neutral	C	A	A	100% profit to charity; CEP Award — Charity; small company
Open Pit	CPB	B	C	B	A	A	A	C	A	Animal testing: non-medical products, significant alternative efforts; CEDC report; on-site child care
Portovista	AHP	C	F	C	B	B	C	C	A	Animal testing: medical & non-medical products, significant alternative efforts; infant formula
Prego	CPB	B	C	B	A	A	A	C	A	Animal testing: non-medical products, significant alternative efforts; CEDC report; on-site child care
Ragu	UN	B	C	C	F	D	C	B	C	Animal testing: non-medical products, significant alternative efforts; foreign-based company; profile
Tamaru-ya	HVAL	A	C	C	A	A	B	A	A	

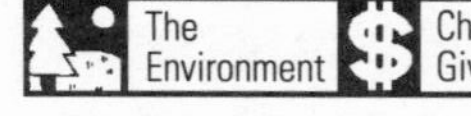

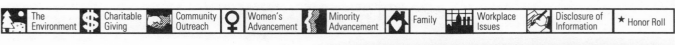

The Environment | Charitable Giving | Community Outreach | Women's Advancement | Minority Advancement | Family | Workplace Issues | Disclosure of Information | ★ Honor Roll

For a more detailed explanation, see pages 7–28.

PRODUCT	PARENT COMPANY									EXTRAS
Thick & Rich	HNZ	B	C	A	B	D	C	A	A	CEDC report; CEP Award — Environment
Thick 'N Spicy	MO	D	D	?	A	A	?	?	F	Animal testing: non-medical products; CEDC report; tobacco; increasing TRI; Workplace Principles
Vlasic	CPB	B	C	B	A	A	A	C	A	Animal testing: non-medical products, significant alternative efforts; CEDC report; on-site child care
Yamaki	HNZ	B	C	A	B	D	C	A	A	CEDC report; CEP Award — Environment
SHAMPOOS & HAIR-CARE NEEDS										
Adorn	G	C	C	B	D	D	B	B	A	Animal testing: medical & non-medical products, significant alternative efforts
Affinity *	JNJ	B	A	A	A	A	A	A	A	Animal testing: medical products only, significant alternative efforts; CEP Award — Disclosure; on-site child care; profile; Workplace Principles
Alberto	ACV	A	?	B	A	D	D	B	B	Animal testing: non-medical products; increasing TRI
Alberto VO5	ACV	A	?	B	A	D	D	B	B	Animal testing: non-medical products; increasing TRI
Apple Pectin	DOW	C	C	B	B	A	A	B	A	Animal testing: non-medical products, significant alternative efforts; CEDC report; on-site child care; pesticide sterilization suits
Aqua Net	UN	B	C	C	F	D	C	B	C	Animal testing: non-medical products, significant alternative efforts; foreign-based company; profile
Attitudes	BMY	B	C	B	B	B	B	B	A	Animal testing: medical & non-medical products, significant alternative efforts; infant formula; Workplace Principles

PRODUCT	PARENT COMPANY	The Environment	Charitable Giving	Community Outreach	Women's Advancement	Minority Advancement	Family	Workplace Issues	Disclosure of Information	EXTRAS
Aveda ★	AVED	A	A	A	A	A	A	A	A	CEP Award — Environment; CERES principles; profile
Avon ★	AVP	B	A	A	A	A	A	B	A	CEP Award — EEO; increasing TRI; on-site day care
Basic White	BMY	B	C	B	B	B	B	B	A	Animal testing: medical & non-medical products, significant alternative efforts; infant formula; Workplace Principles
Beautiful Collection	BMY	B	C	B	B	B	B	B	A	Animal testing: medical & non-medical products, significant alternative efforts; infant formula; Workplace Principles
BeautiLac	DOW	C	C	B	B	A	A	B	A	Animal testing: non-medical products, significant alternative efforts; CEDC report; on-site child care; pesticide sterilization suits
Body Plus	DOW	C	C	B	B	A	A	B	A	Animal testing: non-medical products, significant alternative efforts; CEDC report; on-site child care; pesticide sterilization suits
Body Shop	BODY	A	?	A	A	B	B	C	A	foreign-based company
Bold Hold	ACV	A	?	B	A	D	D	B	B	Animal testing: non-medical products; increasing TRI
Bone Strait	ACV	A	?	B	A	D	D	B	B	Animal testing: non-medical products; increasing TRI
Born Blonde	BMY	B	C	B	B	B	B	B	A	Animal testing: medical & non-medical products, significant alternative efforts; infant formula; Workplace Principles
Botanical	DOW	C	C	B	B	A	A	B	A	Animal testing: non-medical products, significant alternative efforts; CEDC report; on-site child care; pesticide sterilization suits

The Environment | Charitable Giving | Community Outreach | Women's Advancement | Minority Advancement | Family | Workplace Issues | Disclosure of Information | ★ Honor Roll

For a more detailed explanation, see pages 7–28.

PRODUCT	PARENT COMPANY									EXTRAS
Breck	DL	C	A	B	B	?	F	B	C	CEDC report
Brush-On Lights	BMY	B	C	B	B	B	B	B	A	Animal testing: medical & non-medical products, significant alternative efforts; infant formula; Workplace Principles
Brylcreem	SBH	C	D	C	B	B	A	B	C	Animal testing: medical products only, significant alternative efforts; foreign-based company; Workplace Principles
Casting	LORA	B	C	B	A	C	C	B	A	foreign-based company
Clairol	BMY	B	C	B	B	B	B	B	A	Animal testing: medical & non-medical products, significant alternative efforts; infant formula; Workplace Principles
Clear Difference	G	C	C	B	D	D	B	B	A	Animal testing: medical & non-medical products, significant alternative efforts
Co-A Kinetics	DOW	C	C	B	B	A	A	B	A	Animal testing: non-medical products, significant alternative efforts; CEDC report; on-site child care; pesticide sterilization suits
Colorvive	LORA	B	C	B	A	C	C	B	A	foreign-based company
Command	ACV	A	?	B	A	D	D	B	B	Animal testing: non-medical products; increasing TRI
Condition	BMY	B	C	B	B	B	B	B	A	Animal testing: medical & non-medical products, significant alternative efforts; infant formula; Workplace Principles
Consort	ACV	A	?	B	A	D	D	B	B	Animal testing: non-medical products; increasing TRI
Conti	SBH	C	D	C	B	B	A	B	C	Animal testing: medical products only, significant alternative efforts; foreign-based company; Workplace Principles
Dail-Ease	DOW	C	C	B	B	A	A	B	A	Animal testing: non-medical products, significant alternative efforts; CEDC report; on-site child care; pesticide sterilization suits

PRODUCT	PARENT COMPANY	The Environment	Charitable Giving	Community Outreach	Women's Advancement	Minority Advancement	Family	Workplace Issues	Disclosure of Information	EXTRAS
Denorex	AHP	C	F	C	B	B	C	C	A	Animal testing: medical & non-medical products, significant alternative efforts; infant formula
Dimension	UN	B	C	C	F	D	C	B	C	Animal testing: non-medical products, significant alternative efforts; foreign-based company; profile
Dry Style	DOW	C	C	B	B	A	A	B	A	Animal testing: non-medical products, significant alternative efforts; CEDC report; on-site child care; pesticide sterilization suits
Epic Waves	G	C	C	B	D	D	B	B	A	Animal testing: medical & non-medical products, significant alternative efforts
Faberge	UN	B	C	C	F	D	C	B	C	Animal testing: non-medical products, significant alternative efforts; foreign-based company; profile
Final Net	BMY	B	C	B	B	B	B	B	A	Animal testing: medical & non-medical products, significant alternative efforts; infant formula; Workplace Principles
Finesse	HC	A	A	A	B	?	A	B	B	Animal testing: non-medical products
Free Hold	LORA	B	C	B	A	C	C	B	A	foreign-based company
Frosted Lights	BMY	B	C	B	B	B	B	B	A	Animal testing: medical & non-medical products, significant alternative efforts; infant formula; Workplace Principles
Gamma Quotient	DOW	C	C	B	B	A	A	B	A	Animal testing: non-medical products, significant alternative efforts; CEDC report; on-site child care; pesticide sterilization suits

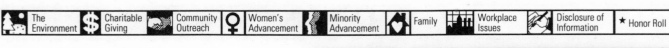

The Environment | Charitable Giving | Community Outreach | Women's Advancement | Minority Advancement | Family | Workplace Issues | Disclosure of Information | ★ Honor Roll

For a more detailed explanation, see pages 7–28.

PRODUCT	PARENT COMPANY									EXTRAS
Get Set	ACV	A	?	B	A	D	D	B	B	Animal testing: non-medical products; increasing TRI
Glaz	DOW	C	C	B	B	A	A	B	A	Animal testing: non-medical products, significant alternative efforts; CEDC report; on-site child care; pesticide sterilization suits
Head & Shoulders	PG	C	B	A	B	B	A	B	A	Animal testing: medical and non-medical products, significant alternative efforts; CEDC report; CEP Awards — Animal Welfare, Employer Responsiveness; increasing TRI; on-site day care; Workplace Principles
Hydravive	LORA	B	C	B	A	C	C	B	A	foreign-based company
ICS	DOW	C	C	B	B	A	A	B	A	Animal testing: non-medical products, significant alternative efforts; CEDC report; on-site child care; pesticide sterilization suits
Infusium 23	BMY	B	C	B	B	B	B	B	A	Animal testing: medical & non-medical products, significant alternative efforts; infant formula; Workplace Principles
Instant Beauty	BMY	B	C	B	B	B	B	B	A	Animal testing: medical & non-medical products, significant alternative efforts; infant formula; Workplace Principles
Ivory	PG	C	B	A	B	B	A	B	A	Animal testing: medical and non-medical products, significant alternative efforts; CEDC report; CEP Awards — Animal Welfare, Employer Responsiveness; increasing TRI; on-site day care; Workplace Principles
Jazzing	BMY	B	C	B	B	B	B	B	A	Animal testing: medical & non-medical products, significant alternative efforts; infant formula; Workplace Principles
Johnson's Baby Shampoo ★	JNJ	B	A	A	A	A	A	A	A	Animal testing: medical products only, significant alternative efforts; CEP Award — Disclosure; on-site child care; profile; Workplace Principles

PRODUCT	PARENT COMPANY	The Environment	Charitable Giving	Community Outreach	Women's Advancement	Minority Advancement	Family	Workplace Issues	Disclosure of Information	EXTRAS
Kaleidocolors	BMY	B	C	B	B	B	B	B	A	Animal testing: medical & non-medical products, significant alternative efforts; infant formula; Workplace Principles
Kiss My Face	KMF	A	?	A	A	Neutral	A	A	A	Small company
Kreml	SBH	C	D	C	B	B	A	B	C	Animal testing: medical products only, significant alternative efforts; foreign-based company; Workplace Principles
La Maur	DOW	C	C	B	B	A	A	B	A	Animal testing: non-medical products, significant alternative efforts; CEDC report; on-site child care; pesticide sterilization suits
Lancome	LORA	B	C	B	A	C	C	B	A	foreign-based company
Logices Colorcreme	BMY	B	C	B	B	B	B	B	A	Animal testing: medical & non-medical products, significant alternative efforts; infant formula; Workplace Principles
L'Oreal	LORA	B	C	B	A	C	C	B	A	foreign-based company
Lustrasilk	G	C	C	B	D	D	B	B	A	Animal testing: medical & non-medical products, significant alternative efforts
Miss Clairol	BMY	B	C	B	B	B	B	B	A	Animal testing: medical & non-medical products, significant alternative efforts; infant formula; Workplace Principles
Natural Woman	DOW	C	C	B	B	A	A	B	A	Animal testing: non-medical products, significant alternative efforts; CEDC report; on-site child care; pesticide sterilization suits

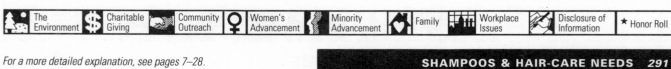

The Environment | Charitable Giving | Community Outreach | Women's Advancement | Minority Advancement | Family | Workplace Issues | Disclosure of Information | ★ Honor Roll

For a more detailed explanation, see pages 7–28.

PRODUCT	PARENT COMPANY									EXTRAS
Neo	DOW	C	C	B	B	A	A	B	A	Animal testing: non-medical products, significant alternative efforts; CEDC report; on-site child care; pesticide sterilization suits
New Dawn	ACV	A	?	B	A	D	D	B	B	Animal testing: non-medical products; increasing TRI
Nice 'N Easy	BMY	B	C	B	B	B	B	B	A	Animal testing: medical & non-medical products, significant alternative efforts; infant formula; Workplace Principles
No More Tangles ★	JNJ	B	A	A	A	A	A	A	A	Animal testing: medical products only, significant alternative efforts; CEP Award — Disclosure; on-site child care; profile; Workplace Principles
N.R.G.	DOW	C	C	B	B	A	A	B	A	Animal testing: non-medical products, significant alternative efforts; CEDC report; on-site child care; pesticide sterilization suits
Nucleic A	DOW	C	C	B	B	A	A	B	A	Animal testing: non-medical products, significant alternative efforts; CEDC report; on-site child care; pesticide sterilization suits
Nu-Heights	DOW	C	C	B	B	A	A	B	A	Animal testing: non-medical products, significant alternative efforts; CEDC report; on-site child care; pesticide sterilization suits
Nu-Pak	DOW	C	C	B	B	A	A	B	A	Animal testing: non-medical products, significant alternative efforts; CEDC report; on-site child care; pesticide sterilization suits
Ogilvie	EK	C	B	B	B	B	A	B	B	Animal testing: medical and non-medical products, significant alternative efforts; CEDC report; CEP Award — EEO

PRODUCT	PARENT COMPANY	The Environment	Charitable Giving	Community Outreach	Women's Advancement	Minority Advancement	Family	Workplace Issues	Disclosure of Information	EXTRAS
Option	BMY	B	C	B	B	B	B	B	A	Animal testing: medical & non-medical products, significant alternative efforts; infant formula; Workplace Principles
Organicore	DOW	C	C	B	B	A	A	B	A	Animal testing: non-medical products, significant alternative efforts; CEDC report; on-site child care; pesticide sterilization suits
Palmolive ★	CL	B	B	A	A	B	A	A	A	Animal testing: medical & non-medical products, significant alternative efforts; CEDC report; profile
Pantene	PG	C	B	A	B	B	A	B	A	Animal testing: medical and non-medical products, significant alternative efforts; CEDC report; CEP Awards — Animal Welfare, Employer Responsiveness; increasing TRI; on-site day care; Workplace Principles
Permasoft	DOW	C	C	B	B	A	A	B	A	Animal testing: non-medical products, significant alternative efforts; CEDC report; on-site child care; pesticide sterilization suits
Permavive	LORA	B	C	B	A	C	C	B	A	foreign-based company
Pert Plus	PG	C	B	A	B	B	A	B	A	Animal testing: medical and non-medical products, significant alternative efforts; CEDC report; CEP Awards — Animal Welfare, Employer Responsiveness; increasing TRI; on-site day care; Workplace Principles
Preference	LORA	B	C	B	A	C	C	B	A	foreign-based company

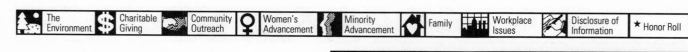

The Environment | Charitable Giving | Community Outreach | Women's Advancement | Minority Advancement | Family | Workplace Issues | Disclosure of Information | ★ Honor Roll

For a more detailed explanation, see pages 7–28.

PRODUCT	PARENT COMPANY									EXTRAS
Prell	PG	C	B	A	B	B	A	B	A	Animal testing: medical and non-medical products, significant alternative efforts; CEDC report; CEP Awards — Animal Welfare, Employer Responsiveness; increasing TRI; on-site day care; Workplace Principles
Premere	LORA	B	C	B	A	C	C	B	A	foreign-based company
Pure Water	SBH	C	D	C	B	B	A	B	C	Animal testing: medical products only, significant alternative efforts; foreign-based company; Workplace Principles
Rave	UN	B	C	C	F	D	C	B	C	Animal testing: non-medical products, significant alternative efforts; foreign-based company; profile
Redken ★	CL	B	B	A	A	B	A	A	A	Animal testing: medical & non-medical products, significant alternative efforts; CEDC report; profile
Rinse Away	ACV	A	?	B	A	D	D	B	B	Animal testing: non-medical products; increasing TRI
Salon Selectives	HC	A	A	A	B	?	A	B	B	Animal testing: non-medical products
Seal 'n Protect	DOW	C	C	B	B	A	A	B	A	Animal testing: non-medical products, significant alternative efforts; CEDC report; on-site child care; pesticide sterilization suits
Second Nature	BMY	B	C	B	B	B	B	B	A	Animal testing: medical & non-medical products, significant alternative efforts; infant formula; Workplace Principles
Shimmer Lights	BMY	B	C	B	B	B	B	B	A	Animal testing: medical & non-medical products, significant alternative efforts; infant formula; Workplace Principles
Shower to Shower ★	JNJ	B	A	A	A	A	A	A	A	Animal testing: medical products only, significant alternative efforts; CEP Award — Disclosure; on-site child care; profile; Workplace Principles

PRODUCT	PARENT COMPANY	The Environment	Charitable Giving	Community Outreach	Women's Advancement	Minority Advancement	Family	Workplace Issues	Disclosure of Information	EXTRAS
Studio	LORA	B	C	B	A	C	C	B	A	foreign-based company
Style	DOW	C	C	B	B	A	A	B	A	Animal testing: non-medical products, significant alternative efforts; CEDC report; on-site child care; pesticide sterilization suits
Suave	HC	A	A	A	B	?	A	B	B	Animal testing: non-medical products
Sudden Beauty	AHP	C	F	C	B	B	C	C	A	Animal testing: medical & non-medical products, significant alternative efforts; infant formula
Summer Lights	BMY	B	C	B	B	B	B	B	A	Animal testing: medical & non-medical products, significant alternative efforts; infant formula; Workplace Principles
Sunsilk	UN	B	C	C	F	D	C	B	C	Animal testing: non-medical products, significant alternative efforts; foreign-based company; profile
TCB	ACV	A	?	B	A	D	D	B	B	Animal testing: non-medical products; increasing TRI
Timotei	UN	B	C	C	F	D	C	B	C	Animal testing: non-medical products, significant alternative efforts; foreign-based company; profile
Tom's of Maine ★	TOM	A	A	A	A	B	A	A	A	CEP Award — Charity; CERES Principles; profile; small company
Toni Lightwaves	G	C	C	B	D	D	B	B	A	Animal testing: medical & non-medical products, significant alternative efforts
Torrids	BMY	B	C	B	B	B	B	B	A	Animal testing: medical & non-medical products, significant alternative efforts; infant formula; Workplace Principles

The Environment
Charitable Giving

Community Outreach
Women's Advancement
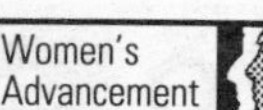
Minority Advancement

Family

Workplace Issues

Disclosure of Information

★ Honor Roll

For a more detailed explanation, see pages 7–28.

PRODUCT	PARENT COMPANY									EXTRAS
Tres	ACV	A	?	B	A	D	D	B	B	Animal testing: non-medical products; increasing TRI
Ultress	BMY	B	C	B	B	B	B	B	A	Animal testing: medical & non-medical products, significant alternative efforts; infant formula; Workplace Principles
Venture	SBH	C	D	C	B	B	A	B	C	Animal testing: medical products only, significant alternative efforts; foreign-based company; Workplace Principles
Vibrance	HC	A	A	A	B	?	A	B	B	Animal testing: non-medical products
Vidal Sassoon	PG	C	B	A	B	B	A	B	A	Animal testing: medical and non-medical products, significant alternative efforts; CEDC report; CEP Awards — Animal Welfare, Employer Responsiveness; increasing TRI; on-site day care; Workplace Principles
Vita Link	DOW	C	C	B	B	A	A	B	A	Animal testing: non-medical products, significant alternative efforts; CEDC report; on-site child care; pesticide sterilization suits
Vitalis	BMY	B	C	B	B	B	B	B	A	Animal testing: medical & non-medical products, significant alternative efforts; infant formula; Workplace Principles
White Rain	G	C	C	B	D	D	B	B	A	Animal testing: medical & non-medical products, significant alternative efforts
Wildroot ★	CL	B	B	A	A	B	A	A	A	Animal testing: medical & non-medical products, significant alternative efforts; CEDC report; profile
SHORTENINGS & OILS										
Adflex	ADM	D	F	?	D	?	?	D	F	CEDC report; increasing TRI
Archer's	ADM	D	F	?	D	?	?	D	F	CEDC report; increasing TRI

PRODUCT	PARENT COMPANY	The Environment	Charitable Giving	Community Outreach	Women's Advancement	Minority Advancement	Family	Workplace Issues	Disclosure of Information	EXTRAS
Crisco	PG	C	B	A	B	B	A	B	A	Animal testing: medical and non-medical products, significant alternative efforts; CEDC report; CEP Awards — Animal Welfare, Employer Responsiveness; increasing TRI; on-site day care; Workplace Principles
E-Z Chef	MO	D	D	?	A	A	?	?	F	Animal testing: non-medical products; CEDC report; tobacco; increasing TRI; Workplace Principles
Good As Gold	ADM	D	F	?	D	?	?	D	F	CEDC report; increasing TRI
Kraft Vegetable Oil	MO	D	D	?	A	A	?	?	F	Animal testing: non-medical products; CEDC report; tobacco; increasing TRI; Workplace Principles
Mazola	CPC	C	A	B	A	B	C	A	B	Animal testing: non-medical products, significant alternative efforts; CEDC report; increasing TRI
Planters	RN	?	A	C	C	?	?	?	D	Animal testing: non-medical products; CEDC report; tobacco; increasing TRI; Workplace Principles
Sunlite	CAG	C	C	C	C	?	?	F	C	CEDC report; factory farming; profile
Wesson	CAG	C	C	C	C	?	?	F	C	CEDC report; factory farming; profile
SLEEPING AIDS										
No-Doz	BMY	B	C	B	B	B	B	B	A	Animal testing: medical & non-medical products, significant alternative efforts; infant formula; Workplace Principles
Sleep-Eze	AHP	C	F	C	B	B	C	C	A	Animal testing: medical & non-medical products, significant alternative efforts; infant formula

The Environment | Charitable Giving | Community Outreach | Women's Advancement | Minority Advancement | Family | Workplace Issues | Disclosure of Information | ★ Honor Roll

For a more detailed explanation, see pages 7–28.

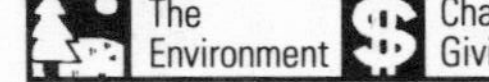

PRODUCT	PARENT COMPANY									EXTRAS
Sominex	SBH	C	D	C	B	B	A	B	C	Animal testing: medical products only, significant alternative efforts; foreign-based company; Workplace Principles
Stelazine	SBH	C	D	C	B	B	A	B	C	Animal testing: medical products only, significant alternative efforts; foreign-based company; Workplace Principles
Unisom	PFE	C	B	A	B	C	A	B	A	Animal testing: medical products only, significant alternative efforts; heart valve suits; Workplace Principles
Vivarin	SBH	C	D	C	B	B	A	B	C	Animal testing: medical products only, significant alternative efforts; foreign-based company; Workplace Principles
SNACKS										
Apple Bakes	HVAL	A	C	C	A	A	B	A	A	
Berry Bears ★	GIS	B	A	A	A	B	B	A	A	CEDC report; CEP Awards — Charity, EEO, Opportunities for the Disabled; profile; Workplace Principles
Borden	BN	C	C	B	A	A	B	B	A	CEDC report
Buenos	RN	?	A	C	C	?	?	?	D	Animal testing: non-medical products; CEDC report; tobacco; increasing TRI; Workplace Principles
Bugles ★	GIS	B	A	A	A	B	B	A	A	CEDC report; CEP Awards — Charity, EEO, Opportunities for the Disabled; profile; Workplace Principles
Cain's	BN	C	C	B	A	A	B	B	A	CEDC report
Carrot Lites	HVAL	A	C	C	A	A	B	A	A	
Casa Vieja	CAG	C	C	C	C	?	?	F	C	CEDC report; factory farming; profile

PRODUCT	PARENT COMPANY	The Environment	Charitable Giving	Community Outreach	Women's Advancement	Minority Advancement	Family	Workplace Issues	Disclosure of Information	EXTRAS
Chee-tos	PEP	B	B	A	A	B	B	B	A	Animal testing: non-medical products; factory farming; increasing TRI
Cheez Doodles	BN	C	C	B	A	A	B	B	A	CEDC report
Chewy	OAT	B	A	A	B	B	D	?	C	CEDC report; Fair Share
Chico-San	HNZ	B	C	A	B	D	C	A	A	CEDC report; CEP Award — Environment
Clover Club	BN	C	C	B	A	A	B	B	A	CEDC report
Combos	MARS	C	A	B	A	?	?	C	B	
Cool Ranch	PEP	B	B	A	A	B	B	B	A	Animal testing: non-medical products; factory farming; increasing TRI
Corn Chips Crisp 'N Natural	HVAL	A	C	C	A	A	B	A	A	
Corn Diggers	RN	?	A	C	C	?	?	?	D	Animal testing: non-medical products; CEDC report; tobacco; increasing TRI; Workplace Principles
Cottage Fries	BN	C	C	B	A	A	B	B	A	CEDC report
Country Chips	HVAL	A	C	C	A	A	B	A	A	
Cracker Jacks	BN	C	C	B	A	A	B	B	A	CEDC report
Crunch Tators	PEP	B	B	A	A	B	B	B	A	Animal testing: non-medical products; factory farming; increasing TRI

 The Environment · Charitable Giving · Community Outreach  Women's Advancement  Minority Advancement  Family 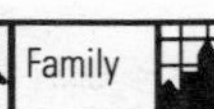 Workplace Issues   Disclosure of Information ★ Honor Roll

For a more detailed explanation, see pages 7–28.

PRODUCT	PARENT COMPANY									EXTRAS
Crunch'n'Munch	AHP	C	F	C	B	B	C	C	A	Animal testing: medical & non-medical products, significant alternative efforts; infant formula
Dipps	OAT	B	A	A	B	B	D	?	C	CEDC report; Fair Share
Dole Nuts	DOL	B	A	B	C	A	C	C	B	pesticide sterilization suits
Doo Dads	RN	?	A	C	C	?	?	?	D	Animal testing: non-medical products; CEDC report; tobacco; increasing TRI; Workplace Principles
Doodle O's	BN	C	C	B	A	A	B	B	A	CEDC report
Doritos	PEP	B	B	A	A	B	B	B	A	Animal testing: non-medical products; factory farming; increasing TRI
Dunkaroos ★	GIS	B	A	A	A	B	B	A	A	CEDC report; CEP Awards — Charity, EEO, Opportunities for the Disabled; profile; Workplace Principles
Fat Free Granola Bars	HVAL	A	C	C	A	A	B	A	A	
Fat Free Muffins	HVAL	A	C	C	A	A	B	A	A	
Fisher Nuts	PG	C	B	A	B	B	A	B	A	Animal testing: medical and non-medical products, significant alternative efforts; CEDC report; CEP Awards — Animal Welfare, Employer Responsiveness; increasing TRI; on-site day care; Workplace Principles
Flings	RN	?	A	C	C	?	?	?	D	Animal testing: non-medical products; CEDC report; tobacco; increasing TRI; Workplace Principles
Frito-Lay	PEP	B	B	A	A	B	B	B	A	Animal testing: non-medical products; factory farming; increasing TRI

PRODUCT	PARENT COMPANY	The Environment	Charitable Giving	Community Outreach	Women's Advancement	Minority Advancement	Family	Workplace Issues	Disclosure of Information	EXTRAS
Fritos	PEP	B	B	A	A	B	B	B	A	Animal testing: non-medical products; factory farming; increasing TRI
Fruit Bakes	HVAL	A	C	C	A	A	B	A	A	
Fruit by the Foot ★	GIS	B	A	A	A	B	B	A	A	CEDC report; CEP Awards — Charity, EEO, Opportunities for the Disabled; profile; Workplace Principles
Fruitquake	OAT	B	A	A	B	B	D	?	C	CEDC report; Fair Share
Fruit Roll-Ups ★	GIS	B	A	A	A	B	B	A	A	CEDC report; CEP Awards — Charity, EEO, Opportunities for the Disabled; profile; Workplace Principles
FundaMiddles ★	GIS	B	A	A	A	B	B	A	A	CEDC report; CEP Awards — Charity, EEO, Opportunities for the Disabled; profile; Workplace Principles
Funyuns	PEP	B	B	A	A	B	B	B	A	Animal testing: non-medical products; factory farming; increasing TRI
Garfield Roll-Ups ★	GIS	B	A	A	A	B	B	A	A	CEDC report; CEP Awards — Charity, EEO, Opportunities for the Disabled; profile; Workplace Principles
Geiser's	BN	C	C	B	A	A	B	B	A	CEDC report
Go-B-Tweens	PEP	B	B	A	A	B	B	B	A	Animal testing: non-medical products; factory farming; increasing TRI
Good Morning	OAT	B	A	A	B	B	D	?	C	CEDC report; Fair Share
Goombay	OAT	B	A	A	B	B	D	?	C	CEDC report; Fair Share

For a more detailed explanation, see pages 7–28.

PRODUCT	PARENT COMPANY									EXTRAS
Grab Bags	PEP	B	B	A	A	B	B	B	A	Animal testing: non-medical products; factory farming; increasing TRI
Graingers	BN	C	C	B	A	A	B	B	A	CEDC report
Granola Bites ★	GIS	B	A	A	A	B	B	A	A	CEDC report; CEP Awards — Charity, EEO, Opportunities for the Disabled; profile; Workplace Principles
Granola Dipps	OAT	B	A	A	B	B	D	?	C	CEDC report; Fair Share
Gushers ★	GIS	B	A	A	A	B	B	A	A	CEDC report; CEP Awards — Charity, EEO, Opportunities for the Disabled; profile; Workplace Principles
Hombres	OAT	B	A	A	B	B	D	?	C	CEDC report; Fair Share
Hostess	RAL	C	C	B	B	B	B	C	B	CEDC report; increasing TRI
Incredibites ★	GIS	B	A	A	A	B	B	A	A	CEDC report; CEP Awards — Charity, EEO, Opportunities for the Disabled; profile; Workplace Principles
Jays	BN	C	C	B	A	A	B	B	A	CEDC report
Jeno's ★	GMR	C	A	A	B	A	A	B	A	factory farming; foreign-based company
Jiffy Pop	AHP	C	F	C	B	B	C	C	A	Animal testing: medical & non-medical products, significant alternative efforts; infant formula
Just Enough	PT	C	D	?	B	?	?	?	F	CEDC report; increasing TRI
Krunchers!	BN	C	C	B	A	A	B	B	A	CEDC report
Kudos	MARS	C	A	B	A	?	?	C	B	
La Famous	BN	C	C	B	A	A	B	B	A	CEDC report

PRODUCT	PARENT COMPANY	The Environment	Charitable Giving	Community Outreach	Women's Advancement	Minority Advancement	Family	Workplace Issues	Disclosure of Information	EXTRAS
Lay's	PEP	B	B	A	A	B	B	B	A	Animal testing: non-medical products; factory farming; increasing TRI
Lyons	ALP	B	C	B	D	?	B	?	B	foreign-based company
Mallomars	RN	?	A	C	C	?	?	?	D	Animal testing: non-medical products; CEDC report; tobacco; increasing TRI; Workplace Principles
Mexican Original	TYSNA	C	?	D	A	B	?	D	D	factory farming; profile
Mini-tacos	PT	C	D	?	B	?	?	?	F	CEDC report; increasing TRI
Mr. Phipps	RN	?	A	C	C	?	?	?	D	Animal testing: non-medical products; CEDC report; tobacco; increasing TRI; Workplace Principles
Mister Salty Pretzels	RN	?	A	C	C	?	?	?	D	Animal testing: non-medical products; CEDC report; tobacco; increasing TRI; Workplace Principles
Moore's	BN	C	C	B	A	A	B	B	A	CEDC report
Munch'ems	UBH	?	C	C	D	?	?	?	F	foreign-based company
Munchos	PEP	B	B	A	A	B	B	B	A	Animal testing: non-medical products; factory farming; increasing TRI
NAB Packs	RN	?	A	C	C	?	?	?	D	Animal testing: non-medical products; CEDC report; tobacco; increasing TRI; Workplace Principles
Nachips	PT	C	D	?	B	?	?	?	F	CEDC report; increasing TRI

The Environment Charitable Giving Community Outreach
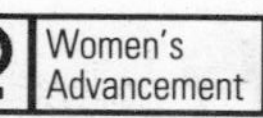
Women's Advancement

Minority Advancement

Family
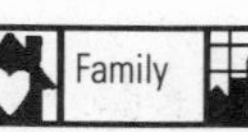
Workplace Issues

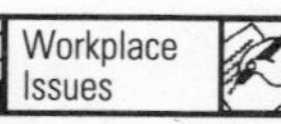

Disclosure of Information

★ Honor Roll

For a more detailed explanation, see pages 7–28.

PRODUCT	PARENT COMPANY									EXTRAS
Nature Granola Bars ★	GIS	B	A	A	A	B	B	A	A	CEDC report; CEP Awards — Charity, EEO, Opportunities for the Disabled; profile; Workplace Principles
Nature Valley ★	GIS	B	A	A	A	B	B	A	A	CEDC report; CEP Awards — Charity, EEO, Opportunities for the Disabled; profile; Workplace Principles
New York Deli	BN	C	C	B	A	A	B	B	A	CEDC report
New York Style	RN	?	A	C	C	?	?	?	D	Animal testing: non-medical products; CEDC report; tobacco; increasing TRI; Workplace Principles
Newman's Own	NEWO	A	A	A	A	Neutral	C	A	A	100% profit to charity; CEP Award — Charity; small company
Nut Harvest	PEP	B	B	A	A	B	B	B	A	Animal testing: non-medical products; factory farming; increasing TRI
Nutri-Grain Bars ★	K	B	A	A	A	A	A	A	A	Animal testing: non-medical products, significant alternative efforts; CEDC report; CEP Awards — Employer Responsiveness, Disclosure; profile
O'Boisies	UBH	?	C	C	D	?	?	?	F	foreign-based company
Orville Redenbacher's	CAG	C	C	C	C	?	?	F	C	CEDC report; factory farming; profile
Pillsbury ★	GMR	C	A	A	B	A	A	B	A	factory farming; foreign-based company
Pizza Crunchabungas	RAL	C	C	B	B	B	B	C	B	CEDC report; increasing TRI
Pizzarias	UBH	?	C	C	D	?	?	?	F	foreign-based company
Planters	RN	?	A	C	C	?	?	?	D	Animal testing: non-medical products; CEDC report; tobacco; increasing TRI; Workplace Principles

PRODUCT	PARENT COMPANY	The Environment	Charitable Giving	Community Outreach	Women's Advancement	Minority Advancement	Family	Workplace Issues	Disclosure of Information	EXTRAS
Popcorn Cakes	HNZ	B	C	A	B	D	C	A	A	CEDC report; CEP Award — Environment
Pop Secret ★	GIS	B	A	A	A	B	B	A	A	CEDC report; CEP Awards — Charity, EEO, Opportunities for the Disabled; profile; Workplace Principles
Popsicle	UN	B	C	C	F	D	C	B	C	Animal testing: non-medical products, significant alternative efforts; foreign-based company; profile
Pringles	PG	C	B	A	B	B	A	B	A	Animal testing: medical and non-medical products, significant alternative efforts; CEDC report; CEP Awards — Animal Welfare, Employer Responsiveness; increasing TRI; on-site day care; Workplace Principles
Quinlan	BN	C	C	B	A	A	B	B	A	CEDC report
Raisin Bakes	HVAL	A	C	C	A	A	B	A	A	
Red Seal	BN	C	C	B	A	A	B	B	A	CEDC report
Rice Cakes	OAT	B	A	A	B	B	D	?	C	CEDC report; Fair Share
Ridgies	BN	C	C	B	A	A	B	B	A	CEDC report
Ripplin's	UBH	?	C	C	D	?	?	?	F	foreign-based company
Rold Gold	PEP	B	B	A	A	B	B	B	A	Animal testing: non-medical products; factory farming; increasing TRI
Ruffles	PEP	B	B	A	A	B	B	B	A	Animal testing: non-medical products; factory farming; increasing TRI

The Environment | Charitable Giving | Community Outreach | Women's Advancement | Minority Advancement | Family | Workplace Issues | Disclosure of Information | ★ Honor Roll

For a more detailed explanation, see pages 7–28.

PRODUCT	PARENT COMPANY									EXTRAS
Salsa Rio	PEP	B	B	A	A	B	B	B	A	Animal testing: non-medical products; factory farming; increasing TRI
Santitas	PEP	B	B	A	A	B	B	B	A	Animal testing: non-medical products; factory farming; increasing TRI
Seyferts	BN	C	C	B	A	A	B	B	A	CEDC report
Shark Bites ★	GIS	B	A	A	A	B	B	A	A	CEDC report; CEP Awards — Charity, EEO, Opportunities for the Disabled; profile; Workplace Principles
Smartfood	PEP	B	B	A	A	B	B	B	A	Animal testing: non-medical products; factory farming; increasing TRI
S'Mores	RAL	C	C	B	B	B	B	C	B	CEDC report; increasing TRI
Snack Logz	PT	C	D	?	B	?	?	?	F	CEDC report; increasing TRI
Snacktime	BN	C	C	B	A	A	B	B	A	CEDC report
Sodalicious ★	GIS	B	A	A	A	B	B	A	A	CEDC report; CEP Awards — Charity, EEO, Opportunities for the Disabled; profile; Workplace Principles
Squeezit ★	GIS	B	A	A	A	B	B	A	A	CEDC report; CEP Awards — Charity, EEO, Opportunities for the Disabled; profile; Workplace Principles
Stella D'oro	RN	?	A	C	C	?	?	?	D	Animal testing: non-medical products; CEDC report; tobacco; increasing TRI; Workplace Principles
Sunchips	PEP	B	B	A	A	B	B	B	A	Animal testing: non-medical products; factory farming; increasing TRI
Suprimos	PEP	B	B	A	A	B	B	B	A	Animal testing: non-medical products; factory farming; increasing TRI

PRODUCT	PARENT COMPANY	The Environment	Charitable Giving	Community Outreach	Women's Advancement	Minority Advancement	Family	Workplace Issues	Disclosure of Information	EXTRAS
Surf's Up ★	GIS	B	A	A	A	B	B	A	A	CEDC report; CEP Awards — Charity, EEO, Opportunities for the Disabled; profile; Workplace Principles
Tato Skins	UBH	?	C	C	D	?	?	?	F	foreign-based company
Thunder Jets ★	GIS	B	A	A	A	B	B	A	A	CEDC report; CEP Awards — Charity, EEO, Opportunities for the Disabled; profile; Workplace Principles
Tiny Tim	PEP	B	B	A	A	B	B	B	A	Animal testing: non-medical products; factory farming; increasing TRI
Tostitos	PEP	B	B	A	A	B	B	B	A	Animal testing: non-medical products; factory farming; increasing TRI
Totino's ★	GMR	C	A	A	B	A	A	B	A	factory farming; foreign-based company
Weight Watchers	HNZ	B	C	A	B	D	C	A	A	CEDC report; CEP Award — Environment
Whipps	OAT	B	A	A	B	B	D	?	C	CEDC report; Fair Share
Wise	BN	C	C	B	A	A	B	B	A	CEDC report
SOUP										
Bovril	CPC	C	A	B	A	B	C	A	B	Animal testing: non-medical products, significant alternative efforts; CEDC report; increasing TRI
Campbell's	CPB	B	C	B	A	A	A	C	A	Animal testing: non-medical products, significant alternative efforts; CEDC report; on-site child care

The Environment · Charitable Giving · Community Outreach

Women's Advancement

Minority Advancement

Family

Workplace Issues

Disclosure of Information

★ Honor Roll

For a more detailed explanation, see pages 7–28.

PRODUCT	PARENT COMPANY									EXTRAS
Chunky Soup	CPB	B	C	B	A	A	A	C	A	Animal testing: non-medical products, significant alternative efforts; CEDC report; on-site child care
College Inn	RN	?	A	C	C	?	?	?	D	Animal testing: non-medical products; CEDC report; tobacco; increasing TRI; Workplace Principles
Continental	UN	B	C	C	F	D	C	B	C	Animal testing: non-medical products, significant alternative efforts; foreign-based company; profile
Cup-A-Soup	UN	B	C	C	F	D	C	B	C	Animal testing: non-medical products, significant alternative efforts; foreign-based company; profile
Fiesta Santa Fe	PT	C	D	?	B	?	?	?	F	CEDC report; increasing TRI
Great American	HNZ	B	C	A	B	D	C	A	A	CEDC report; CEP Award — Environment
Habitant	CPB	B	C	B	A	A	A	C	A	Animal testing: non-medical products, significant alternative efforts; CEDC report; on-site child care
Harris	BN	C	C	B	A	A	B	B	A	CEDC report
Health Valley	HVAL	A	C	C	A	A	B	A	A	
Healthy Choice	CAG	C	C	C	C	?	?	F	C	CEDC report; factory farming; profile
Hearty Soup	UN	B	C	C	F	D	C	B	C	Animal testing: non-medical products, significant alternative efforts; foreign-based company; profile
Hiltons	BN	C	C	B	A	A	B	B	A	CEDC report
Home Cookin' Soup	CPB	B	C	B	A	A	A	C	A	Animal testing: non-medical products, significant alternative efforts; CEDC report; on-site child care

PRODUCT	PARENT COMPANY									EXTRAS
Knorr	CPC	C	A	B	A	B	C	A	B	Animal testing: non-medical products, significant alternative efforts; CEDC report; increasing TRI
Lipton	UN	B	C	C	F	D	C	B	C	Animal testing: non-medical products, significant alternative efforts; foreign-based company; profile
Lots-A-Noodles	UN	B	C	C	F	D	C	B	C	Animal testing: non-medical products, significant alternative efforts; foreign-based company; profile
Mariners Cove	HNZ	B	C	A	B	D	C	A	A	CEDC report; CEP Award — Environment
MBT	BN	C	C	B	A	A	B	B	A	CEDC report
Mrs. Grass	BN	C	C	B	A	A	B	B	A	CEDC report
Pritikin	OAT	B	A	A	B	B	D	?	C	CEDC report; Fair Share
Redding Ridge Farms	UN	B	C	C	F	D	C	B	C	Animal testing: non-medical products, significant alternative efforts; foreign-based company; profile
Soup Starter	BN	C	C	B	A	A	B	B	A	CEDC report
Steero	BN	C	C	B	A	A	B	B	A	CEDC report
Swanson	CPB	B	C	B	A	A	A	C	A	Animal testing: non-medical products, significant alternative efforts; CEDC report; on-site child care
Washington	AHP	C	F	C	B	B	C	C	A	Animal testing: medical & non-medical products, significant alternative efforts; infant formula
Wyler's	BN	C	C	B	A	A	B	B	A	CEDC report

 The Environment
 Charitable Giving
 Community Outreach
 Women's Advancement
 Minority Advancement
 Family
 Workplace Issues
 Disclosure of Information
★ Honor Roll

For a more detailed explanation, see pages 7–28.

PRODUCT	PARENT COMPANY									EXTRAS
SOY PRODUCTS										
Harvest Burger	ADM	D	F	?	D	?	?	D	F	CEDC report; increasing TRI
Midland Fixin's	ADM	D	F	?	D	?	?	D	F	CEDC report; increasing TRI
Nutrisoy	ADM	D	F	?	D	?	?	D	F	CEDC report; increasing TRI
Soy Moo	HVAL	A	C	C	A	A	B	A	A	
Tofu-ya	HVAL	A	C	C	A	A	B	A	A	
Yves	HVAL	A	C	C	A	A	B	A	A	
SUPERMARKETS										
A&P	GAP	A	B	B	B	?	B	A	C	on-site day care
Acme Stores	ASC	A	?	?	C	?	D	B	F	
Albertson's	ABS	A	F	?	C	D	B	C	C	profile
American Stores	ASC	A	?	?	C	?	D	B	F	
Bruno's	BRNO	C	?	?	D	?	?	A	D	
Dillon	KR	A	A	B	A	C	D	B	C	Fair Share
Food Emporium	GAP	A	B	B	B	?	B	A	C	on-site day care
Food Lion	FDLNA	?	?	D	D	C	D	F	F	Fair Share; profile
Fred Meyer	FMY	?	A	A	B	?	?	B	D	

PRODUCT	PARENT COMPANY	The Environment	Charitable Giving	Community Outreach	Women's Advancement	Minority Advancement	Family	Workplace Issues	Disclosure of Information	EXTRAS
Giant Food ★	GFSA	B	A	B	B	A	B	A	A	
Jewel Food	ASC	A	?	?	C	?	D	B	F	
Kroger	KR	A	A	B	A	C	D	B	C	Fair Share
Lucky Stores	ASC	A	?	?	C	?	D	B	F	
Star Market	ASC	A	?	?	C	?	D	B	F	
Vons Food & Drug	VON	?	?	A	B	?	?	A	D	
Waldbaum	GAP	A	B	B	B	?	B	A	C	on-site day care
Winn-Dixie	WIN	?	C	B	F	F	?	?	D	
SUPPLIES: MISCELLANEOUS										
BBQ Bag	CLX	B	B	A	A	A	C	C	A	Animal testing: non-medical products, significant alternative efforts; CEDC report; CEP Award — Community; increasing TRI
Brita	CLX	B	B	A	A	A	C	C	A	Animal testing: non-medical products, significant alternative efforts; CEDC report; CEP Award — Community; increasing TRI
Combat	CLX	B	B	A	A	A	C	C	A	Animal testing: non-medical products, significant alternative efforts; CEDC report; CEP Award — Community; increasing TRI

The Environment | Charitable Giving | Community Outreach | Women's Advancement | Minority Advancement | Family | Workplace Issues | Disclosure of Information | ★ Honor Roll

For a more detailed explanation, see pages 7–28.

PRODUCT	PARENT COMPANY									EXTRAS
D-Con	EK	C	B	B	B	B	A	B	B	Animal testing: medical and non-medical products, significant alternative efforts; CEDC report; CEP Award — EEO
Energizer	RAL	C	C	B	B	B	B	C	B	CEDC report; increasing TRI
Eveready	RAL	C	C	B	B	B	B	C	B	CEDC report; increasing TRI
Flair	G	C	C	B	D	D	B	B	A	Animal testing: medical & non-medical products, significant alternative efforts
GE	GE	D	C	B	C	C	B	C	A	C3; CEDC report; military contracts
Kingsford	CLX	B	B	A	A	A	C	C	A	Animal testing: non-medical products, significant alternative efforts; CEDC report; CEP Award — Community; increasing TRI
Kiwi	SLE	C	B	A	B	B	B	B	A	CEP Award — Charity; on-site child care; tobacco
Liquid Paper	G	C	C	B	D	D	B	B	A	Animal testing: medical & non-medical products, significant alternative efforts
Lustra	MOB	D	C	C	C	C	B	C	A	Animal testing: non-medical products, significant alternative efforts; CEDC report; military contracts; Workplace Principles
Magicube	GE	D	C	B	C	C	B	C	A	C3; CEDC report; military contracts
Match Light	CLX	B	B	A	A	A	C	C	A	Animal testing: non-medical products, significant alternative efforts; CEDC report; CEP Award — Community; increasing TRI
Maxforce	CLX	B	B	A	A	A	C	C	A	Animal testing: non-medical products, significant alternative efforts; CEDC report; CEP Award — Community; increasing TRI

PRODUCT	PARENT COMPANY	The Environment	Charitable Giving	Community Outreach	Women's Advancement	Minority Advancement	Family	Workplace Issues	Disclosure of Information	EXTRAS
Miser	GE	D	C	B	C	C	B	C	A	C3; CEDC report; military contracts
PAAS	SGP	B	C	A	B	A	A	B	A	Animal testing: medical products only, significant alternative efforts; on-site child care; Workplace Principles
Panasonic	MC	C	?	A	?	?	D	?	C	Fair Share; foreign-based company; increasing TRI; same-sex partner benefits
Paper Mate	G	C	C	B	D	D	B	B	A	Animal testing: medical & non-medical products, significant alternative efforts
Raid ★	SCJ	A	A	A	B	B	A	A	A	Animal testing: non-medical products, significant alternative efforts; CEP Award — Environment; on-site child care; profile; Workplace Principles
RIT	CPC	C	A	B	A	B	C	A	B	Animal testing: non-medical products, significant alternative efforts; CEDC report; increasing TRI
Red Devil Enamels	EK	C	B	B	B	B	A	B	B	Animal testing: medical and non-medical products, significant alternative efforts; CEDC report; CEP Award — EEO
Scotch	MMM	C	B	A	C	B	A	B	A	Animal testing: medical & non-medical products, significant alternative efforts; CEDC report; CEP Award — Environment
Sony	SNE	B	B	A	B	B	C	B	A	Fair Share; foreign-based company; increasing TRI
Sterno ★	CL	B	B	A	A	B	A	A	A	Animal testing: medical & non-medical products, significant alternative efforts; CEDC report; profile

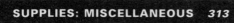

The Environment · Charitable Giving

Community Outreach · Women's Advancement

Minority Advancement

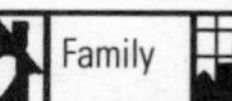
Family

Workplace Issues

Disclosure of Information · ★ Honor Roll

For a more detailed explanation, see pages 7–28.

PRODUCT	PARENT COMPANY									EXTRAS
Thompson	EK	C	B	B	B	B	A	B	B	Animal testing: medical and non-medical products, significant alternative efforts; CEDC report; CEP Award — EEO
Tri-Flow High Performance Lubricant	EK	C	B	B	B	B	A	B	B	Animal testing: medical and non-medical products, significant alternative efforts; CEDC report; CEP Award — EEO
Watco Danish Oil Finish	EK	C	B	B	B	B	A	B	B	Animal testing: medical and non-medical products, significant alternative efforts; CEDC report; CEP Award — EEO
Waterman	G	C	C	B	D	D	B	B	A	Animal testing: medical & non-medical products, significant alternative efforts
SYRUPS & MOLASSES										
Aunt Jemima	OAT	B	A	A	B	B	D	?	C	CEDC report; Fair Share
Butterlite	OAT	B	A	A	B	B	D	?	C	CEDC report; Fair Share
Cary's	BN	C	C	B	A	A	B	B	A	CEDC report
Country Kitchen	MO	D	D	?	A	A	?	?	F	Animal testing: non-medical products; CEDC report; tobacco; increasing TRI; Workplace Principles
Golden Griddle	CPC	C	A	B	A	B	C	A	B	Animal testing: non-medical products, significant alternative efforts; CEDC report; increasing TRI
Hershey's Syrup	HSY	B	B	A	B	C	A	A	A	CEDC report; increasing TRI; on-site child care
Karo	CPC	C	A	B	A	B	C	A	B	Animal testing: non-medical products, significant alternative efforts; CEDC report; increasing TRI
Log Cabin	MO	D	D	?	A	A	?	?	F	Animal testing: non-medical products; CEDC report; tobacco; increasing TRI; Workplace Principles

PRODUCT	PARENT COMPANY	The Environment	Charitable Giving	Community Outreach	Women's Advancement	Minority Advancement	Family	Workplace Issues	Disclosure of Information	EXTRAS
MacDonald's	BN	C	C	B	A	A	B	B	A	CEDC report
Maple Orchards	BN	C	C	B	A	A	B	B	A	CEDC report
Mrs. Butterworth's	UN	B	C	C	F	D	C	B	C	Animal testing: non-medical products, significant alternative efforts; foreign-based company; profile
Old Vermont	CAG	C	C	C	C	?	?	F	C	CEDC report; factory farming; profile
Sunrise	DL	C	A	B	B	?	F	B	C	CEDC report
Vermont Maid	RN	?	A	C	C	?	?	?	D	Animal testing: non-medical products; CEDC report; tobacco; increasing TRI; Workplace Principles
TELECOMMUNICATIONS										
AT&T	T	B	B	A	B	B	A	B	A	Animal testing: non-medical products; CEP Award — Environment; military contracts; Workplace Principles
MCI	MCIC	?	F	C	B	A	?	D	F	profile
Sprint	FON	B	C	B	A	C	A	C	C	
TOOTHPASTE & DENTAL-CARE NEEDS										
Acryline	SBH	C	D	C	B	B	A	B	C	Animal testing: medical products only, significant alternative efforts; foreign-based company; Workplace Principles

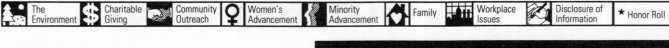

The Environment | Charitable Giving | Community Outreach | Women's Advancement | Minority Advancement | Family | Workplace Issues | Disclosure of Information | ★ Honor Roll

For a more detailed explanation, see pages 7–28.

PRODUCT	PARENT COMPANY									EXTRAS
Act ★	JNJ	B	A	A	A	A	A	A	A	Animal testing: medical products only, significant alternative efforts; CEP Award — Disclosure; on-site child care; profile; Workplace Principles
Aim	UN	B	C	C	F	D	C	B	C	Animal testing: non-medical products, significant alternative efforts; foreign-based company; profile
Aquafresh	SBH	C	D	C	B	B	A	B	C	Animal testing: medical products only, significant alternative efforts; foreign-based company; Workplace Principles
Arm & Hammer	CHD	A	B	A	C	C	A	A	A	Animal testing: non-medical products, significant alternative efforts; CEP Award — Environment
Benzodent	PG	C	B	A	B	B	A	B	A	Animal testing: medical and non-medical products, significant alternative efforts; CEDC report; CEP Awards — Animal Welfare, Employer Responsiveness; increasing TRI; on-site day care; Workplace Principles
Brace	SBH	C	D	C	B	B	A	B	C	Animal testing: medical products only, significant alternative efforts; foreign-based company; Workplace Principles
Breathsavers	RN	?	A	C	C	?	?	?	D	Animal testing: non-medical products; CEDC report; tobacco; increasing TRI; Workplace Principles
Cepacol	DOW	C	C	B	B	A	A	B	A	Animal testing: non-medical products, significant alternative efforts; CEDC report; on-site child care; pesticide sterilization suits
Close-Up	UN	B	C	C	F	D	C	B	C	Animal testing: non-medical products, significant alternative efforts; foreign-based company; profile
Colgate ★	CL	B	B	A	A	B	A	A	A	Animal testing: medical & non-medical products, significant alternative efforts; CEDC report; profile

PRODUCT	PARENT COMPANY	The Environment	Charitable Giving	Community Outreach	Women's Advancement	Minority Advancement	Family	Workplace Issues	Disclosure of Information	EXTRAS
Complete	PG	C	B	A	B	B	A	B	A	Animal testing: medical and non-medical products, significant alternative efforts; CEDC report; CEP Awards — Animal Welfare, Employer Responsiveness; increasing TRI; on-site day care; Workplace Principles
Crest	PG	C	B	A	B	B	A	B	A	Animal testing: medical and non-medical products, significant alternative efforts; CEDC report; CEP Awards — Animal Welfare, Employer Responsiveness; increasing TRI; on-site day care; Workplace Principles
Denquel	PG	C	B	A	B	B	A	B	A	Animal testing: medical and non-medical products, significant alternative efforts; CEDC report; CEP Awards — Animal Welfare, Employer Responsiveness; increasing TRI; on-site day care; Workplace Principles
Dental Care	CHD	A	B	A	C	C	A	A	A	Animal testing: non-medical products, significant alternative efforts; CEP Award — Environment
Dental Floss ★	JNJ	B	A	A	A	A	A	A	A	Animal testing: medical products only, significant alternative efforts; CEP Award — Disclosure; on-site child care; profile; Workplace Principles
Efferdent ★	WLA	B	B	A	B	A	A	B	A	Animal testing: medical products only; increasing TRI; Workplace Principles
Effergrip ★	WLA	B	B	A	B	A	A	B	A	Animal testing: medical products only; increasing TRI; Workplace Principles

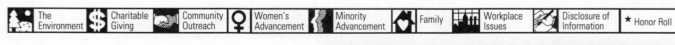

The Environment | Charitable Giving | Community Outreach | Women's Advancement | Minority Advancement | Family | Workplace Issues | Disclosure of Information | ★ Honor Roll

For a more detailed explanation, see pages 7–28.

PRODUCT	PARENT COMPANY									EXTRAS
Fasteeth	PG	C	B	A	B	B	A	B	A	Animal testing: medical and non-medical products, significant alternative efforts; CEDC report; CEP Awards — Animal Welfare, Employer Responsiveness; increasing TRI; on-site day care; Workplace Principles
Fixodent	PG	C	B	A	B	B	A	B	A	Animal testing: medical and non-medical products, significant alternative efforts; CEDC report; CEP Awards — Animal Welfare, Employer Responsiveness; increasing TRI; on-site day care; Workplace Principles
Fluorigard ★	CL	B	B	A	A	B	A	A	A	Animal testing: medical & non-medical products, significant alternative efforts; CEDC report; profile
Fresh 'N Brite ★	WLA	B	B	A	B	A	A	B	A	Animal testing: medical products only; increasing TRI; Workplace Principles
Gleem	PG	C	B	A	B	B	A	B	A	Animal testing: medical and non-medical products, significant alternative efforts; CEDC report; CEP Awards — Animal Welfare, Employer Responsiveness; increasing TRI; on-site day care; Workplace Principles
Kleenite	PG	C	B	A	B	B	A	B	A	Animal testing: medical and non-medical products, significant alternative efforts; CEDC report; CEP Awards — Animal Welfare, Employer Responsiveness; increasing TRI; on-site day care; Workplace Principles
Listerine ★	WLA	B	B	A	B	A	A	B	A	Animal testing: medical products only; increasing TRI; Workplace Principles
Macleans	SBH	C	D	C	B	B	A	B	C	Animal testing: medical products only, significant alternative efforts; foreign-based company; Workplace Principles
Murray	CADBY	B	?	C	C	?	D	B	C	foreign-based company

PRODUCT	PARENT COMPANY	The Environment	Charitable Giving	Community Outreach	Women's Advancement	Minority Advancement	Family	Workplace Issues	Disclosure of Information	EXTRAS
Orafix	SBH	C	D	C	B	B	A	B	C	Animal testing: medical products only, significant alternative efforts; foreign-based company; Workplace Principles
Oral-B	G	C	C	B	D	D	B	B	A	Animal testing: medical & non-medical products, significant alternative efforts
Peak ★	CL	B	B	A	A	B	A	A	A	Animal testing: medical & non-medical products, significant alternative efforts; CEDC report; profile
Pepsodent	UN	B	C	C	F	D	C	B	C	Animal testing: non-medical products, significant alternative efforts; foreign-based company; profile
Plate-Weld	SBH	C	D	C	B	B	A	B	C	Animal testing: medical products only, significant alternative efforts; foreign-based company; Workplace Principles
Plax	PFE	C	B	A	B	C	A	B	A	Animal testing: medical products only, significant alternative efforts; heart valve suits; Workplace Principles
Precision ★	CL	B	B	A	A	B	A	A	A	Animal testing: medical & non-medical products, significant alternative efforts; CEDC report; profile
Prevent ★	JNJ	B	A	A	A	A	A	A	A	Animal testing: medical products only, significant alternative efforts; CEP Award — Disclosure; on-site child care; profile; Workplace Principles
Reach ★	JNJ	B	A	A	A	A	A	A	A	Animal testing: medical products only, significant alternative efforts; CEP Award — Disclosure; on-site child care; profile; Workplace Principles

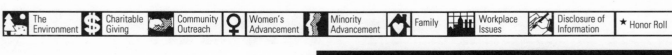

The Environment | Charitable Giving | Community Outreach | Women's Advancement | Minority Advancement | Family | Workplace Issues | Disclosure of Information | ★ Honor Roll

For a more detailed explanation, see pages 7–28.

PRODUCT	PARENT COMPANY									EXTRAS
Scope	PG	C	B	A	B	B	A	B	A	Animal testing: medical and non-medical products, significant alternative efforts; CEDC report; CEP Awards — Animal Welfare, Employer Responsiveness; increasing TRI; on-site day care; Workplace Principles
Signal	UN	B	C	C	F	D	C	B	C	Animal testing: non-medical products, significant alternative efforts; foreign-based company; profile
Sudden Action	AHP	C	F	C	B	B	C	C	A	Animal testing: medical & non-medical products, significant alternative efforts; infant formula
Tom's of Maine ★	TOM	A	A	A	A	B	A	A	A	CEP Award — Charity; CERES Principles; profile; small company
Ultra Brite ★	CL	B	B	A	A	B	A	A	A	Animal testing: medical & non-medical products, significant alternative efforts; CEDC report; profile
Viadent ★	CL	B	B	A	A	B	A	A	A	Animal testing: medical & non-medical products, significant alternative efforts; CEDC report; profile
TOYS										
Aviva	MAT	B	D	B	A	B	A	B	A	
Fisher-Price	MAT	B	D	B	A	B	A	B	A	
Gerber	GEB	C	C	?	B	B	?	?	F	CEDC report; increasing TRI; infant formula
Hasbro	HAS	B	B	B	B	?	?	?	D	
Kenner	HAS	B	B	B	B	?	?	?	D	
Mattel	MAT	B	D	B	A	B	A	B	A	

PRODUCT	PARENT COMPANY	The Environment	Charitable Giving	Community Outreach	Women's Advancement	Minority Advancement	Family	Workplace Issues	Disclosure of Information	EXTRAS
Milton Bradley	HAS	B	B	B	B	?	?	?	D	
Parker Brothers	HAS	B	B	B	B	?	?	?	D	
Playskool	HAS	B	B	B	B	?	?	?	D	
Tonka	HAS	B	B	B	B	?	?	?	D	
VEGETABLES: CANNED, FRESH & FROZEN										
Americana Recipe	MO	D	D	?	A	A	?	?	F	Animal testing: non-medical products; CEDC report; tobacco; increasing TRI; Workplace Principles
B in B ★	GMR	C	A	A	B	A	A	B	A	factory farming; foreign-based company
Bird's Eye	MO	D	D	?	A	A	?	?	F	Animal testing: non-medical products; CEDC report; tobacco; increasing TRI; Workplace Principles
Blue Ribbon	MO	D	D	?	A	A	?	?	F	Animal testing: non-medical products; CEDC report; tobacco; increasing TRI; Workplace Principles
Contadina	NEST	B	?	B	B	B	A	B	B	Animal testing: non-medical products, significant alternative efforts; foreign-based company; infant formula
Dole	DOL	B	A	B	C	A	C	C	B	pesticide sterilization suits
Farm Fresh	MO	D	D	?	A	A	?	?	F	Animal testing: non-medical products; CEDC report; tobacco; increasing TRI; Workplace Principles
Farm Kitchen	CAG	C	C	C	C	?	?	F	C	CEDC report; factory farming; profile

The Environment | Charitable Giving | Community Outreach | Women's Advancement | Minority Advancement | Family | Workplace Issues | Disclosure of Information | ★ Honor Roll

For a more detailed explanation, see pages 7–28.

PRODUCT	PARENT COMPANY									EXTRAS
Glen Valley	OAT	B	A	A	B	B	D	?	C	CEDC report; Fair Share
Green Giant ★	GMR	C	A	A	B	A	A	B	A	factory farming; foreign-based company
Health Valley	HVAL	A	C	C	A	A	B	A	A	
Honey Pod	OAT	B	A	A	B	B	D	?	C	CEDC report; Fair Share
Joan of Arc ★	GMR	C	A	A	B	A	A	B	A	factory farming; foreign-based company
Kounty Kist ★	GMR	C	A	A	B	A	A	B	A	factory farming; foreign-based company
Lean Living	HVAL	A	C	C	A	A	B	A	A	
Le Sueur ★	GMR	C	A	A	B	A	A	B	A	factory farming; foreign-based company
Libby's	NEST	B	?	B	B	B	A	B	B	Animal testing: non-medical products, significant alternative efforts; foreign-based company; infant formula
Luck's	AHP	C	F	C	B	B	C	C	A	Animal testing: medical & non-medical products, significant alternative efforts; infant formula
YOGURT										
Light n' Lively	MO	D	D	?	A	A	?	?	F	Animal testing: non-medical products; CEDC report; tobacco; increasing TRI; Workplace Principles
Stay 'N Shape	MO	D	D	?	A	A	?	?	F	Animal testing: non-medical products; CEDC report; tobacco; increasing TRI; Workplace Principles
Stonyfield Farm	STON	A	?	A	A	Neutral	B	B	A	CEP Award — Environment; small company
Yoplait ★	GIS	B	A	A	A	B	B	A	A	CEDC report; CEP Awards — Charity, EEO, Opportunities for the Disabled; profile; Workplace Principles

Companies That Do Not Appear in the Product Table

The following companies did not provide CEP with enough information to enable us to rate them in more than three categories. They are therefore not included in the product table. The ratings for these companies appear only in the table "Ratings by Company." The companies are: AST Research, Inc., Animal Town, Avery Dennison, Black & Decker Corporation, Brown-Forman Corporation, Brown Group, Inc., Societe Bic S.A., Benetton Group Spa, Carter-Wallace, Inc., Dillard Department Stores, Inc., Dell Computer Corporation, DWG Corporation, Estee Lauder Inc., AB Electrolux, Emily's Toybox, Federated Department Stores, Inc., Fedders Corporation, Farah Incorporated, Gitano Group, Inc., Oshkosh B'Gosh, Inc., Guess Inc., Hartmarx Corporation, Foster and Gallagher, Interco Incorporated, J. Crew Group Inc., L.A. Gear, Inc., The Limited, Inc., R.H. Macy & Co., Inc., MEM Company Inc., Neutrogena Corporation, Olmec, One World Projects, Packard Bell Electronics, Philips' Gloeilampenfabrieken N.V., Perdue Farms Inc., Phillips-Van Heusen Corporation, Revlon, Inc., Russell Corporation, Sebastian International, Inc., Shoney's Inc., Snapple Beverage Corporation, Starter Corporation, Sunshine Biscuits, Inc., Thorn EMI plc, Tambrands Inc., Tyco Toys, Inc., US Shoe Corporation, V.F. Corporation, Seagram Company Ltd, Wendy's International, Inc., Threads 4 Life.

Company Names and Abbreviations

AAPL	Apple Computer, Inc.
ABS	Albertson's, Inc.
ACCOB	Adolph Coors Company
ACV	Alberto-Culver Company
ADM	Archer Daniels Midland Company
AHP	American Home Products Corporation
ALP	Allied-Lyons PLC
AN	Amoco Corporation
ARC	Atlantic Richfield Company
ASC	American Stores Company
ASTA	AST Research, Inc.
ATOWN	Animal Town
AV	Aroma Vera
AVED	Aveda Corporation
AVP	Avon Products, Inc.
AVY	Avery Dennison Corporation
BDK	Black & Decker Corporation
BFB	Brown-Forman Corporation
BG	Brown Group, Inc.
BIC	Societe Bic S.A.
BJICA	Ben & Jerry's Homemade, Inc.
BLN	Body Love Natural Cosmetics
BMY	Bristol-Myers Squibb Company
BN	Borden, Inc.
BODY	The Body Shop
BP	British Petroleum Company p.l.c.
BRNO	Bruno's, Inc.
BTON	Benetton Group Spa
BUD	Anheuser-Busch Companies, Inc.
C	Chrysler Corporation
CADBY	Cadbury Schweppes p.l.c.
CAG	ConAgra, Inc.
CAR	Carter-Wallace, Inc.
CHD	Church & Dwight Company, Inc.
CHH	Carter Hawley Hale Stores, Inc.
CHV	Chevron Corporation
CL	Colgate-Palmolive Company
CLX	The Clorox Company
CPB	Campbell Soup Company
CPC	CPC International Inc.

CPQ	Compaq Computer Corporation
DDS	Dillard Department Stores, Inc.
DEC	Digital Equipment Corporation
DELL	Dell Computer Corporation
DEVA	Deva Lifewear
DH	Dayton Hudson Corporation
DL	Dial Corporation
DOL	Dole Food Company, Inc.
DOMP	Domino's Pizza, Inc.
DOW	Dow Chemical Company
DWG	DWG Corporation
ECC	Ecco Bella
EK	Eastman Kodak Company
EL	Estee Lauder Inc.
ELUXY	AB Electrolux
EMTOY	Emily's Toybox
ESP	Esprit de Corp.
F	Ford Motor Company
FBR	First Brands Corporation
FDLNA	Food Lion, Inc.
FED	Federated Department Stores, Inc.
FJQ	Fedders Corporation
FMY	Fred Meyer, Inc.
FON	Sprint Corporation
FRA	Farah Incorporated
FUJIY	Fuji Photo Film Co. Ltd.
G	Gillette Company
GAP	A&P
GCO	Genesco Inc.
GE	General Electric Company
GEB	Gerber Products
GFSA	Giant Food Inc.
GIS	General Mills, Inc.
GIT	Gitano Group, Inc.
GM	General Motors Corporation
GMR	Grand Metropolitan PLC
GOSHA	Oshkosh B'Gosh, Inc.
GPS	The Gap, Inc.
GUS	Guess Inc.
HAS	Hasbro, Inc.
HC	Helene Curtis Industries, Inc.
HMC	Honda Motor Co. Ltd.
HMX	Hartmarx Corporation

HNZ	H.J. Heinz Company
HSONG	Foster and Gallagher
HSY	Hershey Foods Corporation
HVAL	Health Valley Natural Foods
HWP	Hewlett Packard Company
IBM	International Business Machines Corporation
IMS	Imasco Limited
INDQA	International Dairy Queen, Inc.
ISS	Interco Incorporated
JC	J. Crew Group Inc.
JNJ	Johnson & Johnson
K	Kellogg Company
KMB	Kimberly-Clark Corporation
KMF	Kiss My Face
KO	Coca-Cola Company
KR	Kroger Company
LA	L.A. Gear, Inc.
LE	Lands' End, Inc.
LEV	Levi Strauss & Co.
LIZ	Liz Claiborne, Inc.
LORA	L'Oreal S.A.
LOST	Patagonia, Inc. (formerly Lost Arrow Corporation)
LTD	The Limited, Inc.
MA	May Department Stores Company
MACY	R.H. Macy & Co., Inc.
MARS	Mars, Inc.
MAT	Mattel, Inc.
MC	Matsushita Electric Industrial Co.
MCD	McDonald's Corporation
MCIC	MCI Communications Corporation
MEA	Mead Corporation
MEM	MEM Company Inc.
MMM	Minnesota Mining & Manufacturing Company (3M)
MO	Philip Morris Companies Inc.
MOB	Mobil Corporation
MST	Mercantile Stores Company, Inc.
MYG	Maytag Corporation
NA	Na Na Trading Co.
NATB	The Natural Baby Company, Inc.
NEST	Nestle S.A.
NEWO	Newman's Own, Inc.
NGNA	Neutrogena Corporation
NKE	Nike, Inc.

NOBE	Nordstrom, Inc.
NOVA	Nova Natural
NSANY	Nissan Motor Co. Ltd.
OAT	Quaker Oats Company
OLMEC	Olmec
OWP	One World Projects
P	Phillips Petroleum Company
PCKRD	Packard Bell Electronics
PEP	PepsiCo, Inc.
PFE	Pfizer Inc.
PG	Procter & Gamble Company
PHIL	Philips' Gloeilampenfabrieken N.V.
PRD	Polaroid Corporation
PRDU	Perdue Farms Inc.
PT	Pet Incorporated
PVH	Phillips-Van Heusen Corporation
RAL	Ralston Purina Company
RBK	Reebok International Ltd.
REVL	Revlon, Inc.
RHI	Rhino Records, Inc.
RML	Russell Corporation
RN	RJR Nabisco, Inc.
RTN	Raytheon Company
S	Sears, Roebuck & Co.
SBH	SmithKline Beecham plc
SCJ	S.C. Johnson & Son, Inc.
SCWW-S	Royal Dutch/Shell Group of Companies
SEB	Sebastian International, Inc.
SGP	Schering-Plough Corporation
SHN	Shoney's Inc.
SLE	Sara Lee Corporation
SNE	Sony Corporation
SNPL	Snapple Beverage Corp.
SRR	The Stride Rite Corporation
STA	Starter Corporation
STON	Stonyfield Farm, Inc.
SUN	Sun Company, Inc.
SUNB	Sunshine Biscuits, Inc.
T	American Telephone & Telegraph Company (AT&T)
TBL	The Timberland Company
THOR	Thorn EMI plc
TMB	Tambrands Inc.
TOM	Tom's of Maine

TOYOY	Toyota Motor Corporation
TTI	Tyco Toys, Inc.
TWX	Time Warner Inc.
TX	Texaco Inc.
TYSNA	Tyson Foods, Inc.
UBH	United Biscuits (Holdings) plc
UCL	Unocal Corporation
UN	Unilever PLC
USR	United States Shoe Corporation
VFC	V.F. Corporation
VO	Seagram Company Ltd.
VON	Vons Companies, Inc.
WEN	Wendy's International, Inc.
WHR	Whirlpool Corporation
WIN	Winn-Dixie Stores, Inc.
WLA	Warner-Lambert Company
WMT	Wal-Mart Stores, Inc.
WWY	Wm. Wrigley Jr. Company
X	USX Corporation
XCOLS	Threads 4 Life
XON	Exxon Corporation
YAMP	Yamanouchi Pharmaceutical Co. Ltd.

Product Category Index

Americans and Food

It's 1994: Do You Know What You're Eating?

Reacting to scientific evidence that the way many Americans eat is in itself a bad habit, the U.S. Department of Agriculture and nutrition experts in 1992 revised the configuration of the basic four food groups, which had been in place since 1956. The new plan declares grains, fruits, and vegetables to be the major building blocks of a healthy diet and de-emphasizes the importance of meat and dairy products.

As consumers become more educated about healthy eating, an increasing number of manufacturers and processors are responding to demands for less fatty meats, for organically grown fruits and vegetables, and for foods that are high in fiber and low in cholesterol. Look for these and avoid the fat-ridden, pesticide-laden products that still crowd your supermarket shelves.

Nutrition Checklist

Reduce purchase of food containing the following:

- Sodium—fresh foods contain enough salt.
- Saturated or partially hydrogenated fats and cholesterol—cut down on animal fat; avoid pork and beef, especially fatty cuts; avoid egg yolks, butter, margarine, heavier oils, and fried foods.
- Sugar and alcohol—they provide empty calories, no nutrition.
- Additives—especially avoid sulfites, nitrites, and artificial coloring.

Increase purchase of the following:

- Fiber-rich food—more fruit, vegetables, whole grains, bran, and nuts.
- Fish.
- Olive or canola oils.

- Organically grown foods.
- Fresh vegetables you can steam to retain optimum nutrients—or eat them raw.

Plus:

- If you buy meat, make it well-washed poultry.
- Avoid those fast-food restaurants that do not offer a healthy alternative.

Highly processed foods lose much of their nutritive value and require substantially more energy to produce. You *can* choose alternatives. Fresh foods rich in fiber, for example, not only help guard against digestive diseases like colon cancer, but also generate less waste and use less energy in the production process.

You may have noticed that though CEP includes food products made by tobacco companies in the guide, it does not list cigarettes. If you are interested in living a healthier life, cigarettes have no place on your shopping list. They are responsible for an estimated 1,000 deaths a day in the U.S. alone.

Early in 1991, the board of Johns Hopkins University joined several other institutions of higher learning in selling its investments in tobacco companies. A board spokesperson said, "The holding of tobacco stocks is incompatible with the university's mission to disseminate information on the treatment and prevention of disease and illness."

There are a number of groups working to raise awareness about the effects of smoking on health, eliminate all cigarette advertising, and reduce the use of tobacco products, especially by youth. Among them are ASH—Action on Smoking and Health (202-659-4310); SmokeFree Educational Services, Inc. (212-912-0960); and STAT—Stop Teenage Addiction to Tobacco (413-732-7828).

Nutrition Labeling Act

Many of you have long wished for food labeling that explains in plain English what it is you're eating. But labels with that kind of information were a long time coming. Until recently, few labels spelled out such things as fat, cholesterol, and sodium content. According to the National Academy of Sciences, about 40 percent of all packaged foods offered no nutritional information at all in 1992, despite the fact that in 1990 Congress had passed the Nutrition Labeling and Education Act (NLEA). This law directed the Food and Drug Administration (FDA) to standardize food labels—particularly those claiming to be beneficial to health. The regulations went into effect in May 1994. The law further requires most food manufacturers to cut back on their use of possibly misleading terms such as "light" and "reduced," and to clearly list on their labels the amount of fat, cholesterol, and other nutrients contained. The Agriculture Department (USDA) has agreed to adopt FDA labeling requirements for labels on processed meat and poultry products, which it oversees. Happily for us all, these labels should now be in place.

Advertising Can Still Mislead

Because food advertising falls under the jurisdiction of the Federal Trade Commission (FTC), not the FDA, *no restrictions have been placed on health claims in food ads*. These claims may partially or totally conflict with the label, according to the Washington, D.C.–based Center for Science in the Public Interest.

Hormel, for example, trumpets "Only One Gram of Fat per Serving" for its Light & Lean 97 ham or turkey cuts, but bases this claim on a measly one-ounce serving. The USDA requires nutrition information on luncheon-meat labels to be based on a two-ounce serving size.

Fleischmann's margarine ads state "zero cholesterol," never mentioning the product's high fat content. Similarly, Promise margarine promotes itself as healthy for your heart, though it has been established that a high fat content is associated with higher risk of cancer and obesity. The NLEA prohibits health claims on labels when the food contains "any nutrient in an amount which increases (to persons in the general population) the risk of a disease or health-related condition which is diet related."

Despite evidence that many food manufacturers intend to continue using deceptive or misleading advertising, the FTC has said it would allow health claims in ads that the FDA will not allow on labels. Seeking to remedy this situation, two bills were introduced in 1993, the first by Senator Howard Metzenbaum, "to prevent misleading advertising of the health benefits of foods," the second by Representative Joseph Moakley, "to amend the FTC Act to require nutritional claims in food advertising to meet the requirements applicable to nutritional claims (on the label) for food." Both bills were pending in committee in mid-1994. A broad coalition of consumer, health, and public-education groups, including the American Cancer Society, the American Heart Association, the Center for Science in the Public Interest, and the Council on Economic Priorities have endorsed these bills.

BST Growth Hormone: Doubts Persist

Bovine somatotropin (BST) is a protein hormone produced by the pituitary gland of cows. (It is also known as BGH or bovine growth hormone.) Monsanto and other companies have found that they can alter the hormone genetically, and inject cows with it to increase their milk production. However, consumer groups and worried public officials both here and abroad have raised concerns about the possibility of BST's causing premature growth or breast cancer in humans, and mastitis infections in cows. The controversy has continued for several years, with the U.S. General Accounting Office and Consumers Union saying the use of BST is a potential health risk; other bodies, such as the National Institute of Health, the Congressional Office of Technology Assessment (OTA), and the European Community's Committee for Veterinary Medicine Products, say the substance is safe.

In November 1993, FDA Commissioner David Kessler approved use of the hormone, asserting that after intensive review, he was confident that both "milk and meat from BST-treated cows is safe to consume" and, further, that labeling of such products was unnecessary. Congress asked for a 90-day moratorium, to begin the day of approval, to hear consumer reaction and ponder possible legislation.

Earlier in 1993, the Pure Food Campaign (202-775-1132), which boycotts genetically engineered foods internationally, had asked consumers to request that their neighborhood stores and restaurants provide written statements of policy on BST, and that they not buy from companies selling such products. After the FDA approval, boycott organizers reported that they will continue to boycott all milk, dairy, and meat products from BST-treated herds, and will bring suit against the FDA to demand labeling of these products (*Boycott Action News*, Winter 1994). Call the Pure Food Campaign (see phone number above) to learn how you may obtain a list of companies that do not sell BST-treated products.

Finally: Federal Effort to Reduce Pesticide Use

In June 1993, the Environmental Protection Agency, Food and Drug Administration, and Department of Agriculture announced a coordinated effort to "reduce the use of chemicals in the production of the nation's food," and to pay particular attention to safeguarding the health of children. A National Academy of Sciences report released around the same time recommended changes in chemical regulations "because infants and children consume more calories per unit of body weight and tend to eat fewer types of food than adults." The Academy asked the EPA to make health, not agricultural production, its top priority in determining new regulations. In the past, the three agencies have sometimes worked at cross-purposes, with the EPA and FDA calling for more limits on pesticides, while the USDA promoted pesticide use.

Legislation introduced in 1993 by Senator Edward Kennedy and Representative Henry Waxman sought to address the findings of the Academy's report and a related report by the Washington, D.C.–based Environmental Working Group. The latter study stated, "Millions of children in the U.S. receive up to 35 percent of their entire lifetime dose of some carcinogenic pesticides by age five." The nonprofit Environmental Working Group and the food industry joined together in advising parents to continue feeding their children ample fruits and vegetables, because they are healthful and contain natural anticarcinogens. Until major inroads are made in reducing pesticides, organically grown foods and produce from farmers' markets are still the best bets. Wash all fruit well, especially around the stem.

Americans and Clothes

Wanting It All—at a Bargain

Dressing well is as much a part of the American Dream as job security and a paid-up mortgage. It says a lot about our personal prosperity and lifestyle. Americans have grown used to a clothing industry that can provide everything necessary to help them look their best. In 1992, clothes and accessory shoppers spent $190 billion in stores like Dayton Hudson, Nordstrom, and Macy's—and smaller retail outlets—looking for high style at reasonable prices, plus quality and durability. Nearly every closet in the country contains at least a few private labels: Levi's jeans, shirts from The Gap, a Benetton jacket. Add to that the millions of pairs of Nikes and Reeboks that travel to work or school in the morning and run laps in the evening. You get the picture. It can be a pretty expensive picture.

Looking Good: at Whose Expense?

In the early nineties, as clothing budgets became squeezed by the lingering recession, some consumers bought less or spruced up clothes they already had; some discovered neighborhood thrift shops. Those still shopping for clothes scrambled to look good for a lot less. If the price was right, they bought.

Operating in a highly competitive industry, makers of shoes and apparel have for years sought to keep the price "right" and to maintain profits by continually cutting costs. Many factories moved to low-wage areas of the U.S., causing job loss for thousands of unionized workers left behind. Hundreds more companies moved factories offshore to developing nations where wages are a tiny fraction of the U.S. minimum. During the eighties, the U.S. lost more than 65,000 jobs in footwear manufacturing. Bureau of Labor Statistics records indicate that between 1973 and 1993, more than 400,000 (29 percent) U.S. apparel jobs moved overseas. According to the American Apparel Manufacturing Association (Arlington, VA) in 1992 the United States imported $27 billion in clothing alone, up from $19 billion five years before.

Well, what difference does all this make to us? If manufacturers can hold down expenses and save us money, should we care how they do it? CEP believes that a big reason you're reading this book is that you *do* care how companies conduct their business—everywhere they operate.

The opening up of a worldwide marketplace can be stimulating and beneficial, not only for buyers and sellers of merchandise, but also for production workers and their communities. But it calls for companies to put their good citizenship to work both here and away from home, even if faced with unfamiliar laws and customs. Some U.S. corporations can and do provide decent wages, better working conditions, and educational opportunities wherever they operate. Many more leap at any chance for cheap production costs and high profits. Let's examine just a few examples of overseas sourcing, as now practiced by a majority of U.S. retailers. This will give you an eye-opening glimpse into what may be behind America's constant stream of good-looking apparel at reasonable prices.

Clothes Don't Make the Kid

In late 1992, a "Dateline NBC" TV presentation toured a factory in Bangladesh where clothing was being manufactured for sale to Wal-Mart—the nation's largest retailer—by two of its suppliers, Gitano and Capital Mercury Shirts. Posing as American buyers and using pictures taken with a home video camera, an NBC reporter described what the TV crew saw: ". . . three floors full of children—some as young as nine or ten—making clothes for Wal-Mart." The youngsters said they earned between five and eight *cents* an hour, and that they were kept inside until daily production quotas were met, which sometimes meant 12- and 13-hour workdays. In 1990, 25 workers, half of them children, died in a fire at that factory. They could not escape because gates were locked and exits were barricaded.

This news came as a big surprise to loyal U.S. supporters of Wal-Mart's "Buy American" credo. Though most retailers contract for goods to be made in other countries, Wal-Mart has employed a full-blown public ad campaign and in-house employee pep rallies to emphasize that it "buys American, whenever it can." Yet the Food and Allied Trade Services Department (FAST) of the AFL-CIO found that, in 1992, Wal-Mart imported 288 million pounds of goods from Hong Kong—8,000 times more than it imported before the "Buy American" program began. And when NBC reporters went undercover to nearly a dozen Wal-Mart stores in Florida and Georgia, they found merchandise labeled "Made in Korea" and "Made In Bangladesh" on racks with signs that said "Made in the U.S."

Confronted with the TV show's findings, Wal-Mart countered that "absolutely no illegal child labor has ever been used to make merchandise for Wal-Mart." Technically, they're right. According to a *Harvard Business Review* article on the complexities of child labor in developing countries (January–February 1993), local laws in Bangladesh do not effectively prohibit the hiring of children under 14. Managers there excuse the practice by stating that it is necessary for children to work to help support their impoverished families. CEO David Glass defends Wal-Mart's use of foreign manufacturers as necessary to sustain its level of business, stating that U.S. suppliers cannot meet the store's voracious demand for merchandise. As for the "misplaced" signs: *in each of 11 stores*, Wal-Mart blamed employee error.

Implementing Ethical Guidelines

Levi Strauss & Co. is the world's largest clothing manufacturer. Because it purchases much of its clothing from contractors in developing countries where workplace abuses are rampant, the company devised a set of ethical guidelines to ensure decent working conditions. The guidelines cover health and safety codes, employment practices, and environmental and ethical standards. Child (under age 14) and prison labor, discrimination, and corporal punishment are not permitted. Wages must comply with local laws, and work must not exceed 60 hours per week. Levi Strauss & Co. has sent auditors into 60 countries to ensure that its 700 contractors are adhering to the guidelines.

The company's resolve to "do the right thing" was tested when it moved to terminate a contract in Bangladesh due to child labor employed by the contractor. Upon learning that children were often the families' only source of income in that country, Levi Strauss & Co.

decided to pay all expenses for the children to go to school until they turn 14, when they may be hired by the contractor.

In 1993, Levi Strauss & Co. decided that it would make no direct investments in China and would scale back contracting there because of the country's human-rights record. The company also stopped doing business in Myanmar (Burma).

In June 1994, Seattle-based Nordstrom instituted global guidelines that set standards covering safe work environments, equitable employment practices, and regard for the environment. The guidelines prohibit forced or child labor in the production of Nordstrom goods. Vendors will be monitored for compliance through random on-site inspections.

Nike and Reebok, first and second respectively in sales, manufacture 100 percent of their sports shoes in the Far East. So do many other footwear companies. Shoe-factory workers in South Korea, China, Indonesia, and Thailand commonly labor in poor working conditions for very low wages. On July 2, 1993, CBS-TV's "Street Stories" showed women and girls as young as age 14 making Nike shoes in an Indonesian factory for $1.30 per day, the minimum wage there, which effectively keeps these women below the poverty level. Amazingly, the workers had to strike to get that. When interviewed, Nike factory workers said their company-supplied "free housing" consists of rough barracks, and that they aren't allowed outside the factory fence except on Sundays—and then only with a company pass.

Nike says it has "tried to upgrade both the quality of life and the skills of [its] employees" there, and asserts that Nike workers are better off than most Indonesian workers. "Street Stories" correspondent Roberta Baskin noted that Reebok, Adidas, and other sports-shoe companies make shoes in Indonesia as well. In 1992 when American union activist Jeff Ballinger conducted a survey of wages in Indonesian factories, he found that Nike was "setting the low end of the wage scale"—paying some of its workers 14 cents an hour—even less than the legal minimum wage. The story illustrates one way the top-selling sports-shoe company holds down its costs, but not yours: its labor costs to make an $80 pair of Nikes is about 12 cents, according to Ballinger's survey (*Harper's Magazine*, August 1992). In 1992, Nike had $3.4 billion in sales and spent $180 million on advertising.

Reebok has now established written guidelines and an audit system for its employees' health and safety and for corporate environmental impact overseas. Noted for its awards to persons advancing the cause of human rights, the company developed these guidelines in consultation with Levi Strauss & Co. and the International Labor Rights Education and Research Fund.

Sophisticated Labels, Shameful Wages

Even in 1994, clothing labeled "Made in the USA" may originate in cruel sweatshop surroundings—right here at home! In its November 22, 1993 edition, *U.S. News & World Report* gave the findings of a three-month investigation: "As many as half of all women's garments made in America are produced in whole or in part by factories that pay below minimum wage, flout Federal safety laws, and require workers to spend 60 hours or more" at work each week. There are no insurance benefits; there is no overtime pay. Sadly, in many cases child labor is used.

The article reports that according to records obtained under the Freedom of Information Act, subcontractors who violate basic federal labor laws have manufactured clothes for Casual Corner, Guess, Esprit, J.C. Penney, The Limited, Patagonia, Sears, Wal-Mart, and even some designer labels. For example, CEP has learned that 12 women who sewed dresses for Jessica McClintock, a San Francisco designer, were "paid" $15,000 in worthless checks by a contractor who went out of business. Though not legally liable, the company is being boycotted by the Asian Immigrant Women Advocates, who ask that restitution be made to the workers.

Some apparel companies say they try to hire only law-abiding vendors. Patagonia, maker of premium sturdy outdoor clothing, insists that it "does not knowingly work with any garment contractor that violates Federal or state wage and hour laws." But unfortunately, many manufacturers who obey the law are forced out of business. Agencies charged with oversight—such as the U.S. Department of Labor and the Occupational Safety and Health Administration—are understaffed and unable to cope with the magnitude of infractions.

Retailers themselves could make sure their subcontractors toed a more ethical line by writing into contracts provisions for decent hours and wages—and then checking to make sure that labor laws are heeded. They'll need a push from consumers to do it. Such a step could mean moderately higher clothing prices, but isn't it worth it to ensure your next wardrobe addition wasn't made by someone getting only pennies for piecework? Decent wages and a safe workplace ought to be an elementary cost of doing business.

According to a full-page story in the *New York Times* (July 18, 1994), garment workers from poor Asian countries emigrate to Saipan and other Northern Mariana islands that are U.S. territories with commonwealth status to make clothes for Arrow, Liz Claiborne, The Gap, and several other well-known U.S. companies. Encouraged to emigrate by subcontractors' inflated promises of working "in the U.S.," many went into debt to get there. Most now live in crude communal barracks and make roughly $2.15 an hour (the Marianas were exempted from the U.S. minimum-wage laws in 1976).

Levi Strauss & Co. still subcontracts on the island, but it has made strong efforts to curtail labor abuse there. In 1993, it stopped contracting with the largest local garment maker, citing "unsatisfactory treatment of workers and violations of law." It took this action under its new guidelines prohibiting manufacturing contracts "where there are pervasive violations of basic human rights."

Companies Can Work for Better Conditions

The case of Wal-Mart is particularly interesting, as this company has exerted significant leadership in the U.S. environmental arena, challenging its suppliers to create more earth-friendly products and packaging, and promoting these products in its stores. Such a company could extend its considerable clout to developing countries—helping to bolster and enforce local child-labor laws, and ensuring decent working conditions and wages.

So far, most companies with overseas operations have been slow, either individually or collectively, to use their influence for positive change. Senator Tom Harkin (Iowa) in 1992 introduced a bill that would ban the import of goods made with child labor. That bill was pending in committee as of September 1993. But child labor is just one facet of the unjust and unhealthy conditions that are a hidden backdrop to the inexpensive production of clothing, shoes, toys, and other goods for American consumers.

Reebok, Nordstrom, and Levi Strauss & Co. have taken the initiative in pressing for better workplace practices by adopting "human rights" standards or guidelines for their production facilities in other countries. We hope many will follow their example. These are positive steps and, with ongoing refinement, could form the basis for safer, more humane practices in the world marketplace.

Cotton Without Chemicals

The popularity of cotton has rebounded over the last few years, accounting for about half of textile use worldwide. But American consumers of cotton products are discovering that the hype about cotton's "naturalness" is not made out of whole cloth: cotton production is a potent cause of air, water, and ground pollution, causing attendant health problems in major cotton-farming areas. Not only does cotton growing require more pesticides than virtually any other crop (some 25 percent of yearly pesticide use in the U.S.), but usually it requires chemical defoliants as well. And the creation of cotton cloth routinely involves formaldehyde, chlorine bleach, solvent-laden dyes, and fixatives containing toxic heavy metals.

Consumers have begun to demand a more environmentally sound alternative. And it's happening, at least in a small corner of the market.

Progressive companies, from relatively small Seventh Generation (an environmentally friendly products catalog) and Esprit de Corp. to giants Levi Strauss & Co. and Vanity Fair, have introduced clothes and bedding made of organic cotton. This fiber is truly natural—grown without chemical pesticides or defoliants, then made into products using no bleach, formaldehyde, or artificial dyes.

Few companies have yet made a commitment to use organic cotton and nontoxic production processes in all the garments they produce. One reason is that fewer than 100 out of 30,000 cotton growers in 1993 grew organic cotton. It's an admittedly much harder row to hoe. To begin with, according to Brent Wiseman, Organics Coordinator for the Texas Department of Agriculture, it takes about three years to make the transition from conventional to organic cotton farming. (Texas has between 10,000 and 15,000 acres devoted to organic cotton, more than any other state.) In addition, growers faced with tough problems of alternative pest and weed control must feel reasonably sure there will be continuing demand.

Only one-tenth of 1 percent of all cotton grown in the U.S. is organically grown (*Buzzworm: The Environmental Journal*, July/August 1992). This helps to explain the premium cost of 10 to 20 percent more. Still, demand has materialized and is growing. Esprit de Corp. and Levi Strauss now carry special "natural" lines. Vanity Fair in 1992 acquired Green Cotton Environment, which will continue making organic-cotton sportswear under the name of O Wear. Patagonia sells some green products and has also drastically reduced its overall line, seeking to emphasize less consumption. Small new companies founded on the premise of environmental stewardship have replaced harmful petrochemicals by using beeswax, citrus scouring, and natural oils in their finishing processes. Hackensack-based (NJ) Ecosport, for example, is the originator of the organic "green cotton" line carried by Seventh Generation.

Ancient Seeds Grow New Industry

As in any industry where a revolution is taking place, entrepreneurs implemented revolutionary ideas. Entomologist Sally Fox's work with colored cotton seeds is a case in point. Though the seeds that could produce colored cotton have been around for thousands of years, they attracted little notice because the short fibers produced were not suitable for machine spinning. Ms. Fox, whose hobbies are spinning and weaving, spent years breeding and cross-pollinating colored cotton plants. Her Wasco, California, company, Natural Cotton Colours, Inc., succeeded in producing not only a longer-fiber cotton but new colors, as well.

How They Rate

Levi Strauss & Co. stands out among the clothing manufacturers CEP surveyed for its efforts to be socially responsible. One of our Honor Roll companies, it also received a special America's Corporate Conscience Award for International Commitment from CEP in 1994. At the other end of the spectrum, poor marks in Minority Advancement and Family Benefits marred The Timberland Company's otherwise good showing. Nordstrom performed best among clothing stores, achieving six top grades. May Department Stores Company, though excellent in Community Outreach, and doing well in three other areas, performed poorly in Family Benefits.

The Business of Toys

Play's the Thing

Little kids know how to build elaborate worlds peopled by their stuffed animals. With toys such as Lego blocks or a box full of silvery magnetic shapes, something wonderful begins to happen. Children produce their own creations, unmake them at whim, and make brand new ones. Children without access to these basic diversions have been known to spend hours happily drawing villages on brown paper with nontoxic markers or building space-station controls out of cartons and bottle caps. Older kids learn to explore on bikes and strategize in board games.

Such constructive pastimes, however, are not what children see on Saturday-morning television. Over the last few years, several authors and other analysts have deplored the relentless marketing of toys—especially violent ones—directly to kids. In a prepublication look at Stephen Kline's *Out of the Garden: Toys, TV and Children's Culture in the Age of Marketing* (Verso, 1993), *Kirkus Reviews* reported that the book offers a "well-documented case . . . that the TV market-place transmits not children's culture but that of toy companies."

Deborah Prothrow-Stith, M.D., assistant dean of the Harvard School of Public Health, and author of *Deadly Consequences* (HarperCollins, 1991), said at a May 1993 forum on the subject, "We teach our children that violence is funny, is entertaining, is successful, is the hero's first choice, is painless, is guiltless, is rewarded. The effect is that children see violence as the way to solve problems."

Whether we like it or not, TV—the primary teacher for most American kids from toddlerhood on—continues to provide free lessons in violent behavior. "In the context of making kids less sensitive to effects of violence, some researchers list Saturday morning cartoons among the most socially destructive programs on television," states an August *New York Times* article (Report on Conference on TV Violence and Kids sponsored by National Council for Families and TV, August 3, 1993).

In April 1993, the Center for Media and Public Affairs checked the violence on 18 hours of TV programming. Prime-time network programs showed only two to three violent acts per hour; cable averaged close to 15. Children's cartoons and toy commercials (network) surpassed them all, with 25 violent acts per hour.

A Monster Our Kids Learned to Love

In the early sixties, brief toy commercials appeared between Saturday-morning cartoons. They got a bit more frequent and insistent around the holidays. Ads featured contented children busy with Monopoly (Parker Brothers), trucks (Tonka), Play-Doh (Playskool), and Mr. Potato-Head (Hasbro). Shortly thereafter, Hasbro's G.I. Joe marched upon the scene (1964)—with scads of equipment designed for complete replacement every two years. He was followed by the likes of Rambo, He-Man, and Teenage Mutant Ninja Turtles. By the mid-eighties, more and more American children's playthings had taken a decidedly warlike turn.

With deregulation by the Federal Communications Commission in 1984, it suddenly became legal for toy companies to advertise almost nonstop during kids' programming, *which is often written to showcase the toy*. For an entire generation of parents and kids, things would never be the same: the "program-length commercial" was born. In 1987, the War Resisters League estimated that cartoons promoting toys treated our kids to an average of 50 acts of violence in a single hour. Toy companies were footing the bill for 80 percent of the TV shows aimed at children. Watching these action-figure-centered adventures week after week, children began to learn which toys they "had to have"—and the more violent, the better.

For the toy industry, it was a dream come true. According to the 1990 book *Who's Calling The Shots? How to Respond Effectively to Children's Fascination with War Play and War Toys* (Nancy Carlsson-Paige and Diane E. Levin, New Society Publishers), "By December 1985, all of the ten best-selling toys had TV shows connected to them. . . . To make matters worse, toy manufacturers and other companies that bought licenses to use a toy line's logo began to manufacture a variety of other products, using the logo from the TV character. By 1986, the Toy Manufacturers of America estimated that close to 50 percent of the toy industry's sales were of licensed products." Along the way, G.I. Joe's parent, Hasbro, gobbled up Parker Brothers, Playskool, Tonka, Kenner, and Coleco's (now defunct) Cabbage Patch Kids.

Greatly watered-down 1990 legislation finally put some limits on advertising during children's programs and called for more educational fare. But strong alliances between the television and toy industries had already been forged. That same year, General Electric's NBC announced its new vice president of children's and family programs—the former chief of marketing for Hasbro, Inc., originator of G.I. Joe.

Today, violence remains the focus of major toy companies. Unfortunately, to a great extent our children have been "programmed" to want it. Continuing the media tie-ins originated by TV shows, action figures are now based on film characters like those in the movies *Terminator 2* and *Batman Returns*. By tapping into the natural affinity young kids have for action and excitement, these toys racked up sales of $500 million in 1992.

Beyond Guns

Many kids act out what they view on TV. Thomas Radecki, M.D., of the National Coalition on Television Violence, states, "The cartoon and violent toy studies show that these materials cause children to hit, kick, choke, push, and hold down other children. This repeated teaching of seeing your opponent as someone despicably evil who can only be dealt with through combat is very harmful."

Avidly seeking new and different "hooks" to engage more kiddie customers, manufacturers have introduced an array of products that make most parents squirm, but are popular with their offspring.

Two particularly violent video games, for example, became available in fall 1993 on cartridges compatible with Sega and Nintendo home systems—Sega's "Night Trap" and Acclaim Entertainment's "Mortal Kombat." "Night Trap," which shows bloody attacks on young women, eventually was removed from sale by Toys "R" Us, FAO Schwartz, and some other retailers in the middle of the 1993 Christmas season. Finally, in January 1994, Sega said it would take the CD version off the market, and release an edited version later when industrywide ratings are available.

Still on the shelves, however, was top-selling "Mortal Kombat," which lets players choose bloody attack maneuvers like ripping out their opponents' spinal columns. Though ratings on cartridge boxes may deter some parents, it's doubtful they'll faze the kids who got "hooked" on games like "Mortal Kombat" when they were only available in arcades.

Where the Buck Stops

Organized groups and individual parents have been warning for more than two decades that "violence begets violence," that some playthings and videos and even music geared to youth are pushing dangerous limits. Many parents, feeling cornered by their kids' demands, continue to buy offensive toys for their children. By the time they're age 10, children themselves often do the buying, increasingly with their own money, often with little supervision.

Toy and video-game companies (who love it when the bucks stop with them) may take relatively ineffectual steps like printing movielike ratings or warnings on their packages, but they continue to develop products promoting violence. In the last few years, even music has had its share of violence. Two years ago, after public outcry, popular rapper Ice-T dropped a song called "Cop Killer" from his Warner Brothers Records album "Body Count." The lyrics referred specifically to killing law-enforcement officers. But Tupac

Shakur's 1991 album "2pacalypse Now" features similar lyrics and was not removed. Later songs by Snoop Doggy Dogg, Dr. Dre, and others push violence against women.

In December 1993, WABC-TV in New York reported that many of the top 50 rap songs listed in a current *Billboard* magazine "promoted violence, sex, drug use, and profanity." The Congress of 100 Black Women and other groups called for a crackdown on this kind of music, often referred to as "gangsta-rap." A number of black radio stations, including WBLS in New York and KACE-FM in California, have banned such music from their programs.

Though most major manufacturers provide content labeling, the fact remains that anyone may buy these products. Is it any wonder that our young people grow more violent?

Some Countries Say No

Who's Calling the Shots? notes that in Sweden, the National Board for Consumer Policies, the Swedish Council for Children's Play, and the toy-trade organizations signed a voluntary agreement (1976) to ban the sale or marketing of "modern warfare" toys (post-1914). A decade later, Finland's National Board for Social Welfare and the Entrepreneurs for Toy and Hobby Equipment Manufacturing joined together to voluntarily prohibit the manufacture, sale, or importation of war toys in that country. Business and government groups in Norway have signed a similar agreement. Malta formally bans the import of such toys (WorldPaper Special Report, December 1987).

Germany and Spain have a ban on TV advertising of war toys (*Daily Telegraph* [U.K.], November 14, 1990). The Council on Economic Priorities is in touch with the Peace Pledge Union in the United Kingdom, which is currently in the process of updating information on these agreements. Though new information was, unfortunately, unavailable for this book, we hope that it will be possible to present it in a future publication.

The relationship between toys and media violence is a community, business, and governmental responsibility, not just a parental one. Every adult American—whether a parent or not—can decide not to support the continuing media blitz of violence aimed at children. You can petition the Federal Communications Commission to move beyond the weaker 1990 legislation to reinstate its original provisions: selling a toy by means of a TV show was illegal, and ads on kids' TV shows were limited to a set number of minutes per hour.

Though advertising dollars promote the more violent products, many large toy companies make constructive toys. For example, Hasbro makes Playskool toys and many longtime favorites such as Mr. Potato-Head and Monopoly; Mattel manufactures cuddly dolls and now owns the popular Fisher Price line for infants and toddlers. Tyco toys, producer of electric race car sets and Matchbox cars, has just signed a 10-year licensing agreement with the Children's Television Workshop to develop Sesame Street products. Challenge Hasbro and others to take a hard look at product decisions and marketing practices that affect the youngest members of society.

Alternative Toy Companies

There are companies out there whose mission and products are geared to what is best for the child. Some offer playthings that foster a spirit of cooperation, and introduce kids to other cultures. However, being mostly small and privately owned, only a few of these companies disclosed information to CEP. We do not know the social responsibility of the others, beyond having good products. Here are some you may want to look into: Lego (203-749-2291), a subsidiary of Kirkbi AG in Baar, Switzerland, makes the wonderful plastic blocks that not only engross and educate children, but go right on doing the same for *their* children; Brio Scanditoy Corporation (800-558-6863), also a foreign-based company, offers durable wooden toys that challenge the imagination and delight the eye. Again, these are well-made quality toys to be passed from one generation to the next; Little Tikes Company (216-650-3000), a subsidiary of Rubbermaid, manufactures toys for infants and preschool children. One recent addition to Little Tikes' family of toys is "Wheelchair, Ramp and Friend," the first dollhouse figure from a major toy company to depict a person with a disability.

The HearthSong Toy Company (800-325-2502) was founded

by Barbara Kane in 1983 "to provide parents with access to goods and ideas that would allow their children 'time to be children.' " HearthSong's catalog and stores offer building and action toys, craft and science kits, musical instruments, handmade dolls and books. (HearthSong is now owned by Foster and Gallagher, a private company that declined to answer CEP's questionnaire.)

Olmec (212-645-3660), which makes dolls with authentic black and Hispanic features, was started in 1985 by Yia Eason. This black Brooklyn mother and Harvard graduate decided to leave her well-paying job with Standard & Poor's to found a company that would provide children of color with toys and media images mirroring their own experience. Beginning with Sun Man (to provide youngsters with a black superhero image), and then adding a family of dolls that include Imani, an authentic African-American fashion doll, the company has become the world's largest manufacturer of ethnically correct dolls. Olmec's products are now sold in major outlets such as K-Mart, Toys "R" Us, and Woolworth. In 1993, Hasbro asked Olmec to help develop a line of ethnic dolls dressed in authentic African Kente cloth. Mattel and others now also produce African-American dolls.

The Cultural Exchange Corporation (612-544-1581), founded as a sideline in 1990 by former toy executive Jacob R. Miles III and his wife, in 1994 began making a complete line of playthings that are especially appealing to people of color. The black Minnesota entrepreneurs have introduced such toys as Hollywood Hounds, and will also develop books, puzzles, and cards. The first playthings from Cultural Exchange began appearing in Toys "R" Us and Dayton Hudson during the 1993 holiday season.

A number of mail-order-catalog companies sell similarly positive playthings: Animal Town (800-445-8642), The Natural Baby Company, Inc. (609-771-9233), Emily's Toybox (518-861-6719), The Forest (owned by One World Projects, 800-637-7614), Nova Natural (914-426-3757), Real Goods Trading Corporation (800-762-7325), and Seventh Generation (800-456-1177) are just a few of these.

If you want up-to-date information on the safety or durability of a toy, your best bet is to contact Consumers Union (914-378-2551).

Competition and Worker Exploitation

Many brand-name toys from top U.S. companies—Hasbro, Tyco, Fisher-Price (now owned by Mattel), and Gund among them—are produced by workers in Thailand and other very low-wage countries where firms from industrialized nations go to have goods made inexpensively. Not only do Thai workers often labor up to 14 hours a day, seven days a week, but the factories in which they toil are often firetraps. On May 10, 1993, a Kader Enterprises toy-factory fire near Bangkok killed 188 people and injured 500. According to witnesses, fire escapes were locked. The building's fire alarm and sprinkler system were also grossly inadequate.

Such subcontracting in the name of competitiveness is being practiced by a host of U.S. companies making clothing, shoes, and other products as well as toys. CEP is currently conducting a study (in cooperation with New Consumer, our U.K. counterpart) on benchmark transnational corporate practices in developing countries. Research on exemplary companies shows that it is possible—and can be profitable—for companies to assemble products in developing countries while treating workers fairly.

Mattel Best in Equal Opportunity

Mattel's president and chief operating officer is a woman, who also sits on its board of directors. Forty-two percent of Mattel's officials and managers are female and six women are among the company's 25 highest-paid officers. Mattel received a rating of "A" for Women's Advancement.

Though no minorities are on Mattel's board, there are 10 minority officers, two of whom are among the 25 highest paid. This performance won a "B" for the company.

By comparison, Hasbro has three women on its 15-member board, but no female corporate officers, rating a "B." Tyco has only two women among 38 corporate officers, and none on its board, rating a "C." Neither Hasbro nor Tyco provided any information on minority advancement.

The American Auto Industry

Shifting Gears—Slowly

Over the past several years, the environmental and health problems exacerbated by car emissions have received increasing attention. This, in turn, has put more pressure on car manufacturers to voluntarily increase fuel efficiency and decrease emissions—or face stern governmental regulation. In addition, consumer-advocacy groups point out safety issues they feel are not adequately addressed. And there's plenty of room for improvement in appointing more women and minorities to top positions.

In September 1993, the Clinton Administration sought to rev up innovation and boost conversion by offering $1 billion in federal help to major U.S. car manufacturers. Working with the Department of Defense, manufacturers must develop a cleaner-burning car with fuel efficiency up to three times that of today's cars. Over the next decade, Ford, Chrysler, and General Motors (GM) will aim for production of an auto that goes a whopping 80 miles on a gallon of gas. Currently, new U.S. cars achieve about 30 miles per gallon.

The Colorado-based Rocky Mountain Institute, a research and education foundation that focuses on energy and the environment, predicts the introduction—by 2003—of an "ultralight, ultrasafe, ultraefficient" supercar that would leave many current environmental problems in the dust. This totally new model, exemplified by General Motors' Ultralite "concept car" (built in 1991), would be constructed of synthetic composite materials so light that the cars would be just two-fifths the weight they are now and twice as fast. If a 10- to 20-horsepower " 'hybrid electric drive' that powers the wheels electrically" were used instead of a conventional engine, this would dramatically raise fuel efficiency, according to the Institute.

A California law now requires 2 percent of locally produced vehicles to have zero emissions by 1998 (10 percent by 2003). Delaware, Maryland, Massachusetts, Pennsylvania, and others have followed suit. In California, which is struggling with thousands of layoffs due to loss of defense jobs, a consortium named Calstart was formed in 1991 to build and market components for electric vehicles. Calstart is about 75 percent funded by private capital. It combines 40 regional companies, federal and state governments, labor unions, and academic institutions in a common effort to lay the groundwork for a high-tech transportation industry. The consortium built a showcase electric vehicle that toured the world in 1993. It is now constructing 140 charging and service centers for the vehicles, many of which will run on energy generated by solar collectors.

Research on fuel-cell technology as an alternative to using heavy batteries for electric cars is underway at several companies, including Energy Partners, Inc. (West Palm Beach, Florida), and Ballard Power Systems (Vancouver, British Columbia) (*New York Times*, July 3, 1993). Fuel cells produce electricity by means of a chemical reaction, just as batteries do. But fuel cells continue to provide power as long as the chemical fuel is present, and the new technology reportedly replenishes the chemicals as needed. Some have voiced concern that the method might prove too costly, but mass production may remedy this.

General Motors announced in the fall of 1993 that it would build 50 experimental electric cars that emit zero exhaust, and let 1,000 American drivers try them out (a few weeks each) over the next two years. Fourteen utilities participating in the trial run will help publicize the test-drive program and install chargers in the cars.

Japanese carmakers are also hard at work on development of zero-emission vehicles, and may have models available for market by 1995. Toyota, for example, has put 100 of its top engineers to work exclusively on development of an electric car, hoping to beat the 1998 deadline.

One concern with electric cars is that pollution might simply be displaced from the auto's tailpipe to the site of the generating plant. According to the 1994 edition of *State of the World* (Norton & Co.) produced by the Worldwatch Institute, "Although recharging the battery with electricity generated from coal entails some emissions (including a greater amount of sulfur dioxide, which contributes to acid rain), large power plants tend to be more efficient and less polluting than small internal combustion engines." The electricity needed could be generated from solar power (as Calstart is demonstrating) or, in some areas, from wind or hydro (water) power.

Worldwatch also reports that carmakers in Japan, Germany, and the U.S. are working on refinement of hydrogen-producing technologies, hoping to develop a hydrogen-fuel-cell-powered car that will emit only water vapor.

In accepting the Clinton Administration's challenge to produce a more fuel-efficient car, the U.S. Big Three automakers and the federal defense labs must explore new territory in design and manufacturing, while balancing strong labor demands and the internal need to shape up for competition in world markets, especially with the Japanese.

Japanese Companies Do It Their Way, and It Works

In a 1992 customer-satisfaction survey of 34,000 new-car owners conducted by J.D. Power & Associates, Toyota's Lexus won top honors. Drivers were especially pleased by the provision of a two-hour checkup and test drive for every new car prior to offering it for sale, and free roadside service anywhere in the U.S. (at any time) for four years following purchase.

Honda Motor Co., squeezed by the recession in Japan and in the U.S., was faced in 1993 with the need to temporarily cut car production at its Marysville, Ohio, facility. Instead of laying off workers, it used the slack time for extra training of its employees, investing for greater productivity later on. These are just two examples of a well-financed, innovative process that looks ahead, building a sound business base for the future.

Japan's Big Three automakers—Honda, Nissan, and Toyota—began establishing their own auto-manufacturing plants on U.S. soil in 1982. Most Americans may not realize that these companies were encouraged to come here, by both top U.S. automakers and the United Auto Workers (UAW) union (*Business Week*, August 14, 1989). It was thought that such a move would lead to reduced competition and more American jobs at union wages. But that is not how things worked out.

The United Auto Workers union tried hard but, by 1989, had failed to organize any auto plants owned *solely* by the Japanese. It did succeed, however, in winning bargaining rights at the three companies owned jointly by U.S. and Japanese carmakers (see below).

Plants that are owned solely by Japanese companies have resisted unionization and demand very high productivity. Many provide generous pay at near-parity with union plants and offer opportunities for workers to participate with management in decision making. Unlike American facilities, the Japanese (and a number of European manufacturers) favor a much smaller number of job classifications, and intentionally train their workforce for competence in more than one area.

But Japanese plants have had problems and uneven progress in the area of equal opportunity. In 1988, the Equal Employment Opportunity Commission (EEOC) charged that Honda had deliberately excluded minorities from its workforce. The company later paid $6 million in damages to 377 female and black employees for past discrimination. In 1993, however, a woman headed a Honda facility in Anna, Ohio.

Nissan, also the target of an EEOC investigation, in 1989 was ordered to pay $605,600 in back pay to 92 women, minorities, and older persons, who were found to have been discriminated against. Nissan's Tennessee plant had a female vice president in 1993.

Toyota did not escape EEOC scrutiny. Following a 1987 investigation, it hired five minority employees previously denied positions and paid them $50,000 in back wages. Soon afterward, Toyota established TEAM (Toyota Equal Access for Minorities), a program designed to "bring new business, employment, and education to minorities and women across the country," according to the company. Acting on ideas discussed in consultation with minority business leaders, Toyota now annually funds 30 scholarships to aid students of African-American, Hispanic, and Native American heritage; purchases materials from 80 women and minority suppliers; and works with community groups to stay in touch with local needs. In 1990, Toyota received the Los Angeles Urban League's Social Responsibility Award.

During the last decade, each of the American Big Three has created a joint venture with a Japanese car manufacturer: New United Motor Manufacturing (NUMMI) in Fremont, California, teams General Motors with Toyota; Diamond-Star Motors in Normal, Illinois, was formed by Chrysler and Mitsubishi; and Mazda Motor Manufacturing (USA) in Flat Rock, Michigan, pairs Mazda with Ford.

Women at the Wheel, but Not at the Helm

Forty-two percent of car buyers were women in the 1992–93 model year, according to J. D. Power & Associates. But a 1992 survey of professional women in the auto industry, conducted by the *Detroit Free Press* and the University of Michigan, shows only seven women in top management. Even this poor showing is an improvement over Big Three employment of female managers in 1987.

In 1993, General Motors and Ford each had only one female vice president. GM had two women on its board, while Ford had one. Overall, GM has an edge, with 12 percent of its officials and managerial positions held by women. Chrysler, with not one woman vice president, and only one female board member, raised the number of women in its officials/managers category from 3.5 percent in 1987 to 6.8 percent five years later. The company has indicated it plans to double the growth rate of women (and minorities) in managerial and senior technical slots over the next five years.

Top Opportunities Elude Minorities

Again, General Motors leads the way with programs and opportunities for minorities, but the industry as a whole still has a long way to go. Minorities in management posts averaged around 9 percent at the three companies, and each firm has one member of a minority group on its board.

GM made the "top company" lists in *Black Enterprise* and *Hispanic* magazines due to its strong investment in minority business, programs with minority banks, $1.1 billion in purchasing from minority vendors, and policies to help provide opportunities for promotion.

Ford made *Black Enterprise*'s "Top 25" list, having spent $440 million on purchasing from minority-owned firms. Chrysler is lowest in purchasing ($211 million), and blacks comprise only 4 percent of its senior management. The company has instituted diversity-awareness programs and policies for promotion.

The number of dealerships headed by minorities is infinitesimal, and not getting any better with the recession. More than 600 auto dealerships a year have thrown in the towel during the economic downturn. According to the National Association of Minority Automobile Dealers, only 4.9 percent (249) of Ford's 5,098 U.S. dealerships were minority run in early 1993. Chrysler and General Motors showed an even poorer rate of such dealerships, with 2.8 percent of 4,766 and 2.0 percent of 8,776, respectively. Though each of the Big Three recruits and trains minorities to run dealerships, many of the dealerships launched have continuing financial or other problems. Ford told *Business Week* (February 15, 1993) that for each minority dealership launch, it expends several million dollars in loans and a paid two-year training program.

Overall Performance

Overall, General Motors is marginally the best performer of the Big Three, although Chrysler currently outshines it in the Environment category. GM has been willing to share information, while Chrysler did not answer CEP's questionnaire and Ford omitted important information. In addition, GM—the world's largest industrial company—signed the CERES Principles in early 1994, showing its commitment to continue improving environmental performance. GM does have some safety problems, however (see below).

GM Out of Cleaner Corporations Campaign

In 1992, CEP's Campaign for Cleaner Corporations (C3) released a list of eight egregious polluters chosen by an independent panel of judges, and made cleanup recommendations for each. (See page 391.) GM, named in 1992, received 6,000 letters and calls, largely generated by Working Assets' activist network. In 1993, the company was removed from the list. It was credited for joining with other car manufacturers, defense labs, and the Clinton Administration to develop a super-efficient car; building and testing 50 electric cars; supporting a phased-in gasoline tax that would escalate over five years; extensive disclosure of environmental information; and continuing environmental programs despite the poor economic climate.

Responding to Dual Air Bag Demand

Winning life-saving air bags took at least a decade of pressure from safety groups like Motor Voters (based in Sacramento, California), and the Center for Auto Safety and U.S. Public Interest Research Group (both in Washington, D.C.), culminating in their October 1990 call for a consumer boycott of cars without air bags. It took insistent calls and letters from people like you. Now, more than 75 percent of 1994 Ford and Chrysler car lines and 60 percent of General Motors 1994 car lines are equipped with dual air bags (*Wall Street Journal*, October 12, 1993). The U.S. government will require air bags in all cars by the 1998 model year, and in all minivans and pickups by 1999.

Among major auto manufacturers, GM has the lowest percentage of cars with even driver's-side air bags. Rosemary Shahan, president of Motor Voters, told CEP that GM has actively opposed the introduction of air bags for years, "even mailing letters to its stockholders urging them to write the Department of Transportation (DOT) against requiring air bags."

The Japanese Big Three carmakers—though slow to respond initially—all now offer dual air bags in cars marketed in the U.S. In the 1993 model year, 100 percent of Toyota cars and 93 percent of Hondas featured at least a driver's-side air bag (Insurance Institute for Highway Safety). This compared with 87 percent for Chrysler, 72 percent for Nissan, 60 percent for Ford, and 56 percent for GM.

Safety Concerns: GM Pickup Trucks, Utility Vehicle Rollovers

In April 1993, the National Highway Traffic Safety Administration (NHTSA) requested that GM voluntarily recall all Chevy and GMC pickups made between 1973 and 1987. These vehicles featured gas tanks mounted on the side, outside of the protective steel framework. According to independent research cited by NHTSA, the pickups "have 2.4 times the risk of igniting in fatal side crashes than full-size Ford or Dodge pickup trucks." An April 1993 study performed by an NHTSA statistician for the Department of Transportation indicated there were 349 fatal fire accidents involving GM pickup trucks with "fuel tanks mounted outside the frame rails" (side-mounted) in the calendar years 1979 to 1990.

GM stands behind its pickups, stating that they have had "an excellent safety record over the past 21 years," despite a February 1993 ruling in Atlanta that GM must pay $105 million in the case of a teenager who died in a pickup-truck crash. In November 1993, Federal Transportation Secretary Federico Peña personally took over the GM pickup-truck investigation.

Recent research indicates that rollover accidents can be a serious problem with the proliferation of light minivans and "sport utility" vehicles. Most of these vehicles are designed with a high center of gravity, but fairly narrow distance between the tires. This leads to more instances of rollover. In the 1993 edition of *The Minivan, Pickup and 4x4 Book* (HarperCollins), author Jack Gillis provides a Rollover Index and Rating Chart that lists model names and their ratings for likelihood of rolling over. Among 22 minivan models, for example, Ford's Aerostar four-wheel-drive and Volkswagen's Eurovan have a "very high" likelihood of rolling over compared to a Mercury Villager or Nissan Quest, listed as "moderate." Among 33 sport utility models, Mitsubishi's Montero scored worst and General Motors' Chevrolet Suburban and GMC Suburban models were designated "moderate."

To better evaluate your next utility-vehicle purchase, you may want to check out the 1994 edition of *The Minivan, Pickup and 4x4 Book*. It's available in bookstores or by check ($14.50 postpaid) from The Truck Book, 1518 K Street NW, Suite 302, Washington D.C. 20005.

In 1990, the *Wall Street Journal* reported that Ford Motor Company had received 316 complaints alleging that malfunctioning automatic seatbelts in two of its models (produced from 1987 through 1989) were responsible for 76 injuries and five deaths. At that time, the National Highway Traffic Safety Administration was conducting an engineering analysis of the two cars: the Ford Escort and Mercury Lynx subcompacts.

Other cars have also had problems with faulty seatbelts. Motor Voters' Rosemary Shahan recalled, "In 1979, the Peugeot 504 had the worst head injury score in the history of crash tests." Her organization was instrumental in having Peugeot 1988 and 1989 models recalled after the company's seatbelt system consistently failed to prevent head injuries in crash tests over a decade.

An excellent source for buyers' information on cars and other major purchases is *Consumer Reports* magazine, produced by Consumers Union (914-378-2551), which has performed its own highly reliable independent testing and evaluation for many years.

It may be quite some time before efforts to minimize or end auto pollution make real changes in our environment. Until then, CEP recommends you walk, bike, or use public-transit systems whenever possible. You're contributing to clean air!

The Appliance Industry

More Environmentally Friendly

With an eye toward steady, measurable improvement in new-product energy efficiency, the federal government recently set stricter standards for refrigerators, clothes washers and dryers, and dishwashers. In 1996, there will be new minimum-efficiency requirements for water heaters and air conditioners, as well.

Appliance manufacturers seem to need the push of periodic legislation and special incentives. Then, they regularly come up with energy-saving changes in their products—changes that translate into dollar savings for you and pollution savings by cutting electricity use. Whirlpool, for example, has introduced an award-winning refrigerator that not only uses 25 percent less energy than government standards specify, but also eliminates all use of chlorofluorocarbons (CFCs). Production of these ozone-depleting chemicals, once routinely present in all refrigerator coolants and foam insulation, will end in 1995.

Whirlpool's refrigerator design won the $30 million top prize in a recent contest initiated by the Natural Resources Defense Council and other environmental groups to seek more environmentally friendly versions of this energy-guzzling appliance. The contest was sponsored by two dozen utility companies, some of which are offering rebates of up to 20 percent to encourage customers to buy more energy-efficient appliances. Energy-efficient appliances—though they may cost more up front—in the long run will often be less expensive because of lower energy expenses over the lifetime of the appliance. Right now, the average American household spends more than $1,000 a year running appliances and heating/cooling equipment. If inefficiencies were remedied, this figure would be significantly lower. Over the last 20 years, refrigerator-efficiency improvements have been dramatic. You'll save energy—and pay less on your electric bill—when you purchase a newer model.

Saving Energy with "Green" Appliances

Bright yellow "Energy Guide" labels currently herald annual energy costs or energy-efficiency ratings (EERs) on several kinds of appliances: water heaters, boilers, heat pumps, dishwashers, clothes washers, refrigerators, refrigerator/freezer combos, and room air conditioners. (The manufacturers have ascertained this information by using standardized tests developed by the industry.)

The American Council for an Energy Efficient Economy (ACEEE) has a handy primer, the *Consumer Guide to Home Energy Savings*, which can help you choose the most efficient home-appliance models. The book is $8.95 postpaid from ACEEE (510-549-9914).

CEP's Guide Rates Appliance Companies for First Time

Of the six appliance companies approached by CEP for information on their social-responsibility records, only three—Maytag, General Electric, and Whirlpool—responded with fairly complete questionnaires. AB Electrolux, Fedders, and Raytheon chose to provide little or no information.

Maytag, though its "unneeded" repairmen may be staring at the ceiling, is pretty busy in the charitable-giving department, with gifts totaling 2.87 percent of its worldwide pretax earnings in 1992. It gets average marks in community programs and family benefits, and has traditionally had good labor relations. Employee suggestions have long been valued there as an important source of innovation in productivity and savings for the company. Regular awards of up to $7,500 each are given for suggestions used.

General Electric improved over 1992 in charitable giving and disclosure, finally sold off its aerospace and military businesses, and does pretty well in family benefits. But environmental and workplace problems continue to plague this company. In 1992, CEP listed GE as one of eight egregious environmental offenders in its Campaign for

Cleaner Corporations (C3). The company remained on the list in 1993 as "the worst environmental offender in the electrical equipment industry," and was also cited on *Fortune* magazine's 1993 list of "environmental laggards." According to a Public Citizen report, although GE has designed only 33 percent of all domestic nuclear reactors, they constitute 70 percent of the "Nuclear Lemon" reactors in the U.S.

Whirlpool seems quite responsive to consumers when it comes to improving its products. The company sends out a Standardized Appliance Measurement Satisfaction survey every year to 180,000 households, unflinchingly asking for consumer ratings of all its appliances. It also invites consumers to test products (by computer) at the company's Usability Lab. Whirlpool has acquired several companies. Three times bigger than it was in 1982, it's now the world's largest major-appliance manufacturer.

Considering the huge numbers of women and people of color who purchase their products, there is room for all three of these companies to improve their EEO (Equal Employment Opportunity) programs. GE's "C" grades in the Women's and Minority Advancement categories show that it does only a little better than the other two respondents to CEP's questionnaire. There are two women, one of whom is black, and one Hispanic male on GE's 15-member board. Only five of GE's top 117 executive officers are female. The company has, however, instituted training programs on diversity awareness and sexual harassment at all levels. In 1992, it purchased $123 million in goods and services from women-owned firms and $129 million from minority businesses.

Whirlpool has one woman and one minority member on its 14-person board. One female corporate officer and a Hispanic subsidiary head are among the company's 25 highest-paid officers. At Maytag, there is one female on the 14-member board and one among 13 corporate officers. A Hispanic heads one subsidiary. Whirlpool and Maytag supplied no information on minority purchasing.

It's always a good idea, when buying major items like appliances, not only to check company social performance, but to consult *Consumer Reports* for up-to-date information on quality, safety, and price.

The Computer Industry

Some Products Save Energy and Money

Most personal computers are not actively in use for the majority of the time they are left running, according to recent research. Energy Star™ desktop computers, monitors, and printers are designed to slip into a reduced power phase when not in use. The Environmental Protection Agency reports that computers bearing the Energy Star logo, "could save enough electricity each year to power Vermont, New Hampshire, and Maine; and reduce carbon dioxide pollution equivalent to emissions from five million autos."

Computers account for about 6 percent of commercial electricity usage. Without intervention, this figure could rise to 10 percent by the turn of the century. The generation of electricity leads to hefty emissions of three dangerous pollutants—sulfur dioxide, nitrogen oxides, and carbon dioxide. The EPA joined with top computer manufacturers to introduce Energy Star™ machines that can cut their electricity use in half. In his recent book *The Green PC* (Windcrest McGraw-Hill, 1993), Steven Anzovin says that besides using less power, the newly designed computers will generate less heat, thus lowering costs for air conditioning.

Manufacturers involved in the Energy Star agreement, who sell more than half of the desktops and 90 percent of laser printers marketed in the U.S., began selling Energy Star products in 1993. They promise that a majority of their products will have this "sleep" feature in 1994 or 1995.

All U.S. government agencies are purchasing computers and equipment that meet EPA Energy Star requirements, thanks to President Clinton's Executive Order, which took effect in October 1993. By the year 2000, this effort alone should result in annual energy savings of $40 million for American taxpayers.

For those of you who want to continue using your present computer in a more energy-saving way, the October 1993 *Green Business Letter* notes the availability of a hardware-software device called the PC Ener-G Saver, which automatically puts "any IBM and compatible computer running under DOS or Windows" into a "sleep" mode when not in active use. Contact PC Green Technologies (800-984-7336).

Startling Applications, Greater Convenience

Over the last two years, major companies sought to form alliances—among former competitors and even different industries—in a race to meet the challenge of an "electronic superhighway." Out of this mad scramble, newly configured companies may emerge to provide information and entertainment services never before offered through a single medium.

Right now, there are fascinating computer applications that give new meaning to expectations for convenience and ease of communications. Laptop and notebook computers automatically store the notes you take at conferences, meetings, field trips. Pen-recognition software is in the works at AT&T, IBM, and elsewhere that will translate your own handwriting into typed text.

Blockbuster Entertainment and IBM are working on plans for in-house taping of your favorite CDs or video games, calling them up from huge computer banks located elsewhere. This would remove the need for transporting inventory, and guarantee that your request is in stock. And millions of scientists, writers, researchers—even in the most remote parts of the globe—have discovered that they can brainstorm with colleagues and access or disseminate information through a vast computer network called Internet.

Consumer Health Concerns

With the huge growth of computer use in the last few years, however, have come consumer worries about carpal tunnel syndrome (a repetitive-motion disorder), head and back aches, and the possible health effects of radiation. A corollary industry has come into being to help mitigate these complaints. For carpal tunnel, the most consistent advice from the industry and the medical profession is to take frequent breaks from computer activity, maintain proper posture and keyboard angle, and do regular wrist exercises. A number of labor unions, including the Service Employees International Union (SEIU), Communications Workers of America (CWA), and Retail, Wholesale & Department Store Union (RWDSU), have produced helpful fact sheets on ways to deal with this problem.

In an article titled "The Green Machine" in its May 25, 1993 issue, *PC Magazine* suggested a number of aids, discussed in the following paragraphs, that are available to maintain your overall health when you use computers.

PM Ware (800-845-4843) distributes Tica's User Friendly Exercises, a program that will automatically prompt exercise intervals and teach simple exercises to avoid eye, back, and arm discomfort.

Experts generally agree that the computer user should sit with elbows at right angles to the keyboard, feet touching the floor, and visual display terminal (VDT) at or slightly below eye level. Ergonomic workstations may be assembled from offerings that include adjustable furniture (a good chair is particularly important), newly designed keyboards, antiglare screens, and inexpensive wrist and foot rests. Not all of these live up to expectations, however. CEP spoke to Diane Stein, Safety and Health Specialist at the New York Committee for Occupational Safety and Health (NYCOSH), whose Repetitive Stress Injury Task Force in 1993 tried unsuccessfully to persuade Consumers Union to evaluate VDT accessories. Feeling such a review is in demand, the task force is putting together fact sheets of its own concerning VDT-related furniture and accessories. The first of these should become available in 1994 (212-627-3900).

As for electromagnetic emissions, a primary concern is for women to avoid frequent computer use during early pregnancy. A 1988 study of pregnant California women found that those working 20 hours or more weekly on visual display terminals were twice as likely to have miscarriages in the first trimester. Many newer monitors comply with a standard devised by Sweden's National Board for Industrial and Technical Development. Known as MPR-II, this standard currently provides the best guidelines, though not an absolute guarantee of safety, according to *PC Magazine*. It recommends asking for an MPR-compliant monitor when you buy.

For older monitors, add-on products can reduce emissions, but may run between $200 and $400, depending on the monitor size.

The NoRad Corporation (800-262-3260) is one firm offering such add-ons.

For further insight on computer use and health concerns, read "Comfort Zone" (ergonomics), *Inc. Magazine*, winter 1994; "Computer Users' Injuries Are Often Preventable," *New York Times* Personal Health column, March 4, 1992; and "How to Limit Your Exposure to Electromagnetic Fields," *Popular Science*, December 1991.

Environmental Problems Still Plague Industry

The computer industry for many years has cleaned circuitry using solvents that contain ozone-damaging chlorofluorocarbons (CFCs). The Montreal Protocol will end this practice worldwide by 2000. The EPA has called for an earlier deadline: December 1995. The industry began in the late eighties to achieve aggressive CFC reduction and eventual phaseout. A number of companies, including Apple, have eliminated their use of CFCs before the target dates. Coalitions such as the Industry Cooperative for Ozone Layer Protection helped with this effort. Alternatives, however, sometimes proved equally damaging. One environmentally friendly solution found was an orange-rind-based circuit-board cleaning solvent (Bioact EC-7), now being used by Texas Instruments.

Reducing toxic releases is also a high priority for computer manufacturers. Some companies have signed on to the EPA's Industrial Toxics Project ("33/50" Program). Begun in 1988, this program requires participating companies to work toward cutting in half the release of 17 target chemicals by 1995. IBM and Motorola reached that goal by year-end 1990. Among nonparticipating companies, Tandem, Apple, Digital Equipment, and Compaq showed the smallest amounts of toxic releases relative to sales over the period from 1988 through 1990. This and other factors won them top environmental ratings from CEP.

The downside of environmental performance in computer manufacturing is evident in the 29 EPA Superfund sites and 200 contaminated drinking-water wells located in Silicon Valley alone. The Silicon Valley Toxics Coalition (SVTC), which monitors the environmental impact of the industry, reports that much of the groundwater contamination from underground chemical leaks originates with electronics facilities. One of the firms criticized by SVTC, Advanced Micro Devices (AMD), says that leaks in its underground storage tanks in Santa Clara County have not yet damaged public drinking water, but have caused contamination of surrounding groundwater. Local homeowners have brought a class-action suit against AMD, claiming that property values have been lowered.

Many manufacturers of circuit boards and silicon chips (often under contract to the major computermakers) are lured by lucrative tax incentives to relocate in the Southwest, where residents fear the environmental damage will be repeated. Community leaders from Albuquerque and San Jose (New Mexico) and Austin (Texas) have formed the Electronics Industry Good Neighbor Campaign to prevent further pollution by companies like Intel, Advanced Micro Devices, and National Semiconductor. The group is also working against the tax giveaways offered by state and local governments, and have demanded that the chip-industry consortium Sematech be more responsive to employee and community needs.

Workers Experience Health Problems

According to the Southwest Organizing Project (SWOP), based in Albuquerque, New Mexico, responsible technology is a goal yet to be achieved in its community. Though the computer industry is always billed as a "clean" industry, the electronics-industry employees in this group—mostly Latino women—are allegedly exposed at work to dangerous chemicals, solvents, and gases. In 1984, 200 workers sued the GTE-Lenkurt plant for such exposure, which they say led to illnesses that included cancer, central-nervous-system damage, cardiovascular diseases, and learning disabilities in their children. The symptoms described by these women closely parallel those claimed by Silicon Valley workers. The GTE suit was won by the plaintiffs, but terms were not made public. The company transported its operations to Juárez, Mexico. This is just one story, about one company. There are many more.

A recent Johns Hopkins University study commissioned by IBM found that, during the eighties, one-third of the women who worked in close contact with two chemical solvents in the semiconductor-manufacturing process experienced miscarriages. This was a much higher incidence than that for women working with other chip-plant procedures (62 miscarriages out of 398 pregnancies). Many of the procedures covered in the study have been changed since that time to enhance worker safety. IBM has offered job transfers to concerned employees and held informational meetings for thousands of workers on this subject.

How They Rate

Overall, major computer companies tend to do a good job of promoting women to senior positions. Apple, Dell, Digital Equipment Corporation, and IBM do well here. However, Apple rated a "D" in Minority Advancement, and Compaq does poorly in promoting both women and minorities. It is impossible to choose overall best and worst, because some companies (such as Dell) supplied little or no information and CEP was unable to rate them. Though Digital Equipment and Hewlett-Packard appear on CEP's honor roll, Apple Computer and IBM are close behind in overall performance.

The Telecommunications Industry

Fiber Optics Shapes Its Future—and Yours

By now, you've all seen the ads showing the businesswoman, still at work, saying goodnight to her baby via a TV screen hooked up to her telephone. "You can't do this yet, but you will," runs the copy. Any questions you might have had about this new technology were not addressed by news of company mergers and coalitions seeking to carve out their spheres of influence in the fast-developing field called fiber optics. So you may have been surprised—and a little alarmed—by predictions that you'll soon be using the same central-media receptacle to prepare the PTA minutes, call Uncle Harry, watch "Jeopardy," or shop for a new wardrobe. And maybe one question is not "How can they do that?" but "Do we want to do that?"

What's in It for You?

One issue to look at is whether the new fiber-optics network will really provide you and your family with greater convenience. Will you be able to afford it? Do you want to give up the familiarity of the present arrangement? What are the drawbacks (if any) to the new technology? Because the changeover is still in progress, there remain more questions than answers.

About two years ago, the Federal Communications Commission (FCC) developed the "video dial tone" policy, which means that regional telephone companies may use fiber-optic cable to provide customers with interactive communications capability and information services, in addition to TV programming. However, when the dust settles after telephone and cable companies form working relationships, the telephone companies may end up being in charge. Does that matter?

Yes, according to the Center for Media Education, a group that analyzes media policy. Telephone companies are not required by the FCC to provide public-interest services to their constituent communities, as cable companies are. Educational programming is likely to disappear, because groups wishing to air such programs may have to pay access fees identical to those paid by big corporations. Is this limited fare what viewers really want? And some of you may find the fiber-optic service too expensive—the Center noted in an early 1993 newsletter that some companies may charge by the minute.

The Deep Dish cable access satellite network offers an interview-format program called "Video Dial Tone," which can help you learn more about this new system. Media experts who specialize in public-interest issues air concerns that may match some of yours. Deep Dish also publishes a newsletter.

How to Save with Interactive Shopping

One offering, among an array of new services available using fiber-optics technology, would be a "video mall" cable subscription service.

You, the shopper, would have a box installed on your TV set allowing you to speak with an on-screen salesperson, who would help you by showing videos of the products you are looking for. The service should be priced about the same as an HBO subscription, and could be a big help for people who are housebound, moms with small children, and busy professionals working out of their homes.

Nordstrom, a Seattle-based retailer, is looking to lead the way in interactive shopping. The chain expects to be selling both its private-label and national-brand merchandise via TV by late 1994. It began sending out catalogs earlier this year that featured goods to be available through TV shopping.

How They Rate

According to the information CEP has gathered, AT&T is outstanding or above average in every category; MCI—which appears on CEP's X-rated list—does poorly in three important areas; and Sprint is in the middle, with half of its grades just average and half above average. For the most part, all do better than average in the equal employment opportunity categories.

Investing for a Better World

It's a good feeling to buy an Energy Star (energy-saving) computer, a refrigerator that no longer contains CFCs, or groceries from companies that treat their employees well. But if you have a few dollars to invest—what then? The traditional mutual fund or investment house will be glad to help you invest in a broad array of companies, based primarily on financial return. Chances are, these will include corporations whose major source of income is health-threatening tobacco products or companies that destroy vast sections of rainforest in the process of business expansion. They will likely include companies that lay off thousands of workers with little or no outplacement help as they transfer operations elsewhere to cut costs.

If you don't like the sound of that, there are alternatives: ethical investing and community-development banks.

What Are the Ethical Investment Options?

Ethical (or social) investing is the alignment of one's investments with one's values. It gives you another tool to express dissatisfaction with certain corporate practices, and to encourage more positive ones.

Some $700 billion is now being invested in the United States with the use of ethical screens. Financial returns of screened portfolios tend to be comparable to market returns of similarly managed unscreened portfolios.

Some outperform conventional-fund averages. In fact, on "Black Friday" (October 1987) when the Dow slid 23 percent, the five largest ethical mutual funds (at that time) dropped an average of just 12 percent. The Parnassus Fund (800-999-3505), for example, recently achieved "more than four times the growth of the S&P 500" (*Barron's*, July 26, 1993). *Business Week*, in its year-end 1992 Investment Forecast, placed the fund eleventh on its "Best Performer List" of 48 equity funds. For the year through December 31, 1993, Parnassus had a total return of 17 percent. Calvert Social Investment Funds, Dreyfus Third Century, and New Alternatives Fund are among the longer-established social-investment funds. (Please see chart on page 387 for more funds, phone numbers, and year-end 1993 performance figures.) The Social Investment Forum (202-833-5522), a national professional association founded in 1985, provides a comprehensive listing of ethical-investing funds and practitioners.

You should carefully check the track record of any funds or managers, their financial analysis capabilities, their sources of information, and the seriousness of their social-screening process. CEP knows of some social-investment practitioners who say they use CEP research, but have only a shopping guide, not the appropriately broad and in-depth research that our SCREEN Research Service would provide.

The number of investment vehicles designed for ethical investors has grown over the last two decades. Choices now include more than 30 equity, money market, bond, and mutual funds. In addition, there are community loan funds, credit unions, deposits in community banks, and venture capital funds.

As an ethical investor, you can take advantage of at least five services: (1) investment in companies whose policies and practices match your values; (2) avoidance of investment in companies whose policies you disagree with or whose social performance is poor; (3) divestment of securities already held in poorly performing companies; (4) alternative investment to provide direct aid to communities; and (5) campaigns to influence corporate policy through shareholder proxy proposals.

Where Did Ethical Investment Originate?

As far back as the 1920s, many churches prohibited investment in what they considered "sin stocks" (liquor, tobacco, gambling). By the sixties, however, thousands of average citizens were outraged by social injustices such as investment in South Africa (where the cruel apartheid system was sanctioned by its government), the Vietnam War, the continued curtailment of civil rights, and rampant environmental pollution. A new political awareness galvanized college students, civil-rights activists, members of the clergy, and eventually consumers. They challenged those they felt were exacerbating these problems—and that included American corporations. Many people wished to divest stock in companies whose products or performance were not compatible with their values. And they needed information.

In 1969, Alice Tepper Marlin founded the Council on Economic Priorities (CEP) (800-729-4CEP) to research and provide information on corporate practices relating to such issues. Providing company-by-company ratings of social performance helped people decide how to invest. The Council has been instrumental in helping to curtail the production of antipersonnel weapons, the B-1 bomber, and the MX missile; calling attention to the most egregious polluters in the paper, oil, steel, electric-utility, and hazardous-waste industries; and revealing that nuclear power at that time could not deliver electricity more cheaply than fossil fuels and was considerably more expensive than improvements in energy efficiency. CEP raised awareness of the "revolving door" syndrome involving the military

CEP SCREEN Investor Research Service Broadens Impact

CEP's SCREEN service offers individual and institutional investors concise, comprehensive, unbiased information on a range of social and environmental issues. Quarterly SCREEN reports provide company ratings on 10 issues alphabetically and by industry for ease of comparison, plus profiles and news updates. SCREEN's database covers 800 companies, including Standard & Poor's 500, smaller companies with good social records, and 150 British and Japanese companies.

SCREEN Corporate Ratings Service ($500) is an introductory service that includes quarterly ratings reports on 800 companies, a reference manual that explains the criteria on which ratings are based, membership in CEP, monthly *Research Reports*, a copy of *Shopping for a Better World*, discounts on other CEP and SCREEN publications, and a listing of SCREEN's Client Directory.

SCREEN Corporate Profiles Service ($4,500) includes all of the above plus over 500 one-page company profiles in a binder during the year, and the News Update Service. SCREEN's Profiles Service is available on-line.

SCREEN Full Service ($8,000) includes all of the above plus a CEDC subscription, up to five copies of each SCREEN report, the right to select ten companies for SCREEN to research each year, twenty hours of additional SCREEN research, a discount on additional research above twenty hours, and the right to use CEP's name and permission to quote from SCREEN in materials (subject to CEP approval of copy). The Full Service Subscription is available on-line. **Please see page 395 for a SCREEN order form.**

and senior executives in the weapons-procurement business. And it spotlighted the Strategic Defense Initiative (Star Wars) as a misguided, extravagant drain on commercial research. In 1989, CEP produced its first annual *Shopping for a Better World*, a pocket-sized shopping guide providing company social ratings for consumers. Today, CEP's SCREEN Research Service for Investors evaluates some 800 companies.

In 1971, religious leaders joined together with the Interfaith Center on Corporate Responsibility (ICCR) (212-870-2936) to mount shareholder opposition to corporate practices with which they disagreed. Through proxy organizing and coordinating, this organization spearheaded the ultimately successful campaign to pressure hundreds of corporations to withdraw their operations (and their taxes) from South Africa. ICCR continues to bring shareholder resolutions to some 200 corporate annual meetings on equal opportunity, infant formula in the Third World, the environment, health, and development issues. ICCR is an international coalition of nearly 250 Protestant and Roman Catholic orders, denominations, agencies, dioceses, health-care corporations, and pension funds. Its members have committed their investments to holding corporations socially accountable.

Development Banks Help Rebuild Minority Neighborhoods

In August 1993, a nationwide study of mortgage-lending patterns by Ralph Nader's group, Essential Information, Inc., showed that 49 mortgage concerns in 16 large cities had practiced "redlining" as recently as 1990 and 1991. The study showed that on 62 separate occasions, lenders had ruled out—"redlined"—loans to applicants in minority and low-income communities. Though redlining constitutes a violation of federal fair-lending laws, it has been used for many years to deny loans in what lenders consider high-risk areas. Approached by the *New York Times*, a Mortgage Bankers Association of America spokesperson asserted that by 1993, "the industry [had] launched a nationwide initiative to tear down any and all barriers to home mortgage credit."

Shorebank Corporation in Chicago, Illinois, won a CEP Silver Anniversary Award in 1994. Shorebank provides a wonderful example of what a lending institution and its non-bank affiliates can do to turn around an underinvested community. In the process, the bank helps build pride in the community. Combining hardheaded business sense with ethical principles, Shorebank has invested more

Growth	Assets (in millions) 12/31/93	Most Recent Quarter	One Year (Rolling 12 month)	3 Year Average Annual	5 Year Average Annual	Maximum Load	Expenses	Telephone
Calvert Ariel Appreciation	$219.3	7.6%	7.9%	17.6%	N/A	4.75%	1.44%	800/368-2748
Calvert Ariel Growth	225.8	6.2	8.7	17.3	11.1	4.75	1.23	800/368-2748
Calvert SIF Equity	88.9	3.4	2.1	10.5	10.4	4.75	1.20	800/368-2748
Covenant Portfolio	5.0	2.2	4.1	N/A	N/A	4.50	2.50	800/833-4909
Domini Social Equity	27.0	1.6	6.5	N/A	N/A	0.00	0.75	800/762-6814
Dreyfus Third Century	523.0	1.6	5.3	14.0	12.5	0.00	1.08	800/645-6561
Parnassus	98.0	8.5	17.3	34.8	14.7	3.50	1.28	800/999-3505
Rightime Social Awareness	10.6	-2.7	-2.3	11.0	N/A	4.75	2.44	800/242-1421
Working Assets Citizens Growth	51.6	-0.2	0.0	N/A	N/A	4.00	1.75	800/223-7010
Lipper Growth Fund Ave.		*2.3*	*10.6*					
Balanced								
Calvert SIF Managed Growth	$541.3	0.2%	6.0%	10.3%	10.1%	4.75%	1.31%	800/368-2748
Green Century Balanced	3.2	0.8	-0.7	N/A	N/A	0.00	2.50	800/934-7336
Parnassus Balanced	11.5	-1.0	15.9	N/A	N/A	0.00	0.75	800/999-3505
Pax World Fund	464.4	1.6	-1.0	6.4	10.7	0.00	1.02	800/767-1729
Working Assets Citizens Balanced	44.8	-0.8	4.3	N/A	N/A	4.00	1.75	800/223-7010
Franklin Research Balanced Acct.		*1.7**	6.9*				*	
Lipper Balanced Fund Ave.		*1.2*	*10.7*					
Income								
Calvert SIF Bond	$67.3	-0.1%	11.6%	11.3%	11.1%	4.75%	1.31%	800/368-2748
Muir CA Tax-Free	19.4	1.1	11.8	N/A	N/A	4.50	0.75	800/648-3448
Parnassus CA Tax-Exempt	3.3	1.1	13.0	N/A	N/A	0.00	1.25	800/999-3505
Parnassus Fixed Income	4.2	-0.7	10.6	N/A	N/A	0.00	1.25	800/999-3505
Working Assets Citizens Income	19.8	0.7	10.0	N/A	N/A	2.00	1.25	800/223-7010
Lipper Income Fund Ave.		*1.2*	*12.2*					
Environmental								
New Alternatives	$31.6	1.8%	2.9%	11.1%	10.4%	4.75%	1.04%	516/466-0808
Progressive Environmental	3.0	0.0	10.2	1.7	N/A	4.50	2.05	800/275-2382
Lipper Environmental Fund Ave.		2.4	*3.4*					
Global								
Calvert World Values	$80.6	10.2%	25.8%	N/A	N/A	4.75%	1.12%	800/368-2748
Lipper Global Fund Ave.		*9.7*	*31.0*					

Money Market	Assets (in millions) 12/31/93	Days Average Maturity	7-day Average Yield	30-day Average Yield	7-day Compound Yield	Expenses	Telephone
Calvert SIF Money Market	$139.2	41	2.67	2.64	2.71	0.87%	800/368-2748
Green Century Money Market	3.1	49	2.66	2.69	2.68	0.50	800/934-7336
Working Assets Money Market	121.5	40	2.23	2.20	2.25	1.15	800/223-7010
Money Market Fund Ave.		57	2.72	2.70	2.76		

The Market	Most Recent Quarter	One Year (Rolling 12 month)
S&P 500 Reinvested	2.32%	10.06%
Dow Jones Industrial Average	6.32	16.97

*These figures represent the after-fee performance of Franklin Research's tax exempt managed portfolios. For further information contact Chitra Staley at Franklin Research (617/423-6655).

than $400 million in five neighborhoods over the last 20 years. In 1993 alone, South Shore Bank lent over $37 million, which included rehabilitating 1,075 rental units and financing 63 small businesses. To accomplish all this, Shorebank pioneered what it calls Development Deposits™: converting market-rate deposits from individuals, corporations, charitable foundations, and religious groups nationwide into development loans. Shorebank's mission is to promote "economic development in communities traditionally neglected by the financial marketplace." Considered the model for community development banking by the Clinton Administration, Shorebank operates wholly owned subsidiaries in Michigan's Upper Peninsula, and Cleveland, Ohio, and has multi-year advisory contracts in Kansas City, Arkansas and Eastern Europe. It now consults regularly here and abroad.

America's Corporate Conscience Awards

Each year, the Council on Economic Priorities presents our America's Corporate Conscience Awards, honoring companies for outstanding achievements or initiatives in environmental stewardship, charitable contributions, equal opportunity, community involvement, and employer responsiveness to employees. An independent panel of judges chooses the winners and they are announced at a gala dinner in New York City.

To commemorate CEP's 25 years of working for a better world, in 1994 we presented special Silver Anniversary Awards to Xerox and Shorebank Corporation, in addition to our regular awards. Only companies previously honored with ACCA awards and demonstrating sustained and broad achievements, were eligible for Silver Anniversary Awards.

Once a company is nominated, CEP's research staff carefully examines specific programs, drawing on material provided by the companies themselves and on news clippings, federal-agency files, experts, legal records, and other established sources of information. To qualify as a finalist, a company must not only be outstanding in the area for which it was nominated, it must also earn top ratings in at least four of CEP's *Shopping for a Better World* categories. Furthermore, the company must agree to complete CEP's corporate questionnaire.

Companies may be nominated by CEP staff or advisors, by outside experts familiar with corporate issues, by the companies themselves, and by you. If you wish to nominate a company for an America's Corporate Conscience Award or want information about attending the awards ceremony, please contact CEP directly (212-420-1133). Previous CEP award-winning companies are:

1994

Silver Anniversary Awards
Large: *Xerox Corporation*
Small: *Shorebank Corporation*

Community Involvement
Brooklyn Union Gas Company

Environmental Stewardship
Large: *S.C. Johnson & Son, Inc.*
Small: *Stonyfield Farm, Inc.*

Responsiveness to Employees
SAS Institute

International Commitment
Levi Strauss & Co.

1993

Community Involvement
The Clorox Company

Responsiveness to Employees
Merck & Co., Inc.
Quad/Graphics Inc.

Equal Employment Opportunity
Pitney-Bowes Inc.

Environmental Stewardship
Large: *Digital Equipment Corporation*
Small: *Aveda Corp.*

Conversion Award
Galileo Electro-Optics Corporation
Kaman Aircraft
Kavlico
Science Applications International Corp.

1992

Charitable Contributions
Large: *US West, Inc.*
Small: *Tom's of Maine*

Community Involvement
Supermarkets General Holdings Corporation and
The Prudential Insurance Company of America

Responsiveness to Employees
Donnelly Corporation

Equal Employment Opportunity
General Mills, Inc.

Environmental Stewardship
Large: *Church & Dwight Company, Inc.*
Small: *Conservatree Paper Company*

Special Recognition for Innovative Benefit
Lotus Development Corporation

1991

Charitable Contributions
Large: *H.B. Fuller Company*
Honorable Mention:
The Stride Rite Corporation
Small: *Foldcraft Company*

Community Involvement
Time Warner Inc.

Responsiveness to Employees
Kellogg Company

Equal Employment Opportunity
Hallmark Cards, Inc.

Environmental Stewardship
Large: *Herman Miller, Inc.*
Honorable Mention:
H.J. Heinz Company
Small: *Smith & Hawken*

1990

Charitable Contributions
Cummins Engine Company, Inc.
Honorable Mention: *Patagonia, Inc. (formerly Lost Arrow Corporation)*

Community Involvement
Xerox Corporation

Responsiveness to Employees
Pitney-Bowes Inc.
Honorable Mention: *Fel-Pro, Inc.*

Equal Employment Opportunity
US West, Inc.

Environmental Stewardship
American Telephone & Telegraph Company (AT&T)

1989

Charitable Contributions
Dayton Hudson Corporation
Honorable Mention: *Newman's Own, Inc.*

Community Involvement
Digital Equipment Corporation

Responsiveness to Employees
Federal Express Corporation

Equal Employment Opportunity
Eastman Kodak Company

Environmental Stewardship
Applied Energy Services Inc.
Honorable Mention: *H.B. Fuller Company*

1988

Charitable Contributions
Ben & Jerry's Homemade, Inc.

Fair Employment
Xerox Corporation
Gannett Company, Inc.

Family Concerns
IBM Corporation

Opportunities for People with Disabilities
General Mills, Inc.

Community Action (Job Development)
Best Western International, Inc.
South Shore Bank

Education (Literacy)
Gannett Company, Inc.

Environmental Stewardship
3M

Animal Rights
Procter & Gamble Company

Disclosure
Kellogg Company

1987

Charitable Contributions
Polaroid Corporation
Sara Lee Corporation
General Mills, Inc.

Equal Employment Opportunity
Avon Products, Inc.

Family Concerns
Procter & Gamble Company

Community Action
IBM Corporation
Amoco Corporation

Disclosure
Johnson & Johnson
Ford Motor Company

South Africa
Polaroid Corporation

Campaign for Cleaner Corporations (C3)

CEP's Campaign for Cleaner Corporations (C3), begun in 1992, identifies some of the nation's worst corporate environmental performers in environmentally risky industries. Companies are selected by a blue-ribbon panel of judges, which in 1993 was made up of Dr. Carl Sagan, astrophysicist, Cornell University; author Paul Hawken; Anthony Carfang, President, Covenant Investment Management; Susan Cohn, Stern School of Business; Sophia Collier, Chair, Working Assets Capital Management; Kristin Finn, Senior Research Analyst, U.S. Trust Co. of Boston; Dr. Donald Lauria, New Jersey Medical School; Michael McCloskey, Former Executive Director, Sierra Club; Dr. Andy Smith, Director, Social and Ethical Investments, National Ministries, American Baptist Churches; and Dr. Ariane van Buren, Director of Energy and Environmental Programs, Interfaith Center on Corporate Responsibility.

Judges choose companies based on a careful examination of CEP's research, after which the council recommends measures that the companies may adopt to improve their environmental records. Each year, companies that improve are removed from the list and new polluters are named to it. Companies showing little or no improvement remain on the list. The Campaign's research is used by a wide range of environmental and activist organizations (see below) who help expand awareness and encourage companies to do better.

The 1993 list included Commonwealth Edison, Du Pont, Exxon, General Electric, International Paper, Louisiana-Pacific, Maxxam, Rockwell, Texaco, and Texas Utilities. Every one of the companies named the previous year except Rockwell met with CEP during 1993 to analyze our recommendations for change. Cargill, General Motors, Georgia Pacific, and USX, named in 1992, responded positively and were dropped from the 1993 list in recognition of their improvement.

Activist participants in the 1993 Campaign for Cleaner Corporations were Citizen Action (Columbus, OH, and Washington, DC); Citizens' Clearinghouse for Hazardous Waste (Falls Church, VA); Citizens for a Better Environment (San Francisco, CA); Co-op America (environmentally responsible consumer network, Washington, DC); Environmental Research Foundation (Annapolis, MD); Good Neighbor Project (Waverly, MA); Government Accountability Project (Washington, DC); Greenpeace (New York, NY); Institute for Agriculture and Trade Policy (Minneapolis, MN); Rainforest Action Network (San Francisco, CA); Sierra Club (Washington, DC); Student Environmental Action Coalition (Chapel Hill, NC); 20/20 Vision (letter writing on social concerns, Washington, DC); Women's Environment & Development Organization (New York, NY); and Working Assets Long Distance (free calls for subscribers to talk to companies named in C3, San Francisco, CA).

You can join the Campaign for Cleaner Corporations, too. Contact CEP or any of the organizations mentioned above to see how you can help.

For more information, ask for a free CEP Research Report, "America's Least Wanted: The 1993 Campaign for Cleaner Corporations (C3)." (See the order form at the back of this book.)

Survey

Now that you have had a chance to review *Shopping for a Better World*, we would like to know a few things: Have you used it? Do you find it helpful? How can we make future editions better?

Many changes in this edition resulted from our readers' suggestions, so please take a moment to answer these questions. **Cut out this two-page survey and send it to CEP, 30 Irving Place, New York, NY 10003.**

1. What companies, products or brands not listed in *Shopping for a Better World* would you like to see listed in future editions? (PLEASE SPECIFY)

____

____

2. Please rank, in order of importance, how significant our eight social-ratings categories are to you. Rank from 1, most important, to 8, least important.

___Environment
___Workplace
___Women's Advancement
___Disclosure of Information
___Family Benefits
___Minority Advancement
___Community Outreach
___Charitable Giving

3. Would you like us to rate companies on other issues?

❒ No ❒ Yes

If yes, please list (e.g., executive compensation, PAC contributions, international involvement).

____

____

4. Has *Shopping for a Better World* changed any of your shopping decisions?

❒ No ❒ Yes

If yes, did you:

❒ Use general guidelines, (e.g., look for minimal packaging)

❒ Switch brands

If you did switch brands, how many changes did you make?

❒ 1-3 ❒ 3-10 ❒ numerous

Please give a specific example, (i.e., product/issue area; brands switched to and from).

____

____

5. How often do you take a brand's ratings into account when you decide to buy a particular brand?

❐ Whenever I shop ❐ Often ❐ Occasionally

❐ Seldom ❐ Never

6. Have you written to a company as a result of its rating or profile in the guide?

❐ No ❐ Yes

If yes, please let us know whether you wrote to:

❐ A company you didn't patronize

❐ A company you switched to

❐ Both

7. Please check the attributes you look for when you shop:

❐ Price ❐ Style ❐ Energy efficiency

❐ Convenience ❐ Product quality ❐ Color

❐ Minimal/recycled/recyclable packaging

❐ Company's social and environmental record

8. Now go back to question #7 and circle the three attributes that are most important to you.

9. What other comments, if any, would you like to make about *Shopping for a Better World*?

____

____

10. What size would you prefer future *Shopping for a Better World* guides to be?

❐ Bigger ❐ Same size ❐ Smaller

11. In your opinion, which of the following is the most important information to include in future editions? Please rank in order of preference.

___New companies not yet rated

___New product categories

___Annual update of companies already rated

12. Are you a member of CEP?

❐ Yes ❐ No

CEP Products and Publications

(See Membership/Order Form on page 398.)

Shopping for a Better World: The Quick and Easy Guide to Socially Responsible Supermarket Shopping, $7.49 each includes shipping, 5 for $23.95. Free when you join CEP as a new member.

Students Shopping for a Better World, $7.49 each includes shipping, 5 for $23.95. Rates the major manufacturers of products teenagers buy. Special discounts available for bulk orders. Call 800-729-4237.

Teacher's Guide to Students Shopping for a Better World. Chapter-by-chapter guide to *Students Shopping for a Better World.* Detailed lesson plans and class activities. Call 800-729-4237 to order 25 student guides and one teacher's guide ($100) or a single guide ($23).

Shopping for a Better World: Software Version, $39 includes shipping and handling. All the information in the book at your fingertips. Includes letter-writing program. Available in DOS or Windows.

Corporate Environmental Data Clearinghouse. In-depth profiles of the environmental policies and practices of major corporations. Call 800-729-4237 for prices and list of companies available.

SCREEN. Enables investors to screen their investment portfolios and investment managers and trustees to meet client requests for screened portfolios. See page 385 for more information.

SCREEN SERVICE ORDER FORM

❒ **Corporate Ratings ($500)** ❒ **Corporate Profiles ($4,500)** ❒ **Full Service ($8,000)**

Name ______________________________

Address ______________________________

City, State ____________________ **Zip** __________

Phone ______________________________

Visa/MC/Amex ____________________ **Exp. Date** __________

Free Information

Buyers of *Shopping for a Better World* are eligible to receive *free information* from CEP. To receive any of the free information listed below, please fill out this form and mail it to CEP, 30 Irving Place, New York, NY 10003.

- ❑ Free CEP Research Report on Campaign for Cleaner Corporations
- ❑ Free CEP Research Report on America's Corporate Conscience Awards
- ❑ More information about CEP's Corporate Environmental Data Clearinghouse
- ❑ More information about CEP's SCREEN service
- ❑ More information about CEP and membership opportunities

Name ______________________________

Address ______________________________

City ______________________________

State ______________________________

Zip ______________________________

Please send information about CEP and *Shopping for a Better World* to my friend.

Name ______________________________

Address ______________________________

City ______________________________

State ______________________________

Zip ______________________________

Go Beyond the Guide

CEP's commitment to producing social change is as strong as ever—and we're hoping that yours is, too.

CEP has demonstrated that factual, careful documentation can make a difference to corporate performance and government priorities.

With *your* help we can increase the impact. Our work is supported by our worldwide membership. As a member you will enjoy the convenience of having the facts at your fingertips . . . facts delivered monthly in our Research Report, a respected and reliable source of invaluable information and updates. You'll also receive a free copy of *Shopping for a Better World* and a 20 percent discount on other CEP books and studies.